1 MONTH OF
FREE
READING

at

www.ForgottenBooks.com

By purchasing this book you are eligible for one month membership to ForgottenBooks.com, giving you unlimited access to our entire collection of over 1,000,000 titles via our web site and mobile apps.

To claim your free month visit:

www.forgottenbooks.com/free312566

ISBN 978-0-265-90699-6
PIBN 10312566

Highways and Byways

IN

Shakespeare's Country

BY W. H. HUTTON
WITH · ILLUSTRATIONS · BY
EDMUND H. NEW

MACMILLAN AND CO., LIMITED
ST. MARTIN'S STREET, LONDON
1914

COPYRIGHT

DA

PREFACE

THE writer of this book undertook his pleasant task, with a light and happy heart, more than four years ago. He had known "Shakespeare's country" for nearly forty years, and wandered about in it, whenever he could, in many a holiday. He looked forward to setting down, very quickly, what he had seen, and should see, for the first time or again, of the heart of England, that he might, if he had good fortune, hand on to others something of the pleasure which had been his for so many years. But new work came to him unexpectedly, and only at long intervals could he take up again his travels or his pen. For a long time a bookcase has been stored with the literature of his subject, from the immortal Dugdale down, through the Rev. Thomas Cox, of 1700, to the latest voyager on the banks of Avon, and "the Warwickshire table" has been the name of a desk consecrated to his task. At last it is finished; but it is with a sigh that the pen is laid down, the books put away, the feet no longer turned towards Warwick ways.

The writer cannot hope, for all his care, for all the years he has spent in reading and travelling, to have escaped error: he will only say that he knows well that even to describe what one has seen, or to summarise one's conclusions where others have thought and written too, is no easy thing. Let him only offer what he has written to the memory of the poet who has been his greatest friend for nearly fifty years, in the hope that " never anything can be amiss, when simpleness and duty tender it."

It should be added that Mr. Edmund New travelled with his pencil before any of these impressions were set down in words, and for the limits of " Shakespeare's country " the writer has almost always been content to follow the artist. Some may have wished to see the land larger, some smaller; and there is a great deal to be said for both views. But the truth is that Warwickshire and its neighbours are too full of beauty and of history for one book. The country which Shakespeare knew must be limited when we are to write of it; and it is hoped that these boundaries are not too strait.

Lastly, indebtedness to hundreds of books should be admitted. Many of them have been mentioned : all of them are gratefully remembered by the writer. Yet he must say that, much though he has read, he has studied and investigated for himself; and, pleasant though the reading has been, the seeing has been pleasanter still. For the seeing is mingled in remembrance with the kindness of many people. The writer is grateful indeed to all those who have shown him their houses, or have allowed him to see them, and especially to those who live at Baddesley Clinton and Charlecote, Clopton and Compton Verney, Coughton and Packwood and Umberslade; and most of all to the Misses Knight of Henley-in-Arden, who have helped him so much by their companionship, their knowledge and their kindness. He has had the advantage of Mr. A. C. Coldicott's assistance in proof-reading, which has kept him from many errors and helped him in many facts. What Mr. Coldicott does not know about Warwickshire the author has not discovered —nor will anyone else ; but that devoted student is in no way responsible for the writer's errors of omission or obstinacy.

PETERBOROUGH,
March 4, 1914.

CONTENTS

ix

CONTENTS

CHAPTER IX

LIST OF ILLUSTRATIONS

HIGHWAYS AND BYWAYS

IN

SHAKESPEARE'S COUNTRY

CHAPTER I

FROM THE FOUR SHIRES STONE TO COMPTON WINYATES AND TYSOE

You may begin Warwickshire at one side from the Four Shires Stone about two miles from Moreton-in-the-Marsh. There Glo'ster and Oxford, Worcester and Warwick, meet. A healthy spot, as I suppose ; and once hard by there was a house where people went (1779 is the date) to be inoculated.

"Inoculation, beauteous maid"—is not that how the poet began ? There was also another house for patients " called Gillks's, near Great Rollright." Well, we will leave Moreton-in-Marsh (or Henmarsh, as it was called in the Civil Wars) and go eastwards, and find that little eighteenth century obelisk, with its railings round it, at the roadside—just where you turn up to your left by Wolford Woods. That is really a mark and border line for our book. Leave Gloucestershire behind—you shall not escape Worcestershire, for it dodges you everywhere—and make your journey into Warwickshire through Oxfordshire and Little Compton.

At Little Compton, the manor of which he had bought some years before, and where also lived the Sheldons, Bishop Juxon resided throughout the troublous days from the time when he was turned out by the Parliament men from Fulham to the day when he was moved to Lambeth at the return of Charles II. As at Chastleton, where the good bishop ministered in the house on Sundays, the church is close to the manor house : at Little Compton, indeed, they almost touch. The house is a good, grey, gabled home of the richer yeomen, beautiful but not conspicuous in the beautiful class to which it belongs. Juxon, Whitelocke tells us, diverted himself with a pack of hounds which "exceeded all other hounds in England for the pleasure and orderly hunting of them," and Cromwell heard of it but did not interfere. The Church (in which the law forbade the good man to minister) is simple, with a curious south aisle. It has several memorials of the Sheldons, the family from which came Juxon's friend who succeeded him in London and at Canterbury.

From Little Compton it is but a short way, as we shall see, first along the main road towards Moreton and the Four Shires Stone, and then up a more rural way, to Barton-on-the-Heath. This has a historical connection with many notable names. We need not go back with Dugdale to Domesday and Turkil of Warwick, or Thomas of Arden, but be content to follow him when he says, "There is so little Light in those elder Times from Record, touching this Place, that I can give but a slender Account thereof." With King John comes Simon de Barton, and so on to the Marshalls from Henry III. to Queen Elizabeth. Then the Overburys, under James I., and the rebuilding of the beautiful manor house which you see from the churchyard, to the north. The church was originally Norman, and there survives the fine chancel arch, the tower and the windows looking therefrom into the church, as well as a door. Among the Overburys one married a Sheldon and died in 1739, and had set on his stone the words, not commonly found at that date : "Requiescat in pace." There is no reason, so far as I know, to suppose that he was anything but a loyal member of the English Church. The beautiful position of Barton, with its church looking far across the vale of Moreton-in-Marsh, may well have endeared it to men and women of old as to their successors to-day. Such were Edmund Bury, and especially Elizabeth his wife, seventh daughter of Edward Underhill of Nether-Ettington in the County of Warwick, whose tombstone in the church tells of her that after Master Bury's death in 1588 she took a second husband from Northamptonshire, one Thomas Sawyer, Gent, "whom she outlived and then returning into Warwickshire, her native county, and desiring after this life ended to have her body layd in the chancell of the parish church of Barton-on-the-Heath in the County of Warwick with the body of the said Edmund her first husband she caused " her " tomb to be prepared An. Dom. 1608." Perhaps she had as happy a life as seems suggested by another inscription, which runs thus : " In memory of Willliam Sands Esquire who was born in this parish December 1720 being the Hundredth Year after the enclosure. He was of the Honourable Band of Gentlemen Pensioners in the reign of George III. forty years, and having lived to a good old age in general good health and good fortune finished with a good hope on May 15, 1802, and lies buried in the dust below. Aged 82 years. Resurget."

The date of " the enclosures " is important in the history of this neighbourhood, especially, I think, in that of Long Compton, to which we may now proceed. It is a lovely way through Warwick lanes, not so thick grown or close in summer as those in the heart of the shire, but seeming always on hot days to have still the breath of spring about them. It is a modern poet who sings of this way—or another that leads to the same happy village —in lines the wayfarer will gladly remember of this land of roses :

> " We neither spoke.
> The leafy lyrics of the stripling oak
> Sang us along.
> Hamlet by hamlet passed,
> And yellow sheep,
> We came at last
> Upon the hills that keep,
> As mothers watch their babes asleep,
> Long Compton guarded in the vale :
> There as a dreaming child it lay
> And took the evening light ;
> It was the vocal end of day,
> And larks in giddy flight
> So out of view made music ring
> That clouds, not birds,
> Appeared to sing." [1]

Long Compton stands at the foot of two hills, the steep hill from Weston Park and the long and steep ascent towards Chipping Norton. It is a picturesque straggling place, spoilt here and there by huge advertisements of things that motorists want or

[1] Norman Gale, *Orchard Songs*, pp. 6-7.

B 2

are supposed to want, but still retaining a large number of very charming cottages and houses of larger claims also. The church must have priority of inspection. You come to it through a curious gateway. The upper part thereof is thatched and was evidently a dwelling-house of two rooms, to which a wooden stairway at the side leads up. The church has a long nave with battlements, and a west tower also embattled, with an aisle on the north and at the south a vestry and a porch. The tower is a very fine one, with the curious feature of loop-holes in the battlements, which no doubt were used in the Civil Wars. The nave has a Perpendicular clerestory; and there is a charming sanctus bell turret. In the south porch, Perpendicular, is a stone lady lying perpendicularly, removed from the churchyard, whose headdress is most impressive. The door to the porch, no doubt moved forwards, is Norman. In the nave you will notice the curious winding pattern around the windows, and you will observe that the vestry is beautiful still in spite of restoration, and was more beautiful before that process. In the village you will see a cottage in which Dick Whittington is said to have been born, but most likely was not. And then you will look up Dugdale and find all sorts of curious tales about this place. S. Augustine is said to have been there to excommunicate a man who would not pay tithes, and a dead man had risen to tell the awful fate which befell those who did not pay, with many other mysterious and terrible things. And also if you stay in the village you are like to learn how long old superstitions have lingered there, of witches and the evil eye—as at Tysoe, not far off; and as night sets in and you wander up the hill, not more than a mile to the end of the village, and turn to the right, and you come upon the Rollright Stones, cold and weird in the moonlight, you will not wonder at the strange things men think. For here, on the very frontier of Warwickshire, is a survival which takes you back long before history was written. You are seven hundred feet above the sea, and the road you came by is the border between Oxford and Warwick shires. A circle of unhewn monoliths, belonging to the Neolithic age, is in Oxfordshire and about seventy yards north-east of it a tall single stone, known as the Kingstone, which is in Warwick, and so also are five upright slabs which are called the Whispering Knights. The circle is about one hundred feet in diameter : it probably surrounded a grave, though nothing seems ever to have been found there, not even by Ralph Sheldon the antiquary, Anthony Wood's friend, who died in 1684, leaving his heart and bowels to be buried in the chancel at Long Compton, while his body was interred at Beoley. Sir Arthur Evans thinks the Whispering Knights also sepulchral, but will not say so of the Kingstone, concerning which there are some good ancient tales. In the dim past a king marching to victory was stayed here by a witch, who cried to him :—

" If Long Compton thou canst see
King of England shalt thou be."

The King Stone.

But when he, calling on stick, stock, and stone, rushed forward, he found himself confronted by the Long Barrow that stands in front of the King Stone, and the witch said :—

" As Long Compton thou canst not see
King of England thou shalt not be.

Rise up, stick, and stand still, stone,
For King of England thou shalt be none.
Thou and thy men hoar stones shall be,
And I myself an eldern-tree."

And so king and men became stones, and the witch an elder tree.
There are many about this spot, her children, no doubt, and if
you stick your knife into them you will draw blood. Round
the stones fairies dance at night, and some people—but they are
dead now—have seen them. The Rollright Stones, thus, are far
away from reality : they are no more in Warwickshire than by
Rambin and Rodenkirchen where the little boy was caught by
the elves as he slept in their ring at night. Still, perhaps, people
chip off bits of the stone, as they certainly did not long ago :
perhaps when night has fallen the stones arise and go down into
the valley to drink : perhaps the very name of the stones and the
villages hard by comes from Roland the champion of Christ
against the Pagans, and so when you stand on the hill and look
far away into the mists of memory, you may hear the horn of
Fuentarabia that sounds across the sea. The Rollright stones
(Rowldrich is the correct name for them, it seems) are now alone
in Warwickshire, the survivals of this dimmest past. There were
stones within recent times at Ladbroke and Southam, but they
have been stolen or broken up.

This is a very wandering chapter and so we will go back to
Long Compton for the night, tell a few ghost stories, and take
the road in the morning for Stratford. You may go out of the
way through Weston Park, and see the far from beautiful house,
which belongs to the Earl of Camperdown, built of extraordinary Gothic, Mr. Blore's best combination of Elizabethan
and medieval, which replaced the house that Ralph Sheldon
lived in, who was called " the Great " in his day, people
thinking him a greater personage, it seems, than his namesake the Archbishop of Canterbury. It is interesting to find
Juxon and Sheldon so near each other, by the way. But if
you are fortunate enough not only to see the beautiful park
of Weston but to enter the house, you will find some very
good pictures there, not only, of course, pictures of Duncan, the
hero of Camperdown, but a Gainsborough and a Reynolds or
two, as well as some of the Italian things that everybody picked
up a century and a half ago. And then you shall go, no very long
distance, to Brailes, thence to penetrate into the Feldon, of which

more hereafter. As you go you will look upwards, and know that you have to dip very low down likewise, for Compton Winyates is your objective after Brailes, and then Tysoe. But first take a run up the hill past the wood and see the good church of Great Wolford at the top, then across the valley and up again to Little Wolford and see the fifteenth century manor house, which Lord Camperdown keeps up so well. It has a hall like a college hall, with some pictures in it, and armour, and there some nonconforming folk meet on a Sunday. On week-days they will tell you that Charles II. slept there on his escape from Worcester; but that is not true at all, for he never was near. What Cox says about the Church of Great Wolford is worth reading :—

"The Church is dedicated to S. *Michael,* and was given to the Canons of *Stone* in *Staffordshire,* by *Robert de Strafford,* Grand-child of the first *Robert,* who lived in the Conqueror's Time. In 26 *Hen.* III. the Advowson was disputed between *Hawise,* Widow of *Richard de Gloucester,* and the Prior of *Kenilworth,* to which the Monastery of *Stone* was a Cell; and after a full Hearing was adjudged to be the Prior's Right; and so continued till 51 *Hen.* III. when the Canons of *Stone* passed it away to the Warden and Scholars of *Merton College, Oxford,* to whom it was appropriated the next Year by *Godfrey Giffard,* Bishop of *Worcester, anno* 1268. and in 1291, was valued at 26 Marks. In 16 *Edw.* II. it was again appropriated to them by *Thomas Cobham,* Bishop of *Worcester,* but not valued again till 26 *Hen.* VIII. when the Vicarage was rated at 8*l.*"

As to Little Wolford, on the hill opposite, its history, before the apocrypha of Charles II., was interesting too; *teste* Cox as followeth :—

"*Wolford-parva,* the Estate of the Earl of *Mallent* in the Conqueror's Time; and being held by him of one *Radulphus,* was then certified to contain four Hides and an Half, having before the *Normans* Coming been the Estate of one *Aluric.* From the Earl of *Mallent* it came to the Barons of *Stafford,* who enfeoffed the Family of *Ingram* with the greatest part of it, but the Time when we do not know, but it must be certainly antiently; for 3 *John,* one *Ingram* of *Walworth* levvied a Fine of Lands here, and 36 *Hen.* held Half a Knight's Fee here of the Barons of *Stafford.* In the Record of 7 *Edw.* I. *Thomas de parva Woleward* is said to be Lord of it, and to have two Yard Lands here with certain Freeholders and Cottagers, which were held of the King ; yet the Posterity of the Baron of *Stafford* were reputed the Lords of it, till 12 *Hen.* VIII. when *Edward* Duke of *Bucks* conveyed it, with *Great Wolford*, to *Richard*, Bishop of *Winchester*, and others : However the *Ingrams* still had a manor here, of which *Richard Ingram* died seised 5 *Eliz.* and *Hastang Ingram* was in Possession of it in 1640. At present it has but few Inhabitants ; but antiently had 42 Families."

It is very small now. From Wolford Parva straight for Brailes, Compton, and Tysoe.

And a word about Brailes to begin with. You will look at the " Compton Pike " at the top of the hill, which was set there as a landmark to guide you to the house in a hole. You will not turn aside to see the modern Early English church of Winderton, but will pass on, by the British mound called Castle Hill, up to the great tower of Brailes, the cathedral of the Feldon. I do not think the history of landholding at Brailes, detailed in Dugdale, is of sufficient interest to be repeated here, but before looking at the very fine church it may be worth while to read what Mr. Cox says about its history, most of it quite of the dim past, leaving no mark behind. Thus he writes :—

" The Church here dedicated to S. *George*, was given to the Canons of *Kenilworth* in King *Henry* I.'s Time, by *Roger* Earl of *Warwick, Simon*, then Bishop of *Worcester*, confirming the Grant, whereupon in the Reign of *Richard* I. a Vicarage was appointed by *John de Constantis*, Bishop of *Worcester*, being endowed with all the Alterage and small Tithes, as well of the Demesne as Lands held by Bond Service, together with the third Sheaff ; as also one Yard-Land with haying, and an Orchard belonging to it, which together were valued 26 *Hen.* VIII. at 20*l.* In this Church are several monumental Inscriptions for *John Davis*, Gent. *Helen Davis*, the Wife of *Thomas Davis, Robert* the eldest Son, and *Elizabeth* the Daughter of *Richard Davis*, who died all in the beginning of the last Century ; as also for *John Bishop*, Patron of the Church, and *Helen* his Wife, and *John* the Son of *Barnabas Bishop*. There was also in this Church a Gild founded by *Richard Nevil*, Earl of *Warwick*, by the Name of a Warden, Brethren, and Sisters, with two Priests to celebrate Divine Service every Day, and to pray for the Soul of the said Founder, the Revenue whereof was certified to be 18*l.* 13*s.* 2*d.*

Half-penny, 37 *Hen.* VIII. and out of it a Grammer School was to be maintained here."

No wonder there was so fine a church with all this ado there. The tower is 120 feet high, embattled as usual. The nave has a clerestory, and two lower aisles. There is a fine chancel, a fine south porch. The greater part of the work is of the fourteenth century, with a little that is earlier and later. The vestry at the north is said to be of 1649 ; I know not why—a curious date for church building. In the tower is a room with a fireplace which may have been the abode of a recluse, or of the priest himself ; and there are some good monuments. Perhaps you will leave the villages of Sutton, and Cherington, and Whichford, as you go homewards, but each of them has an interesting church, and the brass of Nicholas Asheton, rector of the last from 1557 to 1582, is worth seeing if only for its mass of Latin verse and its picture of the Elizabethan gown.

Beautiful though these places are, you will not turn southwards to see them. You passed quite near them when you came from Weston. You will rather hurry on to the little " extra parochial " hamlet, close linked in history to Tysoe as well as Brailes, called Compton Winyates.

Compton Winyates is nearly three miles from Upper Tysoe, down a curious wandering wooded road. So from every side is it approached through a network of trees, high hedge rows on banks above the roadway ; and at last it is reached quite suddenly, and you look down to your right and see it stretched out, gardens, water, church and house, before you, a wonderful picture of rose-tinted restfulness. The manor was one of Turchil's eight hides one virgate ; and it passed through his own heirs, not going to Henry of Newburgh, in some way unrecorded in the family named Compton, who held it at least from 7 Edward I., then in subinfeudation from the Earl of Warwick. Already it was called " Wineyate," from a vineyard, " as the inhabitants tell us from Tradition." Camden called it " Compton in the Hole," and Howitt when he visited it made the rustic who showed it give forth a similar discouraging description : " Did ye ever see *sich* a hole ? " One of the sons of the house, the late Bishop of Ely, was very fond of repeating the quaint introduction. But after all, *cwm* means a valley, and Compton, I suppose, the homestead in a hole, and so the " Celt and Saxon " come together in the name.

The first and most obvious thing to observe and remember about the beautiful house is that it *is* a house and not a castle—a most perfect example of Tudor domestic architecture ; and next that it has always belonged to the family that built it, the famous Warwickshire family that takes its name from the little village, Compton. Dugdale is, of course, the person to tell us best about them. He says that after Edward I. he finds " not much that is memorable " till the time of Henry VIII. But he speaks then of William Compton who, as a boy of eleven (so I think one may interpret Dugdale's rather involved sentence) became page to Henry, Duke of York, afterwards King, and then his Groom of the Chamber. He was greatly in Henry's favour, attained to a high post at Court, won a special augmentation of his arms, and so on. He led the rear guard at Térouenne, and was later on the Keeper of the King's Purse. It was he who began the building of this beautiful house, in the year that Henry VIII. came to the throne. He brought the brick from Fulbrook—where the mound may still be seen across the river from Wasperton or on the upper road from Warwick to Stratford—"where a ruinous castle was, whereof he had the custody by the King's Grant and Keepership of the Park ; which castle he pulled down, making use of the materials for that Building." For portraits of this Sir William and his wife, who was Werburga daughter of Sir John Brereton and widow of Sir Francis Cheyney, you must go to Balliol College in Oxford, where is now the glass,[1] figured in Dugdale, a most lovely thing—" a costly window of rare workmanship, the Passion of our Saviour being therein very lively represented ; and in the lower part thereof his own portraiture, as also that of his lady, both kneeling in their surcoats of arms." When he died, of that terrible sweating sickness of which the State papers contain such gloomy records, in 1529, he left some curios to the King, and noted that he had lent money to Sir Thomas Bullen—which accounts for many things. His son Peter

[1] " The Compton Window at Balliol survives in scraps in the third window on the north side of the chapel. The left hand panel contains heads of two ladies in the costume of the reign of Henry VIII. They are supposed to be Lady Compton and her daughter. Sir William Compton with his two sons kneeling behind him is in the centre, below a panel representing Master Chace and his Fellows. Compton has his arms on his surcoat. The glass has been recently overhauled and rearranged. Up to 1912 Sir William Compton was in the rose-window at the west end." So Mr. H. W. C. Davis kindly writes to me.

GATEWAY COMPTON WYNYATES

was made ward to Wolsey, and lived to the very end of Henry's reign, leaving a son but forty-nine weeks old. This son lived till 39 Eliz., and married the daughter of Francis, Earl of Huntingdon. His son was the first Earl of Northampton, " black Northampton " by nickname, to whom a letter from James I. mocking the Turkey-gowned Puritans at Hampton Court is extant. Now this William followed up the connection his father had made between what are now the two great Northamptonshire houses, the Comptons and the Spencers, by marrying Elizabeth the daughter of Sir John Spencer, Knight, Alderman of the City of London. This was a notable match, for it was not lightly adventured. The alderman did not think the young Lord Compton rich enough for his daughter, so the lover disguised himself as the baker's boy, brought in the hot bread one morning and replaced it, in his basket, by the young lady. It goes a little too far for belief that Sir John met him on the stairs and gave him sixpence for being up so early in the morning. But the quarrel that ensued was assuaged by Queen Elizabeth, and the heir that was born became a very rich man. The mother, the first Countess, was a lady who had a very complete opinion indeed of her own goodness and value, as a letter printed by Howitt shows. From that time the fortunes and the loyalty of the family were assured. James I. came to Compton Winyates. Spencer Compton, the second Earl, was Master of the Robes to Charles I., both as prince and king, and went with him to Spain. He set himself to counterbalance the Puritan influence of Lord Brooke in Warwickshire, and raised troops for the king, fought, and was killed at Hopton Heath in 1643. " Pursuing with too much heat, the Earl was left encompassed by a body of the enemy ; and his horse being killed under him, and the headpiece of his armour stricken off by the butt end of a musquet, he was called to surrender, on a promise of quarter. To this summons he replied that he scorned to take quarter from ' such base rogues and rebels as they were ' ; on which he was put to death, receiving almost at the same moment a blow on the hinder part of his head with a halbert, and a deep wound in the face." He left six sons, all of them persons of eminence. Henry Compton, Bishop of London, was the most famous of them, for he taught Mary II. and Anne, and crowned the first with William III. He was a very notable Whig, one of those who resisted James II. to the teeth, and was suspended by him from his bishopric and turned out of the Privy Council and the deanery of the Chapel Royal. He became Lord High Almoner in 1702 : two hundred years later the office was held by another Compton, also a bishop and the son of the Lord Northampton of his day. In the eighteenth century were the days of gambling and heavy election expenses. Compton Winyates was deserted and the beautiful old furniture was sold. After the middle of the nine- teenth came the revival, and from then the house, restored to all its own beauty, has been a favourite home of its owners.

In the Quadrangle, Compton Winyates.

It is indeed a lovely house. As one descends the hill, it is seen, nestling in gardens, to the right. Follow the road, a good way round, and you come to it with the fine gardens and the remains of the moat, a miniature lake now, to your left ; a beautiful water picture there, banks fringed with tall rushes and water flecked with lilies. Pass on and turn to your left and the front of the house is before you. It is built round a large quadrangle, which you enter through an outstanding porch, on which are

the arms of Henry VIII., with his supporters—a greyhound
and a griffin—and his crown, on which is the inscription : " Dom.
Rex Henricus Octav."   There are other royal badges and
devices, including that of Katherine of Aragon.   To the right
is the porter's lodge, with a blocked-up spyhole.   In the middle
of the building to the right is the chapel, divided by a fine Tudor
screen, with a splendid window where once the founders knelt
in their visible presentments.   Out of the chapel is the parlour
which still has the ceiling of the first earl, with the Spencer and
Compton arms.   Next, turning eastwards, you enter the great
hall, not a very large one, after all, but with some old furniture
in it, and pictures, and the gallery, a staircase going up southwards (a new gallery too, added in recent years), and northwards,
under the gallery, opening upon the kitchens.   Upper rooms
are full of interest, notably the room where Charles I. stayed,
Henry VIII.'s bedroom (with some glass with his arms), and
the " Council Chamber " (unfurnished when last I saw it) with
five doors, and three staircases all leading up to one room in the
roof, which they call a chapel.   Was it a chapel ?   There is a
beam there with three crosses on it that may have served for
an altar ; but why should there have been any secret about it ?
I do not find that the Comptons were ever Papists : they seem
to have followed the national Church in its doings quite naturally.   Still there is no reason why this should not have been
a chapel, though it were not a Roman one.   But there is
another little room which is called a chapel too : the sacristy,
no doubt.   And there is the ground floor chapel : I suspect that
was not intended for a chapel at all.   The Tudor chapels were
hardly ever on the ground floor.   But be all this as it may, the
Comptons were certainly a religious family.   Think of those
great mottoes in stone all along the front, and sides, of Castle
Ashby.   " Except the Lord build the house."   Certainly their
labour 'was not in vain who built this beautiful place.   It is red
brick, with stone facings here and there, and some half-timbered
work.   The beauty of it is its homeliness.   It is not too
large for any ordinary person, and I suppose it is not too small
for an earl.   But it is full of secret cupboards—probably they
are closets (that is, small bedrooms), or store rooms, not hiding-
places at all.   People were really not much more fond of hiding in
the Tudor times than they are now ; but to-day there is a passion
for discovering hiding-holes (which hid noboby), and secret

passages (which led nowhere), and instruments of torture, such as those iron hooks which used to frighten the ignorant at Compton Winyates thirty years ago till one of the Comptons plained that they were only meant to hang flitches on. But one may go on for ever looking for beautiful things, and finding them wonderful, at Compton Winyates. One may linger in the house or in the beautiful gardens, which they are trying to recreate again Tudorwise ; but it is best to go out of the gateway tower again and cross to the church. In 1646, when the Parliament men seized the house and dwelt in it, they made a ruin of the church and destroyed the monuments. Dugdale, who had seen the destruction, says that those of Sir William Compton and his wife, and Henry Lord Compton, their grandson, " which were very beautiful and stately," were " utterly razed and knockt in pieces." Anyhow, the new church was built after the Restoration by James, third earl. The spouting bears the inscription : " I. N. 1663." The church is a delightful plain building, reminding one of a Cornish church in little—a double aisle, or rather double nave, which is the same breadth at each end, divided by four arches. The style is that Tudor-Gothic with classical detail which Wren in his early work made such effects with, as at S. Mary's, Warwick ; but of course this is only a small building, an " elegant piece," as Bishop Skinner said at the same date, when he consecrated Mr. Speaker Lenthall's chapel at Burford. The painted roof is quaint and charming : sun, and moon, and stars. The barrel-organ, I fear, is not used. The monuments were fished out of the moat, and here they are, not so very much the worse. Sir William Compton with his collar of SS, his wife at his feet—a position his daughter-in-law would never have occupied ; and, hard by, Henry with his wives, the second of whom was a Spencer like her daughter-in-law, but of the Althorp house. There is also the eighth earl, Spencer Compton, who died in 1796. After him the monuments are to be sought for in the church, even more interesting, of Castle Ashby. You will also rejoice in the banners hung from the walls, a pedigree of the family in themselves, and in the tablet in memory of Sir William Compton, the third son of the second earl, Governor of Banbury Castle during the Wars, who survived the wars to become Master General of Ordnance, and died in 1663. And one last word to ecclesiasticks before they leave the church. There exists a curious Trust for the holding of advowsons which will not allow a structural chancel to any of the churches in its gift.   Let it look at this church and ask what is there in a church that is the same breadth all the way to prevent the very " excesses " of " ritual " which the Trust finds so shocking.

Outside the church again, before you tear yourself away from Compton Winyates, in the churchyard is the grave of a witch (they say) called Jane Story, 1755, and beside is one of those splendid dovecots Warwickshire is renowned for.

Lastly before we go we will quote from Mr. A. W. Ashby's recent book :—[1]

" The burial registers at Compton Wyniates contain eight entries between 1683 and 1812, of receipts of ' £2 10s. 0d. for the poor, according to Act of Parliament for being buried in other than sheep's wool.'   In 1754 £5 was received in a lump sum for the same purpose.   On this occasion the person buried had been a Marquis and a Privy Councillor.   This provision of the law fostered the production of wool and burdened the rates at the same time :   took money from the farmers' pockets with one hand and attempted to replace it with the other, with the risk of losing it in the transfer.   The cost of shrouds made in order to comply with this extraordinary statutory regulation varied between two and nine shillings.   The price of coffins advanced from 5s. 3d. in 1727 to 17s. in 1815, and £1 2s. 6d. in 1817.   In 1727 a set of items of funeral expenditure is recorded thus :—

					s.	d.
To making affidavit ..	..	..	..	..	1	0
Phillip Wells' fees (clerk)	..	..	..	..	2	6
Minister's fees..	..	..	..	..		6
Coffin ..	..	..	..	..	5	6
4 men carrying to church	..	..	..	4	0	
Paid for a shroud	..	..	..	..	2	6
For candles and necessary ware	..	..	1	0		

" For many years the minister's fee for burial was sixpence ; but toward the end of the century it advanced to 2s. 6d. and 3s. 6d., payments being made in a lump sum like any other professional fees."

Compton Winyates has a history, one sees, which touches every side of life, and death.

[1] *One Hundred Years of Poor Law Administration in a Warwickshire Village* (Oxford Studies in Social and Legal History, Vol. iii.)

And now from Compton Winyates to a village, or collection of villages, not so well known as Brailes but worth, perhaps, a fuller record. Perhaps the best way to go is by leaving the park at the gate by which you entered and turn to the right and so on till you join the road from Shipston. That will take you straight to Upper Tysoe, so to Middle and then to Lower, where you are but a mile from the foot of Edgehill. Tysoe, thus familiar to those who make the prilgrimage up hill and down dale to Compton Winyates, is at the south-east end of Warwickshire, close to Kineton. It is in the valley of the Warwickshire Avon, in the corn-growing district called the Feldon. It is a typical justification of what Leland says of the whole shire—" Corn is the cheapest commodity grown in the county, whereof the Vale of the Red Horse yieldeth most abundantly." It was a growing village from Domesday for eight hundred years. Through the greater part of the eighteenth century it had a large number of freeholders. The Earls (now Marquesses) of Northampton were Lords of the Manor.

Let us go to it and look into its history. If you pass through the vale below the Red Horse on your way to Compton Winyates, or to Little Compton, you will come to the very interesting villages which make up the triple Tysoe. On the hill opposite Church Tysoe it is that the Red Horse was originally cut. And Mr. Thomas Cox in 1700 says : " because the Earth is red it is called the Red Horse, and gives a Denomination to the fruitful Vale about it, called the Vale of the Red Horse. The Trenches about the Horse are cleansed every year by a freeholder of the Lordship who holds his Land by that service." First you come to Lower Tysoe, or Temple Tysoe—Temple because the Knights of Temple Balsall held land there, which afterwards passed to the Hospitallers. Of this part of the village there is not much to say, save for the remains of a market house, of the old Cross, and of a fifteenth century house with a doorway two hundred years younger, with the initials " P.I.P." dated 1691. The best house at Upper Tysoe has great merit, with stone doorways on the first floor and a fine window which may have belonged to a chapel. But Church or Middle Tysoe is the most interesting of the three hamlets which make up the parish. You will observe the antiquity of the south wall of the church, where the old windows may still be traced as little slits in the wall. Sceptics (among whom I am one here) may discount the Saxon origin alleged ; but no one will put the date as later than Norman times. In the old windows there are remains of the ancient plaster decoration, but it is certainly not " Oriental" as has been absurdly said. The north aisle, on the other hand, is good thirteenth century work with some Decorated windows, but not so interesting as the south windows. The Perpendicular chancel has been much restored ; so indeed has all the church. But the tombs are unharmed ; one, perhaps that of the benefactor who built the Decorated work, showing only head and feet un-covered ; William Clarke, gentleman, patron of the church, 1618, in trunk hose, with traces of colour now washed away ; a brass of Thomas Mastrupe, priest, 1463 ; other brasses of the Browne family, one of whom bears the remarkable name of Tamizane, which perhaps may be a way of spelling a female Thomas. The font is a very fine Decorated one. Round it are eight figures under canopies of the best style of the time. It is well to say what they are, as the guide-books are puzzled. Beginning from the east, are S. Mary Magdalene ; S. Michael ; our Lady with our Lord in her arms ; the Baptism (the water shown in the traditional style like a series of loaves above each other) ; S. Catherine, and then, opposite to the B.V.M., and between S. Peter and S. Paul, our Lord in judgment, with His right hand raised in blessing and left hand on the orb. In the churchyard the stone of William Kinman, 1799, with lines adapted from the well-known Elizabethan verse comparing the world to a city of crooked streets with its market-place Death. Altogether a most important church, suitable for the highly important parish. For Tysoe has a long history, which Mr. A. W. Ashby has recently elucidated in its social aspect, from docu-ments chiefly connected with the administration of the Poor Law. His description of the position of the place is worth quoting, for comparison with other villages in the neighbourhood. How much difference one sees as one walks about, was made by canals, and by the neighbourhood of great roads. At Tysoe we are close to that buried treasure, Compton Winyates : " Did ye ever see such a hole ? " as a local worthy said to an inquirer almost a century ago (*see* p. 10). But Tysoe's position is unlike that of Compton Winyates. It had no rich lord intimately concerned with its social development. And so its geographical position had its result unhindered. Says Mr. Ashby :—

" It was the misfortune of Tysoe that the village was never

affected, except adversely, by the industrial development of the country. The Oxford Canal was only nine miles distant, but the journey over the intervening hills to Banbury was so difficult that the farmers and haulers preferred to go twelve miles to Stratford, or sixteen miles to Warwick. This fact is by no means negligible when it is remembered that coals at the canal side cost 10*d*. per cwt., and were sold to the poor of Tysoe by the overseers at 1*s*. 6*d*. per cwt., the prices paid to the haulers for carriage being 6*d*. per cwt. However, the distant touch with the canals was good for the district, for with this means of access to distant markets the farmers were not at the mercy of local dealers. Writing on the price of provisions in the county, Wedge said distinctly that the price of corn was much more regular after the opening of the canals than before. Besides the canals, the only means of commercial communication was the turnpike road from Oxford to Birmingham through Stratford-on-Avon. There were daily coaches along this road, as well as pack-horse men plying between Droitwich and London. Thus Tysoe remained and still remains a large, prosperous, old-world, agricultural parish."

A crisis of its history begins with the Agricultural Revolution of the eighteenth century. In 1796 the Enclosure Act was set to work, and in 1798 the Commissioners gave their award for Tysoe. It was a time of great scarcity, due to the hard seasons of 1794 and 1795, and many freeholders—one-fifth, in fact,—sold their rights during the process of enclosure. In spite of this, the number of landed proprietors grew till 1804, chiefly by sub-division of land. At the same time farms began to be consolidated, and in the next quarter of a century the number of owners became much smaller, while the value of the land increased. Lord Northampton's tenants diminished from thirty-one in 1800 to twenty-one in 1815, while, on the other hand, the rent of his estates increased from £1,700 in 1803 to £2,480 in 1911. The population meanwhile was advancing, as it did till 1821, after which a more rigorous enforcing of the Poor Laws caused it to diminish. The population grew between 1665 and 1801 nearly three hundred, and there was evidently good housing and plenty of house-room. But Tysoe was not a self-sufficing village. A great part of the labour at Compton came from it, but the rates were not combined. Hence a gradual decline in the prosperity of Tysoe. A decay of domestic industry followed ; between 1801 and 1820 those employed in trade and handicrafts fell thirty in number. And some of these, it seems, were taken by the pressgang, for the parish paid the landlady of one of the inns fifteen shillings " for eating, beer, and fireing when the chimney-sweep and the razor-grinder were taken for soldiers." The Poor Laws worked hardly. Tysoe never, it seems, allowed a servant (except on marrying) to settle in the village for fear he or she should become chargeable to the parish.

The chief landlords acted well. Though a recent writer states that " the aristocracy and plutocracy of England cared little for what happened to the masses of the people during the period of the French wars," he is constrained a few pages later to quote a minute of the Vestry, December 20th, 1799, which shows that Lord Northampton gave " £30 to lower the price of bread for four months for the relief of the poor," the parish giving the same sum. But the administration was very wasteful. Farmers who failed were paid large sums for hauling coals for the parish, or their rates were paid for them, and even houses found for them at the parish expense. The local charities, besides being used in relief, supported a school " from time immemorial," for which the school-master received a guinea a boy ; but he cannot have made a large income, as the number of scholars seems never to have exceeded twenty. While wages averaged about three shillings a week (as in 1823) several farmers were making their fortunes, but the parish itself seems to have paid for its own special work 1s. 6d. a day. Yet as house-rents and the cost of living much increased and the price of food rose from 100 to 150 per cent. during the century ending in 1830 the incomes of the poor were actually lower after 1790 than before 1760. All this comes out in Mr. Ashby's interesting but somewhat prejudiced study.

One may note here that the stocks still stand in the village. But Tysoe has a more grim and recent record. It is one of the last places where people still fancied witches could be found. In 1875 folk of Brailes thought a neighbour of Tysoe a witch and tried the test of drawing blood. " Blood will I draw on thee : thou art a witch," says Talbot to the Maid of France in *Henry VI*. We are back again in the superstitious days of Shakespeare. But we will not follow these cruel yokels back to Brailes. We are ready rather to go to the limit of our Shakespeare land and find ourselves at Edgehill.

CHAPTER II

How shall we approach Edgehill ? Perhaps the best way, out of very many, is by the long, straight road from Warwick to Banbury. When you have gone from Warwick some ten miles you will find yourself, still rising, at the foot of a steep hill. After you have left Gaydon with its nice modern church, and survived the hills on each side of it, you will find yourself, before you come to the railway, some three hundred feet above sea level: you will then rise forty feet, and at eleven miles from Warwick will see a rise to four hundred and eighty feet before you. In 1910 I read an account of the prospect and the adventures of a cyclist (I give my grateful thanks to C. H. L. G., for I know only his initials) from which I take the liberty of quoting a little for the benefit of travellers like himself, and myself. These byways of Warwickshire are especially delightful. The traveller evidently stopped when this steep ascent was before him, and thus, having consulted his map, he writes :—

" From the high road two lanes led to villages of the names of Burton Dassett and Avon Dassett, which nestled on the western flank of the hill about a mile and a-half from each other. From the nearest one to me, Burton Dassett, the lane was marked as continuing right over the hill. Avon Dassett could be thus reached, and further on was Farnborough, which seemed to offer itself as a likely resting-place. But I had an open mind. So leaving the turnpike I was soon pushing up the lower slope to the hamlet which gives its name to or else takes it from the hill. The situation of the church was romantic in the extreme. The view had already begun to open out."

Indeed it had, one comments. If he ascended the Beacon,

with the windmill by it, he would have seen a wonderful stone erection, *circa* 1450, which I am told is 15 feet 4 inches high, 62 feet round, and 4 feet thick. From its quaint windows you may see the Malvern Hills, or southwards forty miles to another Beacon, just like this, at Ivinghoe. The news of Edge-hill was signalled in this way. A magnificent view from here indeed. Then look at the church of Dassett. This is at Burton, Avon Dassett having one of quite modern date. Close to it is the well, with date [15]34. The church of All Saints (I think it was originally S. James) has a splendid north transept window of four lancets. Two fine Norman doors survive from an earlier church and twelfth century work marks the chancel arch. The decoration of the capitals is extraordinarily interesting, and the whole church is a picture of English architecture in little, going up indeed to the spacious times of great Elizabeth. It has some fine tombs—that of Peter Temple of Stowe, Bucks, 1577, especially, and the tablet to John Temple and his wife with the lines

> " Cur liberos hic plurimos?
> Cur hic amicos plurimos?
> Et plurimas pecunias?
> Vis scire cur reliquerit?
> Tempellus ad plures abiit."

But around the church you will find few dwellings indeed. Why is that? Mr. Cox thus tells us from Dugdale, after a long record of earlier owners of the manor, coming to Henry Belknap who died:

"3 *Hen.* VII. and left Sir *Edward*, his Son and Heir, then 17 years of Age, who became a Man much employed in publick Affairs; for in 2 *Hen.* VII. he was one of the Commanders in the King's Army at the Battle of *Stoke*; in the 6th a Commissioner of Array for this County; in the 12th a Commander in the Battle of *Black-heath* in *Kent*, against the Western Rebels; and in the 17th Keeper of *Warwick Castle*, and Squire of the Body to the King. He was also in Commission for the Peace most of that King's Reign, and sometimes for Gaol-delivery. He was blamed for depopulating and inclosing a great Part of the Parish, contrary to a Statute made in the 3d Year of that King; but he making it appear that his Inclosures were no Prejudice, but a Benefit to the Publick, and that the Benefice was better, the Inhabitants richer, the Children better taught, and God better served ; the King granted him a special Patent of Immunity from any Trouble upon that Account. He continued much in favour in King *Henry* VIII.'s Reign, being knighted by him, and constituted Governor of *Warwick-Castle* ; but died the 12th Year of that King's Reign, in *France*, without Issue, leaving his four Sisters his Heirs ; between whom or their Heirs his Estate was divided; and *Gerard Danet, William Shelley*, and Sir *Edward Wotton* had their several Parts. The Lord *Wotton* was seised of his Ancestors Part, 1 *Jac.* I. and *Danet* sold his Share to *Peter Temple*, Esq ; 2 *Eliz.* whose Posterity enjoyed it in 1640."

Rous indeed (*obiit* 1491) says much of this depopulation ; but the village increased again in the eighteenth century and sank in the nineteenth.

As to Sir Edward Belknap, it may be added that he made the Beacon, and it was shown on his arms, according to one authority. They were thus painted in a coat once fixed above the chancel arch. And now I will go back to the cyclist, whom I left at Burton Dassett with no cheerful prospect of bed or board.

He says now, " I began to wish that some hospitable dwelling might be found among the few to be seen. What a prospect for next morning : first to the west as I faced them, and then from the old windmill at the top northwards and eastwards as well ! But it was not to be. This is evidently a spot which people from afar have scorched and raced by unheeding—a spot only known to the few initiated who reside near at hand. No stranger would seem to have ever desired before to spend a night at Burton Dassett. So very reluctantly I turned away from its enchantment and pushed on, most literally, up to the hanging down which I had not time to explore then, and had to hurry away from with little likelihood of return. The track now passed along the eastern brow and commanded an extensive view. It then dropped gently down to where a road crossed it, leading on the right to Avon Dassett, which looked further off than I had imagined, and on the left downhill to Fenny Compton. I was greatly tempted by hunger to coast down, but Farnborough drew me on, after a little hesitation. Its spire showed up in the distance. It stood, for one thing, higher up than its Fenny neighbour. But, alas ! when I reached its inn there was no room available ! I had better try at Avon

Dassett, only a mile and a-half round the flank of the hill. Like Farnborough, it was another fascinating village—as typical of the ideal English village as one could wish. But, alas ! like Farnborough, the inn's one spare room was engaged."

To this I would add a word of caution from another cyclist, Mr. Douglas Leechman, whose words of wisdom about the roads should be observed. He says :—

"Tourists in this district will do well to keep a sharp look-out for gates across the roads. I forget whether there are seven or eleven in the two miles odd extending between the main roads at Warmington and Farnborough respectively. I know I negotiated the lot of them and some twenty-five miles of road in—well, never mind—one evening, after paying a farewell pilgrimage to Compton Wynyates on a two-cylinder Clement Garrard. I think it must have been on this occasion that I experienced an unpleasant elevation (physical, not mental) near Fenny Compton. There is a narrow pass here through the hills, and the road, canal, and two lines of railway squeeze through a narrow neck. The road falls rather steeply towards the north, and crosses the canal, the bridge forming a kind of ratchet tooth in the slope. I was quite familiar with the place, and recognised that it must be taken slowly. But slowly is a relative term, and as I encountered the bridge I shot right up off the saddle and had time to think a lot before I came down again. Fortunately I ' resumed my seat,' and all was well, but the chances of a nasty smash were all too evident."

Let this be avoided by those who walk or ride or drive or motor through Shakespeare's country. Flying will no doubt be the safest way of going about, when it becomes safe at all.

Now this gives one an account of the geography of this little out of the way bit of Warwickshire. Of Fenny Compton I speak elsewhere (see p. 129). Here I will only say that in Avon Dassett church there is a most important monument to Hugo, the parish priest in 1232, which shows amice, dalmatic, stole, maniple, cassock : I said " priest," but the clerk was clearly only a deacon. Then at Farnborough there is a good church and a quite charming hall with a long terraced walk. From Farnborough go back westwards to Warmington and mount the tremendous hill—a severe strain, as I know, for a motor car. The church is at the very top in a most beautiful position, surrounded by trees. Northwards thirty-seven steps approach it :

it is a fine mixture of styles from Norman to Perpendicular, having been added to century after century. But it is chiefly to be remembered for the little house on the south-west side, which is plainly an " anchorage " where an anchoress or anchorite lived, shut up, up stairs, able to see the altar, but having no mortal consolation except, as the rule allowed, a domestic solitary cat. But there is something else outside, and that is the first memorial we have yet come to of Edgehill fight. Between the south porch and the gate is a low headstone on which are these words : " Here lieth the body of Alexander Gourdin, capitaine, buried the 25 day of October, Ano Domini 1642." The register has further record, thus : " The Battell was fought by our Sovraine Lord King Charles and the Earle of Essex, the three and twentieth Day of October, being Sabbeath Day, Ano. Dom. 1642, partly between Radwaie and Kington. Richard Sauner, captaine of a Foot Companie, a gentleman of Worcestershier, was buried in Warmington Churchyard, the four and twentieth day of October Ano Dom. 1642. Alexander Gourden a Scotsman, was buried the five and twentieth day of October Ano Dom. 1642 ut supra. Also seven others were buried in Warmington Churchyard whose names I know not, and it is reported that one or two more were buried within the field and winde of Warmington aforesaid."

And now it is time we should go to the scene of the battle itself. We take Camp Lane, keeping at the top of the hill and look down through the trees at the quite lovely Arlescote, the house with its gables at the corners rising above the buildings and stacks between us. Then Nadbury Camp, a British entrenchment, to our left, and we get to Knowle End, just where the road descends which takes you the quickest way to Kineton. Just here under a hedge sat William Harvey, the discoverer of the circulation of the blood, while the battle was proceeding that October day. He was put in charge of Charles Prince of Wales and James Duke of York, and he had the boys with him. Down they sat, and he " took out of his pockett a booke and read ; but he had not read very long before a bullet of a great gun grazed on the ground neare him, which made him remove his station." Aubrey, who records this in his " Brief Lives," adds, " He told me that Sir Adrian Scrope was dangerously wounded there, and left for dead amongst the dead men, stript, which happened to be the saving of his life. It was cold, clear weather, and a frost that night ; which staunched his bleeding, and about midnight, or some hours after his hurt, he awaked, and was faine to draw a dead body upon him for warmeth sake." The poor boys, who both lived to be kings, must have seen terrible sights that day, for a bitter fight it was.

Now that we are at the top of the hill, we must walk along, turning, at Knowle End, leftwards. About half a mile onwards we will turn to the left for a moment to see Ratley Church and old houses. In one of the houses is a fine window which suggests an oratory ; the house is fifteenth century. The church is Decorated, and has some good features, while the churchyard has a cross with the Divine Figure still on it though mutilated. Mr. George Miller, whose authority on all that belongs to this district is unimpeachable, tells that the first allotments in the neighbourhood were given here by Lady Lucy Pusey, on the advice of her son, Dr. Pusey. The village itself is not of great interest now. Its days of history are, at least for the time, gone by.

It was on October 22, 1642, that Charles I. marched from Southam, through Wormleighton, to Edgecot, as they say. It would be a very rough way indeed for our generation, and we should take a much better road. But the main road was perhaps not made then (though I certainly think it was) and it cannot have been very easy to get to Edgecot, to the east of Banbury, in a hurry, or to get thence as Charles did on the Sunday morning of October 23. By that time Essex's Parliamentary troops were in the valley at Kineton, and Rupert would have Charles come forward to hold the ridge. So he did. He marched to the Edgehills, I suppose through Warmington, and left his boys at Knowle Hill as he came by. No doubt his troops occupied Ratley too. He himself had breakfast at the Sunrising, a house at the other, the south-western, end of the hills, and then went to the high point at the very centre of the hill, looking down over the plain where the enemy lay. In the morning his troops kept coming up behind him : there were endless delays, in "these stony ways," and often the soldiers could not get their horses shod, for the smiths had run away. It was difficult to get food, and when men were sent out to get something to eat, they were often (Clarendon tells us) "knocked on the head by the common people." And so the battle hardly began before three o'clock. It was over by six, when men could see to fight no more. Charles was in the thickest of the fight, and so was Cromwell. The story of it is well known, but it may well be recalled as we look at the scene from the Radway Tower. The fields have changed much since those days. They are thickly wooded, both on the slopes and in the valley. Then they were bare and there were no houses save in the village of Radway. After he had seen how the land lay, Charles rode down the hill and took place with his foot soldiers in the centre of the field. To his right Prince Rupert, to his left Wilmot, charged with their cavalry upon the foe and scattered them like dust. Rupert cut down the Roundheads, forcing their wing inwards on the main body, and pressing the fugitives into Kineton, where he drove them back down the bank to the river. The narrow streets were blocked with carriages and waggons, Essex's coach stuck among them. So Rupert declared he could " give a good account of the enemy's horse " ; and one of his company who stood by said, " Ay, and of their carts too."

On the left wing Wilmot had been stopped by the ditches and hedges of Little Kineton, and does not seem to have been able to join his fellows in the town ; while in the centre the Parliamentary horse had made havoc of the King's foot men. The main part of the fight took place between two farmhouses, built since then, called Battleton and Thistleton. Lord Lindsey, to whom is attributed the prayer, " Lord, Thou knowest how busy I must be this day. If I forget thee do not Thou forget me " (but really it was Sir Jacob Astley who said it), urged his men forward, as the bells were still ringing to evensong. He was wounded and captured. Sir Edmund Verney, of Claydon, Bucks, the King's Standard-bearer, was killed, giving account, said a letter which told the tale, of sixteen gentlemen before he fell. The Royal Standard was not long in Essex's hands. He gave it to his secretary to hold. Then came Captain John Smith of Skilts (*see* p. 365) with all the loyalty and bravery of an Arden man, and set upon him, telling him that it was no prize for a penman. He recaptured the banner, and then "immediately comes up a great body of his Majesty's horse, which were rallied together, with whom he stayed, delivering the standard to Master Robert Hutton, a gentleman of Sir Robert Willyes's troop, to carry forthwith to his Majesty. The next morning King Charles sent for him to the top of Edgehill, where his Majesty knighted him for his singular valour." So the darkness came on : it was too late for the charge which Falkland urged, and no one knew with whom the victory truly lay. So " in this doubt of all sides, the night, the common friend to wearied and dismayed armies, parted them ; and then the King caused his cannon, which were nearest to the enemy, to be drawn off ; and with his whole forces himself spent the night in the field, by such fire as could be made of the little wood and bushes which grew thereabouts, unresolved what to do the next morning." At dawn, the troops fasting all night, no one was in good stomach for a fight. Charles offered pardon to all those who would give up their arms ; but Essex would not let his men hear the offer, and so, after watching each other all day, on Monday Essex drew back to Warwick and Charles to Edgecot again.

The King's account, after stating that the battle was con- tinued till it was too dark to fight, states that thereupon " both armies retreated, ours in such Order that we not only brought off our own cannon but four of the Rebels', we retiring to the top of the hill from whence we came, because of the advantage of the Place ; and theirs to the Village where they had been quartered the night before "; and adds that, " The next Day after the Battel, the Earl of Essex, finding his army extremely weaken'd and dishearten'd by the great Blow they had receiv'd by his Majesty's Forces, withdrew himself to Warwick Castle ; and the same night the remainder of his Forces went also privately tho' then much distracted." But the report to the Parliament gave thanks for the great blessing they had received, on " the resolute and unwearied endeavours of our soldiers," and de- clared that " the King's Foot are either slain or most of them run away, and are now very weak, and shou'd have been pur- sued by us, but that we must of pure necessity refresh our Men for three or four Days ; and then we shall (God willing) address ourselves to finish the work."

Still memories of the day remain. Mr. Miller tells some tales that came to him from Tysoe, thus :—" On the morn of the battle, a squadron of cavalry passed through Tysoe. As they rode by a farm house, occupied by a farmer named Wells— the farm is still in the hands of a descendant of that family— the soldiers, finding that the farmer's wife was that morning baking, went into the bakehouse and took all the bread out of

the oven. The farmer seeing this, went into the house, collected
all the silver, with every other article of value, and putting
them into a covered pot, sunk them beneath the waters of the
well. The soldiers, having got a supply of bread, rode on till
they came to a lane, where there was a farmhouse with a yard
in front of it. Here they unsaddled their horses, and proceeded to make a meal, washing down the new bread with beer
and cider which they obtained from the farmhouse. Having
rested and refreshed themselves, they resaddled their horses—
the lane has ever since been called Saddling Street—and
proceeded to join the King. As they rode through Temple
Tysoe, a farmer, fearing lest the troopers would seize a handsome cob that he had bred, cut a hole in the barley-mow in his
barn, hiding the cob therein. When the troops drew near,
the farmer was in mortal dread lest his cob should hear the
horses' footsteps when passing by, and, neighing, should dis-
close his hiding place. The cob, to the owner's joy, remained
quite silent. The troop, however, had not proceeded far,
when another incident occurred. Passing a gate just beyond
the village, a stalwart youth stood with his arms over the
gate, gazing at the Cavaliers in their bright array. The captain
stopped and asked the youth which side he wished well. The
youth, taken back at the suddenness of the question, and
having no real opinion on the matter, replied, without knowing
what he said : ' The Parliament.' Whereupon, for a lark,
the soldiers fired several shots over his head. The youth, in
fear for his life, fell down as if shot dead ; nor did he rise from
the ground till the troop was well out of sight, when he ran for
his life to the hills, and did not return for two or three days.
These anecdotes were told to the author by a man over seventy,
who heard it from his grandmother, who lived to be over ninety.
She heard them from her grandfather, who was a boy when
the battle was fought.'

It is said, on the evidence of the Vicar of Kineton, that twelve
hundred were slain. Radway Church shelters the memorial
of one hero. The church itself was rebuilt in 1866. Its picturesque graveyard contains many interesting tombstones,
several which witness sadly to the dangers of the steep descent
of the road from the Sunrising. Within is the monument
of Captain Henry Kingsmill, disfigured and mutilated, but
still showing the figure and dress a little anachronistic,—for it

was erected in 1670 as the inscription tells,—which is worth copy-ing here :—" Here lyeth expecting ye second comeing of our blessed Lord & Saviour Henry Kingsmill Esq. second son to St Henry Kingsmill of Sidmonton in ye county of Southton Knt whoe serving as a Captain of foot under his ^Matie Charles the first of Blessed memory was at the Battell of Edgehill in ye yeare of our Lord 1642 as he was manfully fighting in behalf of his King and Country unhappily slaine by a Cannon Bullett, in memory of whom his Mother the Lady Bridgett Kingsmill did in ye forty sixth yeare of her Widdowhood in ye yeare of our Lord 1670 erect this Monument." " I have fought a good fight I have finished my course henceforth is layde up for me a Crowne of righteousness."

He had ridden a white horse and was conspicuous on the hillside, a mark for the Parliamentary guns. It is still possible to follow the course of the battle, though the fields are now split up and new farms made. The hamlet of Westcot, below the hill and behind the King's lines, seems to have been destroyed during the fight. The Radway church bells rang as the King's troops rode by, and Jeremiah Hill, the parson, read evensong to but a small flock, little knowing that he would be turned out of his benefice before long, yet live to have his own again when the King and Church came back in 1660.

Such are the memories which still survive. Farther back, close to the fight itself, goes the great " ghost-story " of Edge-hill. On the first Christmas Eve after the battle shepherds watching their flocks by night saw ghostly armies come forth on either side, heard the cannon roar, bullets hiss, horses neigh and drums beat, the shouts of warriors and the groans of woun-ded, till with the dawn the hosts vanished into air. Mr. William Wood, " justice for the peace in the county of Northampton," and Mr. Samuel Marshall, " preacher of God's word in Keinton," were told thereof: and they, in spite of hardy scepticism, watched the next night in the open field. Again came the vision ; " and so departed the gentlemen and all the spectators much terrified with these visions of horror, and withdrew themselves to their houses, beseeching God to defend them from these hellish and prodigious armies." From Oxford King Charles hinself sent six " gentlemen of credit " " to search into the truth of the tale : they saw the vision too." But what came of it man knoweth not, and as the war raged it was soon forgotten.

And so you look back to the day when brothers were fated to fight. Modern lines come to your mind as you think of the story, those fine verses of Rudyard Kipling :—

> " Naked and grey the Cotswolds stand
>   Beneath the autumn sun,
> And the stubble fields on either hand
>   Where Stour and Avon run.
> There is no change in the patient land
>   That has bred us every one."
>
> She should have passed in cloud and fire
>   And saved us from this sin
> Of war—red war—'twixt child and sire,
>   Household and kith and kin,
> In the heart of a sleepy Midland shire,
>   With the harvest scarcely in."

It is not strange that, long though the war raged in England and many though the fields were that saw Englishmen fight with Englishmen for King and Parliament, no battle has made more impression on men's memories than Edgehill, the first of the bitter Civil War.

So far of Edgehill, its history and legends. The houses near by must now have each a word. First there is the quite charming grange at Radway, just at the foot of the hill, whence a winding path (private) and road lead up to the Tower, of which more anon. The house certainly contains some of the old Tudor building, but the greater part was designed by Sanderson Miller, merchant, virtuoso, architect, the real pioneer of the Gothic revival, the friend of the Warwickshire literary circle of his day. He was intimate with Fielding, who read " Tom Jones," it is said, in manuscript in this house to the great Pitt, George Lyttelton, and Miller himself. Sanderson Miller the elder made his fortune at Banbury in the late seventeenth century and bought Radway in 1712. His son, also Sanderson, was the friend, not only of Fielding, but of Shenstone and Jago, and it is he whose genius made the quaint and interesting house we now see.

Sanderson Miller is so far known to everyone who visits Edgehill. He ought to be known much better. Country clergymen and squires ought to know him and to hunt in their papers for evidence that he meddled with their churches or houses (or did not). He was in truth the predecessor of Pugin, the precursor of the " Gothic revival." Many people will prefer his classical work, such as the fine County Hall at War-wick, at which he had Hiorns for his Clerk of the Works, who has left at least one notable archæologist as his descendant to-day. Others like the quaintness of his Gothic, which, as Horace Walpole wrote of something or other he did, would win him the freedom of Strawberry Hill. He had a real feeling for medieval architecture, but (like the gentleman in "The New Republic") he wanted the architecture of his day to be a " Renaissance of all styles." He had one advantage over most modern architects—that he really could be original. We need not pursue the subject into an inquiry whether it is advisable to be original in evildoing. But Miller was more than this. He was the friend of a great many interesting people—of Pitt and the Lytteltons and Jonathan Swift's cousin and biographer among men ; and he was at least acquainted with that elegant set of not too ambitious poets and letter-writers which has been dubbed " the Warwickshire Coterie." All this will be found very pleasantly set forth in " An Eighteenth Century Corres-pondence," which may be heartily recommended to all who are fond of quiet, gossipy books that add to our knowledge of the most comfortable age óf English history.

To return to what Sanderson Miller did here. When we rise from Radway and the battlefield to the brow of Edgehill we must not forget that it was he who, as Jago said, crowned " with grace-ful pomp the shaggy hill." The graceful pomp is the Radway Tower, on the spot where Charles stood before the ball. A most curious building indeed it is, with heavy battlements and the absurdest of eighteenth century windows, a cottage below and a room above, where on September 3, 1750, Miller, to celebrate its completion, gave an entertainment for the nobility, gentry, and clergy of the neighbourhood. A wooden bridge connects this with a smaller tower, and other walls near are designed to give the impression that there was once a real castle on the spot. What Miller built seemed to Horace Wal-pole to have " the true rust of the Barons' Wars." Though we do not think so now, we can greatly delight to sit in its garden, look at its curiosities, and perhaps have a simple meal.

The Tower was " opened " thus on September 3, 1750, not with-out prognostications that as it was the day on which Cromwell died, in a great storm, so the elements might destroy it at its very beginning. But it has weathered many a storm since then. The best description I know of it is that by Bishop Pococke of Ossory.[1] "Miller," he says, "has embellished his own house with Gothic architecture, and has made a fine lawn up the hill, with shady walks round it, up to the ruined castle at Edgehill which he has built adjoining to the houses of some tenants. But he has erected a very noble round Tower, which is entire, with a draw-

The Radway Tower.

bridge, to which there is an ascent as by a Mine, and there is a very fine octagon Gothic room in it, with four windows and four niches, and some old painted glass in the windows. In one of these niches is to be placed Caractacus in chains, modeled, under Mr. Miller's directions, by a countryman of great genius now established in London ; it is executed in the yellow free-stone." I wonder if Caractacus ever appeared.

[1] Quoted in that charming book "An Eighteenth Century Correspondence," by Lilian Dickins and Mary Stanton.

From this point, or near it, one may put one's self with Drayton :—

" For, from the loftie Edge that on my side doth lye,
Upon my spacious earth who casts a curious eye,
As many goodly seates shall in my compasse see,
As many sweet delights and rarities in mee,
As in the greatest Vale : from where my head I couch
At Cotswolds Countries foot, till with my heeles I touch
The North-hamptonian fields and fatning Pastures, where
I ravish every eye with my inticing cheere.
As still the Yeere growes on, that Ceres once doth load
The full Earth with her store ; my plentious bosome strow'd
With all abundant sweets ; my trim and lustie flanke
Her bravery then displays, with Meadowes hugely ranke.
The thick and well-growne fogge doth matt my smoother shades,
And on the lower Leas, as on the higher Hades
The daintie Clover growes (of grass the onely silke)
That makes each Udder strout abundantly with milke."

What do you think the " higher Hades " are ?[1]   One thinks of the heroes of past days who have gone from Warwickshire to their rest, from the wide stretch seen from Edgehill and summed up in its glory by Drayton. So with the Northamptonshire poet :—

" Sweet, my sister, Queen of Hades,
Where the quiet and the shade is,
Of the cruel deathless ladies
Thou art pitiful alone."

From the Tower one has a most magnificent view, from Burton Dassett to Moreton-in-Marsh and Malvern, the Clee Hills, the Wrekin, even Shrewsbury, as well as Worcester, Warwick, and Coventry, while at one's feet lies a long level plain which only a long gaze proves to be diversified by churches and farms, mounds and streams. Going further west and south you come to the beautiful house called Sunrising, long a famous inn, where Charles I. breakfasted and many famous folk stayed later in the coaching days. The house is a beautiful one, as well as a famous. Part of it was built in the early seventeenth century, and bears the date 1613, but the front was very skilfully rebuilt in 1807. It was here that James I. rested on August 23, 1619, travelling to Wroxton from Warwick : here the Earl

---

[1] The word "hades" occurs in the Holbeche Estate Book of 1770.   See *Eng. Dialect Dict.*, vol. iii, p. 10.

of Lindsey, taken captive at Edgehill fight, was brought in
to die ; and here Charles I. came again on July 15, 1643,
when he was to meet his wife who had been staying with Shakespeare's daughter at Stratford on-Avon (*see* p. 166). In the house
are many things that have been there since the battle : Lord
Lindsey's sword and several others ; cannon balls, bullets, breast-
plates, what not. During its inn-days the house was a fixed
place for rest at night, and, later, for dining : and Mr. Miller
tells that " it used to be the landlord's boast that more wedded
couples stayed at the Sunrising than in any other inn or hotel
in Warwickshire." Newly-married, no doubt, he means.

Then beyond that and about 200 yards farther you come to
the Red Horse. This is a new one, as time counts in England,
cut only at the end of the eighteenth century, when the Sunrising
was an inn and its owners made a harvest out of the old fair
that was held at its scouring ; as Jago says :—

> " Studious to preserve
> The fav'rite form, the treach'rous conquerors
> Their vassal tribes compel, with festive rites,
> Its fading figure yearly to renew,
> And to the neighb'ring vale impart its name."

He thought it went back to the time of the English conquerors, and was, like the White Horse of Berkshire, an emblem
of their conquest. It is also said to have been cut by the King-
maker in order to commemorate the horse he slew at Towton in
1461, a most unlikely suggestion. Originally the horse, which
· Jago knew, and whose past is so dim, stood in Temple Tysoe on
the hill opposite the end of the church and a particular farm,
Red Horse Farm, was obliged to scour it each year ; and it was
done, of all times in the year, on Palm Sunday.

Now from the Red Horse, unless you turn back to look at
the interesting Upton House, with its fine grounds, its ancient
history going back to the Ardens and part of its buildings to the
fifteenth century, you will go on to Kineton. As to Upton,
the old house, increased in 1698, was altered by Sanderson
Miller for its owner soon after 1730.

But there is a modern story which everyone delights to tell.
Child, the banker, bought it in 1757, and the Earl of West-
morland fell in love with his daughter ; and the lover asked
the father what he would do if he loved a girl and she him and
the father would not consent. " Why, run away with her,

of course," said Mr. Child. No sooner said than done, and married at Gretna Green. But the father was obdurate, and left all his money to his daughter's second child. She became Countess of Jersey, and I think that Lord Jersey still owns, but now lets, Upton.

At the back of the house, some way down the hill, is Temple Pool or Pond, at which the County of Warwick ends, meeting Oxford and Gloucester. And so we will turn back, past the Sunrising and down the steep and dangerous hill. After a mile, unless we wish to continue to Stratford along the

Kineton.

road by which Henrietta Maria travelled to Edgehill, we turn to the right and so on into Kineton. This is a charming little town on the slope of a hill, with pleasant houses in and round it, and streets not much changed since the days when Rupert's men fought in them. The church has been restored, in 1755, but the old thick-set Perpendicular tower remains, and within it a beautiful Early English west doorway, very elaborate. There is a good priest's monument in the aisle. No doubt Sanderson Miller was the architect in 1755, which accounts for the church being as good as it is. So let us say a few words about it. Kineton Church has an architectural history so peculiar as to be, one would say, almost unique. The chancel and tower, about 1340, with the early west door, are completed by the nave and transepts designed by Sanderson Miller, and built about 1755. The present Vicar in a letter to me adds a pathetic postscript to its already unusual history. Speaking of Sanderson Miller, he concludes :—

" Unfortunately a descendant of his—the Rev. Frank Miller —Vicar of Kineton, 1834–89—carried out a drastic restoration of the church—in which he took out all the windows—and added buttresses and parapets. So that nothing remains of Sanderson Miller's work but the bare wall surface.

" An old photograph shows the windows—of a Gothic design with an ogee moulding on the head. It looks also as if he had inserted an east window into the chancel at the same time."

Altogether Kineton and its church, with the warm red stone, have a soothing happy aspect, as befits the heart of England. The town seems far to-day from the sound of civil strife, and we think of it as part, not of Charles I.'s or Cromwell's country, but of Shakespeare's.

While you are at Kineton you may well, after you have seen the town, go forth from it by Little Kineton, between the two ancient tumuli, now called " the Bank " and " Round Hill," to Butler's Marston and some villages beyond. At the first village the church and what I suppose to be the manor house stand at the top of a pretty slope, overlooking, or rather looking across the valley to, the other portion of the village, westwards. The church has a late Perpendicular tower, but the pillars and capitals of the three nave arches are very good late Norman work. There is also an early " squint." The pulpit was used ten years before the Civil Wars, and the occupation of the manor house goes back to Queen Mary's reign in the family of the Woodwards, two of whom were killed at Edgehill. From Butler's Marston a straight road takes you to Pillerton Hersey. This village is by no means so funereal as its name might at first sight suggest. The designation, in truth, comes from a family who held land there, with the patronage of the living, in the late thirteenth century. The church they built is one of the most beautiful in the country, and indeed there can be few more perfect examples of pure Early English architecture than its chancel. The lancet windows are of exquisite delicacy and proportion, the graceful shafts with carved capitals ; and the chancel arch is of the same chaste and simple charm.   As you look eastwards on a summer day the sycamore trees seen through the clear, slightly tinted, glass of the east window, have a surprising effect of sylvan beauty, as though you were in a forest chapel. and S. Hubert about to come to you through the glades.   The roof, though it be but a seventeenth century imitation, does not distract you from the early middle age, for its imitation has none of the lumbering pedantry of some modern architects' work.   The church is in its way a quite perfect thing.   May no innovator come to spoil it !

A mile farther on is Pillerton Priors, where was an alien priory, of which and its church no trace remains save the church-yard.   The church was burnt down in 1666, and there seemed no need to rebuild it.

When you are at the Pillertons, you may go to Stratford through Ettington, or by Walton and Wellesbourne ; but you will be wise if you see something of the little hamlets of Idlicote and Whatcote.   In the last is a beautiful Norman church with many interesting features, a good brass of 1485 among· them, and the epitaph of John Davenport, who was rector for over seventy years, and died in 1668, aged 104.   But better still is Oxhill, which is easily reached over the fields, or round by the part of the main Edgehill road, from Pillerton Priors.   Thus Mr. Thomas Cox speaks of it in 1700 :—

" *Oxhill*, or as it is written in the Conqueror's Survey, *Octe-selve*, was then in the Possession of *Hugh de Grentemaisnill*, and certified to contain ten Hides, and a Mill, having been before the *Norman* Settlement, the Estate of one *Toli*.   In the Reign of King *Henry* II. *Engelram de Dumart* was owner of it ; and because he died without Issue, his Sisters *Emma* and *Eliz.* succeeded him in the Inheritance of it.   King *John* seised upon it, (but for what Reason is not known) and commanded the Sheriff, *Reg.* 18. to give the Possession of it to *Theodoric de Whicheford*, to whom he had granted it by the Name of *Hocte-shulve* ; but in 3 *Hen.* III. *Thomas de Periton*, as Heir to *Engelram de Dummarish*, obtained the Restitution of it ; and dying 11 *Hen.* III. left it his Son *Adam*, who had Livery of it the same Year.   He left only a Daughter and Heir *Margaret*, who by Marriage carried this Manor to Sir *William Keyns*, who left Issue *Robert* ; who in 7 *Edw.* I. held it of the King *in Capite*, by the Service of one Knight's Fee, having one Carucate of

Land in Demesne, five Tenants holding several Parcels of Land under servile Labour, and some particular Rents ; as also diverse Freeholders.   They were an eminent Family, but for Want of Issue Male became extinct ; and this Manor by the Female Issue passed to the *Cressys*."

It has a beautiful church, at the end of the village, and where the road turns southwards to Middle Tysoe, two miles away.   At first it seems of the common Warwick kind, with its embattled tower ; but soon you see that it goes back almost to the Conqueror's day.   There is the nave with its string course still remaining, added to in later times here and there ; an early English porch, on the north with a fine Norman doorway, and at the south a still finer Norman arch, richly carved with zigzag mouldings enriched with rosettes, and above an arcading with a row of heads.   On the north side of the chancel is a low-side window. This is most unusual, for the village in medieval times was more generally to the south of the church, and when the bell was rung out of the window it would be heard best if the window was at the south ; but at Oxhill the village is entirely to the north and east of the church.   There is a good Jacobean altar with eight legs, and what was once a fine chancel screen cut up into a screen for the belfry.   But the most interesting thing in the church is the late Norman font, a most remarkable one. Interlacing arcades   surround it, most with conventional ornament, and within two of them, facing west, Adam and Eve, figures, wearing fig leaves, and very like those on the rude oak work of much later date, showing how much of English medieval work was traditional.   Before you leave the church you will have noticed the six ancient pews, left now at the west end as if of no value, while feeble new ones are above the gang-way as the chief seats ; and also a very much worn brass of Daniel Blackford, 1681—" When I was young I ventered life and blood both for my king and for my country's good, in elder years my care was chief to be soldier for Him that shed His blood for me."   So the civil strife merges in the war of good and evil in these peaceful vales.

CHAPTER III

SHIPSTON-ON-STOUR, formerly one of those detached parts of Worcestershire surrounded by Gloucestershire which make the county histories such haphazard reading, was once noted for being one of the greatest sheep-markets in the kingdom. Now one imagines that most people think of it chiefly because it is on one of the main ways to Stratford-on-Avon. One far from polite writer says that he has never discovered anything in its quiet streets beyond the necessities of meat and drink; but I cannot share his opinion. It has some quite beautiful Georgian houses and a good church much like other good churches, and also a tramway to Stratford-on-Avon (is it ever used?), but more than that perhaps not very much to invite the hurried visitor to pause. But for a place to live in, not to rush through, I should fancy that it is warmly to be commended: it is healthy, quiet, and well built, and what more would you have?

From Shipston you may go by Alderminster, with its fine Norman and Early English church, nestling among ancient trees on the high ground that slopes down to the Stour.

In a most delightful paper on the records of his Court of Arches, Sir Lewis Dibdin, Dean of the Arches, has recently told us that:—

" In 1666 the Vicar of Alderminster was charged with a great variety of misdeeds, from desecrating church ornaments and utensils by turning them to domestic purposes, to hunting, smoking, frequenting ale-houses. and playing games on Sunday. But the head and front of his offence was that he 'boasted a friendship with Oliver Cromwell.' "[1]

So Alderminster church has historical as well as architectural interest. Indeed the two may well be connected. Let us see.

[1] From the full text of Sir L. T. Dibdin's address, in *The Guardian*, January 16, 1914.

The church, which had fallen into sad disrepair, was restored and partly rebuilt in 1873 and 1884. For many years previous to the latter date, the nave, minus the greater part of the south wall which had fallen outwards, was supported by props. The interior was disfigured by damp and whitewash, box pews of deal, and a western gallery. There was a flat ceiling in the chancel dividing the east window. The tiled roofs were low pitched, and soil, in which burials had been permitted, was heaped up, almost to the level of the chancel windows.

Perhaps some light has recently been thrown upon the condition into which the church had gradually drifted, by the remarks of Sir Lewis Dibdin at the Authors' Club, which I have already quoted as well as by the untiring researches of the rector of Whitchurch (the Rev. J. Harvey Bloom) whose church we can see from Alderminster churchyard, standing in a field just across the Stour, but in Warwickshire. At any rate Alderminster has not always been fortunate in its vicars.

The name of the vicar in 1666 appears to have been Swanne. He was perhaps not so bad as the Gloucestershire parson, also referred to by Sir Lewis, who insisted on keeping a cheese all the winter in the font " to the great discomfort of the parishioners sitting near by it," but Mr. Swanne was certainly not a tactful person, even if he was not himself " perverse and obstinate " as he charged the chmchwarden with being. For five years there was difficulty about the church clock (not the present one), and the vicar had a lawsuit over the tithe of wool, as certain letters (unearthed by Mr. Bloom in the Edgar Tower at Worcester) and an entry in the parish register show. We wonder after two hundred and fifty years, whether there was any connection between the alleged malice of the vicar, and the absence of any record in the register of the death of Robert Phipps, who used to be, and possibly is still, commemorated by a stone in the churchyard showing that he passed away on August 10, 1703.

Or you may go to Stratford by Atherstone, with a very delightful farmhouse. The village is below the Stratford-Shipston road. The church, too big and ugly, dated 1876, but with some old features in it, a belfry and two ancient bells. But the farmhouse is more attractive—with its high pitched roof and dormer windows. And at the top of the hill—Atherstone Hill, 200 feet—is the house of Dr. Thomas (1680-1738) who continued and annotated Dugdale, making a great mass of notes in manuscript which appear to have perished. His property was sold to the Wests of Alscot in 1751, and through Alscot park we may go to Preston. This lies on the sharp left bank of the Stour, surrounded on two sides by the park. From the long elm avenue you see the house, famous because it belonged to the antiquary James West, a member of the learned and interesting circle which made Warwickshire delightful in the middle of the eighteenth century. Now James West made the church of Preston interesting, if not beautiful, as a specimen of early Georgian architecture. On to the ancient church he between 1752 and 1757 added some fine features : new walls, or nearly such. great windows such as the age loved, an iron screen (and beautiful gates to the churchyard) and woodwork from the shop of Salmon of Stratford, *circa* 1750. But some of these things have perished in the modern craze for restoration and " Gothic " ; and a fine sounding-board has disappeared from the pulpit too. Do let us keep our sounding-boards—what a help they are to quiet clergymen with tired voices, and what a protection against unnecessary bellowings ! They are planning to take away a most noble one from Castle Ashby itself. But one thing remains that is most curious, the patchwork of glass which James West framed and set up, and part of which he wrote that he purchased " the heads of some of the Abbots of Evesham " of " a rigid Quaker," and that they " were painted on glass and are in my church of Preston upon Stour." These cannot be the medallions in the east window to-day. Where are they ? There is some fine heraldic glass in other parts of the church. Another curious thing is the tablet of Sir Nicholas Kempe (1621) and his two wives, with some very fine words upon his merits, the strangeness lying, not in the tablet, but in its being here at all. It was originally at S. Mary's, Islington, and West seems to have calmly removed it thence—when the new church was built— that it might anyhow be preserved, and dignify "his" church, with which Kempe had nothing to do. The church has also a fine fifteenth century chalice, which the antiquary's wife, Sarah West, gave in 1747—it also not belonging to Preston of old ; and another, Elizabethan, of about 1570. A valuable history of Preston has copied a number of interesting tombstones.

Go out into the village—through the splendid iron gates—and you will see a number of good houses of various sizes and various dates still surviving, and people will tell you of more that have been destroyed or spoiled. Nor can you avoid seeing the model cottages, of which the village mainly consists. The history of the place is well worth following, from the time when it belonged to Deerhurst, then to Tewkesbury, then to those " caterpillars of the Commonwealth " the Dudleys, then to the Hunts, so to Sir Edward Greville, then to the Marriotts (one of whom was a ward of Shakespeare's, John-a-Combe, and another has a very fine monument in the chancel writ in very pompous Latin), and later on by purchase to James West, Esquire, of Lincoln's Inn.

Now from Preston you may either go back into Stratford the way you came from Atherstone, and then by Clifford Chambers, across fields ; or, as I propose you shall, now that we are taking Shipston for centre, return thither, go south-east a mile to see Barcheston and then by Tredington on the Fosse way into the heart of Warwickshire.

It was at Barcheston that Richard Hicks (the name is spelled in many different ways) established his famous manufacture of arras. Sent in the middle of the sixteenth century by William Sheldon, of Brailes and Weston, to the Netherlands, he returned having learned the art which he at once set up at Barcheston when he came back to England. His map of mid-England in tapestry hangs on the wall above you as you ascend from " Duke Humphrey " to the gallery, now a reading room of the Bodleian Library. Besides tapestry his looms wove " arras, moccadoes, carolles, plonketts, grograynes, sayes and sarges." There survived in the district till late in the eighteenth century a good deal of the work that had been made there two centuries before, for Horace Walpole bought some of it for thirty pounds, " very cheap indeed," as he said. There may be some left still, but I expect it has long disappeared. The Hicks family lived long and famously in the Stour valley, and so did their kinsmen, the Crofts, of whom the most notable was William, the organist of Westminster, whose musick still delights us in quires and places where they sing. The places with which these names are connected are Barcheston, Stratford, Tredington, Ettington ; all of the smaller ones, as well as the town of Shakespeare, worthy of many pious visits.

Let us now visit Tredington, perhaps the best of them all. It is a rough road from Moreton-in-the-Marsh, for not all the Fosse

way is still good going. Nor is all straight ; it must have been
deflected at different dates ; but you can still make your way
happily, up hill and down dale, past the woods of Honington and
the woods of Ettington, on the one side or the other, coming
either from Kineton or from Shipston as your way may be, or
(as I came) from Moreton-in-the-Marsh   When you leave the
Fosse way and enter Tredington you are struck at once by the
fine spire of the church standing out of a high tower.   You may
pause as you walk towards it, or while you look at the fine
fifteenth century house to the west of it, which must be one of
the most beautiful rectories in England, and read what Master
Thomas Habington in his "Survey of Worcestershire" says of
the parish :—

"Althoughe our Shyre hath many outlyinge parcells inclosed
with other countyes, yet thys exceedethe all wheare Tredinton
ryngethe lowdest the greatest Rectory of our Shyre, and is
neyghbored with a plentifull marckett at her chappell or infant
chauntry named Shepston, and surnamed on Stowre, a small
ryver yet muche inrychinge thys soyle.   But let not thyne eyes
be so dazeled with the glory of thys Parsonage as to forgett the
Byshop once Patron and styll Lord of thys Mannor."

The patronage was alienated, presumably in the days of the
Tudors, and in Habington's time belonged to Mr. Edward
Sheldon of Beoley.   It was bought later by Jesus College,
Oxford, who still hold it and Shipston.   The Ecclesiastical
Commissioners are the Lords of the Manor.

Having stored yourself with these facts you will enter the
beautiful church.   At the south is a late Norman or " transi-
tion " doorway with Early English pillars and capitals.   Within
are three complete and two half pillars of the same date in the
nave.   The original Norman clerestory windows were embedded
in the later wall when the openings above the arches were enlarged in the fifteenth century.   The chancel is of the most
beautiful Decorated style.   In the Lady Chapel at the east
of the north aisle remains an elaborate niche, deprived of
its saint.   The whole fabric is most seemly and dignified,
and has not suffered much from the destroying hand of the
restorer, but the good north porch, of the fourteenth century,
which has a priest's room above, has lost its figures from the
niches.   There is one low side window visible from without,
and another only seen from within.   The fittings of the church

within are of even more interest than its architecture. There is almost the complete set of the medieval pews, very little restored, a reading desk made out of some of them ; the Perpendicular font of the same date as the pews ; a very good Jacobean pulpit ; the old desk for chained books, with the Homilies still upon it ; and the fragment of an Elizabethan text painted on the wall at the south-west. Then the fine late fifteenth century screen divides chancel from nave. Within are a number of Parker tombs, beautiful marble slabs, grey and white, with the coats of arms in white : the most striking that of Sir Henry John Parker, Bart., who died in 1771, by the entrance to the vault. On this, when I saw it, were placed a number of chairs, threatening the gravest danger to a most beautiful memorial of our ancestors' best taste. Much else in the chancel is connected with a former rector, Thomas Hopkins, who died in 1838. There are some modern altar rails, of no special excellence, for which the good eighteenth century ones have been absurdly moved to the west end of the church. In the vestry, a good medieval one, are the old altar table, and also two parish chests, one medieval, with the three locks for parson and churchwardens, and another Jacobean, and also a most valuable Jacobean chair which is being allowed to perish from rot. These things will no doubt be remedied, for I see that but recently has a new rector come into possession. Some evils may be due to the restoration completed in 1900, when Bishop Perowne re-opened the church ; a suitable historical record of this is set up at the west of the nave, recording a large donation from Richard Badger of Shipston. The brasses on the floor of the chancel complete the interest of the church. one shows a priest in cope, almuce, alb, with at the foot a trefoil, " Ad laudem Dei," and his coat, a chevron between three griffins' heads erased. On the orphrey of the cope are the initials " R.C.," which complete the identification with the brass mentioned by Habington as standing " in the myddest of the chancell." He gives the inscription round the brass thus :—

> " Inceptor legum jacet hic in carne Ricardus
> Cassy, rector erat huius et ecclesiae
> Henrici quinti quondam fuit ipse sacerdos
> Eboracensis canonicus. . . .
> Qui mundo demptus isto ut cum Christo
> Gaudia semper habens hoc roget ista legens."

It seems likely that the lines have long been confused ; the

brass has been reset and half of it is upside down. There may
have been (suggests a learned friend) originally eight lines in all,
and after the first four one has disappeared and we have only
the endings of the last three, and they confused. The brass
commemorates Richard Cassy, whom Henry V. made Prebendary
of Osbaldwick in York Minster in 1414. Its date has been said
to be 1427, perhaps because it was in the December of that year
that a successor was appointed to him at York. He may have
been of kin, indeed very likely was son, to Sir John Cassy,
Chief Baron of the Exchequer. Near this brass is another,
showing a priest in surplice and fur almuce, with this inscription :
" Hic jacet Magister Henricus Sampson quondam rector huj.
ecclïe qui obiit decimo septimo die mensis Novembris año Dni
millesimo quadringentesimo octogesimo secundo cuj. anime propitietur deus. Amen." In Habington's time there was a prayer
from the mouth, to the patron of the church : " Sancte Gregori,
ora pro me."

At the south-west of the church flows the Stour, and on it
stands a mill, like that of Clifford Chambers, with a long history
behind it.

So we pass on up the Fosse way through Halford with its very
pretty manor-house and its restored church, to Compton Verney.
But first we may see Ettington or Eatington to our left.

Nether-Ettington is on the east bank of the Stour, and
Dugdale says, " There is no doubt but the name of this place was
originally occasioned from its situation, *Ea* in our old English
signifying water, and *Dune* or *Don*, an ascending ground ; for
at the Foot of an Hill, and near the River, doth it stand." It is,
more precisely, in the valley watered by the Stour, north of the
Ilmington Hills, and half-way between the Vale of Red Horse
and the Vale of Evesham. Over, or Upper, Ettington is in the
same manor and parish, and it has other hamlets too. The
boundaries of the parish are the Stour at the south, and Tredington in Worcestershire ; westward Aldermarston north
Loxley and Walton ; eastwards Halford, Idlicote, Whatcote and
Pillerton. At Domesday Henry de Ferrers, whose descendants
long held such fame in the Midlands, was the overlord, and under
him Saswalo held seventeen hides. From Saswalo, or Sewallis,
the family of Shirley, which still holds the manor, descend without
interruption. Domesday gives a priest among the dwellers
here, and the Kenilworth cartulary show that the English

owner had endowed a church, dedicating it to the Holy Trinity.
Some remains of it are said still to exist ; but the church which
adjoins the manor-house is later, as we shall see.

First the manor-house claims our attention. The description of

Ettington Old Church.

them both by Sir Thomas Shirley, tempore Car. I., himself not in
the direct line, is worth quoting as an introduction : " There are
divers marks in this town, by which we may judge that it hath
been from all antiquity the seat of a noble and renowned family.
It hath a very ancient church, sumptuously built, and dedicated to

the honour of the Blessed Trinity, and likewise a chantry founded, and a large chapel to the honour of S. Nicholas, which was anciently the place of sepulture for the lords of this manor, who had, at their proper cost and charges, built and endowed both these places of prayer and devotion ; and close by the church is a very ancient mansion-house, built by an ancestor of the family, so long ago that the memory, by the revolution of so many ages, is utterly lost and forgotten ; for the ancient form and structure of the house, is a witness beyond all exception of its pristine antiquity, it being covered with so unknown a covering that the very stuff itself whereof the texture was made is many ages since not only worn out of the kingdom but also the very knowledge that ever any such thing was within the realm." Mr. E. P. Shirley, whose delightful little monograph is our authority, thinks that all this means is Stonesfield slate ; but I can scarce think Sir Thomas to have been a person of so little experience though he did live " in Leicestershire or Huntingdonshire." However this may be, what Sir Thomas saw has long ago disappeared, for in 1641 the house was entirely rebuilt. The Shirleys had other property, and were persons of dignity and eminence, century by century. Sir Ralph whose date, or is it his birth (?) is given by Dugdale as 1279, sat in the Parliament of 1294 as a knight of the shire for Warwick. He is buried in the south transept, with his wife Margaret de Waldershef, daughter of Edward I.'s butler. His son Thomas is remembered, says his descendant, by a pardon for " having caused the death of his neighbour, John Wareyne of Loxley " in 34 Edw. III. Hugh, his son, fell at the battle of Shrewsbury, 1403, being one of those whom Henry IV. dressed up in his own armour :—

> " Another King ! They grow like Hydra's heads :
> I am the Douglas, fatal to all those
> That wear those colours on them. What art thou
> That counterfeit'st the person of a King ? "

His son lived, it seems, chiefly in Nottinghamshire, whose widow leased the manor to the Underhill family, whence law-suits and troubles of all sorts, till the lease ended in 1641. And the head of the family at the end of the fifteenth century married the heiress of the ancient family of Staunton of Staunton Harold, Leicester, from which marriage again came the Earls Ferrers of to-day. Again the ancient manor was let ; and, during one of the tenancies, one person at least of interest in English art was born there, the glorious Dr. William Croft, in 1678. In 1711 the Earldom of Ferrers was created, and Robert, the first Earl, bequeathed the Ettington property to his son George. From him descends the present owner. A redecoration, rebuilding indeed, was undertaken fifty years ago. Of this it is best to use simply the words of the owner (1880): "In 1858 the present Evelyn Philip Shirley, finding the house considerably out of repair, commenced to case and roof it in the advanced Early English style from designs of John Prichard of Llandaff, Esq. These alterations were completed in the year 1862." The deeds of the notable members of the family are recorded on panels on various parts of the outside of the house. Perhaps the most interesting scenes in the long and honourable record are those relating to Sir Ralph Shirley, who built the quaint and delightful chapel of Staunton Harold (represented at Ettington with his friends Sheldon, Dolben, Gunning, and Hammond) and was committed to the tower "by the usurper Oliver Cromwell in 1656, in consequence of his loyalty to his Church and King." There are many fine rooms in the house, and some good pictures. One among many of the latter may be mentioned. It is that of Lady Selina Bathurst (née Shirley), painted by Jervis, 1724, who is wearing a Turkish dress after the fashion of Lady Mary Wortley Montagu. Her husband was the brother of the famous Allen Earl Bathurst, the friend of Pope and of Sterne. There is also a good deal of the famous modern oak carving of the Warwick celebrities, Willcox and Kendall.

Eastwards of the house and quite near it are the remains of the old parish church. (Since 1798, by Act of Parliament, Upper Ettington has been the parish church.) These are the tower and south transept with three of the northern arches and part of the walls of nave and chancel, and at the east traces of what is supposed to be the chapel of S. Nicholas—as a tablet records. "The arches of this chantry of S. Nicholas, founded by Henry, the son of Sewallis, about the year 1200, fell down on the 21st of October, 1875, and were rebuilt within the same year by Evelyn Philip, the son of Evelyn John. Laus Deo. Amen." Several tombs still remain, some fragmentary or imperfect, such as those of Sir Ralph and his wife Margaret, and of later persons, the Rev. John Clarke, vicar of Ettington (ob. 1674) "Ecclesiae Anglicanae propugnator fidelis, phanaticorum malleus"; the

E

restored verses on Anthony Underhill, which some wiseacre ascribed to Shakespeare ; and the great monument to the first Earl Ferrers, who lived to serve Charles II. and Queen Catherine, William III., and Anne, Charles II. making him Baron Ferrers in 1677, and Queen Anne earl thirty-four years later. The south transept of the church survives as a private chapel. The ordnance map does not recognise a distinction of Ettingtons ; but it is the Upper, I do not doubt, which is such a model village to-day, and contains a modern church of the Holy Trinity, with a cemetery on the other side of the road.

So to leave Ettington. Dugdale noted that it was the only parish in the shire which had so long and uninterrupted a succession of owners, for the family can trace direct descent beyond the Norman conquest. - How much more is it now famous, when nearly three centuries more have passed and the line still endures.

From Ettington we pass on, through typical Warwickshire ways, to Wellesbourne (see p. 128), or, rejoining the Fosse way, let us follow it till we reach the park of Compton Verney, passing under the Kineton and Stratford line about a mile across the fields from Ettington station, which is on the road from Ettington to Wellesbourne. Here you cross another road, which runs through the park. On this road from Kineton to Warwick, north thereof, is the delightful park of Compton Verney. Its three delightful lakes (they are really one cut into three by two roads) south of the house, showing no diminution in the driest summer (1911) give a special charm of peace and coolness. The eighteenth century bridge breaks the view from the house in pleasing sort, and as one crosses it one sees the fine trees reflected in the clear water. The main road passes, as it were, through the park, without really entering it : the wayfarer has, as so often in Warwickshire, the pleasure of this great place even if he does not ask to be admitted. The house itself is the main part of the parish of Compton Verney, called even when Dugdale wrote, Compton Murdak, after the lords who held it from Henry I.'s day till they gave up their possession to Alice Perrers, the disgrace of Edward III.'s last days, who robbed the dying king even of the rings from his fingers, but married Sir William Windsor and " lived happily ever after " in spite of having been impeached for her crimes. Her daughter carried it to the family of Skerne. Then came the present family, temp. Henry VI., and thus they came. At that date, says Mr. Cox :—

"*Richard Verney*, Esq ; (afterwards knighted) was in Possession of it, and built a great Part of the Manor-house, as it now standeth. From what Family of the *Verneys* this *Richard* was descended we know not, but find that as soon as he settled here, he was put into publick Employments, as a Conservator of the Peace, a Commissioner of Array, and knighted. He died 5 *Hen*. VII. and left *Edmund* his Son and Heir. He was Escheator for this Country and *Leicester*, and a Commissioner of Array 2 *Rich*. III. He died 11 *Hen*. VII. and left *Richard* his Son and Heir, of whom our Histories relate this Thing memorable of him ; That he was in great Esteem with King *Henry* VIII. who being informed, that he had some Infirmity in his Head, gave him a Licence to wear his Bonnet at all Times, and in all Places ; yea, in his own Presence, without Interruption from any Man. He lies buried with his Wife and Children, in the Chapel, on the North-side of this Church. From him descended Sir *Grevil Verney*, a Gentleman of singular Endowments, whose Son *Richard*, an ingenious Gentleman, had it in 1640. Mr. *Rous* has placed this Town among those, whose Depopulation he laments in this County."

Mr. Cox is, I think, in error in stating that Richard Verney held the house in 1640, for Greville Verney (who married a daughter of Viscount Wenman, of the now extinct Oxfordshire peerage) was still alive. He did not die till 1648. His brother, Richard, the second son, was, however, " a Person happily qualified with a most ingenious Inclination," who gave much assistance to Sir William Dugdale. Dugdale was a great friend of the Verneys. A copy of the first edition of his book is still in the Library ; and with no arms and monuments did he take more pains than at Compton. His illustration of " The prospect of Compton House from the grounds on the south-east side of the house," shows the splendid old house with the rather barn-like chapel near the lake (" the Poole," as Dugdale calls it) with the orchard behind and " the Houses in the Towne " beyond to the east. Most of this is gone, the house replaced in the middle of the eighteenth century by a large classical building (1762, Adam). It has a most dignified portico with huge columns, but is spoiled for the eye, towards the south, by the plate-glass windows. It is a fine house with large rooms, marble pillars, graceful staircases, and " everything handsome about it." Within, the hall, with its four pillars, was decorated with Roman scenes and classical " compositions " by Andrea Zucchi (pupil of that Jacopo Amigoni of Venice who worked mostly abroad and died as Court. painter of Spain, the predecessor of Mengs, in 1752), who painted the scenes on the walls of the dining room and library at Osterley Park in 1767. Other rooms, almost all (except the " serving-room," out of the dining room) large, and all lofty, contain a number of pictures, some of them exceedingly valuable. There are many family portraits, highly interesting and well worth study as a family history, with others of " personages " connected with the Verneys. Perhaps the most interesting are the two portraits, by Reynolds and by Gainsborough, of Lady Louisa, daughter of Lord North, first Earl of Guilford, George III.'s Prime Minister, a determined looking lady with a touch of sadness in her composition ; a set of three splendid Elizabethan ladies, the Countess of Notting- ham among them ; Elizabeth herself in middle life; a remark- ably fine picture ; John Verney, Master of the Rolls, who died in 1741, and married Abigail Harley (named after Mrs. Masham) niece of Queen Anne's minister ; a good Charles I., and a " speaking " Charles II. Briefly, one may say that the eighteenth century pictures are charming, and the Elizabethan ones a very remarkable historical collection.

When Mr. Jago published his charming quarto, through Mr. Dodsley, in Pall Mall, in 1767, the new house had been completed by John Peyto Verney, 6th (14th) Lord Willoughby de Broke, and the poet had very special reason to admire it. Thus skilfully did he express his sentiments, and introduce a compliment to Lady Willoughby and Lord Guilford at the same time. From Compton Winyates he begs that he may " your view "

> " Progressive lead to Verney's sister walls
> Alike in honour, as in name applied !
> Alike her walls a noble master own
> Studious of elegance. At his command,
> New pillars grace the Home with Grecian pomp
> Of Corinth's gay design. At his command,
> On hill, or plain, new culture cloathes the scene
> With verdant grass, or variegated grove ;
> And bubbling rills in sweeter notes discharge
> Their liquid stores. Along the winding vale,
> At his command, observant of the shore.
> The glitt'ring stream, with correspondent grace,
> Its course pursues, and o'er th' exulting wave,

> The stately bridge a beauteous form displays.
> On either side, rich as th' embroidered floor
> From Persia's gaudy looms, and firm as fair,
> The chequer'd lawns with count'nance blithe proclaims
> The Graces reign. Plains, hills, and woods reply
> The Graces reign, and Nature smiles applause.
> Smile on, fair source of beauty, scene of bliss
> To crown the master's work, and deck her path
> Who shares his joy, of gentler manners join'd
> With manly sense, train'd to the love refin'd
> Of Nature's charms in Wroxton's beauteous grove."

A long quotation ; but it well represents the compliments that must have been showered on Lord Willoughby, on his wife, the Prime Minister's daughter (whose " manly sense " is certainly observable in her portraits) and no less on Mr. Lance-lot Brown, " Capability," whose skill it was which had turned the park and garden, from what Dugdale knew, to what we now see.

From the house one may walk out towards the lake and see where the gravestones lie on its grassy slope.

Compton Verney was claimed as extra parochial till one of the owners, fearing that a new line might not use the chapel for its sacred purposes, procured its absorption in the ordinary parochial system. It appears, however, that the claim was not maintained. This was due no doubt to the entire depopulation between 1350 and 1450. But the chapel we now see, built by John Peyto Verney, fourteenth of the old creation, sixth of the new, Lord Willoughby de Broke, is not the old chapel. Till 1772, this stood on the border of the lake, at the south-east of the house, where a clump of trees now hides some of the graves, and other memorial stones are fixed in the grass at their feet. The present chapel is unadorned enough architecturally, though one may justly admire its decent Georgian altar with cloth and cushion, the good Chippendale seats in the midst, and even perhaps the gallery. Its glories belong to older days. And first of these we observe the splendid monuments. In the middle of the chapel, in front of the altar, yet not too near it, for the tiers of pews on north and south allow you to look over, is the beautiful tomb of Sir Richard Verney, 1630, and Margaret his wife, 1631, he, moustached and bearded, in full armour, she in ruff, gown, mantle, and veil. The inscription is " Hic jacent Richardus Verney miles qui oblit vii° die Aug^i. A°. Dni. MDCXXX et aetatis suae LXVII : et D^{na} Margareta uxor eius quae obiit xxvi die Martii Ao. Dni MDCXXXI et aetat. LXX." Dependent upon this is a short pedigree carrying back the line of Verneys, Grevilles, and Willoughbys, and at the end, an eulogy of the piety, loyalty, dignity, and concord of the lives of the knight and his lady. They set the tone of solemn stateliness to the chapel. Then to the north of the altar there is a tablet to the memory of the 6th (14th) Lord Willoughby de Broke's first wife, and others to the Master of the Rolls, 1741, and his wife, 1760, and, to the south, one to the 8th (16th) Lord, 1852 ; and the splendid monument, with its canopy resting on Corinthian columns, of Sir Greville Verney, in his great wig, wearing armour with mantle, ribbon, and badge of the Order of the Bath, with the words " to the memory of Sir Greville Verney, Knight of the Honourable Order of the Bath. The Honourable the Lady Diana Verney, his wife, eldest daughter to the Right Honourable William, Earl of Bedford, erected this monument. He was borne the 20th day of Jan. 1648, married the 29th of August 1667 and dyed the 23rd day of July, 1668." On the floor are five small slabs, and brasses, large and small. The first of these has a knight in armour, and lady with hood and gown, drawn up to show the petticoat, and below them nine sons and five daughters, with the inscription—" Of your charitie pray for the soules of Richard Verney esquier and Anne his Wife which Richard departed out of this present world the xxviii day of the moneth of September a. dni. M°CCCC°. . . ." This, defective in Dugdale's time, is still more defective now. Richard Verney died in 1527 and his wife was Anne Danvers. Near it is the brass of a lady with veil and gown showing petticoat and the words—" Off your charitie pray for the sole of Anne Odyngsale the wyfe of mayster Edward Odyngsale of Long Ygyngeton and sister of Richard Verney esquyer ye whyche deptyde ye yere of o^r Lorde MCCCCCXXIV° on whose sole Jhu haue mcy." And near this again, in armour, with a large collar over which his hair falls, is a portrait of George Verney, of Compton, who married Jane Lucy of Charlecote, and died 1574. There are few houses and chapels where family history can so well be followed. We have the past of the Verneys recorded in pictures, on brass and stone, and in beautiful glass.

To this last we now come. The windows of course are the

great features of the chapel. These were for the most part transferred from the old chapel in 1772. Their history is said to be that, after the Restoration, the Verney of the day bought some foreign glass, said to be of Munich, and then had Munich workmen to fit it to the windows in the old chapel. But this is far from being the beginning of the story. Much of the glass is of the sixteenth century, and English, and was no doubt made for those who set it up. Other glass is of the seventeenth, and some is of the eighteenth; while even the nineteenth, one fancies, had some share in the re-setting. Let us begin with the east window. This is a large circular-headed opening of the well-known eighteenth century type, into which the old glass has been inserted with additions, to make the original pieces fit the curve. On the north is S. Leonard, with his book, gyves, and abbat's crozier. Below, kneeling before an altar of Saint Christopher, is a knight with a tabard over his armour, and six sons kneeling behind him. He is Richard Verney who died in the eighteenth year of Henry VIII. The arms are those of Verney and others. Opposite to him, in the south light, is a lady, also wearing heraldic mantle, who kneels, with her five daughters behind her, at an altar of the Blessed Virgin. Her arms show her to be Anna, daughter of William Danvers, Justice of the King's Bench under Henry VII. Above her is S. Giles with staff and book, and behind him a hind pierced with an arrow. The central light is the Crucifixion, German, one thinks, in tone; but yet very like much other work that one sees in England, such as Fairford, *par exemple*. Below are a great number of coats, of the great families with whom the Verneys were allied. These carry one on well into the eighteenth century, for they include those of Dr. George Verney, Lord Willoughby de Broke, Dean of Windsor, who died in 1726. He, by the way, was a very notable person, well worthy to be of the Windsor Chapter, and much altered the house. The central coats are those of Sir Greville Verney who died May 12, 1642, and married Catherine, daughter of Sir Robert Southwell, and granddaughter of the Countess of Nottingham, whose arms again (she was Catherine daughter of Henry Carey, Lord Hunsdon, akin to the Bullens) and her husband's are in the window. Returning then to the south side easternmost window, we have some of the foreign glass. It has six subjects, and below these three panels. The subjects (1) S. Catherine of Siena before the Pope; (2) a miracle at a feast. Men are at table, a girl turning a spit, and another pouring out wine, all looking with astonishment at the fire. (3) The Annunciation ; (4) the birth of the Blessed Virgin ; (5) the Magi ; (6) the Presentation in the Temple. Below in the central panel is a lady kneeling at a desk, on the side of which is drawn an angel bearing a headless cross. The book before her has on its right leaf the Our Father, on the left the Collects, " Lord make us to have a perpetual fear and love of Thy Holy Name," and " Who never failest to help and govern." Below is the inscription " Anne Lady Verney 1558." The second window, in the middle of the south side, has a crowned female saint, probably S. Catherine, S. Anne teaching the B.V.M. to read, with the motto " O Ave M. Mater gaudens. Gloria Deo et Laus, Honor. . . . ." and S. Margaret of Antioch. These are old figures set in classical niches. Below are coats of arms, apparently quite modern : they carry the pedigree down to the end of the eighteenth century. The westernmost window has two scenes from the life of S. Catherine of Siena, the Lord in the Temple, and the Temptation. Below are the portraits of Sir Richard Verney, died 1630, and Margaret Greville, daughter of Fulke Greville and heiress of the Brookes, who died 1631 ; with other arms. On the north side, west, are again two scenes from the life of S. Catherine, the Crucifixion and the Entombment, with, below, three shields. The central window on this side has S. George, S. Christopher, and S. Anthony, with, below, three shields, again going as far as the end of the eighteenth century. The eastern window, of Gouda glass, dated 1634, contains one large scene of the Ascension, made by cutting to fit this window ; with below in the centre a mother (Alice, daughter and co-heiress of Sir Edmund Tame of Fairford, who died 153$\frac{8}{7}$) with two sons and three daughters kneeling in a chapel whose windows show the Tame arms and the Resurrection.

After the chapel we may say a word about one of the chaplains, Dr. Francis Mead (c. 1800), a Fellow of Magdalen, who, it is said, would only take the office on the stipulation that he should dine with the lord and not the housekeeper. And it was worthy of him, for he came of strong and ancient stock, his father, a naval captain, going to races and balls till he was ninety, and taking a dose of calomel every day.

CHAPTER IV

How shall we enter Warwickshire? This is a question that confronts us continually and very fitly does it meet us at the beginning of each chapter. If we do not make Shakespeare's life the centre of the land in which he lived, and start from Stratford-on-Avon, we may best take one of the natural inlets of stream or valley, road or railway. And, prosaically but inevitably, the first way to be thought of is the Great Western line from London through Banbury.

Go northwards then, and leave still to be explored on your right Wormleighton, and Hardwick and Marston, both in old time the Prior's land of Kenilworth, and Shuckburgh. Leave on your left and behind you the southern and western lands, where you may start from Fenny Compton if you will, and go southwards towards Compton Winyates or westwards to Kineton by Edgehill, which is between the two; and begin to-day at Harbury, or the station which is quaintly called Southam Road.

It is some way from Southam Road to Southam, and we have many places to see on the way. We mount up from the railway, which runs through a cutting, and stand on high ground, and as we approach the edge we shall see splendid views. Harbury itself, which in Domesday is Edburberie, and also Erburgeberie, where the church of Coventry held land, and also tenants held of the great Turchil (or Thurkil), the real lord of Warwickshire, is a hamlet with a beautiful house and a fine church set in the centre of the village. There were surviving at Harbury when William made is survey, two men of English race who had power

57

to sell their land, but could not depart with the land : which must mean that the lordship over the land could not be transferred. That is the contribution which Harbury makes to the obscure problems of the social life of the eleventh century. Otherwise its contributions to history have also an interest. Lands changed hands continually, but so they did in other parishes. The land of the Coventry monks passed to the Canons of Kenilworth, to the monasteries of Combe and Nuneaton, and Combe held also land which came from lay hands, ultimately from Thurkil. The devious course is traced by Dugdale. The manor changed hands—that is, families—five times in less than two hundred years, and not so long ago it changed again.

Monuments in the church of All Saints help to trace the descent. The earliest part of the church is of the thirteenth century. To this belongs the chancel—in its origin—with details here and there, and the north aisle. A modern nave and aisle need not be dated ; but the fine tower is of the fourteenth century. In the west end is a brass to Jane Wagstaffe, who held the manor in the seventeenth century.

" Behold the ende, my children all, and mark yt well or ye begynne
  To deathe are ye subiect and thrall, take heede therefor and flie from synne
  For death on yearthe shall reape and mowe, that liefe therein hath tylde and sowen,
  And liefe agayne shall springe and growe, where deathe hath reapt and also mowen."

The date is 1563. The daughter-in-law, it may be, of this Jane is Anne, whose brass is in the chancel. She came from Stoneythorpe, about two miles away, and died in 1624, " whose vertuous life did well deserve eternall memorie." I do not know if the lovely old Manor house was theirs. You may see a farm as you go towards Chesterton, which belongs to Leycester's Hospital at Warwick, as part of its endowment, charity surviving where families have died out. Beyond this, the church and parish are most to be remembered, because Richard Jago, the poet of Edgehill, was once Vicar here. It is a pleasant walk hence to Edgehill, and Jago was one of the greatest friends of Sanderson Miller, the architect of the tower, whom he generously eulogised in the poem—but not enough to satisfy all the other friends. Harbury was a pleasant halting place

for many of those who came from the south or east to see
Mr. Miller, and the work which he

> "well taught to counterfeit
> The waste of Time."

The Wagstaffes built a school in the village in 1610, which
survives.

Before we leave the village, we may well note that it affords
an example striking enough, of the changes which have marked
the social history of the country. The population is about ten
times what it was in Domesday Book : the rateable value is
nearly twice what it was sixty years ago, the poor rates are
much lower, but the value of the benefice is about half what
it was in 1875 , and two-thirds of what it was in 1844.

From Harbury there is a pleasant walk across the fields to
Ufton, and Ufton has many links with the history of the past.

Ufton is, one supposes, the Ulchetone of Domesday. It
was given by Earl Leofric of Mercia to the Church of Coventry
" at his foundation thereof," and in his charter, says Dugdale,
is Ulfetune. As early as Henry III.'s reign Ufton wood, which
overhangs the valley for a long way towards Long Itchington,
whose wood it joins, was famous.

In spite of claims from one Robert de Pinkney in Edward I.'s
reign—for he " acknowledged their right of Fine, and for so
doing was made partaker of their Prayers and all other their
devout Exercises," which looks very like a collusive action,—
the monks of Coventry held the land till the Dissolution.
Then it was granted to Lord Chancellor Wriothesley, conspicuous, if for nothing else, for the splendid drawing of him
by Holbein. So on to the Spencers of Althorpe in a cadet
branch, and at last to John Snell, who left it in 1679 to Balliol
College, Oxford, for the support of Scottish scholars at that
house. And very famous have the Snell scholars been, down
to the present Archbishop of York.

The church of Ufton is dedicated to S. Michael, and was
endowed, says Dugdale, with one yard of land. It was appropriated to the priory of Coventry in 1260.

This may be told in more detail—because at several points
it links the history of Ufton to the general history of England—
in the words of Dr. Thomas Cox :—

" Upon the Suppression of the Monasteries in the *30 Hen.*

VIII. this Lordship with their other Estates came to the Crown, and there continued, till King *Hen.* VIII. 37 *Reg.* granted it to *Thomas* Lord *Wriothesley,* at that Time Lord Chancellor of *England,* and his Heirs, who past it the same Year to *William Stamford,* Esq ; and his Heirs, who the Year following conveyed the Inheritance thereof to Sir *Andrew Flammock,* Knt. whose Son and Heir *Francis Flammock,* Esq ; 1 *Eliz.* sold it to Sir *John Spenser* of *Althorpe* in *Norhamptonshire,* from whom it came to *Thomas Spenser* of *Clardon,* Esq ; a younger Son of the said Sir *John."* This is the Thomas Spencer whose Stone House we see, and draw (p. 313), and whose fine tomb dignifies the chancel of Claverdon Church.

"The Church, dedicated to *St. Michael,* was appropriated to the Prior of *Coventry,* by *Roger de Molend* [that is, Roger Wesham] Bishop of *Coventry* and *Lichfield* in 1260, 44 *Hen.* III. having been antiently endowed with one Yard-Land. In 1291, 19 *Edw.* I. it was valued at fourteen Marks, but in King *Hen.* VIII.'s Reign it was certified to belong to two Prebendaries in the Cathedral Church of *Lichfield,* who provided a Curate to officiate, to whom they allowed certain small Tithes, valued at that Time at 4*l.* 13*s.* 4*d. per Annum.*"

The beautiful church plate. whereof an exquisite eighteenth century chalice is the most charming piece, bears witness to the last statement, in the inscription : " Deo et ecclesiae de Ufton D.D.D. Ricŭs Dovey Prebendⁱⁱˢ de Ufton ex parte Decani in Cath. Lichen. 1773." Such curiosities of patronage are no more, and the patron is now the bishop. A fine church it is, restored not too bitterly, with (like so many of the churches in the neighbourhood) an embattled tower which completed the building in the fifteenth century, the main building, chancel, nave, and aisles being of the fourteenth, and the south door earlier. A Norman font, I think I remember : certainly I do not forget the pulpit, which is Elizabethan—or was, for only the panels and base of it are original. Just by the pulpit, at the east end of the north aisle, is a delightful brass depicting a clerk and his wife, she in a fine tall hat, with their children, and this pleasing inscription : " Here lyeth the boddyes of Richard Woddomes, Parson and Pattron and Vossioner of the Churche and Parishe of Oufton in the Countie of Warrike who dyed one Mydsomer daye, 1587. And Margerye his wyffe wthe her seven children as namelye Richard John and John Anne Jone Elizabeth Ayless his iiii daughters

whose soule restethe with God." The word " vossioner " is
said to mean " owner of the advowson." Was Woddomes that ?
Or what else can it mean ?   A more modern inscription, unusual
too, but highly to be commended and worthy of imitation, is
that on the north wall of the chancel, also close to the pulpit.
" In memory of Richard Field, a faithful labourer, who, for
good deeds, gained two prizes from the Royal Agricultural
Society of England.   Crushed by a steam windlass, he fell asleep
October 18th, 1878." The churchyard cross has been restored ;
not so the use of the stocks still preserved. Thirty years ago one
could see vagrants set in the stocks in Lincolnshire. The use in
Warwickshire seems not to be so recent. The church stands in a
commanding position at the top of the hill, but only from its
tower can you see so fine a view as you may from the house on the
other side of the road or from Mr. Reed's garden—both of them
Balliol property—farther down the road.   In the distance you
see Malvern, and the Lickey Hills, and nearer the towers of
Coventry, with Warwick and Leamington below and between.
Ufton is a delightful place, fresh and bracing, a contrast on a hot
summer day to the closeness of Leamington in the valley beneath.

To Leamington you may go, down a hill which the cyclist will
rejoice in.   If so you do, you pass through Radford Semele.
The spelling is doubtless an eighteenth or earlier classicism—it
should be Simele.   Ermenfrid held the manor at Domesday and
had bought if from Chetelbert, the brother of Thurkil, the overlord, but yet held—or claimed—it of the king himself. The
manor was once Templars' property. The church, standing
prettily in the fields, modernised if not modern, has one old
Norman window and in the village are two modern Gothic houses
of the style of Mr. Miller, with a tower like his at Edgehill. From
Radford one may go easily and down hill, to Leamington, crossing
the Warwick and Napton Canal.

But return to Ufton and let us take the road to Southam, to
come back again by the woods.   It is a very pretty road ; and
when it dips and you descend into a charming little valley, you
are in the domain of the Chamberlaynes, whose house is called
Stoneythorpe.   " This, of a small hamlet," says Dugdale,
" is now reduced to one House, and hath its name from the rocky
condition of the Ground where it stands, the word Thorpe in our
old English signifying a pretty Village ; but it was originally a
Member of Long-Itchington and had thereof, though when first

granted away by the Lords of that Mannour I have not seen."
In the early nineteenth century the ancient house was "the seat
of Mrs. Fouquier," but the Chamberlaynes had it, I think, before
as well as since.   The house is one of those, not so common, with
double walls, the space within filled with rubble and pebbles—
one wonders if with bats and rats.   The stables, it is said, were
once the chapel of the mansion, which goes back to the fifteenth
century.   Not far away is the Holy Well, very likely an ancient
bathing-place, which may even, one fancies, be Roman.   But
much more probably it belonged to the cell of black canons from
Rowcester, established there in the fourteenth century.   Following the road a mile from Stoneythorpe, we first fall and then
rise into the charming little town of Southam.   Southam being
always on the main road from London and Oxford, was a place of
importance from early times.   It is Sucham in Domesday, and
belonged to the church of Coventry.   It had a fair for eight days
beginning on the day of S. Leodegarius—October 2—till in
1238–9 it was transferred to S. George's day.   In 1226–7 it was
granted a weekly market on Wednesday, transferred twelve
years later to Monday.   The manor, after the Dissolution,
passed through many hands and at one time was divided
into thirty-two parts, which surely was confusing enough even
though my Lord Craven held sixteen of them.   In the town
are some very interesting houses.   There is the Abbey (but why
so called ?), the quite charming " Old Mint " (whose ?) now
the " Horse and Jockey," with a good staircase in it, and the
half-timber house, now a shop, where Charles I. spent the night
before the battle of Edgehill.   Not the first time he had been in
the town, it seems, for the year before the inhabitants were fined
for not ringing their bells when he passed through.

   The Southam Registers of Baptisms, Marriages, and Burials
begin in 1539, and are full of interest, and so are the church-
warden's accounts, which date from 1580.   In 1581 a new bell-
rope was bought for the sanctus bell, and again the following
year, and the great bell was mended.   It was a terribly bell-
ringing age.   But the Southam people were either indifferent
or hostile to Charles.   And yet the town was conservative.
Under Elizabeth it went on celebrating S. Hugh's Day : it
is true that was also the Queen's Accession, but it stands
in the churchwarden's accounts as S. Hugh's; and the
conservatives of Southam could look back far. Up till 1625

at least, there stood one of the great monoliths which are not rare in this district; another survived at Ladbrooke well into the nineteenth century, and the Rollright Stones are not far away. And there are several tumuli in the neighbourhood. There was the less excuse for not ringing for the king, as in recent years the accounts contain such frequent mention of ringing for the bishop, and once for Charles himself when he was Prince. Before we leave the books we may remark one entry which is really not so bad as it seems : "paid to Goode for killing an Urchin April ye 29th 1627 : o. o. iiij." Fourpence is not dear for killing any urchin.

And so we come to the church, which stands on a hill overlooking the valley. From the churchyard you see a lovely pastoral view over hill and dale. A lime walk leads to the south door, and there are many interesting tombstones on either side. On one, they tell you, is the inscription :—

> " In this vain world short was my stay,
>   And empty was my laughter :
> I go before and lead the way
>   For all to follow after."

But the words are obliterated; or, at least, I could not find them in 1910. Then the church itself; a fine broach spire belongs to the ancient part of the church, and the days of Decorated Gothic. For the most part the building is restored and over-restored, and Decorated work is rarely very interesting in a country church. But the clerestory is good, and there is the doorway to the now destroyed rood-loft, and there are monuments on the walls to the Chamberlaynes.

Southam is a very pleasant town, a quiet resting-place on the long high road from the northern midlands. Follow that road and you come to the North Western Railway station, with some ugly lime-works beside it; then you cross the Warwick and Napton Canal, which you will long to explore, and may, very easily and happily; and so you come to Long Itchington. This is a delightful village. It has a large green, on which look some of the finest small houses of Elizabeth's day. The queen herself dined in the half-timbered one, now a surgery, at your left as you enter the village, on August 12, 1575. Three years later she was feasted by Leicester in " a tent which for number and shift of large and

goodlye rooms might be comparable with a beautiful pallais,"
says Laneham the diarist. It was on her way to Kenilworth.
In the church is the monument to Lady Anne Holbourn, one of
the daughters and co-heiresses of the Right Honourable Robert
Dudley, " Duke of the Empire." And indeed in many ways is
the church interesting. The fine heraldic window given in Dugdale has disappeared, but the chancel screen is, in parts, of the
fourteenth century, repaired in the eighteenth, by a gentleman
who was (to adapt Stevenson) " grand at the Gothic." There
was originally a Norman church, and the south doorway, though
altered, shows Norman work still. The south aisle is Early
English. After that the priors of Maxstoke restored the church
in the fourteenth century, and put in most remarkably good
work. There are several monuments of interest.

In the village are more old houses, some even better than
the one Elizabeth slept in, among them the house of the Oding-
sels, of whom Dugdale has much to tell, going back to Henry
III. Village history might well be written in Long Itchington ;
and one old Rate Book, which the Vicar very kindly showed me,
would supply many interesting points. Thus in the late eighteenth century there is constant record of substitutes provided for the militia. Mr. Budd, Constable, of Long Itchington,
pays sums from two guineas to £3 13s. 6d. at different times " to
find a proper man to serve for three years for Joseph Ash [or
some other] except in the case of death," and the entry is " by
one, Thos. Baylis, Sergeant." And the history of the village
has a fine beginning in Domesday Book with Cristina, sister of
Edgar Atheling and of S. Margaret of Scotland, who held a
very large estate here given by the King (I cannot but think
this means Edward Confessor and not William). Did she
marry a Limesi ? And also they say that the last and almost
the best of Early English saints, Saint Wulfstan, Bishop of
Worcester, was born here. There is plenty of work for the
antiquary at Long Itchington. And leaving it to him we may
return to Ufton by Bascote. As we go we cross by a ford
the little Itchen stream,—from which the village we leave takes its
name—which swells not rarely in winter into a torrent, till it
overflows the whole field, drowns sheep sometimes, and spreads
disaster. Up a pretty wooded hill into the village of Bascote,
with its little cosy houses, and over the heath to the great
Ufton wood. Through this runs the road and so we come back

again to the village we came from. On the heath was a skirmish
during the Civil War.

But now I will take you back from Ufton to Harbury and
round into Leamington another way. You shall see it first
with the eyes of him whom we may call the Harbury poet.

> " Weigh the wide champaign and the cheerful downs
> Claim notice ; chiefly strive, O Chesterton !
> Pre-eminent.   Now 'scape the roving eye
> Thy solemn wood, and Roman vestiges,
> Encampment green, or military road !
> Amusive to the grave, historic mind.
> The Tachbroke joins with venerable shade.

So Mr. Jago introduces us to a little known district south
of Leamington, and we will follow him from Chesterton to
Tachbrook. (Chesterton, when he knew it was "a seat of
Lord Willoughby de Broke " : it is still his property, but the
house has gone.) Tachbrook has become almost a suburb of
Leamington. Chesterton, Jago came to know well, for he held
the living with that of Harbury from 1746. And we may pass
from one to the other most easily.

Chesterton, one of the most interesting places in Warwickshire, is one of the most inaccessible. There is no road that
you can call a road. You can go southwards from Harbury,
leaving Bunker's Hill (suggestive of the War of Independence
and of golf, but not really belonging to either) to your right—
or better, past the Leycester Hospital Farm to Windmill Hill.
On this summit, in a large field, is the domed windmill designed
by Inigo Jones for Sir Edward Peyto. A small room, surmounted
by a lead roof which revolves with the sails, is supported on six
circular arches. It is a charming design, most characteristic
of the seventeenth century, but strange indeed in this desolate
place.   It is of a piece with the greatness and dignity which
Sir Edward assumed in all that he did. As you descend the
hill you have to your left a charming pool with a water mill by
it, and a very pretty stone house with good doorway of Caroline
date. The valley is delightful. It leads you, turning left
again, to the three houses which form the village of Chesterton.
There is no road except through the fields, and the church stands
absolutely alone, raised on a mound, behind which northwards
once stood the house of the Peytos. Nothing now remains
but the red brick arch, with good pediment, which led from the

F

garden to the churchyard, the house was destroyed utterly in 1802. It had been rebuilt by Inigo Jones in 1632 for Sir Edward Peyto but before that had a long history, being, as they say, rebuilt once before under Edward IV. The church itself is entered by a south porch, on which is set a sundial with the words, "See and begone about your business." On the wall over this porch has been placed some fine sculptured tabernacle work, perhaps once within. On this three figures, of saints, only remain. The western tower is probably of the seventeenth century,

Chesterton Windmill.

made out of old materials. Then eastwards stretches the long nave and chancel with continuing battlements. The nave is probably of the fourteenth century, but has Tudor mullioned windows inserted. The chancel has two simple early Decorated windows. The division between nave and chancel is marked on the south wall outside by a large buttress. On the north side are five large buttresses. The church indeed seems to have needed continual support. It is again in need, for a great crack shows down the surface of the north wall at its western end. A very fine old door admits you within. The

interior of the church, save for the curious little room under
the tower, is of one piece. There is no chancel arch. The whole
surface is plastered over. There is a Norman font, a beautiful
piscina now used as a credence table, and another at the east
of the nave ; the fine old supports to the roof, and a pulpit
of no great pretensions, from which it is said that an incumbent,
having no sermon at hand, once read an interesting letter he
had recently received from a friend : in these out-of-the-way
places people tell curious stories about clergymen. The fine
series of tombs completes the history of the village as it is given
in Dugdale. Several of them cluster at the west end. There
is the tomb of Humphrey Peyto and his wife, Anne Fielding,
temp. Elizabeth. He wears armour, but his helmet forms a pillow
for his head. She wears a long robe and ruff, and near her feet
nestles a little boy with a red collar. Her husband's feet rest on a
lion. Above are their ten children, one in shroud, some in armour,
some in the gown of civil life. The date of Humphrey's death is
given ; it was 1585 : but the place for her date is vacant ; she
died in 1604. At the west is the large monument, two busts,
under a fine entablature supported by classic columns, of Sir
Edward Peyto (1643) and his wife Elizabeth (*née* Newton)
erected by their son Edward. These monuments, as Dugdale
shows, were once in the chancel. On the north wall, in the first
arch, is Sir William Peyto (1609) and his wife Eleanor Aston (1636)
under a round arch. On the floor is Edward Peyto, 1658, who
married Elizabeth Verney of Compton Verney. The chancel
completes the history by showing how the lands of the Peytos
came to the Verneys, in a monument to the memory of Mrs.
Margaret Peyto, who was born February 10, 1657, and died
May 22, 1746. She was buried in a vault under this church,
June 11, 1746. She was the daughter of Sir Edward Peyto
and his wife Elizabeth, daughter of Sir Greville Verney, and was
born only a year before her father's death. " By the kind
bequest of her will her estate in this county and elsewhere
came to John Peyto Lord Willoughby de Broke and his heirs."
Dugdale has the long history of these people, up to his day ;
and the many coats he gives, from glass in the hall now destroyed,
fill in the tale. One quite recent memorial must be mentioned.
It is that to two parish clerks, named William Blick, who held
the office in succession, the first dying in 1878, aged 78 ; the
second, who was a blacksmith at Harbury, and walked over

to his ecclesiastical duties, in 1905, aged 72. Chesterton, since the days of the Romans, seems ever to have been a secluded place. There, Sir John Oldcastle, political traitor and accused as a heretic, was harboured by the priest John Lacy in 1415. The village then was almost depopulated. When Dugdale knew it it had fourteen families; but hard by is Kingston, alias Little Chesterton, which hath but one house, he tells.

Since the days of the Romans, I said. For at Chesterton, further on, if you go north-westwards from the church and the windmill, where the Fosseway crosses from what is now the Banbury and Warwick road to the Southam and Leamington road, is a Roman camp. The camp has not been excavated, but you can see an earthwork, not exactly rectangular, with a ditch. Through it the Fosse cuts. The camp contains about eight acres, and the ditch is exceedingly wide, probably much wider than it originally was, though it must always have been large. "The earthwork," says Professor Haverfield, "may be an early Roman fort, abandoned as the tide of Roman conquest swept swiftly north. Or like Brinklow it may not be Roman at all. In either case the late coins and burials seem to suggest a wayside village in the third or fourth century. But the spade alone can solve the problem." Enough has been said at least to show that Chesterton with its camp, its windmill, its church, and its houses scattered scantily on the grassy slopes, is a village which no traveller in Shakespeare's land who wishes to go back to the old times must fail to see.

Following the Banbury road towards Warwick, and turning aside to the right at Oakley Wood, you reach the villages of Bishop's Tachbrook and Tachbrook Mallory. The latter has its history, and that of the Mallorys, in Dugdale. The former has also a history, which illustrates the English Reformation. It belonged to the Bishop of Coventry till the first year of Edward VI., when the Bishop (of Lichfield) Richard Sampson (consecrated on June 11, 1543, to the see of Chichester—very likely Barlow received consecration at the same time) alienated it, for what consideration we know not, to Thomas Fysher, Esquire. In Tachbrook Mallory are the remains of an old chapel in a house recently restored. At Tachbrook Bishop is a good church with Perpendicular embattled tower at the west, a Decorated chancel (which looks entirely modern) eastwards, just above the road— the churchyard is surrounded south and east by road, and stands on a little hill—and an Early English nave with late Decorated additions. The north side has a Norman door now blocked up, and three large buttresses. The memorials are chiefly to the Wagstaffes and the Landors. John Wagstaffe (1681) and Alice (Stanton), his wife, are notable. Of him the epitaph says that "His Religion did not make him insociable nor his mirth irreligious." There are also Sir Thomas Wagstaffe, 1708, who, when he died, was the last of his race, and John, his third son. On the north side of the north aisle is the tablet of John Rous, 1670, who married Mary, the widow of Thomas Wagstaffe, and co-heir of William Combe of Stratford. "He had the honour," it says, "to be chose one of the burgesses for Warwick in that renowned Convention (afterwards a Parliament) which restored King Charles ye 2nd to his throne." He died without issue. The monument was put up by Lady Crewe, who died at Fawsley, but wished to be buried here with "her dear relations" 1696. The record concludes with these words : "This was placed here by the kind permission of ye present Dean of Lichfield in ye time of his visitation." The other family connected with Tachbrook is of course that of Walter Savage Landor. On the floor we see the record ; "Savage vault full," and "Landor vault" ; on the wall Walter's beautiful Latin memorial of his brother Robert and a tablet to himself.

Continue the road from Tachbrook to Leamington, and turn aside for a few minutes to Whitnash, a very pretty village with many black and white houses. The church stands on a height above the village green, surrounded by trees. It has been very much restored, but there are some surviving signs of very early, even herring-bone, work. The church, restored inside out of all knowledge, contains the good brasses of Benedict Medley and his wife, whose inscription is lost. He bought the manor from Sir Henry Willoughby in the time of Henry VII., to whom he was Clerk of the Signet. A brass to Richard Bennett, rector 1492–1531, shows him vested in an alb, stole, chasuble, and holding the chalice with the Host. On the north wall of the chancel is a slab with record of Nicholas Greenhill, forty years rector, who died in 1650, aged 70. He was headmaster of Rugby, aged 22, in 1602, but remained there only three years. The inscription begins in Latin and ends in English, the latter part perhaps his wife's, for she set it up, and it is in verse very indifferent, save that he is described as a "Greenhill periwig'd with snow." A touching instance of local piety is near, in the memorial to the Rev. Thomas Morse (who died in 1784, aged 84), his wife and children, with the concluding words : " Friendly regard has inscribed this marble to the memory of a family now totally extinct."

Our journey's end is at Leamington. Some writers are so precise as to think this elegant town not worth a word because Shakespeare never saw it. Of such we will not be. Let us consider it thus.

Warwickshire might be regarded by the vulgar as insignificant if it had not a watering-place. As a matter of fact, it has several. But of these and their somewhat dim merits, this is not the place to discourse. Let it suffice that Leamington still retains the fame which it acquired a hundred years ago. The passion for curing real and imaginary ills by the drinking and washing in unpleasant waters was discreetly directed by Dr. Jephson to what was then a little village, which, indeed had mineral waters as good as anywhere else ; and eminent physicians have quite recently declared that "there is no known reason why the Leamington springs may not prove equally efficacious as " those of Kissingen and Homburg. Let us be content with this without an analysis of the waters, and recognise that Leamington, especially in the winter and the spring, is a most pleasant place to stay in. It is not far from hills, on its south and east, and is surrounded by woods and bisected by the river from which it takes its name. The long main street, going up the slight hill, is well built. The Jephson gardens are eminently pleasing. There are good walks among trees, and houses with all the merits which belong to the era of 1820–1840. Queen Victoria, who had visited the town in 1830, allowed it the title of " Royal Leamington Spa " in 1838. It is an excellent centre for Warwickshire expeditions.

Whatever else one associates with Leamington it is certain one cannot forget Mr. Dombey's sojourn there. A letter of Dickens's in 1847 shows that he and " Phiz " visited the town together, and there is an illustration " Major Bagstock is delighted to have the opportunity " which shows a possible semblance to the Parade, in which the Native has become all that his creator (in his instructions to the artist) desired, earrings and an outlandish appearance, and a dark brown countenance and " Mosesy." When Mr. Carker " strolled beyond the town and re-entered it by a pleasant walk where there was a deep

shade of leafy trees and where there were a few benches here
and there for those who chose to rest," guide-books (and I
am rather inclined to think the Town Council also) identify
this with Linden Walk ; but another authority says Holly
Walk.   Such are the contentions which delight the heart of the
local antiquary when he finds that a writer of fiction has presumed to touch his native town.   At any rate the hotel (" The
Crown ") at which Mr. Dombey stayed, is no more.   The railway ruthlessly demolished it.   Mr. Dombey, Major Bagstock,
Mrs. Skewton, Mrs. Granger, and, not least, Mr. Carker, went, of
course, to Warwick, and saw all that they ought to see ; but there
is nothing very remarkable that they did there to connect them
in our memories with the place.   Thackeray knew Leamington
also ; and you must find your way to Lansdowne Crescent—out
of Holly Walk, to the left—and see No. 10, a semi-detached
house in which Nathaniel Hawthorne lived when he was writing
about Warwickshire.

The discovery of the spring goes back as far as Camden,
but it was not till 1786 that the Baths were founded.
William Abbotts developed them, and according to his tomb
in the churchyard, "devoted his whole time and fortune to
accomodate the public, and lived to see his benevolent works
merit the approbation of the most eminent physicians."   He
died in 1805.   He had been assisted by Benjamin Satchwell,
a shoemaker and poet, who lived till nine years later.   The
original spring, now covered by a stone building, is at the west
side of the church.   A little further on, across the Leam, you will
come to the Jephson Gardens on the right, and the Pump Rooms,
with the Corinthian columns, without which no Pump Room
could exist, on the left.   The Pump Rooms are worthy of their
associations, and they have all the proper healing arrangements.
Alas ! the Assembly Rooms, in Regent Street, which were built
by the great Elliston (familiar name to all readers of Macready's
Diary) are now no longer used, for assemblies ; and the Bedford
Hotel, in which Jack Mytton (1796–1834) performed one of his
unpleasing feats—jumping on horse-back over the dining-table
and the guests, and then from the balcony into the street—has
ceased to exist, and is replaced by the London and Midland Bank.
William West, in his "History, Topography and Directory of
Warwickshire" (1830) which is, I think, almost the first book to
give its due importance to Birmingham, when he is noting how

many famous buildings of the past have fallen into ruin, such as " Kenilworth, Maxstoke, the halls of the Templars at Balsall," and how many once populous villages have passed away into silence, as Hurst, Oltchurch and Cesterover—two of the three now passed even beyond the view of the historian—points a contrast by the example of Leamington, " a hamlet which, at no very different day from the period in which the author now writes, was composed of only two or three very humble rural dwellings, and occupied by a few poor and unlettered inhabitants; but which has now arisen, like the palace of Aladdin, into all the proportion, beauty, and magnificence of a fashionable watering-place ; adorned with buildings, for ornament and use, which display the most luxurious specimens of modern taste ; thronged by thousands of inhabitants, busy in commercial enterprise, and wealthy in the intellectual endowments, and surrounded by country fertile, diversified, and rich in historical and poetical associations."

The growth of Leamington is illustrated in a curious way by the local history of the old Poor Law.   When it was of the greatest importance to keep the paupers to their own birth-place lest they should become chargeable to the parish where they settled, we find the overseers of this new town issuing a notice to householders urging them to keep down the number of their servants and to engage them for fifty-one weeks only, so as to give them no " local habitation."

It need hardly be said that all sorts of royal and illustrious persons have adorned Leamington by their presence ; but Dr. Jephson, whose statue is to be seen in the gardens named after him, was the real creator of its fame.   Two landlords also greatly aided its growth, Mr. Willes, of Newbold Comyn, whose house and park are at the end of Holly Walk, and Mr. Wise, of Shrubland Hall, a handsome house just a century old, with a very good library, outside the town to the south.

The attractions of Leamington may be described as wholly therapeutic.   The waters benefit some people, the cheerful society others, the excellent hunting to be had from this centre others, and the mild climate the aged.   To these may be added the walks round, which are still beautiful and attractive, though the ways to them are gradually being built over, and the excel-lent shops.   No doubt it would be true to say now, as in 1814, that " provision is made for the gay as well as the sick and drooping."

. The history of this very modern town goes back, however, very much farther as a village.   Mr. Cox records, from Dugdale of course, that :—

" *Lemington Priors,* so called to distinguish it from *Leamington Hastings,* was the Estate of *Roger de Montgomeri* in the Conqueror's Time, when it was certified to contain two Hides and two Mills ; but before the Conquest 'twas the Freehold of *Oluuinus,* Father of *Turchil de Warwick. Robert de Belesm,* Son of *Roger,* inherited it after his Father, and having forfeited it to the King, it was given to one of the Bishops of *Chester, i.e.* of *Coventry* and *Lichfield,* who enfeoffed *Jeffrey de Clinton* with it, and he granted it for ten Marks, a silver Cup, and a Besantine of Gold to his Wife, to *Gilbert Nutricius* of *Warwick,* and his Heirs, to hold by the Service of Half a Knight's Fee. In which Grant it is said to be *De Feodo Episcopi. G. Nutricius* is supposed to die without Issue, and thereupon this Lordship returned to *Jeffrey de Clinton,* who gave it to the Canons of *Kenilworth,* together with the Church and Mill of this Village.

" But it seems, that the Service of Half a Knight's Fee, by which the said Canons held it, was by the Bishop made over to the Monks of *Coventry,* for in 20 *Henry* III. the Prior there certifying what Knights Fees were held of that Monastery, mentions Half a Knight's Fee in *Lemington* near *Warwick,* held by those Canons, as was again returned 36 *Henry* III. What these Canons held here is particularly specified in 7 *Edward* I. to be a Water-mill, three Yard-Lands and a fourth Part, Half a Mill in the Demesne, nine Servants holding three Yard-Lands and three Quarters, and performing servile Labours, eight Cottagers holding so many Cottages, and eight Acres of Land, and eleven Freeholders holding thirteen Yard-Lands and a fourth Part, with another Half of a Water-mill ; and besides all these a Court-Leet, Gallows, Assize of Bread and Beer, by the Grant of K. *Henry* III. together with the Church appropriate endowed with two Yard-Lands :   All which were enjoyed by them till the Dissolution of the Monasteries by King *Henry* VIII."   Thence to the Crown, and thence to the Dudleys.

The churches of Leamington are modern and none of them is of the highest merit.   A recent Roman Catholic writer says they " are all modern and uninteresting, the most striking being the Catholic [he means Roman] church of S. Peter in Dormer Place," a sentence a little difficult to understand. But the Parish Church does not attempt to be both striking and uninteresting ; it really has very considerable merit, and now that weather has toned it might well be taken for a late, and rather unusual medieval type.   There was an ancient one —it was a chapelry to Leek-Wootton dedicated to All Saints. This underwent various transmogrifications in the seventeenth and nineteenth centuries.   But it seemed unsuited to the dignity of a watering place and the neighbourhood of a pump room, and so from 1843 the new church began to be built.   It is excellent for its date : the nave and aisles are Perpendicular, the transepts (1849 and 1869) Decorated.   The framework of the ancient tower remains within the nave.   The windows are good, at the west—bad, at the east.   The reredos is an excellent representation of Leonardo da Vinci's Last Supper ; and there is, or was, a fine painted cloth representing the Flight into Egypt. The whole building is by no means unworthy of the position and wealth of the town.

The consecration of the church we now see took place on July 17, 1845.   The *English Churchman* gives an account which is worth noting.   It says, " At about eleven o'clock a *procession* of more than fifty clergymen in their surplices, stoles, and the hoods of their respective degrees, left the vicarage, and passed round the east end and south side of the church to the western entrance.   They were preceded by the choir, and chanted (to the 8th Gregorian tone, 2nd ending) the 126th, the 122nd, and the 132nd Psalms.   The procession, which was conducted by the Rev. E. Fortescue, entered the church at the western door, and proceeded to the altar, within the rails of which the Rural Deans and distinguished ecclesiastics from distant parts, were accommodated ; the rest of the clergy sat in the choir on either side."

Now to this, Mr. Fortescue's son-in-law (since himself called to his rest) gave me a most entertaining addition, which follows naturally on the italicised word " *procession*."

" Edward Fortescue was an enthusiastic volunteer.   He has described it to me.   There was published an account of the event to come—an open-air procession, unheard of, and glorious—all the neighbouring clergy and great men to walk in the open air to the Church—of course Mr. Fortescue did all he could to persuade to the use of some kind of ecclesiastical, or at least university, habit and not tall hats and coats—no one thought of anything so *outré* as a banner or a Cross, but at any rate it was thoroughly ecclesiastical and was to be honoured by the presence at the culminating point of the procession of the LORD BISHOP of Worcester (Dr. Pepys). Well—my father-in-law said that the Bishop had arrived, and was ready, and he moved the procession forward through the streets, and did what was natural to keep people at a proper distance apart to look effective and not all huddled together, and it started off, and the proper people fell into their places gradually—and he then went respect- fully to the Bishop and asked him to take his place.—Of course no one expected in those days anything more than decent pomp, but they did expect that.

" The Bishop listened, and moved a little to one side where he found *Mrs. Pepys,* and said Now my dear, or the like, and moved off *arm-in-arm.* How my father used to burst with laughter, at the collapse of his expectations."

So much for Leamington's ancient history in the Middle and the early Victorian ages. More we need hardly say to commend its antiquity or its waters or its general pleasantness ; but a word must be given to its *environs.* It must be admitted that for antiquarians and Shakespeareans the first thing to inquire at Leamington is the way to Warwick. There are two ways : the one, leafy and sandy, with a canal, that seems disused, to your left, and the Leam across fields and behind houses to your right, starts from the Great Western station and brings you to Warwick past the King's School and by the bridge with its glorious view. The other starts from near the top of the hill and the trams take you past every variety of Victorian building, by Emscote with its quaintly painted modern church standing just aside from the noisy road, past the Milverton station of the L.N.W.R., into Warwick by the east gate.

But there are other places to visit from Leamington. No one should neglect to go along Holly Walk, take a field-road and climb the hill to Offchurch, where a Norman Early English and six- teenth century building (not to mention other periods) is throned upon the hill. The Early English porch is an especially good one. In the tower are marks of shot said to remain from a skirmish at the beginning of the Civil War. There is a very good timber roof dated 1592. I blush to say that I have not penetrated to Offchurch Bury, where in the grounds there are pillars which are said to resemble in decoration the capitals at S. Sophia —and people say they belonged to Offa's house—or his church, if Offchurch was named after the Mercian king. But I have been to Offchurch both by the fields and by the lovely road from Radford ; and no one must go without pausing again and again to taste the view, and the air, and the scent of the trees.   Or Lillington on the Rugby road may be inspected, and Cubbington beyond it : both have churches of interest, the latter with much good Norman work.   But our way has been that from Warwick.   No one goes to Leamington without going on to the county town. Very much surprised indeed would Dugdale have been to find little Leamington Priors regarded as an introduction to Warwick ; but certainly nowadays the watering-place is more important than the county town.   Or shall we put it that no one who comes to Leamington is likely to be content without seeing Warwick, while those who come to Warwick may be unwilling to mar their memory of ancient glories by the contrast with trim or faded modernism ?

CHAPTER V

AFTER Leamington, of course Warwick. The Castle of Warwick is, certainly to the ordinary sightseer, probably to the historian, the centre of Warwickshire. If the county is the land of Shakespeare, it is also the land of the great lords who have made so much of English legend and English history. " Guy of Warwick " was known long before Shakespeare gave glory to the shire, and the castle had been built and besieged and won renown long before the spacious days of Great Elizabeth. And if the quiet beauties of Stratford-on-Avon delight all those who love true English scenery and honour the memory of the greatest of Englishmen, the splendour of Warwick Castle impresses everyone who is not blind and deaf to the glories of the past.

As you approach Warwick by train from Leamington you see the castle towering over the town to the left. But if you are wise you will come by the " low road," smooth and leafy, bordered by pleasant houses to the right, and the sluggish, choked canal to the left, past Myton, now only a row of modern houses, but one of those villages of medieval times which have now quite ceased to exist—even in Dugdale's day it was no more than " a grove of elms "—past the school, great in its newness, till you reach the Avon, and are stopped on the fine bridge—one of those bridges in which the eighteenth century excelled—by the view of the castle to your left. It stands high up on the rock, the river flowing below—and, with all the changes that have befallen it, all the destructive wars and fires and restorations, it still bears the appearance of a fine medieval fortress. In Dugdale there are two quaint and beautiful views of it, and the town, embowered in trees ; and yet I do not think it is any less beautiful to-day.

The Courtyard
Warwick
Castle

And indeed its history goes very far back. It is one of those places which are naturally designed for fortification and for legend. Of course it is traced to the Romans, and of course it has its mythical heroes.

Dugdale justly argues the antiquity of the place from the "commodities which surround it," but he wisely goes on to the records which John Rous collected, and from them indeed he extracts sufficient wonders. One need not be careful to disentangle the town from the castle in these tales, or to tell minutely of Cymbeline or Artegal, of Morvidus who "slew a mighty Gyant in a single Duell," or Dubritius, "who made his episcopal seat here," or Guy who became a hermit (and about him more elsewhere). But then Dugdale fastens himself upon "that King Warremund from whom the Kings of Mercia did descend" who "from his own name caused it to be called Warrewyk." And Warrewyk it continued to be written for many centuries. Those who have seen of the signature of the king-maker will remember the bold letters, " Ri. Warrewyk."

After King Warremund we come in Dugdale to more certain history in the person of Æthelfleda, the daughter of Alfred the Great, the "lady of the Mercians." She undoubtedly gave the town its prominence in central England, and with her the history of the castle begins. But what shall we say of her work ? Of the castle as built by Æthelfleda Mr. Freeman (*carum et venerabile nomen*) wrote that " the lady wrought between the town and the river one of those vast artificial mounds which played so important a part in the early history of fortification," and added that " the mound itself still remains, a monument of the wisdom and energy of the mighty daughter of Ælfred, while the keep of William has so utterly perished that its very site can only be guessed at." This he wrote when he was telling the story of the great achievements of the greatest of early English heroines. Later, when he summed up the history of the Normans in England, he said, " At Warwick the mound of the Lady of the Mercians still remains ; for the castle of the Conqueror we seek in vain." But later investigations, summed up by Mr. J. H. Round in a communication to the Society of Antiquaries in 1902, lead to the conclusion that the castles built at the time of the Norman Conquest by the Conquerors were not stone buildings but " moated mounds, crowned with a palisade : " the moated flat-topped mound was the

Norman invention in which the English found an instrument of oppression. This, the *motte*, was what the Normans set up, and it is this, not Æthelfleda's work, which survives at Warwick. Later came the buildings which we now see ; and what remains of Æthelfleda's work, we may presume, is only the choice of the site with perhaps the decision of its boundaries. Æthelfleda may have built a wall for the town ; the Normans made a mound with palisades from which to overawe it. And that no doubt was not the work of Thurkil the Englishman, who, if he was not strictly Earl of Warwick, was certainly the chief landowner in the shire in King William's day. Thurkil was one of those who came not to the assistance of Harold against the Normans, and so he was allowed to hold his lands till his death, when they were given to Henry of Newburgh, the son of Roger de Beauchamp, Count of Meulan. The castle itself seems to have been first built by William the Conqueror as he marched northwards, 1068–1069.

Briefly may the history of the castle then be told. What we see of the building dates at earliest from the end of the thirteenth century, and the chief additions, are Guy's tower (1394), Cæsar's tower (*c.* 1360), a large part of the dwelling-rooms at the beginning of the seventeenth century, and more in 1770. The vicissitudes which befell it in the Middle Ages begin with the Baron's Wars, when Earl William Mauduit was taken prisoner by Sir John Giffard of the Barons' party, and the walls of the castle were demolished ; demolished, that is, after the fashion of which we hear so much in the chronicles, which did not prevent their being very soon built up again. This was in 1264. In 1266 Henry III. was there, preparing for the siege of Kenilworth after the victory of Evesham. Again the castle was restored—this was probably the time of its chief building—by Guy, the earl in Edward I.'s time, whom Piers Gaveston in the next reign nicknamed " Black dog of Arden." And it was there, perhaps in the great hall itself, that Gaveston in 1312 had his hasty trial, and thence that he was led forth to Blacklow Hill beyond Guy's Cliffe to meet a traitor's fate. Within two years the Black Dog received Edward II.'s pardon for this ; but he did not serve him with any cordiality and was conspicuously absent from the Scottish War. Says Dugdale : " as I cannot commend his Demeanor in those things last spoke of, so do I not discern that he had any great comfort there of himself, for it is plain enough that he enjoyed not the felicities of this world full xiv. months after." After his death Hugh le Despencer had custody of the castle, for a debt which the king declared Guy had owed him. Earl Thomas, Guy's heir, married Catherine, daughter of Roger Mortimer Earl of March. A second Thomas left a second Richard who died *anno* 17 Hen. VI., leaving a daughter, Ann, who married Richard Nevile the king-maker, and a son who wedded Cecily, Richard Nevile's sister. This son, Henry, the last of the Beauchamp earls, died in the twenty-third year of Henry VI., and the great inheritance came to the Neviles. How short a time it stayed is written in every history book. The earldom passed through Isabel, the king-maker's daughter, to Edward her son, whom Henry VII. slew, and Margaret her daughter (who married Richard Pole) whom Henry VIII. slew. And then—Dugdale's pedigree shows the curious line of kinship—John Dudley was made Earl of Warwick and held the earldom with the duchy of Northumberland. He, like his father, perished on the scaffold ; but Elizabeth renewed the earldom to his son Ambrose, who died at last without issue.

Before we speak of the new line we may tell briefly what the medieval earls had done for the fabric and the history of the castle. It was the first Thomas Beauchamp who built Cæsar's tower in the last half of the fourteenth century. And in his time too was built the gateway, with the barbican and gatehouse, while his son Thomas the second built Guy's tower, a defence as skilful as solid. Then, in the completed castle, Henry V. was received by Richard Beauchamp in 1417 as guest ; and fifty-two years later Richard Nevile received Edward IV. as a prisoner. When Richard III. was king, and through his wife son-in-law of the dead king-maker, he twice visited the castle, in 1483 and 1484. Ambrose, Elizabeth's Earl, entertained the queen in 1572 and in 1575.

In Elizabeth's reign Warwick was undoubtedly at its highest glory. It had rich benefactors, a " good earl " to watch over its interests, commercial prosperity, and security from war. "The Black Book " of the Corporation, a most interesting and curious record, tells of the prosperity and happiness of the town. When Elizabeth came in 1572 she was greeted with much speaking— which is the invariable sign of mercantile prosperity—and many indifferent Latin verses. She came on a Monday from Itchington, " went by Woodloes the fairest way to Kenilworth," stayed there on Monday and Tuesday nights and returned to Warwick

G

Castle on Saturday night very late, and rested all Sunday. In the town's jubilation fireworks played a great part—and with disastrous results. Four houses were burnt by them, and by " a Dragon flieng casting out huge flames and squibes."

What Warwick was like in Queen Elizabeth's reign may be gathered from a variety of sources, especially Leland's "Itinerary," Dugdale's "Warwickshire," the " Book of John Fisher " (1580–1588) and some old plans. Of course the east and west gates stood as they do now, but they seem to have been in a ruinous condition. Above the east gate was S. Peter's chapel, above the west S. James's. The north gate had gone ; the Castle was the south gate. The chancel, with vestry and chapter house, of S. Mary's, were little different from what they are to-day, but the ancient nave of the church still stood. It was rather smaller than Sir Christopher Wren's, and its tower was lower. Over the south porch, as so often, was a room, where John Rous had lived.

S. Nicholas Church by the river was pulled down in 1779 and rebuilt. The bridge was then close to the castle, and the castle was then much more closely attached to the town. A road led up from the bottom of Mill Street, called Castle Street, came by the walls to the High Cross which stood where is the present Court House in Jury Street. It was at the end of the eighteenth century that the Castle grounds were enlarged, the wall moved northwards, and part of Castle Street taken in. The Park, which had been open fields, was enclosed at the same time, and the new castle bridge was built in 1790, replacing the old one which had been made to the west. Remains of the old bridge can still be seen. When Elizabeth came in 1572 she was received at Ford Mill Hill. The population was about 2,600. Tuesday and Saturday were, by Philip and Mary's charter, market days, and on S. Bartholomew's and S. Simon and S. Jude's days were fairs. The government of the town was in the hands of a bailiff and twelve principal burgesses and twelve assistants. All this and much more can be learned from the Black Book, most piously transcribed and published by Mr. Thomas Kemp, deputy-mayor, in 1898, and twice mayor of the town. Most of the entries in it were made in Elizabeth's reign by Mr. John Fisher, town clerk, but it was continued spasmodically till the eighteenth century. The meetings of the Corporation seem to have been often turbulent— " I lye not, you lye," was a not uncommon rejoinder—and "stick to yt fellowes," a cry of the commons to those who bore their part among the notables. But persons who "leawdly behaved in language and speech" against the bailiff and burgesses were set in the stocks. Yet we must not forget to set against such rudeness the good behaviour and charity of Thomas Oken, the most famous benefactor of Warwick. He died in 1573, having lived through all the reformation. His brass is on the east

Mill Street, Warwick.

wall of the north transept; he had ordered the words "Jesu have mercy upon me" to be set on it. And in his will he directed a sermon and a dinner and other things annually. At the end of the dinner a paternoster to be said and praise given to God for the soul of himself and his wife. His house is a small gabled half-timbered building in Castle Street, looking towards S. Mary's Church "at the head of a block of buildings, having the road on one side of them and a narrow passage on the other."

G 2

Another house that is still standing, though it is much changed since Elizabeth's day, is the Priory, within a high wall and surrounded by large gardens. It is some way to the north of the main streets, between Priory Street and the Great Western railway. In Elizabeth's day it belonged to Thomas Hawkins—nicknamed Fisher, because his father had sold fish in the town —a dependant of Dudley Duke of Northumberland, who survived through Mary's reign, and then came to great wealth. He pulled down the buildings of the ancient priory, founded by Henry of Newburgh, and built a fine house, finished in 1568. He lived till 1576, a great person in the town. Leicester stayed with him at his visit in 1571, and it was there that the Marquess of Northampton died. In 1572 Elizabeth herself supped there, with the Earl and Countess of Warwick, and visited Fisher, who was grievously suffering from gout. His son Edward ran through his father's wealth very quickly, and sold the Priory to Serjeant Puckering, Lord Keeper. His granddaughter was the heroine of an exciting case of abduction, being stolen away by one Joseph Walsh, as she was walking in Greenwich Park, and carried to Flanders. She was recovered after nearly a year, and married Sir John Bate, but lived only two years afterwards. The house received many additions in the eighteenth century, but the north side of it remains much as of old. It has, like so much Church property, often changed hands, but has now been more than half a century in the possession of the same family.

In 1576 the east gate, S. Peter's Chapel, and the Shire Hall were granted by Lords Leicester and Warwick to the Corporation.

The government of the town, with a good deal of squabbling from time to time, continued to be as ordered by the charter of William and Mary till James II. annulled the charter, in pursuit of his plan to secure control for the Crown over all Corporations. In 1694 a new charter was granted, which lasted till the Municipal Corporations Act of 1835.

The report of the inquiry into the "present state of the Warwick Corporation," held in 1833, was published at Warwick m 1834. This was on behalf of the Municipal Corporations Commission, and led to the Act dissolving the old Corporation. Many curious details are to be found in the evidence, and much vehemence: the evidence of Mr. Innes, sometime Fellow of

Magdalen College, master of the school, is exceedingly quaint. He held his post for fifty years, and for thirty seems to have had hardly any pupils, and to have been crippled by gout. But he was a gentleman and a good master.

.The later history of the town is uneventful. Its politics, internal and external, cause no disturbance ; and it deservedly enjoys parliamentary representation still, though in union with its mushroom neighbour Leamington.

Let us return to the castle. After the death of Ambrose, the good Earl, in February, 1590, the castle was for a time in the hands of the Crown. The title was given 16 James I. to the family of Rich. The castle was granted to Sir Fulke Greville, a descendant of the famous woolstapler of Chipping Campden, and it remains still in the hands of his descendants.

Warwick Castle, in the early days of James I., is thus described by Bishop Corbet (the delightful friend of all who have read Aubrey's " Brief Lives ") in his *Iter Boreale*.

> " Please you walk out and see the castle ?   Come,
> The owner saith, it is a scholar's bome ;
> A place of strength and wealth : in the same fort
> You would conceive a castle and a court.
> The orchards, gardens, rivers, and the air,
> Do with the trenches, rampires, walls, compare :
> It seems nor art nor force can intercept it,
> As if a lover built, a soldier kept it.
> Up to the tower, though it be steep and high,
> We do not climb, but walk ; and though the eye
> Seem to be weary, yet our feet are still   •
> In the same posture cozen'd up the hill ;
> And thus the workman's art deceives our sense,
> Making those rounds of pleasure a defence."

And the merry ecclesiastic gives a cheerful description too of his host, the great Fulke Greville, whose every word " was wine and musick," and by whose side was

> " A prelate, by his place
> Arch-deacon to the bishop, by his face
> A greater man ; for that did counterfeit
> Lord abbot of some convent standing yet,
> A corpulent relique."

The Puritans would be shocked at him, the good man says, but not he.

Sir Fulke Greville was not only a generous host but a great

builder. He entertained James I. in 1617, 1619, 1621, and 1624. Part of the castle, when he came into possession of it, was in a ruinous state, and part of it was used as the county gaol. He set to work to " " reedify it," and spent the huge sum, for those days, of £20,000 on the work. He, and George Earl of Warwick at the end of the eighteenth century, were really the creators of the castle as we see it now. But each of them was a conservative architect. Little at Warwick has been destroyed except by time. It was Sir Fulke's work to make it, as Dugdale says, " a place not only once more of strength, but also of extraordinary delight ; being planted with the most pleasant gardens, walks, and thickets, forming the most princely seat within the midland parts of this realm." In 1636 Charles I. stayed at the castle, and attended service, with the Mayor and Corporation, · in the choir of S. Mary's Church. The Earl of Lindsey was brought there from Edgehill, a prisoner, and died almost as he entered. In 1642 the castle, then belonging to Robert Lord Brooke, the son of Fulke, was besieged for a few days. This was he who has been compared by the present Countess of Warwick to Lord Morley, and she adds with candour her opinion that the latter " has displayed Mr. Chamberlain's vigour without his inconsistency, and Mr. Balfour's cleverness without his hesitations." Then came more peaceful times. The great fire of 1694 which destroyed so much of the town left the castle unharmed ; and in the next year William III. paid it a visit. When the earls of the Rich family died out the descendants of Fulke Greville, who had already been ennobled as Lords and then Earls Brooke, received the ancient title—Francis Greville Earl Brooke being in 1759 created Earl of Warwick. George, his son and successor, completed the building as we see it now. And thereby hangs a tale. This is a very curious point in the history of the earls of Warwick, who seem at certain times to have been inclined to run into debt and live extravagantly : it is to be elucidated perhaps, but only perhaps, by a pamphlet published in 1816 called " A Narrative of the Peculiar case of the late Earl of Warwick, from his Lordship's own manuscript," which is prefaced by the note that " the following narrative was intended to have been published in the lifetime of the noble Earl, which his Lordship has left as a memorial of his peculiar case, &c., who died a Martyr to Treachery, Delusion, and Pre-judice.' The vehemence of the paper is considerable. It seems to have been issued as a stroke in a quarrel between two legal figures representing different sides of the family ; but the inter-esting part to the visitor to-day is to see what of the present castle and its surroundings is due to the work of the owner just about a century ago. Thus the pamphlet :—

" I found almost everything out of repair, in and out of the castle. I began the arduous task of putting everything in the most perfect order imaginable. The floors, the windows, the ceilings, the chimney pieces, the wainscots, the furniture, are all put in by me, and they are the most beautiful in the kingdom, as is generally admitted. I collected a matchless collection of pictures, by Vandyke, Rubens, &c. The marbles are not equalled perhaps, in the kingdom. I made a noble approach to the castle, thro' a solid rock ; built a porter's lodge ; made a kitchen garden, and a very extensive pleasure garden ; a book room, full of books, some valuable and scarce, all well chosen. I made an armoury ; and built walls round the courts and pleasure garden, &c. I built a noble green house, and filled it with beautiful plants. I placed in it a vase, considered as the finest remains of Grecian art extant, for its size and beauty. I made a noble lake, from three hundred to six hundred feet broad, and a mile long. I planted trees, now worth one hundred thousand pounds, and which are now rapidly increas-ing in value, estimating them at only one hundred thousand trees, and to increase one shilling a year, it makes the additional value of five thousand pounds per annum. Besides, I planted one hundred acres of ash, which should be, if properly taken care of, one thousand pounds per annum, cutting ten acres a year at one hundred pounds per annum. I built a stone bridge of hundred and five feet in span, every stone from two thousand to three thousand eight hundred pounds weight. The weight of the first tier on the centres was estimated at one thousand ton. I gave the bridge to the town, there being no toll on it. I will not enumerate a great many other things done by me. Let Warwick Castle speak for itself."

And so it shall, for what George Earl of Warwick is thus made to say is an excellent introduction to what we now see.

We enter by the gate-house which he constructed, opposite to S. Nicholas Church. This is a plain embattled structure very

Warwick
Castle
from the
Bridge

inoffensive and not unpleasingly delusive in its appearance—for probably only experts would recognise it as a work of A.D. 1800. This gives entrance to a way cut through the solid rock, whence we enter the open space, called of old the Vineyard, and we see at once, in one view, the greatest part of what Walter Scott, in his delightful enthusiasm, called " the fairest monument of ancient and chivalrous splendour which yet remains uninjured by time." And that indeed is the outstanding fact about the buildings before us.

The most obvious characteristic of the present-day Warwick Castle is that without change of its main ancient parts it has remained habitable by each generation as it has been adapted to the needs of each.

The original gate-house is dated by experts in the fourteenth century. It gave access to the barbican—a term used " indiscriminately to denote any outwork by which the principal approach to a castle or a gateway of a town was covered " ; at Warwick it is a narrow way, a straight lane between two walls. When you have come out again from this narrow way you see that " the plan of the castle consists of a bailey or enclosed space, with a tall mount on the line of its outer defences, and on a side or at an angle of the *enceinte* remote from the main entrance." I quote from Mr. Hamilton Thompson, our latest expert. And if you follow the same writer you will observe under his guidance that while in the fourteenth and fifteenth centuries large private houses took the place of the great castles, there still remain " a few striking exceptions which belong to the later part of the fourteenth century. The two polygonal towers, Guy's tower and Cæsar's tower, which cover the angles of the eastern curtain at Warwick and flank the gate-house with its barbican, are cases in point. Few castles show features of the military architecture of all periods to such an advantage. The plan is that of an early Norman mount-and-bailey castle, which has in course of time been surrounded with a stone curtain ; while a magnificent residence, in the main a building of the sixteenth century, has grown up on the south side of the bailey next the river. The most commanding military features, however, are the towers just mentioned, 128 and 147 feet high respectively. The whole character of these towers is French rather than English."

As you enter the Vineyard on your right is Guy's tower, finished in 1394, an edifice of many angles and loop-holes and machicolations, its walls ten feet thick.   On your left, towards the river, is Cæsar's tower, some thirty years older, and some twenty feet higher.   Splendid though it is when seen as you see it now, it looks still finer from the river, more massive, more obviously terrific as a work of defence.   Its most striking feature is its irregularity, specially designed to enable the defenders to shoot from numerous points, by obtaining " the largest available space at the least obstruction to the line of discharge from the walls." It is built on the solid rock, and thus could not be undermined. It is so high that no military engines known to the Middle Ages could overlook it.   It has four stories, from each of which arrows could be discharged through the skilfully protected outlets ; above them a parapet with battlements ; above this again another story with wide windows, and on the top of all a flat roof, protected again with battlements, on which a large number of men could stand and employ every weapon of offence.

Inside at the lowest part was a prison where many inscriptions still testify to the courage of the prisoners, chiefly Royalists of the Civil War.

Between these two towers stands the gate-house, through which you enter the inner court.   The moat has gone, and one enters peacefully by a stone arch.   Then you come to the barbican, which projects nearly sixty feet from the main wall.   An octagonal turret is on either side, and within is the portcullis, above which are the holes from which evil things could be thrown upon the heads of assailants.   Through this is a small court, where again an attacking force would be exposed on every side to attack from gallery, towers, and walls.   After this is the gate-house itself, with still again portcullis and its accompaniments.

At last through this you find yourself in the inner court, to the left the main building of the castle, to the right the less terrible and probably uncompleted towers ; first the Bear tower, attributed to Richard III., and then the Clarence tower, said to be the work of his brother.

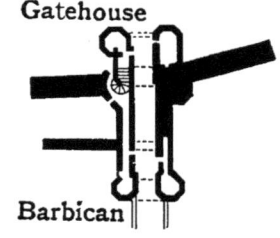

Gatehouse

Barbican

Warwick Gateway, Barbican.

Ramparts are continuous round the court, passing the smaller Northern and Hill towers, and showing above them the original Norman mount.

The main building has an ancient undercroft; and that fine

view from it towards the river, much though it has suffered, yet shows a good deal of the ancient, perhaps the original, wall. "At the western end there are seven bays of various projections "—I quote from the book of the present Countess, who says the description is "drawn up for" her "by a technical expert"—these "rising to three stories, and lighted by rectangular windows, with transomed mullions and cusped headings of the early seventeenth century, all surmounted by a battlement with plain merlons. The sixth and seventh bays form a tower of five stories, the westernmost of the two having three angles and an entrance at the basement. The other is also of the same number of angles, but has plain window openings. These bays seem entirely the work of Sir Fulke. The succeeding two bays have in the basement two blocked arches of wide span, rising from a central hexagonal column and half hexagonal piers—the original main entrance to the basement. The windows, of which there are two tiers, are transomed, and have cusped heads; the tower lights the long corridor. Part of this wall is at least as old as the fifteenth century."

The interior of this has a long corridor, and a beautiful vaulted hall, of earlier date than Sir Fulke, probably late thirteenth century, with three windows overlooking the river. From this come smaller rooms, leading into the kitchen, which is of Fulke Greville's time, and beyond it is a little ancient room with a flight of steps down to it, the last of them a newel staircase.

The chapel has been much altered and modernised, but it has some fragments of old glass. Below it are two rooms.

The dining room, the work of Francis Earl of Warwick (1770), designed after Greville's work, is a curiosity in one style, the great hall in another. This, restored since the fire of 1871 to practically its former condition, contains the so-called Guy's porridge pot—a cauldron for boiling soldiers' rations—and some fine armour. From it comes the Almonry passage, a long corridor leading from the great hall; part is ancient and vaulted, part seventeenth century, and ceiled in plaster. "Behind the vaulted portion lies first the ancient Solar, now called the Red Drawing Room, or the ante-room, which itself opens into the Cedar Drawing Room." Of these rooms a little must be said, but it would be impossible to particularise the fine features of the house or to tell of its treasures in detail. It needs a guide book to itself.

In the great hall you are shown the armour which is called Earl Guy's. It is really a collection of different dates. The headpiece is of Edward III.'s date ; the shield (which they call a breastplate) of Henry VII.'s ; another shield, which is Jacobean, is called his back armour ; a tilting lance and a two-handed Tudor sword are added to complete the set, and some horse armour of Henry VI.'s day. More interesting is the mace of Richard Nevile, the king-maker, and the baby set, said to have been made for " the noble impe," Leicester's son, who died before he was four years old.

From the great hall—sixty-two feet by thirty-five, and forty feet high—whence the most beautiful view over the river compels one to linger as long as fate, or guide, permits, we enter the Solar, which has the famous Rubens portrait of Spinola, and an Assumption attributed to Raffaelle. To name all the Vandykes here and elsewhere would be an unending task ; but the best of them, perhaps, are in the next room—the cedar drawing room— the beautiful Marchesa di Brignola, so often exhibited in London, and the Montrose. The green drawing room, next, has at least three fine portraits, the Rubens of S. Ignacio Loyóla, the famous Strafford by Vandyke, and the Prince Rupert by the same artist. The state bedroom has beautiful views without and a state bed within. Then the Boudoir is most interesting for two pictures of Henry VIII. and Anne Boleyn, which are ascribed to Holbein, and for the statement of the guide books that a boy's portrait here is of Henry VIII. by Vandyke. Now we come into the Almonry Passage, and so by the Billiard Room and the curious little room, all angles, called the compass room, into the chapel. Then you must see the great dining room, with the interesting pictures of " Prince Fred " and his wife, George III.'s father and mother ; you may ask to see the private apartments if you are inquisitive ; and if you are fortunate you may be allowed to look at the seventeenth century MSS. of Shakespeare and some of the quartos in the Shakespeare room.

The gardens are delightful, and the park, though it is quite a modern invention, is more delightful still, and makes you feel quite certain that Shakespeare walked in it. You will look, by the way, at the graceful " Warwick Vase," graceful in spite of its huge size, which Lady Hamilton's husband sold to his nephew George Earl of Warwick (*see* above). And then you will think how glorious it would be to go down the Avon those two miles through the park, and look back for what is perhaps the finest view of the castle.

Instead of that you will go back again quite humbly, and out of the gateway, and walk across to look at the church of S. Nicholas. It will be well to arrange your itinerary thus : S. Nicholas, then up Castle Hill to Jury Street, so up by the Court House and the High Street to Leycester Hospital and the West Gate ; back by Brook Street to the Market Place ; thence by Old Square to S. Mary's Church, then along North-gate Street to the County Hall, along and turning right by the Butts to the East Gate, looking at Landor's house, and so down Smith Street to S. John's Hospital. But before you see any of this, it is well that history should step in for a moment and remind you of something very ancient but now in quite a modern dress. For Warwick's extreme antiquity does not rest only in its castle. The very modern school which you see, so well built and so well situated on your left hand as you go by the low road from Leamington to Warwick, is in its history almost as ancient as the castle. In the summer of 1123 Henry I. confirmed to Theodwulf Bishop of Worcester, among other things, the school as in King Edward's day belonging to the church of All Saints. All Saints' Church was the church in the castle. S. Mary's was founded, it seems probable, by the Count of Meulan, after the Conquest and before the creation of the earldom of Warwick. Grants to it are found from Henry I.'s reign. Earl Roger, son of Earl Henry, now called Earl of Warwick and Newburgh, " fulfilled the virtuous purpose of his father, making one college of that of All Hallows, the castle, and S. Mary in the town of Warwick." All Saints, it seems, was the mother church of Warwick ; and Mr. A. F. Leach, whose authority I would be the last to dispute, thinks that it owes its dignity to being the creation of Æthelfleda, the Lady of the Mercians, who built the burh at Warwick. Earl Roger granted the school away from All Saints to S. Mary's, which was already becoming the important church of the town, growing in importance as the town grew, " that the service of God in the same church may be improved by being frequented by scholars." It was but a step in the absorption of All Saints by S. Mary's which was completed before 1143. To the Collegiate Church of S. Mary belongs most of the ecclesiastical history of Warwick. Now one of the officials of the church was the schoolmaster. He had his stall in choir, where he was to attend when he was not teaching his boys, wore a silk cope on the greater festivals, and his place among the precentors in processions. It must be remembered that there were two schools, the grammar and the song schools, and it was over the former that the schoolmaster presided. That school, it is clear, continued without break. In the fifteenth century it produced John Rous, historian and antiquary, chantry priest of Guy's Cliff. Its local habitation was a dissolved church in the market place. And so it lasted on until the dissolution of the monasteries. The school would then have disappeared, had it not been for the Guild of Holy Trinity and S. George in the town ; the guild, it appears, to which the buildings of the Leycester Hospital once belonged. When it too was dissolved, it procured the refoundation of the school as the property of the town, now incorporated, May 15, 1545. King Henry thus declared his purpose in the founding (as he of course claimed it to be) of the school. "Led by the singular love and affection with which we are no little moved to the youthful subjects of our realm in the county of . Warwick, that henceforth more imbued from their cradles with more polite letters than was customary before our day, when they come to a riper age they may turn out better instructed ; thinking assuredly that so the Anglican Church of Christ, Whose immediate vice-gerent we are, may be adorned and glorified not only by learned men in the world of letters but by wise men for the commonwealth of the realm . . . . do establish for all future times a free school in the said town of Warwick, under a master or pedagogue ; and [that it shall be] called in the vulgar tongue 'The King's New Schole of Warwyke.'" The schoolmaster was to be appointed by the Crown, and to be a corporation sole. It appears that Henry left all the money of his "charity" to the school ; but that the mayor and citizens later on secured some share of it, after Philip and Mary had granted to them a charter of incorporation.

Under Elizabeth the school was taught in what is now Leycester's Hospital. In 1576 the earls of Warwick and Leicester granted the chapel over the East Gate for the school, with the Stewards Hall (now replaced by the Shire Hall in Northgate Street).

The master of the school was given £50 a year, double the salary of the Vicar of S. Mary's.

The list of schoolmasters contains some distinguished names, notably that of John Owen, 1595–1620, pupil of Bishop Bilson. He was a famous epigrammatist, of the kind that would delight the heart of William Shakespeare. Here is one on the familiar theme that everything was saleable at Rome :—

> " An Petrus fuerit Romae, sub judice lis est.
> Simonem Romae nemo fuisse negat."

Among later masters was Mr. Thomas Dugard, who made an " oracion " when Charles I. visited the town in 1636.

On September 5, 1694, there was a great fire at Warwick which began with a spark lighting a thatched roof in the High Street, destroyed the nave of S. Mary's (not directly, but through some of the furniture of houses being carried there for safety when they were really alight) and about two hundred and fifty houses. In consequence of the old school being burnt the school was moved to what had been the college of clergy attached to the church. Up to the middle of the nineteenth century the churchyard was the only playground. In 1836 the school was placed under the municipal charity trustees, and under the mastership of the Rev. Herbert Hill (1843–1876) it began a new life. He was a man universally beloved : when burglars stole his plate, parents and friends subscribed to replace it. But the school could not prosper till it got a new scheme in 1875, and new buildings in 1879.

Mr. Leach says that " nothing of the college now remains but the old wall which still surrounds the vacant site," which was purchased in 1905 by the Vicar of S. Mary's " with a view to its preservation."

Having taken this interlude from our walk, resting, I think, on the bridge, whence we may look on those two ancient things, the old castle and the modern school, we are ready to resume our itinerary.

Well, then, to begin with S. Nicholas. This must be looked at for what it contains, but its date is 1780. The history of S. Nicholas as a parish is very ancient, and the site of the present church has been used for religion since a very dim age. Rous says that a nunnery there was destroyed by the Danes in 1016. The history of the parish (now the only parish in Warwick

Entrance to Warwick from the West.

except S. Mary's, which has engrossed All Saints', S. Helen's, S. Michael's, S. John Baptist's, S. Peter's, S. Laurence's, S. James's, and the Holy Sepulchre, churches or parishes) is interesting, but not to be detailed. The ancient church was entirely demolished in 1778, and the new building was begun in 1779. I am glad to say that though a local architect was responsible it was neither Miller nor Hiorns. The judgment of our Early Victorian critic on it is not to be gainsaid :—

" The present church, though faulty in general outline, in its proportions, and in detail, is nevertheless interesting, from the fact of its being one of the earliest churches in this country erected, towards the close of the last century, on the incipient revival or renaissance of ancient Ecclesiastical architecture, and when as yet the principles of construction, adaptation and arrangement, were scarcely, or at best but imperfectly, understood.

" The whole of the work of this church, externally as well as internally, is altogether faulty in design and meagre in detail, and the mouldings are clumsy ; whilst the outline of the building appears heavy and devoid of due proportions. It must however be considered as erected in an age when the mere form of the pointed arch appears to have been, though erroneously, regarded as the predominating principle of medieval architecture, and as an early instance of the revival of the so-called Gothic style."

The matters of interest in the church are the monuments of the Stoughtons, a family which once owned S. John's Hospital —to be seen hereafter ; and a most interesting brass described by Dugdale, missing in the mid-nineteenth century, and now affixed to the east wall of the vestry, of which this is the description :—

" An incised brass effigy (in length 21¼ inches) of the first vicar of the Church. He is habited in the mass vestments, viz.— amice, alb, chesible, stole and maniple, with the apparels on the wrists and at the feet in front of the alb. The hands are united in supplication.

" Ꜧíc jacet Robertus Wíllardsey prím. Vícarí. ístí. Ecclesíe qui obíít ríí díe mens. marcíí anno dní. Míll. cccc° rríííí°. cujus anime propícíetur deus. Amen."

So we may leave S. Nicholas without reluctance and proceed up Castle Hill to the centre of the town.

Leicester's Hospital Warwick

We go up Castle Hill, with the castle wall on our left, into Jury Street, one of the main streets of the town, a continuation or part, in fact, of the road which runs straight through the town from Leamington, under the east gate, up the hill out through the west gate, and so on to Barford and Stratford-on-Avon, one of those two streets which Leland called the beauty and glory of Warwick. Jury Street, says a writer in 1815, was " so called from the *matted room* in it where the juries were formerly impanelled." In it, at the corner, is the Court House, a fine stone building of 1730. We then come to the High Street; resisting the temptation to do more than look at S. Mary's as it stands on the hill above us to our right, and passing straight on to the Leycester Hospital. This indeed may be described as one of the glories of Warwick, and, standing on the brow of the hill, its picturesque black and white, the trees by its entrance, and the chapel on the gate beyond make a picture which reproduces perhaps better than anything else in the town the visible presentment of Elizabethan England. The building was originally erected in the reign of Henry VI. as the hall or mansion of the United Guilds of S. George and the Holy Trinity. These guilds were founded in the reign of Richard II., and four priests were endowed to say Mass for Richard II. and his wife, Thomas Beauchamp Earl of Warwick and his wife, and for the souls of Edward III. and his son, the Black Prince. The chapel over the Hongyn or west gate has its origin so far back as Roger of Newburgh, 1123, and was given to the church of S. Mary ; but the advowson of the chapel was given to the guild of S. George by Thomas Beauchamp, the builder of the tower. Something of the history of these guilds has already been mentioned. It need only be added that when the guilds were dissolved—Thomas Oken, Warwick's great benefactor, being the last master—the buildings were used by the citizens, and the Corporation held them for thirty years till, after some haggling, Robert Dudley Earl of Leicester obtained possession in order that he might, according to the vicarious manner of the time, create a charitable foundation. He established a market and twelve men who were to be " impotent persons, not having above £5 per annum of their own, and such as had either been or should be maimed in the wars of the said Queen's service, her heirs and successors," so says Dugdale ; and if there were no such old soldiers, born in the counties of Warwick or Gloucester, then other poor folk not soldiers might be chosen from

Kenilworth, Warwick, Stratford-on-Avon, or Wootton-under-Edge or Erlingham in Gloucestershire. The men were to wear, and still wear, "gowns of blew cloth, with a ragged staff embroidered on the right sleeve." These badges are silver, and all but one of those still used are the originals. The pensioners are "not to go into the town without them." The patronage of the hospital passed, on his death without issue, to Leicester's sister Mary, wife of Sir Henry Sidney, and it remains in the hands of her descendant, Lord De L'Isle and Dudley. The master, who is a priest and acts as chaplain, has a delightful house, all up and down, with panelled rooms, and great cupboards and quaint stairways, and in his garden is the Norman arch which alone remains of the ancient chapel of S. James. The house occupies the north side of the quadrangle, to which access is obtained first through the arched gateway with the inscription, "Hospitium collegiatum Roberti Dudlei comitis Leycestriae." This has the date 1571, with the double-tailed lion of the Dudleys and the barbed dart of the Sidneys on either side. Over the entrance to the quadrangle is the Leicester cognisance of the bear and ragged staff, with the initials "R.L." and motto "Droit et Loyal." Rous declared that the bear " was taken from the name of one of the British Earls of Warwick, Arthal, which signifies in the British language a bear ; and when another British Earl named Morvi had vanquished a giant in a duel, with a young tree plucked up by the roots, and stripped of its branches, in token of that event, to the bear was added the ragged staff." This, I need not say, is not to be accepted as the origin of the Dudley badge.

The quadrangle is a rich gabled and pargetted curiosity of building, on whose walls are arms of the families connected with Dudley, and white bears figured on the gables. Over the master's house is inscribed "Honour all men : love the brotherhood : fear God : honour the king." The master's house communicates with the southern side of the court by a cloister, above which is a gallery : at the south is the kitchen. At the top of the stairs is the old Guild hall, now split up into rooms : each brother has two rooms and a pantry. The kitchen is at the south, while the brethren's meals are cooked by a cook who belongs to them in common : it has some old oak furniture, including the chair in which James I. sat when Sir Fulke Greville entertained him, the signature of Robert

West Gate
Warwick

E.H.N.

Earl of Leicester to his will and a piece of curtain said to have come from Cumnor and to have been worked by Amy Robsart, as to which again you may be sceptical. The ancient hall still awaits restoration to its original purpose ; at present it is used as a laundry and coal hole. Its gallery is now part of the master's house, and has a most beautiful tie beam. The hall itself still retains its fine roof timbers, from which most of the carving has departed: and an inscription on the wall recalls its great day of glory—" Memorandum that King James the First was right nobly entertained at a supper in this hall by the Honourable Sir Fulk Greville, Chancellor of the Exchequer, and one of his Majesty's most honourable Privy Council, upon the fourth day of September, Anno Dom. 1617. God save the King." The present master tells us that " there is one other record of the use of this hall, in A.D. 1454, when the Duke of Suffolk, afterwards beheaded in a boat off the coast of Kent, sat in this chamber to hear some complaints by the Warwick commoners."

The chapel, it must be admitted, bears too obvious signs of the handiwork of Sir Gilbert Scott (1863) ; but it has a good screen and stalls, and there is still about it a lingering flavour of old time, before architects and parliaments and commissions meddled with the good deeds of good men. It leaves over the whole Hospital the sense that it is sanctified by the word of God and prayer. How beautiful such a life may be, peaceful . at its close in the care provided of old, it is easy to guess. When towns and castles change may this house of the grace of God still survive in blessing.

Leaving then the chapel on the west gate we turn for a look at the long street stretching eastwards. There are many old houses in it which survived the fire ; most of them perhaps a little too much freshened up with paint and whitewash ; but still they must have looked new once, and then not so unlike their appearance now. But there are also a number of very fine eighteenth and early nineteenth century houses, patterns of solid building and comfort ; and certainly there is nothing out of harmony in the street, a picture of English town homeliness as of many centuries.

You may now go either outside the walls, up Bowling Green and Smith Street, or within by Brook Street and Swan Street, past the old but modernised Woolpack Inn, which has

S. Mary's Church, Warwick.

not the "pretensions" of the Warwick Arms in the High Street, to the Market Place: the old city walls, of which pieces are here and there remaining, were between those two routes. The market place is small and comely. The museum is worth inspection. Out of it, Old Square takes you straight to S. Mary's Church.

It has been told how the ancient church was destroyed by the fire. It had a nave with four bays and six windows in the clerestory, aisles, and transept, the aisles having three windows each, the transept windows resembling the east window of the chancel. In the south arch was the tomb of Thomas Beauchamp Earl of Warwick, the builder of the nave, with his wife. This perished in the fire, but the effigies are now on the east wall of the south transept. The choir, the Lady Chapel, and the other buildings on the south survived as well as the "lobby," but the nave perished. Dugdale's account of all the glories of the church as it was when he knew it is as pitiful as delightful to read ; diversifying his record of the Earls and interspersing many a quaint conceit. When he comes to the Lady Chapel, he gives a more close description, which may be compared with what still survives. Meanwhile let us look at the nave. I am by no means of those who disparage it. "Fine proportions and incongruous detail" is not an unfair description, but at least it is ten times more interesting than what Street or Scott would have given us. It is original, if only in its combinations ; and that in post-Reformation English architecture is not a thing of no account. Out of the subscriptions for the relief of those who suffered from the fire a certain part was set aside for rebuilding the church. It seems that Sir Christopher Wren was first consulted, and the designs which he made are among his papers in All Souls' Library, marked "not executed"—but, though most books deny it, I feel convinced that the tower really is his work, for the design among his papers is entitled "orthography of the tower of the parochial church of S. Mary at Warwick, executed after an unsuccessful attempt in execution of a defective prior design by other hands." The other hands were those of Sir William Wilson, who built Nottingham Castle, and designed the nave ; and the nave, aisles, and transept are undoubtedly his. The success of the tower lies in its height and its proportions. The detail is that mixture of classic and Gothic which modern architects

abhor, but simple persons may regard as at least an attempt
to advance towards a new style after the manner of the medieval builders. The aisles, nave, and transepts continue the same
attempt, but not so successfully. The design of the windows
cannot be said to be good, though the tracery is, to say the least,
curious. Sir William Wilson did not attempt a clerestory; and
this should by no means be counted to his discredit; he ended
with a cornice and a balustrade. I do not think Sanderson
Miller would have done that, but still the effect is not entirely
displeasing. The old organ in the west gallery well befits its
place. Below it is a good bust of Landor. In the north transept
is the brass of Thomas Oken and his wife, with the curious
" accomodation," " on whose soul Jesus *hath* mercy "; in the
south, besides the Norton monument, 1615, is the white marble
slab on which now rest the brass effigies of Thomas Beauchamp
Earl of Warwick, 1401, and Margaret his wife, 1406. While the
ancient nave perished, the crypt remains, and contains some
work undoubtedly of Roger of Newburgh's time.

Now the Choir, late Decorated and in parts Perpendicular,
is ascribed to Thomas Beauchamp in 1392, but no doubt contains additions of Earl Richard more than fifty years later.
It has four windows on each side, and an east window of the same
fifteenth century design on a larger scale. The roof is the most
interesting and beautiful part of the chancel; it is in four bays
groined, divided again four times by cross ribs; in the centre
of each an angel bearing Beauchamp arms, in two cases impaling other coats (Mortimer and Ferrers). The roof is also
supported by flying ribs, coming from between the windows
and crossing each other. The sedilia and piscina are good
early Perpendicular work, and opposite to them is an arched
recess where was probably the Easter Sepulchre. There is a good
black and white marble reredos, modern. The niches on either
side the great east window are vacant. In the very centre
of the choir is the great tomb of Thomas Beauchamp Earl of
Warwick (the first) and Catherine his wife, daughter of Roger
Mortimer Earl of March, both of whom died in 1369. They
lie facing the altar, he in complete armour, she in a rich gown
with a jewelled belt. Each head rests on a double cushion
supported by a small seated figure. Their right hands are
clasped. His feet rest on a bear, hers on a lamb. Below are
thirty-six niches, each containing a standing figure, and below

again are shields of families connected with the Beauchamps. It is a fine impressive tomb, but its splendour pales before those we are still to see.   There are many slabs and brasses in the choir, among them the pretty little memorial of Cecily Puckering, who died in 1636, aged thirteen—" Mistress Cisseley Puckering.   I sleep secure, Christ's my King "—an anagram. But there is no memorial of that Marquess of Northampton, Queen Catherine Parr's brother, whose funeral we have mentioned, for the sufficient reason given in the Black Book of Warwick.   " This marquesse so decessed not the richest man in England."   On the north side is the vestry, vaulted like the choir, and the lobby, beyond which is the Chapter House, now a mausoleum, which contains the great tomb of Sir Fulke Greville, first Lord Brooke, concerning whose death it is impossible to avoid Dugdale's sardonic comment on the elaborate provision which the good man had made for his burial, under this tomb with its canopies and columns and its heraldic memorials, and on the simple inscription which recalls the brevity of the Campden monument to his ancestor—" Fulke Grevil, servant to Queen Elizabeth, concellor to King James, and frend to Sir Philip Sidney.   Trophæum Peccati."   What Dugdale says is this: " Delaying to reward one Hayward, an antient servant, that had spent the most of his time in attendance upon him, being expostulated with for so doing, [he] received a mortell stab in the back, by the same man then private with him in his bedchamber at Brook House in London, 30 Sept. ann. 1628, who, to consummate the tragedy, went into another room, and having lock't the door, pierced his own bowells with a sword."

About the middle of the south side is the entrance to the passage which admits to the Lady Chapel, or Beauchamp Chapel, as it is more generally called, from the man for whose memorial it was built, Richard Beauchamp Earl of Warwick.   It was begun in 1443, finished in 1464, and consecrated in 1475.   Its cost is calculated at some £40,000 of present money.   Between the actual chapel and the choir is a small chantry chapel, with a plain two-light east window, two beautiful canopied niches on either side of the altar [removed] and a remarkable piscina made with wood.   Between the chantry and the chapel is a fine stone screen ; between the chantry and the choir of the church a small lobby or pew, as again at the west end, by which

The Beauchamp Chapel, S. Mary's Church, Warwick.

access down six steps is obtained into the Beauchamp chapel. The chief feature of the chantry is the exquisite fan tracery of the roof, the design extending from pillars at each side and from central bosses, work very early of its kind and suggestive of the Eastern chapel at Peterborough Minster or the Baylie chapel at S. John's College, Oxford, the one fifty, the other a hundred, years later.

The Beauchamp chapel itself is the glory of the church. The entrance from the transept is said to be of the eighteenth century, and so no doubt it is, but a copy of earlier work. Within, there is a gallery over the door, probably for an organ. The building is lofty and of good Perpendicular vaulting, groined so intricately that it looks, as has been said, like network. The windows are large and high in the wall, with stone canopied niches below, and oak stalls. The east window of three large lights, the central divided by two transoms, the north and south by one, has its stonework filled with niches containing a number of charming small statues. There is still much of the fine fifteenth century glass remaining, though it has suffered a good deal; it is well worth detailed examination.[1] At the north side of the chapel close to the east wall is a small vestry.

Almost in the midst and facing the altar is the tomb of Richard Beauchamp—a magnificent work of grey Purbeck marble, on which the effigy in full armour and wearing the Order of the Garter, but with head bare, lies under a hooped framework, of brass gilt like the figure itself. Round the monument are niches, alternately large and small; the larger containing statues of fourteen of the earl's kindred, going down to his sons-in-law, including the king-maker, the small angels carrying scrolls with the words, "*Sit Deo laus et gloria : defunctis misericordia.*" Over the hearse, or hoops, hung the velvet pall, till a century or so ago. The inscription runs thus[2] :—

𝕻reieth deboutly for the Sowel whom god assoille of one of the moost worshipful knightes in his dayes of monhode & conning‡Richard*Beauchamp‡late Eorl of Warrewik*lord Despenser of*Bergebenny & of mony other grete*lordships whos body resteth here under this tumbe in a fulfeire bout of Stone set on the bare rooch the whuch bisited with longe siknes in the Castel of‡Roan therinne decessed ful cristenly the last

[1] See C. F. Hardy in *Archæologia*, lxi. (1909), p. 583.
[2] * Denotes figure of a bear ; ‡ a ragged staff.

day of *April the yer of oure‡lord god A M CCCCxxxix,‡he
being at that tyme *Leiutenant gen'al and goberner of the
Roialme of flraunce and of the Duchie of Normandie by sufficient‡
Autorite of oure Sou'aigne lord the King *Harry the vi.
thewhuch body with grete deliberacon' and ful worshipful
condiut *Bi See *And by *lond was broght to Warrewik the
iiii day of‡October the yer abouseide and was *leide with ful
Solenne exequies in a feir chest made of Stone in this Chirche
afore the west dore of this‡Chapel according to his last wille *
And‡Testament‡therin to rest til this‡Chapel by him debised
i' his lief were made Al thewhuche Chapel founded‡*On the
Kooch And alle the membres therof his‡Executours dede fully
make And Apparaille **By the Auctorite Theydide *Translate‡
flul *worshipfully the seide Body into the bout abouseide,·
Honnred be god therfore *‡*‡*‡

The figure is a magnificent presentation of a fifteenth century
noble equipped for war. Meyrick's description of the armour is
worth quoting, as we see so much armour in the Warwickshire
churches, and this is the best of all. He says :—

" The monumental effigy of the Earl of Warwick is all brass,
exactly like a suit of armour, and laid on his sepulchre ; his breast
and back plates have each placates or placards, rising up with
scalloped edges, to points, before and behind, and on the front
one appear the screw holes which held the lance rest. Each of
these placards is fastened at top, with a strap and buckle. The
elbow pieces, particularly that part within the bends of the arms,
are very large, that on the bridle arm being the greatest of the
two, and are so ridged as to look like several successive plates.
Upon the espaulieres are placed pauldrons, also ridged, with the
edges turned up, so as to form the prototypes of pass-guards.
Pendant from the last tassett is the apron of chain, which is continued all round, being likewise behind appended to the last
culette, which, from the appearance of the buckles and straps,
might, it seems, be removed at pleasure. Besides the two large
tuilles over the thighs, there are two tuillettes at the hips, and
these are elegantly ridged. The cuisses are also ridged all the way
up, so as to resemble so many distinct pieces, and in this specimen
we have a distinct display of those lateral pieces attached by
hinges to the cuisses, by which we learn that they did not en-
velope completely the under part of the thigh, but only reached

to where the saddle could meet, allowing the rider a better seat on his horse. These pieces were held in their places by a buckle and strap. This warrior has the garter round his left leg a little below his knee."

The other monuments are of a later and more tawdry magnificence, but illustrate the pomp of Elizabethan decoration. The tomb on the north wall, of Robert Dudley Earl of Leicester and Lettice, his Countess, is huge and elaborate, with arms, and figures, and ornamentations of all kinds. The couple wear the dress of the late Elizabethans ; but whereas the Earl died in 1588 his widow survived him forty-six years, and died at the age of ninety-four. At the south-west is the tomb with recumbent effigy of Ambrose Dudley Earl of Warwick, which is more interesting because simpler and smaller, though it is rich enough indeed in the costume of the good earl. The inscription is a little history of his life :—

" Heare under this tombe lieth the corps of the L. Ambrose Duddeley who after the deceases of his elder brethren without issue was sonne and heir to John Duke of Northumberlande to whom Q: Elizabeth in ye first yeare of her reigne gave the manor of Kibworth Beachamp in the county of Leyc: to be helde by ye service of beinge pantler to ye Kings and Qvenes of this Realme at their Coronations which office and manor his said father and other his ancestors Erles of Warr: helde. In the second yeare of her reigne ye said Qvene gave him the office of Mayster of the Ordinavnce. In the fowrth yeare of her sayd reigne, she created him Baron Lisle and Erle of Warwyk. In the same yeare she made him her Livetenant Generall in Normandy and dvringe the tyme of his service there he was chosen Knight of ye Noble order of ye Garter. In the Twelvth yeare of her reigne ye said Erle & Edward L: Clinton L: Admerall of England were Livetenantes Generall joinctely and severally of her M^{aties} army in the north partes. In the Thirteenth yeare of her reigne the sayd Qvene bestowed on him ye office of Chief Bvtler of England, and in the xvth yeare of her reigne he was sworne of her Prevye Covnsell. Who departinge this lief wthovt issve ye xxi day of Febrvary, 1589, at Bedford Howse neare the city of London, from whence as him self desired his corps was conveyed and interred in this place neare his brother Robert E: of Leyc: & others his noble ancestors, wch was accomplished by his last and welbeloved

wiefe yᵉ Lady Anne Covntes of Warr: who in fvrther testimony
of her faythfvll love towardes him bestowed this Monvme't as a
reme'brance of him."

There remain two more monuments. One which attracts
most attention of all, for its pathetic interest, is the quaint figure,
richly dressed, of the seemingly deformed little child, the one
legitimate son (according to later decisions) of Robert Dudley,
" the noble impe," who was Baron of Denbigh and " a child of
great parentage but of far greater hope and towardness," but
died before he was four years old. And also there is the tablet
on the north wall of the child's niece, Lady Katherine Leveson,
widow of Sir Richard Leveson, and daughter of the famous
Duchess Dudley and her husband, that Sir Robert Dudley who
was not recognised as the great Earl's lawful offspring.

So we may turn from this chapel rich in decoration and this
church rich in memories, still the centre of Warwickshire church
history. We bear with us the remembrance of many great folk
whom Shakespeare must often have seen, and of past heroes
whom he must have been taught to venerate.

And it is to be hoped that the needed work of restoration may
be done through a fund that is being now raised. What the
appeal says is worth quoting, both for its truth and as a historic
record of the condition of the chapel in May, 1913 :—

" The present condition of this historic monument of Gothic
architecture is such that, in order to arrest further decay due
to the friable nature of the stone used in its construction, considerable repair is urgently needed.

" A recent inspection has been made, and a report prepared
by a representative of the Association for the Preservation of
Ancient Buildings. This expert supports the views of the archi-
teet, under whose direction the restoration of the remaining
portion of S. Mary's Church (of which this chapel forms part)
has been carried out. This work has cost over £20,000, and it is
needless to state that the raising of so large a sum has been a
heavy drain on the resources of the town and immediate locality.

" We feel, therefore, justified, having regard to the national
interest attaching to this ancient monument, in appealing for
financial help to the general public, to our brethren over the seas,
and to Americans, to many of whom the chapel is a familiar
object as being closely identified with the history of Warwick
and its earls, apart entirely from its high architectural merits."

From S. Mary's Church, turn at the west door by the road in front of you which goes slightly to the right ; it is Northgate Street, and led originally from the castle to the north gate. It is now eminent by reason of the County Hall, one of the most important works, and perhaps the best, of Sanderson Miller (*see* p. 31). His correspondence shows the great pains he took to collect money in the county to build a place worthy of the shire, for county business and county gaieties. It was completed in 1753, I believe, and there was a great ceremonial opening ; but so careless was Miller of fame, and so soon was he forgotten, that we find at least as early as 1815 the design as well as the building attributed to Mr. Hiorne, or Hiorns, of Warwick, who was really, as Miller's letters show, his clerk of the works or chief workman. The front of the building is really imposing, in the style which the eighteenth century used so well : the tall front, with its Corinthian pillars, is worthy of Bath. It has stood wind and weather well, and will probably look none the worse for the repairs which I saw in 1912. It is a pity that the common English custom of neglect is in evidence here ; the two niches with no statues, and the large space with no inscription. The great hall is a very fine room which I do not think any county can surpass. Out of it are the criminal and civil courts ; and the eulogist in 1815 tells you that " once a year, at the time of the races, it is converted into a ball-room ; the stone floor is then covered by a boarded one; the circular recesses are fitted up in the manner of card-rooms; the pillars are encircled with wreaths of lamps ; and the whole solemn appearance of a court of justice is changed into the brilliant and sportive scene of gaiety and fashion."

Next to the County Hall is the old gaol—which also has a fine front, with Doric pillars, and is now part of the barracks—that is, what used to be called the Militia Barracks. I presume that the county police station is the building of which the early nineteenth century writers are so proud, as containing everything that the wit of man could devise for bringing up paupers in the way they should go. A quotation from the *Gentleman's Magazine* of 1810, which declares that there " industry is encouraged, and the product of labour is appropriated to promote its exercise," may be capped by another, and official, statement of the same era :—

" House of Correction or Bridewell, Warwick, nearly opposite the entrance to the gaol, and enclosed within a high stone wall ; having been enlarged at different times, the arrangement is rather inconvenient, the entrance from some of the wards to the chapel and other parts of the prison requiring an ascent of many steps ; the same regard to classification, order and cleanliness, prevails here as in the county gaol. The boys and the women were formerly employed in heading pins for the manufacturers of Birmingham, and the men in drawing and preparing the wire for that purpose, but it was found to be

Landor's Birthplace, Warwick.

attended with loss, owing to the waste of material ; consequently was declined a few years ago. A flour mill worked by crank, with hand labour, employing one hundred men, who relieve each other at intervals, grinds sufficient quantity of corn to supply the county gaol and Bridewell and for hire."

After we have left the police station, we may go down Saltisford and out in the country ; or by the Butts where anciently the bowmen practised, inside the walls; or by Chapel Street where is Mr. Kendall's wonderful house full of elaborate and

graceful wood carving—his hand is seen in many a Warwickshire church and house, and the skill of workmanship, and the
Victorian style, are not to be mistaken.   You will come out

The East Gate, Warwick.

anyhow by the east gate, with the chapel of S. Peter over it ;
and so you pass out of the old town, but down a street which
looks old enough, and narrow enough, to have been medieval—
but is not—Smith Street ; and this leads you to Leamington.

The chapel of S. Peter is of Henry VI.'s date, they say. It was once used as a school and is now turned into a dwelling house. Close to it, on the north side of the street, is the prim and stately house, in the best style of the second half of the eighteenth century, where Walter Savage Landor was born in 1775. Memories of him may be gathered at Tachbrook and Ipsley and Hatton, but yet one hardly thinks of him as among the War-

S. John's House, Warwick.

wickshire poets. Here he was born, but it was at Bath and in Italy that he "warmed both hands before the fire of life." Still one may think of Dr. Parr coming in here to discuss the oddities of his pupil, and of Landor, one may be sure, discoursing upon the oddities of his tutor. Perhaps he would be pleased to know that the house—on which a plate now records his birth—has become a girls' school.

But you will stop, where the Coventry road turns to the left to take you to the Great Western station, and at least look through the fine iron gates, very high and quite simple in design, across the circle of the grass, to the splendid front of the Elizabethan house known as S. John's Hospital. The history goes back to Henry II.'s time—the date of all others for founding hospitals—when it was set up "for entertainment and reception of strangers and travailers, as well as those that were poor and infirm." The greedy parliament, of course, dissolved it, as it was religious; in 1563 Elizabeth gave the site to Anthony Stoughton, who set about building the house, which was completed in 1626. The front is the best part of it; its five gables, rich porch, and two huge bay windows are in the very best Elizabethan domestic style. It has recently been bought for use as a family mansion; and a beautiful one it will make, for it has many fine rooms, and a splendid staircase, and all sorts of nooks and crannies. A quarter of a century ago, and later, one could lodge there, in somewhat primitive fashion. One morning when I looked out of my bedroom door I found a duck quacking at it, who had waddled up the great Jacobean staircase on the chance of getting a meal from the visitor. I was told there were ghosts there also, but I never saw them.

When you turn from S. John's Hospital to the station you are on the road to Guy's Cliff, one of the most charming places in the county. Leland calls it "an abode of pleasure, a place meet for the Muses, with its natural cavities, its shady woods, its clear and crystal streams, its flowering meadows, and caves overgrown with moss, whilst a gentle river murmurs among the rocks, creating a solitude and quiet most loved by the Muses," and Dugdale says it is "a place of so great delight, in respect of the river gliding below the rocks, the dry and wholesome situation, and the fair groves of lofty elms overshadowing it, that to one who desires a retired life either for devotion or study the like is hardly to be found." So, it seems, thought King Henry V., for when he was staying at Warwick Castle he visited it, and determined to build a chantry there. But this he did not live to do, and Richard Beauchamp took the duty upon himself, and he ordered the ancient oratory (which was said to date from the time of Dubritius) to be rebuilt. Among the chantry priests was John Rous, himself a Warwickshire man, and the first of Warwickshire's great antiquaries. It was there that he wrote his many chronicles, of the kingdom

Guy's Cliff Mill.

and the shire, of which Dugdale made good use ; and those
who have seen the Roxburgh Club edition of the life of Richard
Beauchamp, with its wonderful drawings, will not fail to bless
his memory.   After the dissolution, the property changed
hands frequently, and the house is an erection of many dates ;
seen from the river it is most picturesque, whatever the architects may say about it.

But one ought not to visit Guy's Cliff without saying something about Guy Earl of Warwick, who here turns up again
in all his glory, with his dun cow (a vehement animal which
he killed), his armour, his statue, his porridge pot, his faithful
Phillis, and his life as an undiscovered hermit here till she came
to close his eyes.   It is a legend common enough in most countries, not older than the thirteenth century.   There never was a
Guy Earl of Warwick, alas ! or any Earl of Warwick at all, at the
time he is said to have lived.   Our history then begins quite
late.   The chapel is ancient, and some parts of the house, and,
in the eighteenth century it is described as a small country
mansion approached by the fir avenue along which it may still
be seen from the high road.   Samuel Greatheed built most
of the present house, after 1750, particularly the present entrance, with its steps, looking on the rocky courtyard.   You enter
through a stone archway and find yourself in a dell surrounded
by a wall of rock on three sides, with the house added on to your
left.   The rock is pierced here and there, for stables and such
like, and in front as you enter is the large cave which is called
Guy's.   An inscription carved on the rock partly in Runic
characters and partly in Roman lettering of the twelfth century,
says (being translated) " Cast out, Thou Christ, this burthen
from Thy servant, Guhthi," which may be the origin of the
Guy legend.   The chapel, built *tempore* Henry VI., is small
and a good deal spoilt by restoration.   It contains a huge mutilated figure which again is set down as Guy's.   The tower
is early fifteenth century, and has battlements with four crock-
eted pinnacles at the corners.   Overhanging trees shut in the
little courtyard and give it a romantic if not gloomy aspect,
as romance was understood by the artist whose works we see
within.   The house, says an old guide, " consists of numerous
apartments, formed more for use than show, agreeably to the
prevailing taste of our private English gentlemen," and this
is quite true.   Its interest lies in the fact that in 1772 and

Caves at Guy's Cliff.

1773 Mrs. Siddons, then Sarah Kemble, stayed here for some time as a companion to Lady Mary Greatheed. Her visit, which was supposed to keep her from matrimony, ended by her marriage at Holy Trinity, Coventry. At the beginning of the nineteenth century, Mr. Bertie Greatheed was the owner, and his son, who died in 1804, aged twenty-two, left a daughter through whom eventually the property came to Lord Algernon Percy, the present owner. Bertie Greatheed the younger, was an artist of considerable pretensions. You see several portraits from his hand, including one taken in 1803 of Napoleon, by whom, according to a well-informed writer, he " was greatly caressed," and was, after the war began, again " suffered to retire to Italy while so many of his countrymen were retained captive." His great work is the Cave of Despair (Faerie Queen I., ix), a collection of life-sized horrors, now darkened by age and dirt, and only visible by an ingenious arrangement of reflected light. There are busts and portraits of Mrs. Kemble and Mrs. Siddons, and many good pictures of the kind that dilettanti picked up in Italy so readily a century and more ago; but the views from the windows over the river, through the gardens, and towards the mill across the pool are what one lingers over longest.

Few of the thousands who visit Guy's Cliff see the house, but everyone sees the view from the Coventry road, up the fir avenue across the garden to the curious, worse than Strawberry Hill Gothic of the west front, and sees the more beautiful and distant view from the Mill. This is quite a modern building, some ninety years old, but it is quaint and pleasing in effect, and one may stand by the broad stone parapet in front of it and look across the river, enlarged by the mill pool, to the gables and chimneys of the house that is built on a rock. The water mill itself goes back as far as Domesday, and beyond.

If you follow the Avon here you come to Emscote bridge, and so along to Warwick itself. If you turn back into the Coventry road, you find, a few yards further on your way, buried in trees at your left, Blacklow Hill, where, if you could climb the fences and pierce the thickets, you should see the monument put up in 1821 to commemorate (with curious inaccuracy) the murder of Piers Gaveston on that spot. The inscription is set down by some to Dr. Parr (whose Whiggism it reflects) by others to Mr. Greatheed. Or you may cross the river by the mill, climb the hill by a path through a pleasant meadow, and find yourself in Leamington.

The Avenue, Guy's Cliff.

CHAPTER VI

IF highways in Warwickshire are "good going," byways are delightful in their repose. There are two good roads from Warwick to Stratford-on-Avon, those at the west and at the east of the river, which are called locally the high road and the low road. Let us take the low road and turn away from it as occasion calls us. We descend the steep hill, after passing the Leicester Hospital and the west gate; and we go along good level ground still mainly eastwards. The Avon and the castle path are now to our left, that is, southwards. Rejecting the turn to the right at Longbridge, where Nicholas Brome killed John Herthill (*see* p. 321), which would take us by the "high" road, we pass Sherborne Park, and perhaps turn aside to Sir Gilbert Scott's elaborate and expensive church, with its fine marbles and its alabaster reredos. If we so turn aside it "will not escape our notice" that Clayton and Bell were responsible for the windows. But for the moment I wish to leave aside Hampton Lucy and Fulbrooke and the rest of the sights and sites we may best observe from the "high" road, and to go past Sherborne Park, and come to the fine bridge which spans the wide but shallow Avon at Barford. Thence the river winds so much in its course before it reaches Wasperton as to be at least three times the length of the way by road. Turn aside in the village, which has many excellent seventeenth and eighteenth century houses, to the church, on the road to the left. It was rebuilt in 1844, and the tower is the only old part remaining, but that—rather too much overgrown by ivy—is a fine one. It bears, they say, the marks of the guns fired on it by the Parliament's forces when the Royal Standard was flying there, just before the battle of Edgehill.

So back again into the main road, till you turn aside, half a mile later (there is a pretty walk along the river bank just after you pass the Forge Cottage), to your right and come to the village of Wasperton. This, with its outlying farms, has a good deal of historical interest. But before we mention this, let us go straight into the church. The parsonage at the west end has a lovely garden with fine trees. The churchyard itself is well kept, like most of these Warwickshire ones, and has many interesting gravestones. The church was restored, not very cruelly, by Sir Gilbert Scott. What old (seventeenth century) glass there was has been turned out into the porch for an east window by Pugin. Of the bells one is the sanctus bell from Thelsford Priory, which was a mile away on the river bank, but has now entirely disappeared. The chalice is pre-Reformation, and the rest of the plate is 1571. The most interesting thing visible in the church is the little brass on the south wall near the door :—

> " Reader inquirest who interrd here lyes
> Tis honest Henry Collins who to rise
> To endless glory rests till the great day
> Of Judgment summons mortalls from the clay
> His pious soule's already gone to dwell
> Surely in Heaven which on earth liv'd so well
> Sober and just in conversation
> A loyall subject and the Churche's son
> More might be engraven but this shall suffice
> Us for example him to eternize
> Honest Henry Collins who put off his
> Earthly tabernacle May the 27 1664."

There was a long while ago in the churchyard a gravestone thus inscribed : " Hic jacet Thomas Crosse, quondam Firmarius de Wasperton, qui obiit xiii die mensis Aprilis anno D. Mcccclxxiii cujus animae propitietur Deus. Amen." There are now other good old stones, notably those of the Seelys, but not this.

Dugdale has not a great deal to say about Wasperton. The property there was given by Leofric to the Church of Coventry, and at the dissolution Henry VIII. gave it to William Whorwood, through whose family it passed to the Walters. The estate was bought by Dr. Richard Rawlinson, the famous antiquary and non-juror, by whom it was bequeathed to S. John Baptist College, Oxford. (The parish church is dedicated to S. John Baptist, by a happy coincidence.) A letter-book of Dr. Rawlinson's still exists at S. John's. The letters deal mostly with the

Wasperton property, and that at times rather querulously.   In June, 1736, he took great interest in the restoration of the church.   The parish had been "presented" in the Bishop's Court for its bad state, and it was time to interfere ; and Dr. Rawlinson, though he wrote, "I can't stand any personal applications," was very generous in gifts towards the good work.   In August, 1736, he wrote : "For the church, between ourselves at present, I design two brass branches of candlesticks, and a fine marble table for their altar.   These came to my hands by accident and at a reasonable rate, and will be ornaments few of our county churches can boast."   These have not escaped the "restoration" of the nineteenth century, though one still sees many a marble table in churches, even in Warwickshire, I think.   Rawlinson, one may note, was already a non-juring bishop.   He was consecrated in 1728, but it was kept a profound secret.   In 1736 he had not yet bought the outlying farm of Heathcote, to round off his property.   Of Heathcote, Dugdale writes : "This is in the Parish of Wasperton but whether it was ever a Village or not I cannot affirm : Howbeit the appellation shows, that there hath been a House at least, the last Syllable, viz. Cote, signifying as much ; and it is probable that the Ground hath formerly been of a Heathy Condition, for so doth the first part of the name intimate, though now, by good Husbandry, it be of a better kind.   As it was originally a member of Wasperton, so it did pass therewith from the Monks of Coventrie to Walter the son of Thurstan de Cherlecote, being confirmed by King Richard I., but in that grant it is called 'Terra de Hethcote,' so that it had not then the Reputation of a Village."   It passed later to the monastery of Thelsford, and thence to the Walters.   Heathcote now has a very handsome seventeenth century farmhouse on the brow of the hill, overlooking two other farmhouses, each of which has old work in it, and the third, near the Warwick road, has a special interest.   This was long held by the Seely family, four of whose delightful portraits adorn the walls of the dining-room.   The first of the family buried in the churchyard has the date 1678 ; the portrait of the head of the family in the house is 1719.   The descendants still hold the land, from S. John's College, while the other farms are held by an equally old family, the Garners, one of whom, Mr. Thomas Garner, the architect, will ever be remembered by those who study the best art of the later nineteenth century.

There are quaint records of the doings of old time preserved in the MS. diary of John Morley, Vicar of Wasperton in the later years of the eighteenth century. There was living in the parish at the time one Mr. William Welsh, also in Holy Orders, as his monument in the church shows. Now see how he behaved :—

"1787, *Dec. 1st.*—Mr. Foster called and informed me of a considerable altercation which happened last night at the Talbot, Wellesbourne, between Mr. Welch of Wasperton and Mr. Lucy, which ended in the former turning the latter out of the room, striking him and giving him a black eye.

"*Dec. 2nd.*—Dined with Mr. Lucy Confined to house from the blow received the previous night.

"*Dec. 17th.*—Called and dined with Mr. Lucy conversed with him on the subject of the quarrel with Mr. Welch permission to ask Mr. Welch next Wed: to interchange and apologize and terminate the affair amicably."

And here may be added another of the worthy Mr. Morley's notes, though it refers to another place in the county (dated March 22, 1800) :—

"Went to Hatton and while Dr. and Mrs. Parr, and I were sitting in the summer house, two City officers came in a Post Chaise with the Order made last Wed: by the council of Aldermen that the Bishop of Chichester and Dr. Parr be requested to preach the Spital Sermons at Newgate Christ's Church the next Easter Monday and Tuesday. My friend the Dr. went in his cellar and produced a bottle of Champagne, 1 of Burgundy, and 1 of his best Port, which the City Officers drank, praised, and returned still able to find their way to the chaise again."

Things are much more peaceable at Wasperton now ; it has been whispered that the greatest excitement is the bathing in the Avon ; a tent is visible, the passer-by may say, as evidence, but surely that does not carry one far. Wasperton also has many pigeons, and a remarkable dovecot, with stone base and superstructure of brick with tiles ; and a turret remains, one of three that stood near not long ago. A house hard by has a splendid Tudor chimney ; and the cottages are, many of them, whether in brick or in half timber, distinctly interesting. Wasperton is a village to linger in.

Beyond Wasperton, when you have returned to the lower road and crossed the Thelsford brook and farm, you may turn to the right and pass through the village and by the park of Charlecote. Leave them if you will for a while, for they belong to the Stratford, the Shakespeare, interest, and keep on, across the bridge over the Avon and by the King's Mead, up a little hill a mile or two further on, to the delightful solitude of Loxley Church. To the south of this you shall see a charming parsonage, discreetly turning its best face away from the road, to the left a large modern hall which fitly represents the architecture of the early

King's Lane, near Stratford-on-Avon.

twentieth century, though I believe its date is earlier. But the church itself shall enchain your interest. It was given —that is, the church in the sense of property—to the house of Stone in Staffordshire, a cell of Kenilworth, by Robert Fitz Odo in Henry II.'s time. On the Sunday next after the feast of S. Thomas the Martyr, 1286, it was reconsecrated after rebuilding by Godfrey Giffard, Bishop of Worcester, who preached on the text, "Sanctificate domum hanc quam aedificasti." This Dugdale tells. The lowest part of the tower belongs, I presume, to the period before this ; the upper part to a later date, and the present form of the church, with its round-headed windows, is due to the further restoration in the eighteenth century. Then were the charming semi-circular steps to the west door laid ; then was the pulpit, I imagine, stuck in the wall so that you enter it from the vestry suddenly, for all the world like a Jack-in-the-box. Then perhaps were the monuments cruelly turned outside, and was the quaint vestry porch constructed ; then certainly were the square pews fitted with their comfortable adornments. The chancel stands high above the nave, three steps up, the sanctuary one step more. Of the Edward I. church remains an early English lancet on the south ; of the oldest of all, some herring-bone work on the north. Altogether it is an exceeding quaint place ; long may it remain undisturbed. I will end my memory of it by quoting verbatim the excellent doings of one of the former parish priests, as recorded on the north wall, and hoping that many others who have succeeded and will succeed him shall have so good a record. It runs thus :—

GEORGE HUDDESFORD M.A.

Vicar of this Parish

Only surviving son of George Huddesford D.D. President of Trinity College Oxford.

Born 24th Octr 1749   Died 7th Oct 1809

He was a man of various and highly cultivated talents
And of unspotted innocency and integrity of life
The blameless vivacity of his wit
Exhilarated the moments of social intercource :
The purity of his heart and the soundness of his principles
Exalted the value of his friendship
And insured its disinterestedness and constancy
Throughout the course of his laborious ministry
He explained, inculcated and inforced
The invaluable doctrines and the practical obligations of
    Christianity
With zeal diligence energy and fidelity,
And he powerfully exhorted and assisted his hearers
In the pursuit of the only lasting objects of human concernment

His precepts and his practice alike tended to prove the depend-
ence under the mercy of God
Of happiness temporal and eternal
Upon a life of piety and virtue
He is gone to receive the reward of his labours.

From Loxley we may return by Wellesbourne Mountford and
Wellesbourne Hastings. The church is in Wellesbourne Hastings ;
it has a good tower, with battlements like most of those about
here (Loxley included). It is a dignified building, but it has
suffered horribly from the restorer, some seventy or eighty
years ago, whose work cost £4,000, believe me. On the
north of the chancel a good Norman arch with cable moulding
has been suffered to remain. There are a great many good
eighteenth century monuments in the church, but the gem
is the fine brass of Sir Thomas le Straunge, who died 1432,
and is shown in his plate armour as he may have fought the
Irish kernes, for he was Constable in Ireland. Among modern
things of merit are the Salviati mosaics on the east wall of the
sanctuary. The village need not detain us long. It has a
number of very good seventeenth and eighteenth century houses.
Nor again need we linger at Walton Hall, deep in woods at the
brow of the hill not far away. It is the property of the Mordaunts
and has a long history behind it. There is a house by Sir Gilbert
Scott, who was certainly let loose in these parts. Also not far
away is one of the numerous spas the eighteenth century was so
fond of—the Bath Hill with the Bath House, which has some
really interesting books and pictures in it.

CHAPTER VII

ON your way from Ufton southwards, or northwards if you are going from Banbury to Southam, you will pass through the very pretty village of Ladbroke, houses black and white, deep in trees, and with a good manor house of mid-nineteenth century style suggestive of Leech and Cruikshank, Miss Trotwood and Lewis Arundel—at least so it seems to me as I not too clearly remember it. The church I remember quite well, but I have never been able to get in. It looks as if it had been " thoroughly restored " ; but what is the good of that if one can't see it ? No doubt one could get in if one fetched the key ; but one gets tired of getting people up when one is an early caller. Dugdale has something to say about the name of the village, which he supposes " had its Name originally from the dirty Soyland Clay where the stream runneth *Llaid* in the old British signifying the same with *Luton* and *Licnus* ; but it is frequently written in all antient authorities *Lodebroc,* the a being changed into an o." There is nothing very interesting in the history of the manor, though it brings in the names of Catesby (which family won it after a long dispute) and the great Alice Duchess Dudley and her unsatisfactory husband. There was some very good heraldic glass in the church windows in Dugdale's time. I suppose it is all gone, but the book tells you there is an Easter Sepulchre and an effigy of a priest, with other good things.

So on to Watergall at your right, some way from the road, where there is a great reservoir, made perfect, it seems, in the seventeenth century, but originally much older. Then Fenny Compton, a pretty village with good brown stone houses, and some of brick, and the fragment of a religious house, possibly. This has a good fourteenth century window at the west end, the room for the priest below, the chapel window above—the chapel now a bedroom ; it is joined on to an eighteenth century house.   But the church, on a slight elevation in the village, with a hill to the west of it, is the chief attraction of the place. And it has had many notable Rectors ; among them, in the nineteenth century, two whom Oxford greatly honoured, Charles Abel Heurtley, for 32 years, and Charles Bigg, for fourteen, the former long Margaret Professor, the latter Regius Professor of Ecclesiastical History, each tenure ended only by death. How good a parish priest, how quaint and arresting a preacher, was Dr. Bigg will very long be remembered ; his remarkable personality will not be allowed to be forgotten so long as one remains of the many who admired and loved him.   The church he tended is of beautiful brown stone—they say the tracery of the windows is from Kenilworth, to which house the village once belonged ; the late Decorated doorway of the north porch is marked by bullets ; they tell that soldiers took refuge here after Edgehill.   Is the western door (blocked up) of the eighteenth century ?   There is a good early thirteenth century font with a pleasing cover of the eighteenth.   That last good century also supplies some most excellent altar rails.   The parish chest with its three locks is also a good thing to be looked upon.   There are remains of an ancient font (besides the one in use) : there is a good aumbry ; you will look at the fine original oak doors.   Then you will turn to the monuments. There is one to Elizabeth Croke, only daughter of Charles Croke, who is described as " A most dutifull child in y^e most difficult tryals, carefull to please and fearfull to offend."   She died on February 19, 17$\frac{18}{19}$, aged " 22 yere."

Let us away to Wormleighton.   Cross the main road and mount the hill, and see on the Oxford Canal, a most winding and river-like piece of water, a canoe, and a barge, horse-drawn, going its solemn way.   This may be a good place just to note what was said in " England Display'd " (1769) before the water system was perfected—soon again to fall into disuse.   Things have altered since then, for the Avon cannot be considered—the landlords do not allow it—to be navigable to Warwick.   The canals, however, do a fair amount of work, but several of them are in parts quite neglected.   I have never seen anyone on the canal between Warwick and Leamington. But to quote our author :—

" The only navigable river in this county is the Avon, the navigation of which is extended to Warwick : but a navigable canal is now making, which is to extend from the city of Coventry by Nuneaton, Atherstone, and Tamworth, to Fradley Heath near Litchfield, and there to communicate with the Stafford-shire navigation, which is to connect the Trent and the Mersey. Another canal is intended to be cut from Coventry, by Warwick, to Stratford, there to communicate with the navigation of the river Avon. A navigable canal is also now making from the Coventry canal, already mentioned, to the city of Oxford ; particulars of which have been already given in our account of Oxfordshire. These canals, when finished, will be of the greatest importance to this county, as they open a communi-cation with many parts of the kingdom.'

This shows you something of the position Fenny Compton, with its wharf, holds on the artery that connects Birmingham with Oxford. The canals certainly caused great excitement at the time of their construction. Daniel Pulteney, member for Bramber (who declared that he had only one constituent), wrote constantly, *circa* 1785, to the Duke of Rutland, and was much concerned with the growth of canals—" all my eloquence," he says at one time, " will be damned up [so he spells it] in canals and turnpikes." The real objection to them, Pitt told him, appeared to be that they obstructed hunting. People at Grantham protested against the Warwick canal. How could they be affected by it ?

But this by the way. Wormleighton is metal more attrac-tive. It stands on the brow of a hill. The manor had a chequered history before it came to the Spencers ; the end whereof, when it had reached William Montfort of Coleshill, temp. Hen. IV., is thus epitomised by Mr. Cox :—

" Being come to *William* it was left by him to Sir *Simon Mont-fort* his Son, who being attainted 10 *Hen.* VII. this Lordship was forfeited to the King, who granted the Inheritance of it out of the Crown, *Reg.* 13, to *William Cope*, Esq; Cofferer of the House-hold of that King, to be held in Socage, paying 20 Marks *per Ann.* into the Exchequer. He in the 14 *Hen.* VII. depopulated twelve Messuages and three Cottages here, and inclosed 240 Acres of Land. One Sir *Edward Raleigh,* Knt.

also wasted six Messuages more ; at length the said *William Cope* sold this Lordship to *John Spencer*, Esq; who soon after built on it a fair Manor-House, wherein making his Abode with a large Family of sixty Persons, he became a great Bene-factor to the Church in Ornaments and other Things. From him descended Sir *Robert Spencer*, Knt. created Baron *Spencer* of *Wormleighton*, 1 *Jac.* I. whose Grand-child *Henry* Lord *Spencer* enjoyed it in 1640.'' To the Spencers it still belongs, and the well-kept village, with its good cottages, bears witness to their care.

And the Spencer house is what brings us to see Wormleighton. Begun by John Spencer, it was continued by later possessors. Much of it has been destroyed. But the gatehouse under which you enter is as fine as ever. It reminds one of Wadham College at Oxford. The archway has lost its double doors, but the building above bears the royal arms, and the date 1613, the thistle and the crown also with the same date. Within, facing north, are the Spencer arms, twice, and the Willoughby coat. (The wife of the first Lord Spencer was co-heiress of Sir Francis Willoughby.) Westwards is a two-storied building with good windows, eastwards a tower with four stages, from which you may see to Malvern, and to Billesdon Coplow in Leicestershire. The height of the hill is given in the Ordnance Survey as only five hundred feet above sea-level ; but the waters from it part, going different ways, those on the north towards Leamington, and so by Avon to Severn, those on the south to the Cherwell and the Thames. Behind the fine yellow building of the gatehouse and the tower, you come to the main building, once a noble quadrangle, but now of only one block, with some detached fragments. It is a good ex-ample of the late Henry VIII. style. An old print shows the bay as once carried up to the second story, yet perhaps the whole front has been less changed than at first one thinks, for a recent writer even goes so far as to say that, with the excep-tion noted, " the building seems practically unaltered." The main house bears the Spencer shield with seven quarterings, and the same with coat, mantling, and supporters complete, and the motto " Dieu defend le droit." The north side of this house, which has not been spoiled by modernised windows, is very fine. It is a large battlemented piece of dignified Tudor, or early Jacobean work, with large windows on the first floor, red brick with stone mullions. Within there are some good rooms, including an oak-panelled parlour, on the ground floor, but they have been much altered, and the only one which remains very much as it was, save that the two large windows on the north have been blocked up, is on the ground floor, a large chamber of state no doubt in old days, now little used if at all. Above it is the " Star Chamber " of the same size, which has gilt stars on the woodwork of the panels, and the old oak door which leads to the back stairs of the house. The beautiful fireplace has the Spencer shields. At the east of the lower room is a very fine Tudor window of six lights, most beautiful from without. There are several fine doorways within. One with the arms above has been defaced to make a bathroom, only two of the coats remaining intact.

The house was famous till the midst of the seventeenth century. It was at Wormleighton that the great Spencer library began its honourable history. The glorious Leicester of Queen Elizabeth stayed there, and it is said Queen Elizabeth did likewise. When the royal army was drawing towards Edgehill, and Charles stayed the night of October 21 at Southam, Prince Rupert slept at Wormleighton. Between them was Shuckburgh, of which more hereafter. The position of Wormleighton in the centre of fighting during the next few years was a dangerous one, and at last on January 7, 1646, it was burnt by the royal troops lest it should be made a garrison by the enemy. It has never been rebuilt.

Passing straight on from the gateway and leaving the house to the right you come, down a little slope, to the church, once belonging to the canons of Kenilworth. You first notice the western tower, of the end of the twelfth century, strong and impressive. Then through the early fifteenth century south porch, by the twelfth century door, into the fine late Norman nave, to which a Perpendicular clerestory has been added. The windows—some of them—are of the Kenilworth sandstone which the canons so constantly supplied to their churches. The chancel arch, of the fourteenth century, admits, up three steps, to the dignified and beautiful chancel, through an exquisite fifteenth century oak screen, well restored, its fine groining (seen from the east) unharmed. This is said to have been brought from a monastery, but it certainly looks extraordinarily well where it is. There is a good east window, Perpendicular ; but the modern has been at work with his passion for Early English, which he reproduces so badly, in two lancets at the south.

On the floor, notice the tiles with the arms of the Botelers. The altar and the rails are of good Restoration work (1664). And then you come to the monuments. On the north is the marble tablet which has this inscription : " This is the monument of John Spencer, Esquire, sonne and beire of Sir Robert Spencer, Knight, Baron Spencer of Wormleiton, which John Spencer departed this life at Blois in France the sixt of August after the computation of the Church of England and the sixteenth after the new computation in the yeare of our Lord Christ 1610 being 19 yeares old 8 monethes and odd dayes, neuer marryd of whom his brother Richard Spencer hath made this epitaph— Blaesis evasit spiritus ossa jacent—Hoc posui frater fraterno junctus amore—Tertius invita morte secundus ero." Opposite is the curious monument to the wife of Thomas Barford, vicar, 1686. The heart of Robert Spencer, the builder of the house, was buried, as a slab shows, at the north of the altar. In the chancel too are a number of very touching memorials of late vicars, in the nineteenth century. To the eighteenth belongs the slab of " Mr. William Pettiphar, 29 years vicar of this church and curate of Ufton " dated 1754. But the most famous family connected with Wormleighton has left no memorial. It is that of Washington, allied by marriage to the Spencers. From 1585 they lived at Sulgrave near Banbury. Robert Washington, second son of Robert Washington of Sulgrave, was married at Wormleighton, and the son of Laurence Washington, an elder brother, was baptized there. This Laurence was the direct ancestor of George Washington the President.

From Wormleighton, after a short walk eastward, you follow the road to Priors Hardwick. This church belonged, not to Kenilworth, but to Coventry, and the manor also. Thus Mr. Cox :—

" *Herdwick Priors* was one of the 24 Towns, given by Earl *Leofrike*, to the Monks of *Coventry*, in King *Edward* the Confessor's Time, when he founded that Monastery. In the Conqueror's Survey it is certified to contain fifteen Hides, and is called in that Record, *Herdwiche*. It continued in the Monks' Hands till the Dissolution ; and in that Time there is nothing remarkable said of it more than that the Monks had Free Warren granted to them in all their Demesne Lands here in 41 *Hen.* III. which were five Carucates, the rest being held by 29 Tenants who occupied 17 Yard-Lands, for which they paid certain Rents, and performed divers servile Works, and besides had a Court-Leet.

"After the Dissolution of the Monastery, it was granted by King *Hen.* VIII. *Reg.* 34. to Sir *Edmund Knightley,* and Heirs Male, which he dying without, it descended to *Valentine* his Brother, then a Knight. He died seised of it 8 *Eliz.* and left it to his Son and Heir *Richard,* who sold it in the same Reign to one *Ralph Blount,* an antient Servant of Sir Valentine's. He had Issue *Richard,* who inclosed all that belonged to the Manor, and then sold it to Sir *William Samuel,* of *Upton* in *Northampton-shire,* Knt. who gave it to *Arthur* his younger Son, who sold it to *William* Lord *Spencer,* whose younger Son *Robert* was in Possession of it in 1640." To the Spencers it still belongs.

The church is Early English and Decorated, but has been restored, with bad new stone work in the nave windows. There is a good south porch of the end of the twelfth century, and the south door of the chancel is Early English, the embattled tower Decorated. The old oak door at the south is refaced and painted. Within, a modern vestry and good modern pulpit and reredos ; the seventeenth century rails ; the gem, perhaps, the chancel roof as of old, and the leaves sculptured on the chancel arch. The tomb to be noted is that let into the chancel floor, of which only the feet of a man resting on a splendid large dog with a curly tail are all that can be seen now. Walk across the fields back to the road, and so on to Priors' Marston. This was once but " a lordship in the parish of Priors Hardwick " and belonged to Coventry also, and the chapel belonged to the same house, being attached to the manor. It is a quaint wandering village, with cottages covered with ivy and creeping plants, among them a good brown house of the eighteenth century, and a pretty inn, "The Falcon," of the seventeenth. The church has been much restored (in 1863), but the lower part of the tower may be Norman—or is it one of those interesting eighteenth century works, like Berkeley, perhaps the concoction of Sanderson Miller ? But Priors' Marston (though I believe there is, or was, a girls' school there) will not detain you long. You follow the road, if such it be, across many fields and through many gates, till you see Napton standing on the hill in front, the red houses and the trees delightfully mingled, and spreading down the hill from its summit to the valley below.

You must pass through Lower Shuckburgh, with an uninteresting rebuilt church, and then rise by a steep continuous ascent
to the wooded height of Shuckburgh superior (as Dugdale hath
it). The family of Shuckburgh, to whom it belongs, is traced
back by Dugdale, as holding land in the parish, to the time of
King John ; but they may well be much older ; it is one of the
oldest continuous possessions in England. Thomas's edition of
Dugdale, which occasionally adds valuable matter to the original
store, has a fine tale of the Shuckburghs of the Civil War. As
Charles was coming from Southam before the battle of Edgehill
he saw Sir Richard Shuckburgh's elder son hunting, " upon
which it is reported that he fetched a deep sigh and asked who
the gentleman was that hunted so merrily that morning, when he
was going to fight for his crown and dignity, and being told it
was this Richard Shuckburgh, he was graciously received. Upon
which he went immediately home, armed all his tenants, and the
next day attended him in the field, where he was knighted, and
was present at the battle of Edgehill. After the taking of
Banbury Castle, and his Majesty's retreat from those parts, he
went to his own seat, and fortified himself on the top of Shuckburgh Hill, where, being attacked by some of the Parliament
forces, he defended himself until he fell, with most of his tenants
about him ; but being taken up, and life perceived in him, he
was carried away prisoner to Kenilworth Castle, where he lay a
considerable time, and was forced to purchase his liberty at a dear
rate." His memory is preserved in the church. To the church
you must come through the park, a beautiful park with lovely
views, and black cattle pasturing therein. So you come to a
good house of, I suppose, the early nineteenth century, and a
garden with trim clipt yews. So up a steep little path to the
church, once belonging to the nuns of Wroxall, " but there never
was any Vicar endowed, the Cure having been served by a
Stipendary," says Dugdale ; and indeed it has all the appearance of a private chapel, and is still a peculiar. The building
has some Norman work in it, but has been " thoroughly " restored, and its interest is to be found in the splendid series of
Shuckburgh tombs from the recumbent effigies (in the south
chapel) of John Shuckburgh, Alderman, and his wife beside him
also in a ruff, dated 1549, down to quite modern days. There
are a very large number of most interesting tablets and brasses.
Among the latter is the figure of Margaret Coles, and there are

other beautiful Shuckburghs, figured in Dugdale. King Charles's convert is Richard Shuckburgh, Knight, of whom the inscription tells that " Dilexit Deum et Ecclesiam, regem, pauperem atque patriam," and adds, " Ecce (lector) viri imaginem " ; and his " image " shows him in armour with pointed beard and moustache. Among the great number of interesting monuments of more modern days it is difficult to make a selection. Let us take some, almost at random. Here is Julia Annabella Lady Shuckburgh, the only surviving daughter of James Evelyn of Felbridge in the county of Surrey, Esquire, and of Annabella of the Sussex family of Medley—" two families of approved worth and most respectable lineage ; but whatever is illustrious in a long line of virtuous ancestry was far outshone by her own private virtues " ; and she died in 1717. Or read what is said of the Lady Shuckburgh who died in 1783—·" whose unaffected innocence and singular sweetness of manners were the delight of all who knew her, Her piety and purity of heart a bright exception to the general dissipations of the age." She tried the Bristol waters, it seems, but in vain. Does anyone try them now ? Before we leave the church we must not forget to notice a most interesting inscription, witnessing to the true relation between so ancient a family and those who serve it, to the memory of Anne Jones, an old and valued servant for nearly fifty years, who died in 1846 aged 85. The quiet charm of this sheltered church is not easily to be described. You look southward over the park, far away it seems from the world. Flecknoe you might see perhaps, and Willoughby far away, from some point in the park, where Magdalen College rules, and where is the monument of the President on whose death James II. began all that encroachment on college statutes which was one of the things to lose him his crown. And Daventry is about six miles away. You are on the road there from Southam when you leave the Shuckburgh gates.

Of the history of the Shuckburgh family, loyal, steadfast, dignified and perhaps proud, there are many stories. There is no disrespect, I hope, in quoting a famous correspondence in which a Sheridan, the Lady Seymour who was Queen of Beauty at the Eglinton Tournament, met a Shuckburgh with results humorous if not conclusive. Thus it runs :—

" No. 1. ' Lady Seymour presents her compliments to Lady Shuckburgh and would be obliged to her for the character of

Mary Steadman, who states that she has lived twelve months, and still is, in Lady Shuckburgh's establishment. Can Mary Steadman cook plain dishes well, and make bread, and is she honest, sober, willing, cleanly, and good tempered? Lady Seymour will also like to know the reason she leaves Lady Shuckburgh's house. Direct under care to Lord Seymour, Maiden Bradley, Wiltshire.'

" No. 2. ' Lady Shuckburgh presents her compliments to Lady Seymour ; her ladyship's letter, dated October 28th, only reached her yesterday, November 3rd. Lady Shuckburgh was unacquainted with the name of the kitchen-maid until mentioned by Lady Seymour, as it is her custom neither to apply for, nor give, characters to any of the under servants, this being always done by the housekeeper, Mrs. Couch, and this was well known to the young woman. Therefore Lady Shuckburgh is surprised at her referring any lady to her for a character. Lady Shuckburgh, keeping a professed cook, as well as a housekeeper in her establishment, it is not very probable she herself should know anything of the abilities or merits of the under servants ; she is therefore unable to reply to Lady Seymour's note. Lady Shuckburgh cannot imagine Mary Steadman to be capable of cooking anything, except for the servants' hall table. November 4th.'

" No. 3. ' Lady Seymour presents her compliments to Lady Shuckburgh, and begs she will order her housekeeper, Mrs. Couch, to send the girl's character, otherwise another young woman will be sought for elsewhere, as Lady Seymour's children cannot remain without their dinners because Lady Shuckburgh, keeping a professed cook and housekeeper, thinks a knowledge of the details of her establishment beneath her notice. Lady Seymour understands from Steadman that, in addition to her other talents, she was actually capable of cooking food for the little Shuckburghs to partake of when hungry.'

" This is illustrated by a drawing of a round table, with all the little Shuckburghs at their mutton chops cooked by Mary Steadman.

" No. 4. From the housekeeper :—

" ' Madam,—Lady Shuckburgh has directed me to acquaint you that she declines answering your note, the vulgarity of which she thinks beneath her contempt, and although it may be characteristic of the Sheridans to be vulgar, coarse, and witty, it is not that of a lady, unless she chances to have been *born in a garret and bred in a kitchen*. Mary Steadman informs me that your ladyship does not keep either a cook or housekeeper, and that you only require a girl who can cook a mutton chop ; if so, I apprehend that Mary Steadman, or any *other scullion*, will be found fully equal to the establishment of the Queen of Beauty.

" ' I am, Madam,

" ' Your Ladyship's &c., &c.,

" ' Elizabeth Couch.' "

The correspondence is given in Mr. Boughton Leigh's " Memorials of a Warwickshire Family," a book now unhappily out of print. The manuscripts are preserved at Brownsover Hall.

A famous run, by the way, and a famous hound, are connected with Shuckburgh. Men have gone on hunting there since Edgehill day, and long before it no doubt. Lord Willoughby de Broke remembers a day, many years ago now, when they found at Shuckburgh, and, he says, "the hounds ran their hardest, straight for a thick fence, about a hundred yards the other side of which was a shooter who had not seen the fox; but the fox had seen him, and when half through the fence had twisted round in it, jumped out the same side he went in, and ran along the side." Now was the time for a good hound to show his quality. "All the pack, bar Ravager, charged the fence and flashed on up to the shooter; but he, turning half-way through the fence, as the old Brocklesby whipper-in used to say, ' like an eel in the mud,' jumped out exactly where the fox had done, and threw his tongue, so that we did not lose a minute." And the run was worthy of the clever hound, for " that was a pretty good day's sport, as we killed that fox seven miles from where we found him, went back to Shuckburgh, ran another a seven-mile point in the opposite direction, and killed him in the Bicester country."

At Shuckburgh you are on the very verge of Northamptonshire. Before long you can be at Catesby, or Staverton, or Daventry. The last may well be the end of your journey. It is a town famous in the Civil Wars, whether it go back to the Danes for its beginning or no; and there Charles stayed a week just before Naseby, and Lambert made a stand for the old

Cromwellians when the Restoration was on foot, and he was captured at Staverton. Daventry Church is of 1752. Had Sanderson Miller a hand in it? That is all I will ask. The answer is that he had not directly, though to look at it you would think he had. But Miller was not only, amateur though he was, an architect himself but the cause of architecture in others, who were professionals. And at Daventry the church was designed by a Warwickshire man. The *Gentleman's Magazine* in 1826 records that its first stone was laid on April 8, 1752, and that it is " a handsome edifice, from a design by Mr. Hiorn of Warwick," and that " it appears by the vestry-book November 9, 1758, that the whole expense, including hanging of bells, clock, and chimes, amounted to £3,486 2s. 5½d. The only entrance is at the west end, where the vestibule is divided into three doorways corresponding with the nave and aisles. The interior is very neatly fitted up, and has north, south, and west galleries ; and the nave is divided from the aisles by four lofty Doric pillars, supporting low, circular arches, etc., and a covered roof." This description, so particular in its facts down to the halfpenny, is the best introduction I can give to the church.

But I cannot forebear to add another sentence from the *Gentleman's Magazine* of the same year. "There has recently been erected as part of the site [of the priory] from a neat design, a town gaol, with a national school room over it, and behind, or to the north-east, a parochial poor-house." Could anything be better? The children cannot fail to learn the choice before them.

But when I leave this chapter in Northamptonshire, without disputing about whether the fashion of calling this place " Daintree is comparatively modern and never of popular usage," I bethink me that we are still in the country of Shakespeare, who knew the red-nose innkeeper of this town well enough.

Broadway.

CHAPTER VIII

FROM EVESHAM BY CAMPDEN TO STRATFORD

FROM Evesham to Chipping Campden one should go, I think, not by the great road through Broadway ; I will not describe that great road, which I purpose to leave to my right, but only say that if you go by it you must see, a little off the road, the beautiful manor-house of Wickhamford, and then pass, descending to it, and rising again when you have come into it, the famous long street of Broadway. There are beautiful houses, beautiful inns, famous memories (of quite modern days), and Mr. New's picture will show you something of the beauty. Then the long rise, with here and there a twist in it, till you get to the top of the great hill, by the tower with its quite recent history as the dwelling-place of William Morris and his friends, and so after a few more miles, turn sharp to the left and down a hill into Campden. But the way I would take you is through Bengeworth and Bretforton and Weston. The really exciting thing about Bengeworth is its beautiful bridge with the fine ribs underneath.

Church and history are good, and many things you may read in the Evesham *Notes and Queries*. But I propose to hurry on to Bretforton. Take the first turn to the left after you have crossed Bengeworth bridge; avoid then the first houses to left or right; and turn aside to Badsey if you like and see the very interesting pictures in the church. The church itself was "restored" in 1885, and then two pictures were presented, the

The Grange, Broadway.

"Madonna" by Carlo Cignani (1628–1719), and "The Raising of the Widow's Son" by Van Veen (1556–1634); but anyhow go on to Bretforton. There you will see the fine Early English church, restored, of course, and with later additions, but retaining its Norman font. It was dedicated in its renewed state, on S. Thomas of Canterbury's Day, 1295, by Llewelyn, Bishop of S. Asaph. In the windows are still fragments of ancient glass. The tower, with battlements of course, was built in the fifteenth century. All through the early history

it was in the charge of the abbey of Evesham, and everything for the church seems to have been done by the
abbats.   In later times, but for some cruel destructions in
1817, it seems to have fallen into very góod hands.   The ancient
customs of the church and of the village are recorded.   The fish-
pond and dovecot remain, and so does the large vaulted
room, of Norman date, now a cellar in what was the abbey grange.
The famous Bretforton family throughout the Middle Ages
was Jwens or Hewins, yeomen who supplied many priests
also to the village.   At the Reformation period one of them was
Auditor of the Court of Katherine of Aragon, and one was witness
(or overseer) of the will of John Hill of Bearley, who died in 1545,
and whose widow was the second wife of Shakespeare's grandfather, Robert Arden.   In 1586, or about then, the manor was
sold to the tenants, and a class of yeomen owning their own land
was so established.   John Watson, a nephew of the Bishop of
Winchester, secured some 250 acres and claimed to be lord of
the manor ; but his claim was always resisted.   The new yeomen
built a large number of good houses, which still remain.   The
manorial rights lapsed, and the village till the end of the eighteenth century was a sort of oligarchy of gentlemen farmers.   Of
these I find in the history of Bretforton some very pertinent
remarks which I take the liberty of quoting, with gratitude to
the learned author, (the Rev. W. H. Shawcross) who has studied
the village so closely :—

   "The various Shakespearean controversies have given rise to the
most absurd misconceptions with regard to the position and status
of the old families of this district, and the documents are read and
interpreted in the light of the social organisation of the eighteenth
century and even of ideas derived from purely nineteenth century
history.   In the Vale of Evesham and the North Cotswolds nearly
all the families from which people are now proud to trace their
descent were yeomen,—ranging from the landowner, or ' large
freeholder ' of Gregory King down to the small holder of a few
acres.   Of these yeomen many were the direct descendants and
representatives of ancient feudal families of position and influence ;   many others came into existence subsequent to the
Reformation, either by private acquisition of land or by deliberate
creation by the State.   From these yeomen are descended not
only many of the most powerful noble families of modern times
but frequently, through the crushing out of the small holder or

proprietor by purely economic causes, the agricultural labourer employed on their estates. The Bretforton wills show an extraordinarily high degree of comfort in the village for this period, just as the inventories show the possession of wealth fully commensurate to the beautiful houses the yeomen families of the district have left for the admiration of later generations. It may be noted here that at least a dozen yeomen families of Bretforton habitually used arms, of unquestionably ancient origin, in sealing their deeds and other documents."

From Bretforton the road veers southwards, a way going to the two Honeybournes on your left, and you are taken into the charming village of Weston-sub-Edge. There the church is " restored," but there is a beautiful green and there are some good Jacobean half-timbered houses. In this village, and in part of the rectory which remains, lived William Latimer (not Hugh) the friend of Tyndale. The church has some good monuments. There is a brass of Thomas Hodges, and monuments of the Lord Saye and Sele who died 1708, and of a famous seventeenth century chirurgeon John Ballard (1678). An interesting point about Weston is that it remained unenclosed some eighty or ninety years later than the neighbouring parishes. Though the lord of the manor seems for all practical purposes to have died out there at the Reformation, the old open field system of husbandry continued. What was practically a corporation of fieldsmen (who have been truly described as the aristocracy of the village and " did not represent more than one-sixth of the population ") managed the agricultural arrangements of the land. This old system remained in the midst of many social changes up to the time of the enclosure, when land was more valuable, the railways had brought the most undesirable people, as Mr. Stratton shows, to the games, and everyone was willing to get rid of the plague and let the open fields be used for more productive husbandry. The " Field Account Book " from 1826 to 1852 has been published as one of the charming productions of the Essex House Press, printed at Campden. It gives interesting evidence of the condition of common holdings, in the hands of a few, as they were between the seventeenth century and two centuries later. The " fieldsmen " were gradually dying out before the climax of 1852, when the Dover's hill games were stopped and the enclosures were carried out.

But while the agricultural system was changed, we have the

authority of Mr. C. R. Ashbee, who has a first-hand knowledge of the arts and crafts of the neighbourhood, for saying that the old crafts lingered on, handed down in a family, and producing skilled thatchers and glaziers, wattlers, and the makers of those wonderful Cotswold walls, which it is an education to watch in the making, walls which look so simple when thay are made, yet last for a century or more.

Weston-sub-Edge has some good gabled houses, as I said, and so has Aston-sub-Edge which you next come to, at the foot of a hill three hundred feet high, by which you rise into Chipping Campden. This is really the chief town of the wool-growing district of old times, as Evesham is chief of the vale. It was well said a year or two ago in the *Times*:—

" The western edge of the Cotswolds yields one of the noblest views England has to show ; the road after a long gentle rise suddenly breaks over into space and all the glories of the world are spread before one—the rich wooded valley of the Avon and of the further Severn, beyond which rises the shapely line of the Malvern Hills, with the Clees more remote, and in the vaporous distance fold after fold of the foothills of the Welsh marches. The face of the escarpment falls 400ft. in a single wave to the fertile Evesham Vale, but the road zigzags down into a little coombe where lies Broadway, most admired of the Cotswold villages with their comely houses of brown stone."

But let those who admire Broadway turn aside when they have seen this wonderful view, from Campden Hill, or from Broadway tower, to Chipping Campden itself.

Campden is the most beautiful town of its district, and it has at least four points of special interest : the splendid fifteenth century church, in design almost exactly resembling that of Fairford at the south-eastern point of the county, some thirty miles away ; the almshouses ; the remains of Baptist Hicks's great buildings ; and the splendid village street, with houses as good as Grevil's house and the Lygon Arms in it. Let us take the first last, as we enter it. It is a wide street and a long one, and the houses in it are all old, the majority, perhaps, of the seventeenth century, but many much earlier. The most famous house is that of William Grevil, " flos mercatorum Angliae," as his brass in the church calls him. He was the head, one may suppose, of the Cotswold wool trade at the time of its greatest prosperity, and his splendid house with its great windows lighting great rooms shows how rich he was, as his gift to the church shows how generous.   Beyond this is what was the Woolstaplers' Hall, now a private house, beautifully, and justly, restored ; with a fine open-timbered fourteenth century hall.   Then there is the Market Hall, and many another building of simple excellence. Indeed, all the building in Campden is good : that is the impres‐ sion you have of the whole place.   And there is another thing to notice about it : would that it were true of other places.   The beauty of Campden has this special interest, that it has never

Chipping Campden.

been seriously marred.   Campden is not like Broadway, a village made up to please modern taste, on the model of the old houses, beautiful indeed, which survive there : it has never been taken in hand by a benevolent landlord or an enterprising house agent. Mr. Ashbee, who knows it so well, says : " None with any senti‐ ment for beauty or fitness can to this day pass down Campden High Street, perhaps the loveliest thing of its kind in England, without a sense that on the whole the local craftsman, even into our own time, has felt this too.   His work is not so good as the work he often repairs or replaces, but if he is left alone, he makes no flagrant error of taste and still works with some sense of reverence and conservatism."

Next in the street we must note the church, splendid for its size and openness. It was in building when Grevel died in 1401, but it must have been rebuilt or completed very much later, for it closely resembles both Northleach and Fairford. It has been so well described by Mr. Herbert Evans ("Oxford and the Cotswolds," pp. 191–2) that I feel I can best describe its excellences by quoting him—and the more so because I so entirely agree with his strictures :—

" The impression made upon the stranger by the great church of Campden is best described as that of a perfect combination of unity, magnificence, and strength ; in this respect it is not surpassed by any one of the many churches mentioned in this volume. Moreover, the unity of the effect is enhanced by the solemn uniformity of the colouring of the exterior, which is a rich dark brown unbroken either by creeping plants or by patches of unweathered stone. But the greater our admiration for the exterior, the greater will be the shock to our feelings on entering the building ; it is the old story of nineteenth century atrocities —scraped walls, encaustic tiles, stained deal, and flat ceiling. The reader, I fear, must be getting weary of my frequent lamentations on this subject, but the fault is not mine, and this instance is too flagrant to be passed over in silence."

The warning remonstrance of Mr. Evans is very far from being unnecessary, for where they are not prevented, mechanical firms and, I grieve to add, ignorant country clergymen are still destroying the beauty of the past. Perhaps William Morris's views were extreme ; but with a policy of " anti-scrape " all lovers of the memorials of the middle ages must be in accord.

However, Campden Church still retains a great deal of its ancient glory. The brasses have been moved, but they have their beauty and interest still. The curious Hicks chapel, with its record of the second family which made Campden famous, remains unharmed. This is at the south-east of the church. Baptist Hicks was a London merchant who made his fortune, not unhelped, no doubt, by the political influence of his brother Michael, secretary to the great Lord Burghley. In a recent book, " A Cotswold Family : Hicks and Hicks-Beach," by Mrs. William Hicks-Beach, family papers are utilised to tell us a great deal about the lives of these brothers. Michael Hicks becomes real to us, through many interesting letters printed for the first time in these pages. We see the closeness of his association with Elizabeth's Minister, the friendly yet rather servile nature of the relation, the kindnesses done in a rather lordly way, the loan of carriages or lodging, ending still in the fact that "the measure of Cecil's honourable favour towards Michael was not very tremendous. He was not advanced to any office. He remained secretary always." Baptist Hicks nevertheless is really the most notable person in the family, at least till modern times, a successful mercer and money-lender, whose tomb in Campden Church and whose buildings in Campden village delight us to-day. His, too, was the notable residence of Campden House in Kensington and the Hill and region that bears its name. In 1609 he bought the manor of Campden, when he had become a rich man. He was a free-man of the Mercers' Company in 1580, and became Master in 1611, and again eleven years later. He had supplied silks and damasks for the coronation of James I. at the cost of £3,000, and with that monarch he had much close dealing, helping him on several occasions with large loans—and in 1606 the interest on these loans amounted to £4,000. No wonder James had knighted him even before he was crowned. And he lived prosperously through all this to be seventy-eight, dying at last on October 18, 1629. His splendid tomb, with a great marble canopy, supported by twelve marble pillars, where his wife lies beside him, says that he "by the blessing of GOD on his ingenious endeavours arose to an ample estate, and to the aforesaid degrees of honour—[he died a Viscount]—and out of those blessings disposed to charitable uses in his lifetime a large portion, to the value of £10,000," and adds that he "lived religiously, virtuously, and generously." So, "in all peace and contentment" did his wife Elizabeth May, of a famous Merchant Taylor family; The Hicks tomb is a remarkable thing, more so than beautiful; but eminently characteristic of the mercantile idea of commemoration. His honours passed through his daughter Juliana to the Noel family, now Earls of Gainsborough. His magnificent mansion, south-east of the church, was hardly completed, and accustomed to its inhabitants, before it was destroyed. There remains in a large field, once the garden, several terraces that can easily be traced, and at each end two charming gazebos (or garden houses) where the good man could sit and enjoy the splendid views and bracing atmosphere of the Cotswolds.

With the Woolstaplers of the Middle Ages and the rich Hicks before the wars, the story of Campden is one of successful commerce. Note that as a parallel or contrast to that of Chipping Campden, the history of Chipping Sodbury in later Stewart times is interesting. It was one of the towns to be deprived of its charter under the " reforming " process · of the later years of Charles II. Till then it had a bailiff and ten burgesses, a survival of the old Guild association, but in 1681 a new charter gave it a mayor, six aldermen, and twelve burgesses. In 1688 when James II. was making effort too late to regain his popularity, the old constitution was restored, and so it remained till the Municipal Corporation Act of 1882. But Chipping Campden's guild organisation was replaced by James I., whose interest in the neighbourhood was no doubt evolved by Master Dover (to whom he gave his coat). James gave Campden a steward, two bailiffs, twelve capital burgesses, and twelve inferior burgesses; and these held power, elected annually, till the Municipal Corporation Act of 1882, which spared this comparatively free body no more than the close one of Chipping Sodbury. The remains of former glory are to be seen at Chipping Campden in the Town Hall, a small building restored a few years ago, close to the beautiful market house. In the town hall is Sir Gerard Noel in his habit as he lived, as High Steward of the borough, in 1824, and two most beautiful silver maces, one bearing the date 1605 and two brass-gilt ones given in 1773, keep him company. Interesting details of the history of the bailiffs have been published in the *Evesham Journal* of recent years.

The beautiful almshouses, so simple, yet so dignified and impressive, which you pass on your left as you go to the church, were the gift of Baptist Hicks, and they show that rich traders could be generous. They are architecturally the surviving memorial of the great tradesman ; for besides the ruins of the great house of Sir Baptist Hicks, destroyed in the Civil War, and leaving nothing, practically, but the two beautiful garden houses or banqueting houses, there is an existing possessor of the title of " Campden House." This is the Earl of Gainsborough's, a beautiful building as one sees it from the opposite hill, itself on a slope well backed by trees.

Chipping Campden Church and Almshouses.

But another hill is more famous, because of "Dover's games." Of the sports themselves we have many records. They were held on a piece of high table land above Broadway, in the parish of Weston-sub-Edge easy still to discover, because it is universally called Dover's Hill, and the point where Warwickshire, Worcestershire, and Gloucestershire meet. No doubt the origin of the sports goes back to the ancient Whitsuntide festivities, and Dover only gave them a new life in 1610. Robert Dover, a lawyer who lived at Barton-on-the-Heath, was an eugenist before his time, a health fanatic, an open-air devotee, perhaps even an advocate of total abstinence. At any rate he thought his games would draw folk from the pothouses, to which the Puritan banning of festivity had driven them. Endymion Porter, of Mickleton and Aston-sub-Edge, the friend of all the wits of the day, and well known at Court, encouraged him in his scheme, and presented him with a hat and feather, and a ruff that had belonged to King James himself. There is the record of all they did in the *Annalia Dubrensia, 1636,* a most entertaining book, to which most of the wits of the day, including Drayton and Ben Jonson, contributed. "A heroic and generous minded gentleman," and much like it, is the description of Mr. Dover, whom Ben declares to have been his "jovial good friend" (so he was probably a moderate drinker). The picture of all they did, in the book, is delightful—quite an illumination of English sports ; and ever so decorous. But now look on. The Puritans suppressed Mr. Dover and his games. The Restoration revived them. Eighty years or so later, Richard Graves, who being brought up at Mickleton, knew them well, thus describes them, in *The Spiritual Quixote,* the record of the days of Mr. Geoffrey Wildgoose and his Sancho Panza :—

"They now approached the place of rendez-vous, where the revel was held ; which was a large plain on the Cotswold-hills. Their ears were saluted with a confused noise of drums, trumpets, and whistle-pipes : not those martial sounds, however, which are heard in the field of battle ; but such as those harmless instruments emit, with which children amuse themselves in a country fair. There was a great number of swains in their holiday-cloaths with their belts and silk handkerchiefs ; and nymphs in straw hats and tawdry ribbands, flaunting, ogling, and coquetting (in their rustic way) with as much alacrity as any of the gay flutterers in the Mall.

"A ring was formed about the wrestlers and cudgel-players, by the substantial Farmers on their long-tailed steeds, and two or three forlorn coaches sauntering about with their vapourish possessors; who crept out from their neighbouring seats, to contemplate the humours of these aukward rustics, and waste an hour of their tedious month in the country, where (as a great modern observes) 'small matters serve for amusement.'"

There is a long passage too in Somervile's *Hobbinol* which evidently has them in mind, and certainly shows some of the sports to have been rough and scarce seemly to modern view. But they lasted on till 1852. A late memory of them shall be quoted here, which Mr. G. M. Stratton contributed some years ago to the *Evesham Journal*, which has the most excellent Notes and Queries relating to all the district, edited by Mr. E. A. B. Barnard, a devoted and skilled antiquary. Mr. Stratton thus gives his reminiscences :—

"In connection with Dover's Hill festivities, the writer would like to recall a few incidents related by his mother. But as an introductory he would say :—My father, Charles F. Stratton, was born at Chalford, Gloucestershire; he was about four years old when his father, George Matthias Stratton, died. There were four children—viz., George Matthias, Charles Frederick, Matthias, and Ann Minchin. My father, C. F. Stratton, was adopted by his grandfather, Matthias Stratton, gin distiller, wine and spirit merchant, Vine-street, Evesham, where he remained for some years. My father used to relate how in 1813 he had a holiday from school on purpose to make balls of clay to stick against his grandfather's house (who was that year Mayor), to place candles in to illuminate on the occasion of peace caused by the victory over the French at Waterloo.

"My father when quite a young man was appointed foreman at his grandfather's silk mills, situated at Badsey, where he re-mained until he married Miss Ann Knight, daughter of Mr. Knight, a famous long-wooden plough maker. He then took a beer-house in that village, where he remained for two years; then he removed to the Plough and Harrow, Vine-street, Eves-ham. Just across the street was the Police Station and the Town Hall.

"One day a stranger was locked up for some trivial offence; my father, hearing the man had no money or friends, gave him food and employed legal assistance, and the man was eventually discharged. Hereby hangs a tale.

"My mother at that time used to go to Dover's Hill each year, taking a large tent, a good supply of ale, cider, wine, spirits, and eatables to sell during the gaming week. She made a good sum of money, and the surroundings were so alarming that as fast as her silver changed into gold she would drop the sovereigns into the large barrels of ale or cider through the bung-hole (this was her safety bank). She also had a couple of loaded revolvers under her serving table ready for use. She never left the tent day or night until the festivities were over, as no one was safe from the lawlessness of the crowd of card sharpers, thimble-riggers, pick-pockets, thieves, confidence-men, vagrants, and criminals of the deepest dye, the riff-raff of society. During the daytime the turmoil was terrible, but all night long it was a perfect pandemonium. Cries of murder were often heard, and disorder and rapine held full sway. If the shadow of a person showed through the sheeting of the tent at night he would almost sure to be struck with a heavy bludgeon from without, and the miscreant would crawl underneath and rob his victim. One year every stall and tent (except my mother's) was levelled to the ground and their contents pillaged. Scores of persons, nut sellers and others, found a safe asylum in my mother's tent. The scenes, she said, were indeed terrible. Yet my mother went there each year with her serving-maids and her men, and with eatables and drinkables for sale, and was never molested or robbed. Neither was any pedler or benighted person who sought shelter in her tent for the night ever molested or injured. The reason for this was—The man who was locked up at Evesham and whom my father befriended and assisted, proved to be a sort of leader of the lawless band who attended Dover's Hill. It happened one day at the next Dover's Hill meeting that this man and several of his confederates entered the tent for refreshments. He at once recognised my mother. He immediately turned and addressed his companions in a slang understood by them, and every year afterwards she and all who sheltered within her tent were always safe from molestation. One day while she was attending to her business, a large crowd of the light-fingered gentlemen rushed into the tent, preceded by a gentleman (I believe it was a Lord North), who suddenly tripped up. He immediately placed his hands into his trousers pocket to protect his money. The prigs at once surrounded him and commenced tickling his ears to induce him to remove his hands. The posse of police who was following arrived and rescued him from his ludicrous position. The sharpers did him no injury, but they told my mother that if they could only have got his hands out of his pockets they would soon have had his money. The reason of this incident was : Lord North at the head of the squad of police had made a raid upon the thimble-riggers, card sharpers, etc., overturning their tables, stands, etc., and breaking them up. North North and his men gave chase to the fleeing sharpers, several of whom made for my mother's tent. Lord North outstripped his escort, slipped upon the ground, and thus caused the laughable episode. My mother also used to get a permit from the excise authorities, and would take a tent and refreshments to sell during the days of sale at all the farm sales that took place around Evesham and its neighbourhood."

Thus the memory of those great feasts is not so far away ; and the remembrance is a subject somewhat exploited of Socialists, who quote with glee the lines of Shackleford Marmion from the *Annalia Dubrensia*:—

> " Hear, you bad owners of inclosed grounds
> That have your souls as narrow as your bounds,
> When you have robbed the earth of her increase,
> Stored up that fading treasure and spoke peace
> Unto your wretched thoughts ; the barren field
> Of Cotswold, and those emulous hills shall yield
> A crop of honour unto Dover's name
> Richer than all your stacks or barns contain. "

One more quotation before we leave these famous Cotswold games. It shall be from the *Life and Letters of Mr. Endymion Porter sometime Gentleman of the Bedchamber to King Charles the First*, by Mrs. Dorothea Townshend. It may link Dover's Hill for us to the next place we shall visit :—

" Mr. Dover," says Mrs. Townshend, " was master of the revels, riding about on a fine horse, arrayed in a suit of clothes which had belonged to King James himself, and had been presented to him by Mr. Dover, through Endymion Porter, for the greater encouragement of his patriotic undertaking. And among the assembled gentry around Mr. Dover in his high hat and padded suit were young Mr. Porter with his Spanish elegance, and a tribe of Porter cousins from the neighbourhood ; and more distinguished guests were there. D'Avenant and the great Ben Jonson himself came to honour the sports with their presence, and write sonnets in their praise ; and who knows whether a certain Mr. William Shakespeare may not have ridden over from Stratford, through the orchards, on one of those gay Whit Thursdays, to see Justice Shallow's grey- hound outrun on Cotsall."

We may go to Dover's Hill either directly from Campden or from Aston, about a mile either way, by roads fringed with woodland.   At Mickleton is a most beautiful manor house, with a delightful scallop over the central first floor window and below the middle dormer in the roof—a house built in the very perfection of delicacy and cleanliness and solidity, with its wall and its fine gate posts, and good iron gate, in front.   It was not in this house, I suppose, that Endymion Porter lived, but in an older one—and Mickleton is full of good houses.   The history of the place belongs chiefly to Endymion Porter, whose charming letters show that all through the atmosphere of Court intrigue, civil war, popish plots, and the discreditable escapades of unworthy children, the honest cavalier, the friend of the greatest and the wittiest men of the day, pursues his course, anxious only to fulfil his duty, which he thus once expressed to his wife when she wanted him to leave the king at a time of danger—" My duty and my loyalty have taught me to follow the King my master, and by the grace of God nothing shall divert me from it."   It is the tone of all the letters to his wife, a charm- ing collection.

> " I could not love thee, dear, so much
> Loved I not honour more."

He was loyal to his king, indeed, through many a sacrifice as well as in prosperity ; but none the less was he a devoted husband and a lover of his wife all the years he lived.

And, next to Porter, Mickleton brings us the memory of the honourable family of Graves, antiquaries and country gentlemen. In the good Decorated church, with its priest's chamber and its fine spire, there are many monuments to the Graves family. Perhaps more interesting is the tablet which Mr. Richard Graves put up to the memory of Utrecia Smith, daughter of a rector of the parish who lived to be ninety, and " bred up in a genteel manner " two sons and two daughters on about eighty pounds a year. Utrecia was a young lady of learning, whose early death was most deeply mourned. There are allusions in Shenstone's writings, and the writings about him, which make one think that he might have married her. And he wrote when all that was mortal of her rested in this church :—

" Sure nought unhallowed shall presume to stray
    Where sleep the reliques of that virtuous maid,
Nor ought unlovely bend its devious way
    Where soft Ophelia's dear remains are laid."

The house of Graves, where Shenstone's life-long friend and biographer was born, had, he tells us, " many natural beauties; of surrounding hills and hanging woods, a spacious lawn, and one natural cascade ; capable of great improvement, though, from various circumstances, the place is to this day in a very unfinished state." The successors and heirs of the Graves family did beautify their mansion, and then one of them moved it—an act of heroic daring—to the top of the neighbouring Kiftsgate Hill, whence it sees all the glory of the western Cotswolds.

Leave Mickleton then, and journey northwards, that you may follow the road Mrs. Townshend would imagine Shakespeare, rather anachronistically, to have taken when he came to see the Dover games. As you go towards Stratford, about ten miles, you have the Shakespearean villages on your left, that is to the west of you ; but the road you go by is quite solitary, through arable land, not much wooded, till you come to the borders of the Stour and the village of Clifford Chambers. We will approach this village, then, as if we walked out with Master Shakespeare towards Campden. Clifford Chambers is but a short way from Stratford. Go out towards Shipston, and turn to your right, and by a very good road, with woods about it, you will come to a charming village on the Stour—and mind that you make the river rhyme with " flower." Of old the village belonged to the great Abbey of S. Peter at Gloucester, and they tell you that its name meant no more than the ford by the cliff. More truly it is Clifford Chamberer, for the manor granted to Gloucester in 1099 was allotted to this official. A ford there is, and two mighty good mills, to which the carts come from many a mile away. The church (which like the village is off the main road) as I saw it on a hot summer morning, seemed spick and span. Is the chancel new, or only renewed? The nave is good Norman, but there is a new tower. The south door is Norman, but has a new porch. The families whose memorials are to be found in the church are Parry and Harris. Among the best things is the tomb of Hercules Raynsford and his wife (a Parry), a splendid brass, the man in armour of 1583. Another brass gives his daughter Elizabeth, who married one Marrow. Then there is a splendid monument with kneeling figures, to Henry, son of Hercules, who has below him two sons, and one baby in a shroud, with

Church and old Vicarage, Clifford Chambers.

the label "Of Such is the Kingdom of Heaven." The coat of arms is magnificent. On the other side of the chancel is the touching remembrance, by his parents, of a young surgeon, John Parry Nash, who died in 1816, aged only 29; a descendant, I suppose, of the family named above. In the churchyard there is the tombstone of Susanna Lovell, the "Gipsy Queen."

But no account of this interesting church can be complete without a word on its chiefest treasure, the chalice and paten of 1494–5. The chalice is described as silver parcel-gilt, the bowl standing on a hexagonal stem divided by a knob with six facets, one with a cross on it, the others with one letter each of the word *Jesus*. On the front panel is the crucifix, with foliage at each corner. The work is exceedingly rough, and some think also that it has been maltreated, but I should consider this doubtful. The paten has for central ornament the Holy Face imprinted on the cloth of S. Veronica, equally rough. The nimbus around has a fleur-de-lis. At the date of the making of both the incumbent was John Dorseley.

Clifford Chambers Manor House.

Close to the church is the exquisite house, black and yellow, which was the old vicarage, and just beyond is the most charming seventeenth century manor house, standing at the end of a fine lawn closed by good iron gates.

At Clifford you can either cross the fields to Atherstone or go on, having Quinton to your left and Long Marston to your right, till you come, slowly rising, to Mickleton, and so to Campden. But we will go the other way, to Stratford.

CHAPTER IX

STRATFORD-ON-AVON

WE are come to the centre of our shire—the goal of our quest. Say what you will, Stratford is the heart of Warwickshire, even of England, for all who visit it to-day; and the small stream of Avon is the most famous of all English rivers. Washington Irving quoted the verses, little better than doggerel, of Garrick (at a time when there were those who still remembered him in the town, " a short punch man, very quick and entertaining "). Let us quote them again, for a pleasant " sentiment " as we enter the town :—

> " Thou soft-flowing Avon, by thy silver stream
> Of things more than mortal sweet Shakespeare would dream,
> The fairies by moonlight dance round his green bed,
> For hallow'd the turf is which pillowed his head."

The poet and the river are certainly the two governing factors in the life of Stratford. Shakespeare is to be seen and heard everywhere. The river, which half encircles the town, is more easily forgotten, yet it gives the setting which bestows on the place its only distinction of beauty, and it no doubt founded the prosperity which has never wholly deserted it. Something of this you see as you enter from Charlecote or Shipston over the great stone bridge and see Sir Hugh Clopton's work beside you, dignified as of old. The little streams, canal and river, which make the island upon which the Unicorn inn stands, show how important water transit has been in the past history of Stratford. There is a pleasant reach just above the town for boats and the little steamers which are on the watch to allure visitors ; and below the bridges is a good stretch of clear water past the church —a view painted by innumerable artists—till you come to Lucy's

Clopton Bridge, Stratford-on-Avon.

Mill and the beginning of a series of locks. The best view of Stratford by far is from the meadows at the east. There you see the church with its graceful spire rising from the solid Decorated tower, and the curious tower and theatre of the Shakespeare memorial, not unpleasing, as it is mellowed by time, the great bridge of Clopton, the wharves, and a few old houses by the river bank, and at the back, in nooks and crannies peeping out on here and · there a little rising ground, larger houses, gabled, a tower of guild chapel, or town hall. Time has long gone by since Stratford, in Jago's day, hailed

> " The freighted Barge from Western Shores
> Rich with the Tribute of a Thousand Climes."

The river had been made navigable from Tewkesbury in 1637 by William Sandys of Fladbury ; it is navigable no longer ; but a tour by boat down the stream is still greatly to be commended, and those who have essayed it have left very pleasant memories of their trip. At least everyone should go to the Wyre (or weir) Brake, a coppice by the river's brim, whence you can see Stratford spire, or on to Luddington Dam, with its three weirs, overshadowed by great elms. From thence, if you will, you may find your way, by pretty lanes, to Bordon Hill, on the road from Stratford to Binton (*see* p. 232), whence you will have the other good view of Shakespeare's home—the spire still straight in the foreground, the town sprinkled with trees, and Shottery to the left, asleep among its meadows. Stratford is a town in the heart of the country, owing its charm to the river which enriches its fields.

Stand then, when you return, at the entrance to the town, past the big cattle market, across the often crowded bridge, and remember how difficult was the way in the old days before the generosity of Clopton. Leland, the first of the archæologists of modern England, in his tour of our land, as Henry VIII.'s antiquary-in-chief, between 1534 and 1543, thus spoke of Clopton's great benefaction. (Miss Toulmin Smith's edition is a book every student of local antiquities should possess. I quote here from vol. ii., p. 27) :—

" The bridge ther of late tyme was very smalle and ille, and at high waters very harde to passe by. Whereupon in tyme of mynde one Cloptun, a great rich marchant, and Mayr of London, as I remember, borne about Strateforde, having never wife nor

M

children, converted a great peace of his substance in good workes
in Stratford, first making a sumptuus new bridge and large of
stone, where in the midle be vi great arches for the maine
streame of Avon, and at eche ende certen smaul arches to bere
the causey, and so to passe commodiusly at such tymes as the
ryver risith."

You can pass commodiously enough now. And so you enter
the town and pause for a moment to think of its antiquity, for
Stratford-on-Avon is a really ancient town. The name is genuine
and very likely marks a position on a Roman road. What road
that was it is not easy to say ; none can be traced east of the
town ; but on the west the road to the Roman station of Alcester,
passing no village, only Drayton Bushes and Red Hill inn, is
singularly straight ; and Roman coins are very abundant in the
town and neighbourhood. But this is dim, and perhaps guess-
work. The town emerges into history very clearly in Domesday
Book. It was among the manors of the Bishop of Worcester,
who had the envied right of a mill there on the river, which
brought ten shillings a year or a thousand eels. Wulfstan,
Bishop of Worcester, made twenty-five pounds a year by his
rights in Stratford when William the Conqueror was king ; only
five pounds had been made in the Confessor's day. The Norman
Conquest must have started the town's prosperity. Alveston,
the property by Wulfstan's gift of the priory of Worcester, was
for a time its rival, stretching its boundaries up to the other side
of the river. But many trades began to find a home in Stratford,
and by the middle of the thirteenth century its supremacy in the
district was assured. The Thursday weekly market, dates from
Richard I., and was revived in 1314, and the " Rother (cattle)
Market " dates from that time. Sir Sidney Lee has noted how
Shakespeare uses the unusual word in " Timon of Athens " : " the
pasture lards the rother's sides." Fairs were added later, on the
day before Trinity Sunday and the two following days, on
S. Austin's Eve and two days later, and others. In the fourteenth century " the Stratfords," famous prelates under
Edward III., came from there, two of them Chancellors, all
bishops, one Archbishop of Canterbury, one of the three beginning
his ecclesiastical work as Vicar of Stratford. John, the Archbishop, gave great benefactions to the parish church, founding
a chantry, in the chapel of S. Thomas of Canterbury, in 1322 ;
and his nephew built " a house of square stone " for the five

priests who were to serve it.   Under Henry V. this became form-
ally known as a college of priests, and the church as collegiate.
Later benefactions included one for four choristers who were to
have a bed-chamber in the church (the parvise, no doubt) " so
hereunto they were to repair in winter at eight of the clock, and
in summer at nine ; in which lodging be two beds, wherein they
were to sleep by couples ; and that before they did put off their
clothes they should all say the prayer of *De profundis* with a loud
voice, with the prayers and orisons of the faithful, and afterwards
say thus : God have mercy on the soul of Ralph Collingwood
our founder, and Master Thomas Balsall, a special benefactor
of the same."

The part played in the town life by the guild was as important
as that played by the church.   The Stratford guild, of Holy
Cross, the B.V.M, and S. John Baptist, was of the early thirteenth
century, and it received a special chapel from Robert of Stratford.
Its statutes, most interesting, are still extant.   The guild hall,
with its parlour, counting-house, and school, date from the
fifteenth century, and at the end of the century the chapel was
repaired.   It still stands, as we shall see, opposite to the site of
New Place.   The guild became one of the most famous in England.
Men as far away as Peterborough joined it, and personages as
great as George Duke of Clarence, his wife, the king-maker's
daughter, and their children.   The Grammar School, built and
endowed by the guild, dates from 1427.   The destruction of the
guild in its religious aspect was one of the great misfortunes of
Stratford, and, with the destruction of the canonical foundations,
marked the beginning of the town's decline.   It is curious how
important a place the guild chapel had come to take in the town's
life.   The Commissioners of 1547 noted that its position in the
centre of the town was " for the great quietness and comfort of
all the parishioners there ; for that the parish church standeth
out of the same town, distant from the most part of the said
parish half a mile and more ; and in time of sickness, as the plague
and such like diseases doth chance within the said town, then
all such infective persons, with many other impotent and poor
persons, doth to the said chapel resort for their daily service."
How much comment is incited by this refreshing passage, quoted
by Sir Sidney Lee !   One finds that the excuse of half a mile—
a very short one from the church to the guild chapel, surely—
was in vogue in the sixteenth century ; one notices that the daily

services were really attended ; and then one wonders how the guild brethren liked the presence of " infective persons."

In 1553 the new government, mayor, aldermen, and council was founded on the ruins of the guild, and received much of its property. And under that rule the town still remains. A very strict and severe government it was in the sixteenth century, though it did suffer thirty ale-houses to exist in the town. To it belonged John Shakespeare, who began as ale-taster and constable, and rose to be chief alderman. In his later years it is clear that he fell on evil days. In 1586 he was deprived of office in consequence of his failure to pay the charges imposed upon him by his office. Sir Sidney Lee thinks his failure was due to an unfortunate speculation in corn, or to the dearths out of which the law forbade him to take any advantage. It was a time when Stratford as a town was distinctly prosperous ; and the prosperity of the town encouraged its young men to seek greater prosperity still. Many a Stratfordian went to London to make a greater fortune than he could make at home ; but those who stayed at home for the most part did not lack, when good Queen Elizabeth sat on the throne. Among those who went was William Shakespeare : why, it seems that we shall never know. He made an imprudent marriage, it seems likely ; at any rate a rash one, if not worse. Perhaps he got into a scrape about deer stealing (see p. 209). More probably he was bitten with stage fever, after seeing the players who came so often to Stratford ; and he knew that he could both act and write. No one with powers such as his could be ignorant of his capacity. It seems likely that he tried his hand first at village school-mastering,—so an old actor told the indefatigable gossip and recorder, Aubrey ; and certainly he learnt to hit off the humours of schoolmaster pedants to the life. He married in 1582, he left home in 1585, he came to London in 1586. And there we leave him, remembering only that he lodged with a wig-maker, disliked going into great society, became a noted actor and a famous dramatist. In ten years he had made something like a fortune. He probably returned to Stratford in 1596, the year when his father had a grant of arms, and his own boy Hamnet died ; he bought New Place, once the property of Sir Hugh Clopton, in 1597 ; and he amassed more riches and garnered greater fame till he came back finally to live in the town of his birth in 1611. He had a house in London too, at Black-

friars, from 1613, and he often visited his old friends and con-
tinned to write for the theatres. In 1602 he had bought more
land, from the Combes, and added to his garden in Chapel Lane.
In 1605 he purchased also " the unexpired term of a moiety of
the interest in a lease, granted in 1554 for ninety-two years, of
the tithes of Stratford, Bishopston, and Welcombe." He had
become a rich man, and so he lived and died. His father died
in 1601 ; his mother, who had lived still in the house in Henley
Street, in 1608 ; he himself on April 23, 1616. The anniversary
of his birth (probably April 23 also) and death is now kept by
travellers from all parts of the world in the place which he made
famous. His wife lived till
1623. He left two daughters,
both married, Judith, the
younger, to Thomas Quiney
(in the birthplace is the letter
of his father Richard, asking
a loan of £30 from the poet),
and Susanna, the elder, to
Dr. John Hall, who inherited
New Place. John Hall was
buried in the chancel of the
parish church, November 25,
1635, and his wife, "witty
above her sex," was laid
beside him in 1649. Their
only child, Shakespeare's only
surviving grandchild, married

first Thomas Nash of Strat-
ford, and then John Barnard of Abington, close to Northampton, knighted in 1661 at the Restoration. She died in 1670.
Her second husband died in 1674. All these little facts are of
interest to the traveller to-day. It was not always so. Look
back two centuries for an example. Among all the testimonials
to the worth of Mr. William Shakespeare I know none more
curious than that of the Reverend Thomas Cox. Remember
that it was published in 1700 :—

" *William Shakespear* an eminent Poet, but no Scholar ; and so
in him the Maxim holds good, *Poeta nascitur not fit ; a Poet is
born, not made so*. His Genius was jocular, but he could be serious
when he pleas'd ; for tho' his Comedies were so merry that

Heraclitus himself could hardly forbear Laughter, his Tragedies were so mournful that *Democritus* could not keep from sighing. He had many Wit-Combats with *Ben Johnson,* who tho' he excell'd much in Learning, yet was as much excell'd by him in quickness of Wit and Invention, which gave him the Advantage of a more valuable Man. He dy'd and was buried in this Town in 1564."

Let us hope at least that the date is a misprint. And consider the sentence about his genius again and again ; for it is as an open window to the Queen Anne period in its literary taste. After this we turn back gladly to the simple sentence of the great antiquary : " One thing more, in reference to this antient town, is observable," says Sir William Dugdale, " that it gave Birth and Sepulture to our late famous Poet, *William Shakespeare* whose Monument I have inserted in my Discourse of the church."

Thus briefly is the Shakespeare tale told. It is that which brings most people to Stratford. There are a few points outside it which should not be forgotten, but even they link themselves to the chief " motif."

To continue the town's story. The ancient college of priests was destroyed in the eighteenth century, and a new Town Hall was erected, the old guild hall falling into disuse. In July, 1643, New Place received a visitor whom it would have done Shakespeare's heart good to welcome, Queen Mary as she was called, Charles I.'s wife, Henrietta Maria, whose wooing one might almost picture as having some little resemblance to that famous one of Catherine by Henry V. On July 11, 1643, her Majesty left King's Norton attended by " above two thousand foot, well armed, and one thousand horse and six pieces of cannon and two mortars and about one hundred waggons," and arrived the same day, at New Place, where her nephew " Prince Rupert mett her " with " a large body of troops." She became the guest of Mrs. Susanna Hall, widow, Shakespeare's eldest daughter, with whom was then living Thomas Nash and his wife Elizabeth, daughter of John and Susanna Hall, and grand-daughter of Shakespeare. The queen left Stratford-on-Avon July 13, meeting the king in Kineton field at the foot of Edgehill about 4 o'clock in the afternoon. Her staying at New Place may be taken to show that it was regarded as the chief house in the town : " When it is borne in mind," wrote Mr. Halliwell Phillips, " that it had a frontage of more than sixty feet, while its breadth in some parts was at least seventy, and its height over twenty-eight feet, there is no difficulty in assuming that, in those days of low ceilings, Mrs. Hall and the Nashes were perfectly at their ease, so far as space was concerned, in their reception of the queen and her personal attendants."

Old House, Stratford-on-Avon.

In the eighteenth century the town began to have a special fame because it was Shakespeare's town ; and it was Garrick, one may fairly say, who made it famous. " The Beauties of England and Wales," 1814, contains such a delightful description of the occasion, and what it seemed to the Georgian folk to mean that I cannot forbear to quote it :—

"Until the early part of the eighteenth century polite literature was confined to so few, that the national love of Shakespeare (whose birth was so momentous an era in the fortunes of this town) was not sufficiently ardent to lead numerous pilgrims to Stratford, for the purpose of poetical devotion. But with the spread of letters inevitably kept pace the progress of Shakespeare's fame. His readers must needs become innoxious idolists ; and, for very many years, Stratford has witnessed throngs of visitors, anxious to tread the ground which Shakespeare's feet had pressed in boyhood ; and to express, by mournful contemplation over the spot hallowed by his ashes, their gratitude for the banquet of intellectual joys afforded by his all-but superhuman talents. The public inclination to visit this favoured neighbourhood was promoted by the man who, perhaps of all others, was best able to appreciate the poet's merits—the celebrated Garrick. In the year 1769, he instituted at Stratford a festival in honour of Shakespeare, which was termed the JUBILEE. This interesting celebration commenced on the morning of Wednesday, Sept. 6, 1769, and terminated with the evening of the following Friday. An octagonal amphitheatre was erected on the Bankcroft, close to the river Avon, which was capable of holding more than 1,000 persons. The interior was arranged with much taste ; but the most gratifying ornament was a statue of Shakespeare, cast at the expense of Garrick, and afterwards presented by him to the Corporation, to be placed in a niche of the Town-hall. The amusements consisted of a public breakfast at the Town-hall ; the performance of the Oratorio of Judith in the church of Stratford ; a public ordinary at the amphitheatre ; an assembly ; a masquerade ; the recitation, by Garrick, of an ode and oration in praise of Shakespeare ; an exhibition of fireworks ; and a horse-race for a silver cup. The town was illuminated ; cannon were fired ; and bands of music paraded the streets. The concourse of persons of rank to assist in this poetical festival was so great, that many were not able to procure beds in the town, and are said to have been constrained to sleep in their carriages. The weather was wet and unfavourable, but much good humour prevailed among the parties assembled. The whole of the festivities were afterwards subject to some satirical remarks from persons who were unfeigned admirers of the bard ; and it must be confessed that, with the exception of the ode and oration, the performances were of a character quite commonplace. But, perhaps, it would have been difficult to render ceremonies more classical sufficiently gratifying to popular apprehension ; and it must never be for-gotten that the festival was a national tribute, which exalted genius and high rank concurred in rendering respectful to the memory of the great poet."

Several opinions of the Jubilee were much less polite. It has been generally supposed that it was Garrick who began the idea of commemorating Shakespeare by an institution in his native town, but a recent book (" Shakespeare and Stratford," by Henry Shelley) attributes the idea to Charles Matthews in 1820, who suggested a " Theatre, a National Monument and Mausoleum to the immortal memory of Shakespeare." The birthplace (so believed) was bought by national subscription in 1847, the New Place estate in 1862, in 1891 the Birthplace Trust was incor-porated by Act of Parliament, and in the following year Anne Hathaway's cottage was acquired. The two houses to the south of the birthplace were given by Mr. Andrew Carnegie in 1903 ; they are now used as the offices of the Trust.

Thus the ages have left their marks on Stratford, from the Domesday of William Conqueror to the generosity of an Ameri-can millionaire. Much that is truly ancient survives in this town of restorations and, one must admit, of occasional impos-tures. Let us take one example of survival. Stratford still preserves its ancient fair or " mop." How few are left of these historic festivals ; and how keenly those that remain are en-joyed ! Stratford Mop, like S. Giles' fair at Oxford, is fed from all the neighbouring villages and by excursion trains from distant towns. A description in journalese, of the scene on October 13, 1909, is worth preserving :—

" Stratford-on-Avon rose to the occasion in gallant style, and for a few hours the old-world town ran riot with frolic in which young and old joined with happy disregard for age or decorum. Hiring evidently belongs to bygone days. Buxom youths with bronzed brows and comely maidens with rose-coloured cheeks no longer sport the tri-coloured streamer—that token of bond of union, the promise of twelve months' faithful service between master and servant. The seriousness of work and wages is brushed on one side, and the thoughts

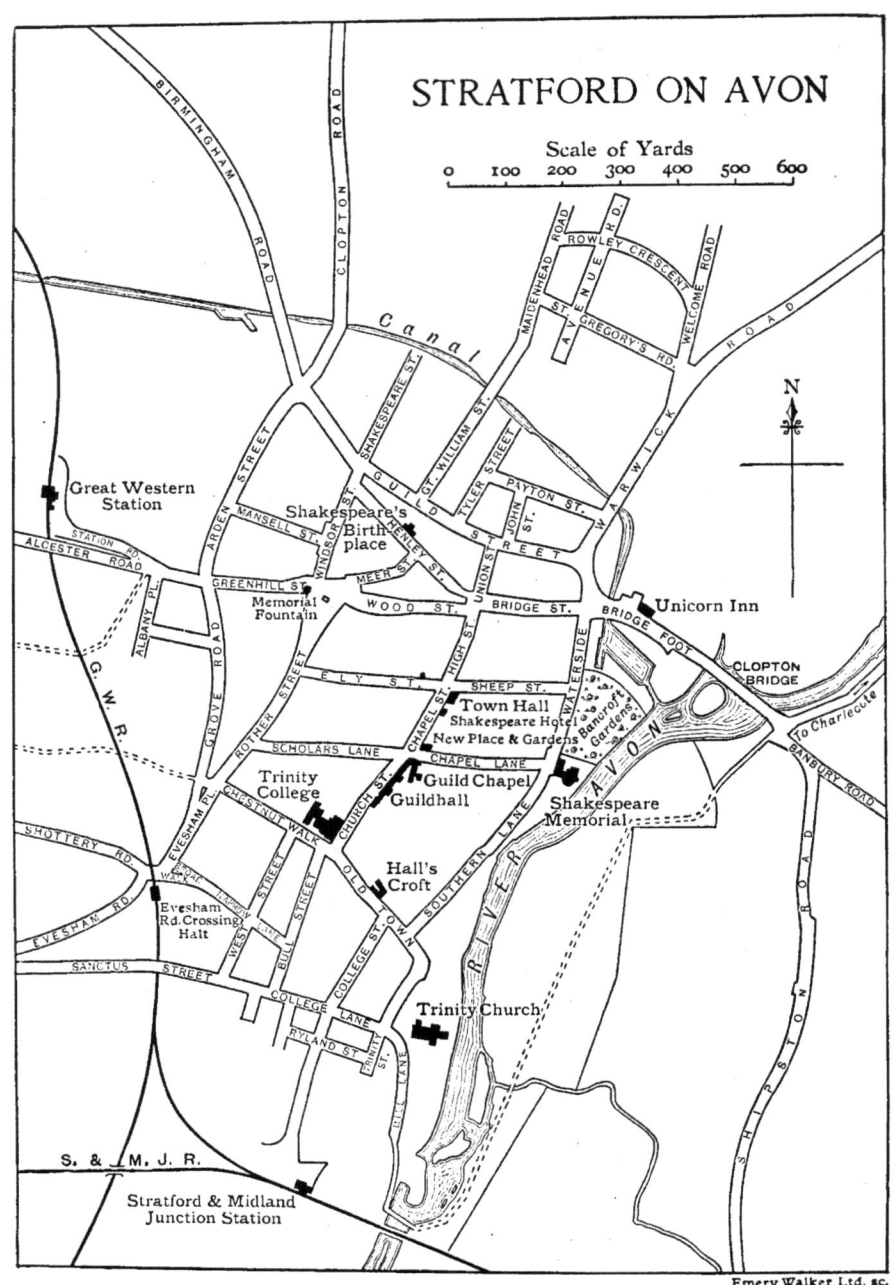

Plan of Stratford-on-Avon.

uppermost in the minds of the rural element is how to get the maximum amount of enjoyment in the minimum time.

" To assist them in carrying out this intention there is no lack of means, provided they have the wherewithal. First and foremost, there were eight prime oxen and close upon a dozen porkers to be consumed, and the work of turning the beasts, which were impaled upon great spits, before blazing wood fires, and the basting of the same by cooks in white garb, was followed with interest by the crowd.

" Then there was sightseeing. ' Cheap Jacks ' with varying supplies of Birmingham jewellery were in old haunts in the High Street, and it was astonishing the value for the money here offered. Imagine a gold watch, with two or three sovereigns into the bargain, for one sovereign ! Vendors of pirated music were here, there, and everywhere, and visitors were reminded not to forget the little ones at home, for whose delectation wonderful creations in the form of the ' Dying Duck,' or golliwog, ' all alive,' were to be had for a copper or so."

No doubt Shakespeare saw a " mop " very like this, though " Bremicham " was far inferior to Stratford in those days, and the hiring part of the fair would be a much more serious matter. It is certainly worth seeing Stratford on mop day ; but it is not a day to choose if one wants to meditate upon the scenes of the poet's life.

Such is the history—all one needs to know when one goes there—of the centuries which have made Shakespeare's town what it is to-day. How shall we begin to visit it ? No doubt the first thing to do is to see how the land lies. The chief sites or " sights " of the town may be seen on this rough plan.

Arriving, as most people do, at the Great Western station, the way into the town is straight and simple enough ; and equally simple is the way if one enters from Charlecote (p. 205) or Shipston (p. 40).

The first thing a traveller may be expected to want is an inn, though I am inclined to believe that it is almost the last thing he thinks of. Stratford is well stocked with hostelries. Across Clopton Bridge the first thing he sees on the right is the unpretentious but pleasing Unicorn, where he may feel quite modern unless he happens to occupy a large room which has actually no window, and no light at all except from a skylight. But everybody who goes to Stratford ought to remember that

The Red
Horse
Stratford
on-Avon

Washington Irving made one inn famous. Thus he wrote in
an unforgotten passage :—

" To a homeless man, who has no spot on this wide world
which he can truly call his own, there is a momentary feeling
of something like independence and territorial consequence,
when, after a weary day's travel, he kicks off his boots, thrusts
his feet into slippers and stretches himself before an inn fire.
Let the world without go as it may ; let kingdoms rise or fall, so

Washington Irving's Sceptre.

long as he has the wherewithal to pay his bill, he is, for the
time being, the very monarch of all he surveys. The arm-chair
is his throne, the poker his sceptre, and the little parlour, some
twelve feet square, his undisputed empire. It is a morsel of
certainty, snatched from the midst of the uncertainties of life ;
it is a sunny moment gleaming out kindly on a cloudy day :
and he who has advanced some way on the pilgrimage of existence knows the importance of husbanding even morsels and

moments of enjoyment. ' Shall I not take mine ease in mine
inn ? ' thought I, as I gave the fire a stir, lolled back in my
elbow-chair, and cast a complacent look about the little parlour
of the Red Horse, at Stratford-on-Avon."

In spite of this description which has made the inn one of the
famous sights of the town, it is not spoilt.   Washington Irving's

The " Red Horse " Yard.

room is kept as he described it, with the poker, guarded as a
relic.   There is still an old-world air about the Red Horse,
perhaps due to the fact that from its position in the middle of
Bridge Street it cannot be indefinitely enlarged, except at the
back where it extends to Guild Street.   It remains an eighteenth

or early nineteenth century inn, not an Elizabethan hostelry or a modern hotel.   Of such there are plenty in Stratford.   There is the Shakespeare Hotel in Chapel Street with many pleasing old features.   There is the Falcon at the corner of Scholar's Lane, looking on Chapel Street and almost exactly opposite to New Place.   If you find this house very full—it is a very pleasant one, and they will even tell you that Shakespeare visited it often (which is not at all unlikely)—you may even have the chance to be given a bedroom not far off in the restored and redecorated Tudor House, and the bedroom will be panelled entirely with old dark oak up to its fine plaster ceiling.

The Church Porch.

The town has also many smaller inns, and many good lodgings. It certainly " lays itself out " for visitors.

But now for the things we have come to visit.   These may be taken in the following order—the Church, the School and Guild chapel, New Place, the Birthplace, the old houses, the Memorial Theatre and Library, and the river.   You approach the church, either along Southern Lane, beside the river, coming from the theatre, and having a way, long known as " the wash," down to the stream, where boats are waiting for you ; or down the winding street called Old Town, which has many good houses in it. You go up an avenue of fine limes, which quite shade the way in summer, to the north porch. "This walk," said an inscription now destroyed, "was paued and pich't in ye yeare of our Lord God 1719 at the onely cost and charge of Mr. John Hunt, an alderman and a standing Justice for the Borough of Stratford and village of Old Stratford." The porch has a room above the entrance way, the top embattled, the sides buttressed. This is probably of the same date as the west door and the chancel—so now we had best make our guesses at the date of the whole building. There was a church here at the time of Domesday Book. Nothing of this early time, unless it be under ground, I think, survives. The main part of the church is of the thirteenth and fourteenth centuries. It owed much, as did the town, to the generous benefactions of the three Stratfords, John, Robert, and Ralph. As we go round it and within we may see how the centuries enriched it. The north and south transepts, with certain parts used up in the present tower, belong to the early thirteenth century. The north and south aisles, the piers of the nave, and the tower are the work of the Stratfords, and date from the last twenty years of the thirteenth century to about 1330. More than a century later Dean Balsall, the head of the Collegiate Chapter, and Dean Ralph Collingwood were benefactors who built the chancel, the clerestory, the west window, and the north porch, between 1480 and 1520. In 1800 a grim "charnel house," which stood on the north side, where Shakespeare must have seen it every time he went to church, and refreshed the abhorrence of disturbing the dead which dictated the doggerel lines on his grave, was pulled down; and the graceful spire, the feature of the church which is most characteristic, most quickly observed and longest remembered, belongs to a period not much before about 1765. It replaced a timber steeple about forty-two feet high, which was pulled down in 1763. The architect of the new spire was a Warwick man, probably Hiorns, the disciple of Sanderson Miller, a name to be honoured by all Warwickshire men. Though the church has thus had much reconstruction, it seems probable that the nave and chancel as we now have them were built after the thirteenth century design. As is not uncommon in medieval English churches, "the nave is deflected five feet from the line of the chancel."

The west dooorway is a fifteenth century insertion into the older masonry, and the door is of beautiful, and typical, Perpendicular design. The interior of the south porch has remains of two holy water basons, and a figure mutilated perhaps when Shakespeare's father was showing a lively spirit of Puritanism. The doors are fine fifteenth century work. On the left is the

The Clopton Tombs, Stratford Church.

great knocker, which it is supposed was used when a fugitive
in haste demanded sanctuary. The attribution is doubtful,
but the knocker at any rate proves that church doors were no
more often kept open before the Reformation than after.

Till late in Queen Victoria's reign the church was divided by
a huge screen on the top of which had been placed a great
organ : under this those who would stand by Shakespeare's
grave must penetrate. A picture in the church still shows
what it was like. Restorations, not always judicious, but generally necessary, have swept much away, and the whole length,
nearly two hundred feet, can be seen as soon as you stand in

Figures from the Clopton Monument, Stratford Church.

the midst of the nave. But before that, as you enter the church,
stop at the west end of the north aisle and see the old Register
which lies open at the baptism and burial of the town's great
son. " 1564. April 26. Gulielmus filius Johannis Shakspeare " : and " 1616. Ap. 25th Will Shakspeare, gent." The nave
is a wide dignified space with six-sided fourteenth century pillars,
a clerestory of a century later, the windows so large that they
seem to be continuous. The pulpit was Sir Theodore Martin's
memorial to his wife Helen Faucit, the greatest actress of the
Macready period, who acted on the first night of the opening
of the Memorial Theatre in 1879.

The Clopton chapel occupies the east end of the north aisle ; you go up three steps to it and enter a beautifully decorated "pew." It was formerly the Lady Chapel ; and besides its other interest, it is to be specially regarded because it was the pew in which the owners of New Place sat, and thus Shakespeare and his descendants occupied it. There is the altar tomb of Sir Hugh Clopton, without effigy or inscription, but recognisable as his by the arms on the arch above it. It is probable that this was prepared by him in his lifetime, for he left directions that he should be buried at Stratford if he died there ; but he died in London and was buried in

Mrs. Amy Smith, from a Tablet in the Clopton Chapel.

S. Margaret's, Lothbury. Thus the inscription was never written. On the north wall is the fine tomb of William Clopton and Anne his wife, 1592 and 1596, in armour and in a rich robe. Above are their children—" The Right Honorable Joyce, Countess of Totnes, their Eldest Daughter, caused this their Monument to be repaired and beautified anno 1630 "—and another inscription recording the restoration by Sir John Clopton in 1714. To the west of this is Sir John Clopton's own monument, 1719, and his wife, daughter of Sir Edward Walker (who built the new part of the house) 1692. Sir Edward Walker has also his monument here—and then at the east is the gorgeous tomb of George Carew Earl of Totnes and Baron of Clopton, with Joyce his wife—their effigies in painted alabaster under an arch supported by Corinthian columns with all sorts of emblems of war and heraldry.   The inscriptions record the Earl's son, Sir Thomas Stafford, the Earl and the Countess.   This is a typical rich Jacobean monument.   At the right, southwards, is a little figure of a woman kneeling in prayer, who is Mrs. Amy Smith, 1626, for forty years waiting gentlewoman to the Countess.   Above, a tablet to Thomas Clopton (1643) and his wife Eglentine (1642).   The Latin inscription for Sir Edward Walker, Garter King at Arms, was written by Dugdale.   The whole chapel was very carefully and skilfully restored, with a reproduction of the old colouring, by Sir Arthur Hodgson in 1892.   A window commemorates him, in the south aisle, with scenes in the life of S. George.   In the Clopton Chapel is a window which he himself placed in memory of his wife in 1902, who died in May, two months after they had celebrated their " diamond " wedding. He died on Christmas Eve of the same year.

The south aisle was entirely rebuilt in 1332 by John Stratford, then Bishop of Winchester.   It ends, like the north aisle, in a chapel dedicated to S. Thomas of Canterbury.   Here is the fifteenth century font in which Shakespeare must have been baptized.   We now come to the tower, standing on four simple early thirteenth century arches.   This is the earliest part of the church.   The north transept is now shut off by the fifteenth century rood-screen and used as a vestry.   The south transept has the American Memorial Window, unveiled by the Honourable Thomas Bayard, the American Ambassador, on Shakespeare's birthday in 1896.   It bears the inscription :   " The gift of America to Shakespeare's Church," and conspicuous in it are the figures of Charles I. and Archbishop Laud.

On the west wall is the tomb of Richard Hill, " thrice bailiff of this borough," who died in 1593, and is glorified by an inscription in Hebrew, Greek, Latin, and English.   There is a beautiful brass chandelier here, given in 1720.   But all the interest of the rest of the church pales before that of the chancel.   It was rebuilt by Dean Balsall (1465–1491), and is a beautiful piece of late Perpendicular work. The glass of that date, given by Sir Hugh Clopton, was centuries ago broken and dispersed ; fragments of it are now in the Clopton chapel.   The windows are very large, the glass, to the memory, some of it, of Halliwell Phillips, not unpleasing; and the whole appearance of the choir with its fine stalls (the screen is hardly worthy of them) is very rich. The rails are, unfortunately, modern brass.

The altar has for its mensa a stone slab which was found in the south transept eight years ago. It has still three, of the usual five, crosses visible, and it is believed to be that erected, in 1332, by John Stratford, Archbishop of Canterbury, and dedicated to his predecessor S. Thomas.

To the north is the altar tomb of Dean Balsall. Eastwards are the tombs of Richard and Judith Combe, with a touching inscription; and on the east wall the recumbent figure of John Combe, 1614 (*see* p. 221). (*see* p. 221) Westwards of this is the bust of

Effigy of John Combe

Shakespeare. It is one of the two portraits (the other being the Droeshout engraving in the First Folio) which were certainly almost contemporary. It was the work of Gerard Johnson (or Janssen), a Dutch sculptor who lived in Southwark, and was put up before 1623. The colours are believed to reproduce the original, but the bust was whitewashed by Malone's orders in 1793, a crime not redressed till 1861. The side view shows the face as refined, intellectual, humorous; the full face is almost as heavy as the Droeshout prints.

In front, within the altar rails, are the graves of William Shakespeare, his wife Anne Hathaway, his daughter Susannah Hall, and her husband, and their son-in-law Thomas Nash. They had the right to lie there, as Shakespeare had bought a

portion of the tithes of the parish and was thus part-rector.   The
graves lie thus :—

Anne Shakespeare	William Shakespeare (*Name not inscribed.*)	Thomas Nashe	John Hall	Susannah Hall	Francis Watts	Anne Watts
1623	1616	1647	1635	1649	1691	1704

Two inscriptions give the record of the poet's fame.   On the
bust are the words :—

> " Judicio Pylium, Genio Socratem, Arte Maronem
> Terra tegit, populus mœret, Olympus habet."

> " Stay passenger, why goest thou by so fast,
> Read, if thou canst, whom envious death hast plast,
> Within this monument ; Shakespeare, with whome
> Quick nature dide; whose name doth deck this tomb,
> Far more than cost, sith all that he hath writt,
> Leaves living art, but page to serve his witt."
> Obiit anno Domini, 1616.   Ætatis, 53, die 23 Ap.

On the stone covering the grave are the famous lines :—

> " Good friend for Jesus' sake forbeare
> To digg the dust enclosed heare,
> Blest be ye man yt spares thes stones.
> And curst be he yt moves my bones."

The earliest attribution of this doggerel to Shakespeare (though
he was quite capable of it, as a warning to gravediggers) is found
in a book of 1777, which says that the guide told the author that
the poet was so affected by the charnel-house " that he wrote
the epitaph for himself to prevent his bones being thrown into
it."   And indeed it may well be true.   The other inscriptions,
too, are worth remembering, so I set them down :—

This is Shakespeare's wife, who lies north of his grave : " Heere
lyeth interred the body of Anne, wife of Mr. William Shakespeare,
who depted this life the 6 day of Avg: 1623 being of the age
of 67 yeares.

> " Vbera, tu mater, lac vitamq. dedisti.
> Vae mihi : pro tanto munere saxa dabo
> Quam mallem amoveat lapidem, Angel' ore'
> Exeat Christi Corpus imago tua
> Sed nihil vota valent, venias cito Christe, resurget
> Clausa licet tumulo mater, et astra petet."

The Shakespeare Monument.

On the south of Shakespeare's grave is that of his grandson by marriage :—
" Heere resteth ye body of Thomas Nashe Esq. he mar Elizabeth, the davg. and beire of John Halle, gent.   He died Aprill 4.A. 1647 aged 53.

> " Fata manent omnes, hunc non virtute carentem
> Vt neque divitiis, abstulit atra dies ;—
> Abstulit ; at referet lux ultima ; siste viator,
> Si peritura paras, per male parta peris."

Then comes Dr. Hall, a famous man in his time indeed, a physician of no mean ability, and a Puritan with the best of them.   He it was, no doubt, who took the Puritan preacher to New Place in 1614 when he was given " one quart of sack and one quart of claret wine."   He doctored all the great folk of the county, and also " Mr. Drayton an excellent poet."   The epitaph very fitly eulogises his medical skill.   It may well be that he had many manuscripts of his father-in-law.   What became of them ?
" Heere lyeth ye body of John Hall, Gent: he marr: Svsanna, ye davghter and coheire of Will. Shakespeare, Gent.   Hee deceased Nover 25 Ao. 1635 aged 60.

> " Hallius hic situs est medica celeberrimus arte,
> Expectans regni gaudia laeta Dei.
> Dignus erat meritis qui Nestora vinceret annis.
> In terris omnes sed rapit aequa dies ;
> Ne tumuloque desit adest fidissima conjux,
> Et vitae comitem nunc quoq. ; mortis habet."

Next to Dr. John Hall lies his wife ; but not undisturbed. Richard Watts bought the tithes some time after her death, and claimed to be buried in the chancel.   He was placed in her grave, and her epitaph was erased and his substituted.   In 1844 this epitaph was erased and the old inscription put back " by lowering the surface of the stone and recutting the letters."   Thus it runs :—
" Heere lyeth ye body of Svsanna, wife to John Hall Gent: ye davghter of William Shakespeare Gent.   She deceased ye 11th of July, Ao 1649 aged 66.

> " Witty above her sexe, but that's not all,
> Wise to Salvation was good Mistris Hall,
> Something of Shakespeare was in that, but this
> Wholy of him with whom she's now in blisse.

> Then, Passenger, ha'st ne're a teare,
> To weep with her that wept with all?
> That wept yet set herself to chere
> Them up with comforts cordiall.
> Her love shall live her mercy spread
> When thou hast ne're a teare to shed."

Next are the other members of the Watts family who retained their inscriptions undisturbed.

And now we may leave the church. Reverential care has made it a worthy house of God ; and those who visit it for remembrance of him who is buried there will not forget to worship as well as to dream of the past. The history, by those who would know more, may be read in " Shakespeare's Church," by the Rev. J. Harvey Bloom (1902). We pass now to the school and guild chapel.

The Guild Chapel, the successor of one built after licence granted to Robert Stratford, is next to the church, the most interesting building in the town from the purely archæological point of view. Of the ancient chapel nothing remains. What we see is much later. The main part is that which Sir Hugh Clopton " restored " in 1492, the tower, the porch (facing New Place), and the nave. The chancel is a century or more earlier. Leland calls it " a right goodly chapell," and so it is still, though little of its decoration remains. Once it had a splendid series of frescoes ; they were destroyed (at least I suppose the white-wash over them destroyed them) little more than a hundred years ago. A reproduction of them was made before they perished, but one need not speak of it now, as nothing can be seen in the chapel. What does remain, however, is a tablet to the memory of Sir Hugh Clopton in which he is called a " charitable Gent," and compared to the centurion who built the Jews a Synagogue. The tower is fine, and the porch is finer. Next to the chapel, southwards, is the Guild Hall, the ground floor of a building which is now used as the Grammar School. It has fine oak beams in the roof, and wood and plaster decorations, and there are some remains, carefully preserved, of a fresco of the Crucifixion. Here the Corporation sat for centuries. But the chief interest of the hall is that in it plays were acted by travelling companies in the sixteenth century; and here no doubt Shakespeare himself saw " Henry VI," in its original form, a play which he rewrote

The Guild Chapel Stratford.

and in which he very probably acted the king. His father was high bailiff when the players came in 1569. The Earl of Leicester's company acted here in 1587, and it has been thought probable that Shakespeare joined them as an actor there, going over to Lord Strange's company in 1588. Richard Bradshaw's company, about the validity of whose licence there was question, played there in 1631 or 1633 (and also at Charlecote). A few years ago old mystery plays were acted again in this hall, and remarkably indeed did they recall the old atmosphere. One could even fancy the schoolboys struggling for seats, and the weary apprentice asleep outside, concerning whom it is recorded that a quarrel arose (though not here) because one who saw the slumberer " dyd turn upon the too upon the belly of the said prentice." If the hall has certain claim to be Shakespearean, little less certainly has the big schoolroom above, for here the boys of Stratford have been taught for centuries, learning, no doubt, most of them, little Latin and less Greek, and profiting nothing in the world at their books, as Master Page thought of his son William. The schoolmastership in Shakespeare's day was something of a prize, it seems ; and one of the schoolmasters, like enough, is preserved for us for ever, under the *nom-de-théâtre* of Sir Hugh Evans. This was Thomas Jenkins, who became master in 1577, and was, I am inclined to think, of S. John's College in Oxford, a place well known to Shakespeare, through his friend Davenant of the Crown Inn in that city, who gave books to the college.

The big school, the upper room still used, is a delightful place, with its large windows and its huge oak beams. Out of it is what was once the Council room, with an ancient oak table, beams and plaster, two York and Lancaster roses on the walls, and such like remembrances of past days. The Armoury, too, must not be forgotten. It is at right angles to the Guild Hall. " It has some fine Jacobean panelling, and over the fireplace there is a large painting of the arms of the Kings of England, which, as we learn from the town records, dates from 1660, and points to the public rejoicing at the restoration of the Stuarts,". says Mr. Richards in his guide to the school. There was the good black and white schoolmaster's house across the court, or small playground. Westwards of the school is a row of almshouses, which survive from the times of the Guild.

New Place was, of course, quite close to the school, and from

Grammar School
& Guild Chapel
Stratford-on-Avon

E·H·NEW

W&S

his garden Shakespeare could see the boys with their satchels and shining morning faces, just as one may see them now, creeping to school, or running home with shouts of glee. Nothing now remains but the foundations of the house. It stood from 1483—when it was built by Sir Hugh Clopton, rebuilt by Sir John Clopton in 1702—till 1759, when it was demolished by the Rev. Francis Gastrell, Vicar of Frodsham, Cheshire, who had bought it three years before. · This testy personage was vexed by continual requests to see the house of Shakespeare, and with equal vandalism he cut down a fine mulberry tree which the poet was said to have planted. A visitor to Stratford in 1760 gives, I think, our earliest record of this— in the following words :—

" There stood here till lately the house in which Shakespeare lived, and a mulberry-tree of his planting ; the house was large, strong, and handsome ; the tree so large that it would shade the grass-plot in your garden, which I think is more than twenty yards square, and supply the whole town with mulberries every year. As the curiosity of this house and tree brought much fame, and more company and profit, to the town, a certain man, on some disgust, has pulled the house down, so as not to leave one stone upon another, and cut down the tree, and piled it as a stack of firewood, to the great vexation, loss, and disappointment of the inhabitants ; however, an honest silversmith bought the whole stack of wood, and makes many odd things of this wood for the curious, some of which I hope to bring with me to town."

New Place, or the site and foundation of it, must certainly be examined by every visitor to Stratford.

Between 1597 and his death, Shakespeare had been its owner. There he died on April 23, 1616. He left it to his daughter, Susanna Hall, who lived there till 1649, succeeded by her daughter who lived till 1670. Only the foundations of this house are now visible, covered over by wire, in the space at the corner of Church Street and Chapel Lane. The great garden, at the back of this site, is now a public garden, and in it, on the central lawn, is a mulberry descended from the poet's own tree.

If Shakespeare's house is destroyed that of his grandson, Thomas Nash, survives. It has been completely altered. Awhile ago it was an eighteenth century house to look at, within and without, but a thorough " restoration " has given it something of the appearance it had in Shakespeare's day.

Following the notice of the Birthday trust, on which it is difficult to improve, one may observe that the house, "portions of which are four hundred years old, became in the early years of the seventeenth century the property of Mr. Thomas Nash, who was born in this town on 20th June, 1593, and was married in the Parish Church on 22nd April, 1626, to Elizabeth Hall, Shakespeare's only granddaughter and last surviving descendant. Nash died on 4th April 1647, and was buried in the Chancel of the Parish Church next day." He " left this house to his wife for life ; at her death in 1670 it passed to his cousin Edward Nash.

" In the course of the next two centuries the house was tenanted by a succession of private owners, and underwent from time to time much structural change and disfigurement. In 1862 it was purchased for the nation as part of the New Place estate, the whole of which was conveyed in 1891 to the Trustees and Guardians of Shakespeare's Birthplace. In 1912, the Trustees re-adapted the house to public uses. Surviving features of the sixteenth century were freed of modern accretions and the fabric was restored in all essentials to its early condition." The newness it bears now will no doubt soon wear off. The transformation is certainly wonderful to those who remember it only a few years ago. It now contains a very interesting collection of "relics of the Poet's demolished Residence, of Garrick and of the Shakespeare Jubilee of 1769, his letter to the Corporation when he was given the freedom of the town, and some boxes made from the mulberry tree. There are also a number of Roman coins found in the neighbourhood, from Mark Antony (B.C. 33) to Arcadius (A.D. 408), and of English silver coins, and of local tradesmen's tokens of the 17th century." Among the odd objects you must please observe a munkle-swingle, and then wonder what in the world it was, or is. Why, it is a watchman's whip with two heavy balls on it, of course. " Round the walls of the front room on the ground floor hang carefully executed copies of authentic contemporary portraits of personal friends of Shakespeare, several of whom are known to have visited him at New Place. They include Shakespeare's fellow actors—Richard Burbage, Nathaniel Field, and John Lowin—the poet Michael Drayton (a native of Warwickshire), and the dramatist Ben Jonson. The "Tudor" rooms on the first floor preserve precisely their original dimensions. In these rooms are exhibited a series of coloured engravings of the medieval frescoes on the walls of the Guild Chapel, and a small collection of paintings in oil by Edward Grubb" (*see* p. 185). I have not spoken of these frescoes because they no longer exist; but the reproductions are well worth study, as illustrating the popular religion in which Shakespeare's contemporaries had been brought up.

From New Place, where Shakespeare certainly died, it is not far to Henley Street (whether you go along the succession of streets which terminate at the top of Bridge Street, past the clock, and bending to the left, or approach the house at the back, from Guild Street, where a charming view is obtained across the old garden planted with Shakespearean flowers) and the house where he was very probably born. It may be well to remember that, as a pilgrimage place, what is now called the Birthplace has a much shorter record than the church and New Place. Apparently not till after 1760 was this double house in Henley Street regarded, or made famous, as that in which Shakespeare was born. Even the sexton who showed the church to Washington Irving, years after that, insinuated a doubt as to the house; and Halliwell-Phillips tells that "a house near the river, called the Brook House, now pulled down, was some years since asserted to have been the birthplace of Shakespeare." But John Shakespeare had property in Henley Street, for certain, as early as 1552, when he was fined for having a dungheap in front of his house. In 1556 he bought a freehold house in the street; in 1575 he bought the house now called the Birthplace. No doubt the earlier purchase was that house which adjoins the Birthplace. They are to all intents one house; and the poet's father may well have been the tenant of one before he purchased it and after he bought the other. William Shakespeare was born in April, 1564. From these facts one may draw what conclusion one can. There is no doubt what conclusions the public, 'those who purchased the house, by public subscription, in 1847, as a National Memorial, and the Shakespeare Birthplace Trust to-day, have drawn. Indeed, though Sir Sidney Lee, their chairman, is content with the statement that " the fact of its long occupancy by the poet's collateral descendants accounts for the identification of the

western rather than the eastern tenement with his birthplace, the
trustees officially issue their statement of fact in these words:

"The detached building in Henley Street, known as Shakespeare's birthplace, is formed of two houses communicating with

each other.   Of these houses, that to the west, which visitors
enter first, is the house in which Shakespeare was born and where
he spent his childhood.   The visitor passes immediately on entry
into the kitchen or living room of the residence of Shakespeare's
parents.   In the large room on the upper floor Shakespeare was
born on 23rd April, 1564."   I could not be so precise myself
but at least, it is certain that Shakespeare's father lived in the
house and that at his death it became the poet's own.   He left
it to his elder daughter, Mrs. Hall, and after her to his only grand-

Shakespeare's Birthplace.

daughter, who, when she died in 1670, as Lady Barnard, bequeathed the property to her cousin, Thomas Hart, who was the
grandson of the poet's sister, Joan Hart.   Joan, it is thought,
had lived there all her life, from 1569 to 1646.   Early in the
seventeenth century the eastern part of the house was let separately as an inn, called at first " The Maidenhead," and afterwards " The Swan and Maidenhead."   The western part was
lived in by the Harts down to 1806.   During the eighteenth
century it was used as a butcher's shop.   When Nathaniel

Hawthorne saw it, there was still trace of the base uses to which it had come. Both houses were then bought by Thomas Court, whose widow's death in 1847 caused them to be sold by auction, when they were bought for the nation. Since then they have been public property, and are held by trustees, with New Place and Anne Hathaway's cottage, under powers conferred by Act of Parliament when the Trust was incorporated in 1891. The two cottages at the eastern boundary of the Birthplace garden, which belonged to the Horneby family in Shakespeare's time, were given by Mr. Andrew Carnegie in 1903, and are now the offices of the Trust, where the assiduous and learned librarian, Mr. Wellstood (successor of the long famous and devoted servant of all Shakespeareans, Mr. Richard Savage) may be consulted, and the distinguished forms of the Trustees in their meetings sometimes be dimly descried.

The front of the house has undergone many changes. It were, perhaps, both tedious and cruel to particularise them. Suffice it to say that attempts at " restoration " were made in 1857 and the next year, and finally, by easy stages, the house assumed the very decent and comely, and comfortably aged, appearance which it bears to-day.

You enter into the eastern part of the house, a large room, with open fire-place, and this is supposed to be the " living-room " of the Shakespeare family. Within is the kitchen, a rather higher room, which is lighted by one small window at the right. Opposite to this is the fire-place, and near it a hatch to the bacon-cupboard. Behind are the pantry and wash-house, and, underneath, a cellar, not too large. Once this back part used to be shown as the room in which the poet was born ; but now a tradition has grown up which, we see, the trustees sanction, that the true birth-room is that at the front on the first floor. Of this Washington Irving wrote :—

> " Of mighty Shakespeare's birth the room we see ;
>   That where he died in vain to find we try,
> Useless the search, for all immortal he,
>   And those who are immortal never die."

The room was no doubt the " best bedroom." It has a fire-place, and good windows looking on to the street. Contemporary furniture—two carved oak coffers which were sold from this room in 1847—and an oak desk-box from the Grammar School have been placed here : some call it with pleasant faith the .

desk at which Shakespeare wrote when he was at school. The ceiling, the walls, the windows, are covered with names of visitors, highly distinguished persons some of them—I regret to say that Walter Scott is among the number—who ought to have known better than perpetrate such an offence. There is an amusing story about this. A virago of a caretaker was once dismissed from her post; she spent her last night in white-washing the walls, thinking to destroy these records of interest, but she forgot to size her work and it was easily removed. Was this the person whom Washington Irving saw and immortalised?

In Shakespeare's House.

" A garrulous old lady," Irving wrote, " in a frosty red face, lighted up by a cold blue anxious eye, and garnished with artificial locks of flaxen hair, curling from under an exceedingly dirty cap. She was peculiarly assiduous," he continued, " in exhibiting the relics with which this, like all other celebrated shrines, abounds. There was the shattered stock of the very matchlock with which Shakespeare shot the deer on his poaching exploits. There, too, was his tobacco-box, which proves that he was a rival smoker to Sir Walter Raleigh ; the sword also with

O 2

which he played Hamlet ; and the identical lantern with which Friar Laurence discovered Romeo and Juliet at the tomb ! There was an ample supply also of Shakespeare's mulberry tree, which seems to have as extraordinary powers of self-multiplication as the wood of the true Cross."

Of these, or other relics—for the doubtful articles are removed to New Place or abolished altogether—let us speak later on. Meanwhile, look at the room at the back of the house, formerly two small rooms. It has what is called the Stratford portrait. This much resembles the bust in the church, but its history is not a long one. It was given by Mr. William Oakes Hunt in 1864, whose grandfather had bought it at a Clopton sale. Investigation of the picture revealed that a beard was an addition, and its removal brought the picture to its present, and very pleasing, aspect. There is an attic above, but nothing therein. None of the furniture of the house is actually original, with a possible exception noted above. We must do our best with our imagination to recall the table-boards, the joint stools, the truckle beds, the coffers, the spinning-wheel, the pails and pots, the wooden and leather bottles, the pot-hooks, gridiron, frying-pan, candlesticks, kneading-troughs, which appear in the list now preserved here of Richard Baker's possessions (*circa* 1595). It is but a shell that we see ; yet the links with Shakespeare's boyhood are certain.

The eastern portion of the house is now a museum. Each floor has two rooms, the wall between them being destroyed to give ease of access. Much that one sees is interesting only through somewhat remote connection with Shakespeare or his time. There is an excellent and detailed catalogue of all that is to be seen, printed for the trustees, and to be bought in the house. Among the objects worth examining are the old sign of the " Falcon " at Bidford (*see* p. 241), the pocket dial-ring (" a dial from his poke "), the Garrick Jubilee medals, the old corporation maces, the very doubtful " sword of Shakespeare," and his finger ring, " W. S." You will read in the very interesting story of these in the catalogue how this last was picked up by a labourer's wife on the ground in the " mill-close " hard by the churchyard. It was quite black when found, but when the metal was " proved " in aquafortis it resumed its natural colour. The purchaser of the ring in 1810 was Mr. Robert Bell Wheler (1785–1857), a keen hunter of Shakespearean relics, to whom the town owes much. He showed it to Malone, and noted that he " had nothing to

allege against the probability of any conjecture as to its owner."
Wheeler, from the fact that no seal was attached to Shakespeare's
will and that the words "and seal" were crossed out of the
manuscript, concluded that he had lost his seal.

There are more certainly authentic relics than this in the room.
There is a deed of sale of two tenements in Henley Street, 1575,
witnessed by John Shakespeare, a conveyance of land in Shottery
to Anne Hathaway's brother, the will of Lady Barnard, the
begging letter of Richard Quiney to the poet, a conveyance by
his father and mother of land at Snitterfield; a signature of his
daughter (one, alas! but "her mark," Judith, it seems, could not
or would not, write), a number of tradesmen's tokens contemporary with him. The upper rooms contain a number of very
interesting pictures, engravings, books, and all sorts of objects
illustrating the life and times of him who made Stratford's fame.
Many of the original editions of his works, including the four
folios, are in the lower room.   There is also the "Ely House
portrait," which belonged to Bishop Turton of Ely (who only
died in 1864). The best that can be said for this is that it is a good
picture, which seems to have been modelled, perhaps in the seventeenth century, on the Droeshout engraving. There are many
interesting objects in these rooms, and there has long been a succession of kind and cultivated persons to direct attention to them.
You may well spend a couple of hours in this Elizabethan company.

Then you will beg leave, if you are wise, to walk in the trimly
kept garden. You will go out by that old garden door with its
two oak pillars with brackets carved with a staff and lily, and
three crowned heads, which some think may have represented
the Magi. It came from a house near the churchyard now pulled
down. Along the broad path you walk, past the base of the old
market cross, and between trees and flowers which are named
in the poet's works. The garden is not too spruce, and yet it
is tidy. It is not too full, and yet it is well covered. It is not
too public, and yet you may get into it for the begging. You
can hardly fancy Shakespeare the boy playing in it, yet you
may certainly see his ghost smiling kindly at this fragrant
memorial of him.

And so out again into the street. Whatever its authentic
history there is nothing in Stratford quite like the Birthplace. It
has at least the "aura" of many centuries of devotion. It
stands alone among the Stratford houses.

Now let us see houses of inferior interest but perhaps greater beauty. Stratford has not a few. Along the street which is called by three names in the course of its length—Church Street, Chapel Street, High Street—you see many interesting houses. Coming from the south you pass at your right several quaint little shops, at your left a pretty late seventeenth century house called Mason's Croft; at your right again, the Grammar school and Guild Chapel at the corner of Chapel Lane ; then opposite, and at the beginning of Chapel Street, New Place ; opposite to that again, the Falcon Inn ; further up on the right the Shakespeare Inn, with its picturesque five gables ; then the Town Hall ; and opposite to it, at the corner of High Street and Ely Street, the pretty half-timber dwelling not too elaborately restored, now called Tudor House. This last is by no means the least attractive of the old Stratford houses. It has a history, too, as the house of John Hannys in 1459–60, of Roger Paget in 1482, then the property of the Cloptons, let at the end of the sixteenth century to one John Ballamy, and emerging again early in the seventeenth as the property of Mr. John Woolmer, who is commemorated in the nave of the parish church. He died in 1710, aged 85, having been •thrice mayor. His kindred did much for Stratford. Two especially deserve remembrance, the one because she gave the fine brass chandelier to the church (*see* p. 180), the other because she is thus commemorated on her tomb. (The latter's date is 1704.)

> " Mirrour of curtesie adieu !
> 'Till the last trump, thy Life renew ;
> Belov'd by all ;—of all bewail'd;—
> O that our teares might have thee bail'd."

The two ladies seem to have been the second and first wives of Joseph Woolmer. The other interesting houses are not very many, but they include the house of Julius Shaw, next to Nash's house, where all that is old is within, timber chiefly ; Thomas Hathaway's two doors further on, Dr. Hall's house with its three gables, in the " Old Town," near the church, where there are several panelled rooms and a fine Jacobean staircase—the door is often open, says my experience, and one sees it ; and Harvard House further down High Street, near Ely Street, the most elaborate of all the houses, with its highly carved barge boards and ornamental corbels, all happily unrestored, where Thomas Rogers lived, whose daughter Catherine married John

Harvard of Southwark, and was the mother of John Harvard, the pious founder of a college across the Atlantic, many indeed of whose sons have come as pilgrims to this town. Further on, at the corner of Bridge Street and High Street, is the house, very greatly transformed indeed and with an entirely new front, in which Judith Shakespeare, the poet's daughter, lived from 1616 to 1652. It was the house of her husband Thomas Quiney, a vintner. You may still see the great cellar where he kept his wine, and the slopes down which the casks were sent. He was for a while successful, being Chamberlain of the town in 1621, but eventually he fell on evil days, " suffering townsmen to tippell in his house," and departed to London. His father's letter, seeking to borrow money from Shakespeare, is in the Birthplace.

This brief list does not exhaust the good private houses; nor does it include the many modern shams. Among public buildings the Town Hall naturally takes the chief place. It is at the corner of Sheep Street and Chapel Street, and Mr. Ribton Turner's excellent guide book calls it, most unkindly, "a commonplace building of the Tuscan order." It is really a very pleasant place, as it ought to be, having been built in 1768. Outside it is the Shakespeare statue, which Garrick gave after the Jubilee to the Corporation. There is a large ballroom on the first floor, which has Gainsborough's famous portrait of Garrick with the bust of Shakespeare. Garrick, it must be remembered, was made a freeman of Stratford, as was, a few years ago, Mr. Benson. In the same room is a good Romney of the third Duke of Dorset, who was High Steward of Stratford at the time of the Jubilee. The picture in the mayor's parlour of Mrs. Hitchman is to be noticed, because it is the work of one of those local artists of the eighteenth century whose work is now beginning to be discovered to be far from negligible, Edward Grubb (1740–1816), who was also a monumental sculptor, as the parish church witnesses..

From the Town Hall it is not much more than a good stone's throw to the Memorial Theatre and Library. This has, I always think, been very unjustly decried. It is a curious and quite Tudor-looking erection of red brick, with a tower not unlike the old engravings one sees of Elizabethan theatres. It dates from Mr. Charles Flower's generous gift of a site and a sum of money in 1872. The theatre was finished and opened on April 23, 1879, when Helen Faucit, the last of the great actresses of the old style, played Beatrice, with a deliberation and at the same time a fire which were a revelation to those of us who were present. America was represented too : Miss Kate Field read the dedicatory prologue. And Ireland sent Barry Sullivan, who played Benedick with rather elephantine spirit that night, and Hamlet the next with more than funereal

The Memorial Theatre, Stratford-on-Avon.

state. These were the days before Henry Irving and Ellen Terry had showed how Hamlet and Beatrice were people of our own as well as of all time, or, I should say, before the lesson had sunk into the hearts of actors and audiences. Since then Ellen Terry has made the sorrows of Queen Katherine live again for us on this Stratford stage, and represented that exquisite approach of death in the garden at Kimbolton, where at the sound of sweet music " killing care and grief of heart fall asleep, or, hearing, die." And Mr. Benson, with his company of earnest students, fired by his own passionate enthusiasm, has made himself a very Stratford man, and all Englishmen his debtors, by the revivals he has given in this theatre, of almost every play that Shakespeare wrote. Stratford has made him a freeman, as she made Garrick; and he is almost worshipped by Stratfordians. The service he has rendered cannot be exaggerated. He has made Shakespeare to live again as a dramatist who can appeal not only to the cultivated students of great cities, but to the country folk of his own shire ; he is as much alive to-day, one feels when one sees a Stratford audience, as he was when his first play was acted, perhaps in his own town. Here in the last twenty years we have seen even " Troilus and Cressida " and " Pericles " (though sadly distorted, not by Mr. Benson), and revelled in the perennial charm of " Love's Labour's Lost " ; the tragedies have sounded their solemn note, the comedies tinkled with fresh laughter, and the long line of histories made their great patriotic appeal. Truly a great achievement. The memory of Frank Benson will ever be cherished in Stratford, with that of the great Garrick, at the feet of their master himself.

But in this theatre there will always abide that happy memory of its first opening, as Lady Martin recorded it in her charming study of Beatrice which she wrote as a letter to Mr. Ruskin six years later. The happy personal note is ended by a word of timely warning which those who have acted in this theatre have always borne in mind :—

" It was at Stratford-upon-Avon, on the opening, on 23rd of April, 1879 (Shakespeare's birthday), of the Shakespeare Memorial Theatre. I had watched with much interest the completion of this most appropriate tribute to the memory of our supreme poet. The local enthusiasm, which would not rest until it had placed upon the banks of his native stream a building in which his best plays might be from time to time presented, commanded my warm sympathy. It is a beautiful building, and when, standing beside it, I looked upon the church wherein all that was mortal of the poet is laid, and, on the other hand, my eyes rested on the site of New Place, where he died, a feeling more earnest, more reverential, came over me than I have experienced even in Westminster Abbey, in Santa Croce, or in any other resting-place of the mighty dead. It was a deep delight to me to be the first to interpret on that spot one of my great master's brightest creations. Everything conspired to make the occasion happy. From every side of Shakespeare's county, from London, from remote provinces, came people to witness that performance. The characters were well supported, and the fact that we were acting in Shakespeare's birthplace, and to inaugurate his memorial theatre, seemed to inspire us all. I found my own delight doubled by the sensitive sympathy of my audience. Every turn of playful humour, every flash of wit, every burst of strong feeling told, and it is a great pleasure to me to think, that on that spot, and on that occasion, I made my last essay to present a living portraiture of the Lady Beatrice. The success of this performance was aided by the very judicious care which had been bestowed upon all the accessories of the scene. The stage, being of moderate size, admitted of no elaborate display. But the scenes were appropriate and well painted, the dresses were well chosen, and the general effect was harmonious—satisfying the eye, without distracting the spectator's mind from the dialogue and the play of character. It was thus possible for the actors to engage the close attention of the audience, and to keep it. This consideration seems to me now to be too frequently overlooked."

It is a charming theatre indeed, and the library adjoining it is a very good one. So is the picture gallery, with its delightful collection of theatrical portraits. What a comfort, some must feel, to get away from the solemn memorials in the rest of the town which seem sometimes to try to make you believe that Shakespeare was a University Professor, and find yourself in surroundings which remind you that he was the greatest representative that ever lived of a continuous and ever youthful art.

Whatever Shakespeare might say about the men of letters who write his life, the pathologists who dissect his character, or the pedants who fight about the details of his sonnets, there can be no doubt at all that he would be at home among those who, in each generation since his own, have bodied forth his characters to the people. Ada Rehan and Ellen Terry, and the host of men and women who have spoken his lines on the stage, which is the memorial he would have loved best, need not doubt that he would have lingered in the picture gallery which shows how they looked as they imagined his characters. As to

The Church, Stratford-on-Avon.

the picture of himself, given in 1895, it is interesting in relation to the Droeshout portrait, but Sir J. C. Robinson, in 1898, conclusively, as I cannot but think, showed it to be a forgery.

There is a memorial outside, too, which one is sure that Shakespeare would have tarried to look upon. It is the really fine monument designed by Lord Ronald Gower, in the garden to the south of the theatre, where the poet sits thinking, and below him are the vivid figures of Henry V. and Hamlet, Lady Macbeth and Falstaff. The memorial stands in the pleasant Bancroft garden, whose name seems to be an old one, and means the croft on the bank. It was here that the chief performances of Garrick's jubilee took place. Now you can sit here quietly and think, or take—it really can be forgiven—the too insistent steamer and go up and down the river for a while, or, better still, get a little boat and row up under Clopton Bridge past Tiddington, for a swim, or, in sight of the Welcombe Hills, to Hatton rock or Alveston mill, even to Charlecote. In a few minutes you can be away from all the noise and bustle of tourists ; you can lie down under shadow of the bank, and ponder over the old days, wonder at the memories that have brought you so far, then fall asleep and dream of Shakespeare, in whose country, the very heart of England, you have found yourself.

Stratford-on-Avon, Church and Mill.

CHAPTER X

ROUND STRATFORD :: CHARLECOTE AND CLOPTON AND SHOTTERY

THOUGH Charlecote lies at the east of Stratford, and some three miles away, and Clopton House just at the north, as it were, at the very doors, and there is no link between them, they are the two houses which undoubtedly the Shakespeare lover first, or, at least, most, associates with the poet, among the villages that are near his home.   One, of course, on account of legend, one through a true and tragic story.   And the first people the Shakespearean remembers after the kindred at Stratford are the Lucys, the next the Cloptons who did so much for the town.

Let us go, then, to Charlecote first. The way out from Stratford is over the Clopton bridge, with the Unicorn Inn to your left.   Then take the road to the left and pass the outskirts, not ugly, of the town—the Tiddington road.   After a little way do not turn to the right, which would take you to Loxley, but go straight on.   At Tiddington, where there

are a number of pleasant houses, if you keep straight on, or
again from Charlecote returning to Stratford, you come to the
delightful village of Alveston. This has its modern church, of
1839, and the ancient church, now unused, near the river, remains in part—its chancel and its bell turret. Of this
more anon. The village, according to "The Beauties of
England and Wales" (1814), was "called by the late Dr. Perry
the Montpelier of England, on account of the salubrity of the
air." Alas! the fame of Montpelier and Alveston alike, among
world-renowned health resorts, has departed. But there is
an interest more recent and more ecclesiastical which is worth
preserving—I mean that belonging to the life of Mr. Francis
Fortescue Knottesford (1771–1859). The story of a famous
Warwickshire squire and parson, though not every word of it
belongs to Warwickshire, has so full a flavour of a time unlike
our own that I quote it as it comes to me, by the kindness of
some of his kindred. It runs thus :—

"The Reverend Francis Fortescue Knottesford, born April,
1771, was the only child of Captain Fortescue, who died when his
son was about four years old. His devotion to his mother was
so great that when by the death•of a rather distant relative he
became owner of a property in Warwickshire (which carried
with it the obligation to take the name of Knottesford) he would
not leave his curacy at Hadley, Suffolk, because of her love for
that place. Such removals were then thought much of, and his
daughter, Mrs. Jackson, used to tell how the children's nurse
'Bye,' a Suffolk woman, could very imperfectly understand the
language of an old weeding woman who worked on the Alverston
estate. They managed, however, to quarrel a good deal.

"Francis must have been a thoughtful, precocious child. On
his sixth birthday a servant found him trying to burn some of
his toys, and when she exclaimed in dismay he replied, 'I must ;
it's my birthday and I am putting away childish things.' His
desire for the ministry showed itself early, and when sent to
Eton his one grief was that he could not wear a surplice as the
foundationers did. His love for Eton was stronger even than his
love for Oxford, and in his old age he delighted to tell his grandchildren stories about it. It was in or just before his time that
windows in the foundationers' dormitory were first glazed, and
he told us that the 'boys' were so indignant at the effeminacy (?)·
that they smashed or pulled them out (they were little leaded

panes) two or three times, and it took all the power of the authorities to induce them to submit.

" On his mother's death, which closely followed that of his eldest boy, Mr. Knottesford removed to Alveston Manor, an old religious house which had belonged to the monastery of S. Mary at Worcester. It had come into the Knottesford family by purchase, not by robbery. The drawing-room had been the chapel, and has large windows east and west. The whole house, as it was then, plainly showed its original use, as did the fish-pond connected with the Avon, and the bowling-green and large lawn, said to be the same size as the site of Worcester Cathedral. It has since been altered. It is a picturesque, timber-built mansion, surrounded by trees and facing the large bridge beyond Stratford. It contains a large library, in which Mr. Knottesford and his son amassed a collection of books of Catholic theology.

" On both sides of the house are glass conservatories. Up and down these the old gentleman, so tradition in the family says, used to pace reciting the 119th Psalm. This would lead us to suppose that he said at least the small hours and perhaps the whole daily office of the breviary in Latin. His confessor was Dr. Routh, the long-lived president of Magdalen College, Oxford. Though the latter part of his life ran parallel to the Oxford movement, yet his religious training was entirely previous to it and apart from it. Thus he is one of the proofs that confession never really died out in the Church of England.

" Mr. Knottesford was a very learned man, using seven or eight languages in his library ; he was also very musical and a good casuist. Men used to come to consult him from many parts besides Oxford. His great friend, besides Dr. Routh of Magdalen, was Dr. Stillingfleet who lived near Edgehill. He greatly enjoyed laying out his grounds, which had been much neglected, and planted rare and beautiful trees. He encouraged swimming among the younger servants and used to go down to the river with them on summer evenings accompanied by a large Newfoundland dog who was trained to assist if need arose. He afterwards erected bathing sheds on his property for the use of the Stratford youth, which were still standing and utilised till quite recently. In later years his son and his daughter, both married, lived with him, and the two families of grandchildren were successively born and brought up in the old manor-house, and played in the gardens and orchard.

" Mr. Knottesford was also a generous helper in the building of Alvestone Church (not on the same lines), and in the improvements made from time to time at the Collegiate Church of Holy Trinity at Stratford-on-Avon, which he dearly loved. Missionary bishops, especially Bp. Field of Newfoundland, used to stay at his house. As age came on friends preceded him to Paradise, and his powers lessened generally, but his quiet life of study and prayer continued to the end. He was at church on Sunday ; on Monday his son-in-law heard him saying the Pss, as was his habit when rising, then the sound of a fall. He was unconscious when they rushed upstairs, and passed away on Tuesday night, May 31st, 1859. R.I.P." Of his work in other parishes something is said elsewhere (p. 246).

Alveston must not be left without seeing the old church. It is near the river, and nothing remains but the chancel and the belfry. There is a remote Shakespearean connection here. Nicholas Lane, whose effigy is affixed to the wall, was he who had a lawsuit with John Shakespeare, who had become responsible for a debt from his brother Henry. The tedious details may be read in Halliwell-Phillips' "Life of Shakespeare." Henry Shakespeare was he of Snitterfield, whose pecuniary affairs were generally in disorder. He died on December 29, 1596, and his wife on the following 9th of February. Nicholas Lane predeceased him, dying on July 27, 1595, as the copper plate on his monument records. The monument itself is of considerable interest. It shows the man in his doublet and hose, with curly hair, moustache and beard, with cuffs at wrist and ruff at neck, a rough thing at best ; and two sons kneeling at his side. There is also in the church a marble tablet to the memory of a Colonel Peers, who received fatal wounds at Dettingen, and another to William Hiron, murdered on November 20, 1820, near Littleham Bridge, nearer Charlecote, by four men with the Elizabethan, and even Shakespearean names of Quiney, Adams, Sidney, and Heytrey. As to the scene of the murder, it was said quite lately that the hole in which the dead man's head was found lying will never fill up. But I have not attempted to verify this. We return now to the main road (which turned to the left at Alveston) before we come to Littleham Bridge, and then, in little over half a mile, to the fine gate which gives the nearest entrance to the park, of Charlecote. This way, however, you cannot take unless you are private visitors to the house.   Those whose visit is more that of the tourist must go by the main entrance from the village.

Now everybody knows why Charlecote is famous among Shakespeareans.   The story is that told by the credulous Archdeacon Davies—in a manuscript at Corpus Christi College, Oxford, writ before 1708—that William Shakespeare was " much given to all unluckinesse in stealing venison and rabbits, particularly from Sir . . . . . Lucy, who had him oft whipt and sometimes imprisoned, and at last made him fly his native country, to his great advancement; but his reveng was so great that he is his Justice Clodpate, and calls him a great man, and that in allusion to his name bore three lowses rampant for his

I·H·N

Charlecote in Spring.

arms."   No one would attach more value to this tale than to the Archdeacon's spelling, or to his conclusion, which is certainly false, that Shakespeare " died a papist," were it not that Rowe tells much the same story in 1709.   Sir Sidney Lee is satisfied to call it " a credible tradition," but Mr. Charles Elton (a name always to be honoured among Shakespeareans) simply says, when he tells how Shakespeare went to London, that " about a century after someone invented the story of his robbing a park."   Rowe and Davies, indeed, cannot be considered independent witnesses—the phrases are too much alike.   But the Lucys had no deer park at Charlecote or (as was later suggested by rationalists) at Fulbrooke : Sir Sidney Lee is content to think it was in a rabbit warren that " a few harts or does

P

doubtless found an occasional home." There is much virtue in " doubtless," and likewise in a home that is only " occasional." But still the story is persistent ; only you must notice that it all, including some absurd lines in which Shakespeare is supposed to call the owner of Charlecote a bloated just-ass, "a parliament member, a justice of peace," is of the early eighteenth century, when the gossips began to stir about literary men. The most plausible argument comes from the similarity of the non-existent " Justice Clodpate " to the immortal Shallow, and of the "three lowses" and the " dozen white luces" of "The Merry Wives," to the real arms of the Lucys (three luces hauriant argent), with the further point that Shallow had come to Windsor to carry to the Star Chamber (a pleasing anachronism) the matter of a poaching affray. It looks as if it all comes from the plays—as if Shakespeare did make a joke about the Lucy arms, and clever people, and gossips, manufactured the rest. If he did mean to mock the Elizabethan justice in his plays he made amends by much honour to other Lucys. So a little scepticism is justifiable. At any rate there is not so much evidence to connect Shakespeare with deer-stealing as there is to connect him with the marriage licence of November 27, 1582 (or so I should say).

Let the Shakespeare association then lie, and we will turn to the Lucys themselves. Sir Thomas Lucy, the elder (1532–1600), held the property in descent from ancestors who had been there more than three hundred years. Cox says, here and there making Dugdale more emphatic than he was :—

" *Charlecote*, or as it is written in Domesday-book *Cerlecote*, from *Ceorle* the *Saxon* Owner, before the Conquest ; but after it was given to the Earl of *Mallent* by the *Norman* King. It was then certified to contain three Hides and two Mills, and belonged to the Parish of *Wellsburne*. From him it descended, with his other Lands, to *Henry de Newburgh*, his Brother, the first Earl of *Warwick*, whose Son and Heir *Roger*, 23 *Hen.* I. gave to the Collegiate Church of *Warwick*, then newly by him founded, one Hide of Land lying here, with the Tithe of the whole Lordship, and two Mills. This *Roger* enfeoffed *Thurstane de Montfort* (a great Man in those Days) with this Lordship, and other large Possessions ; and his Son *Henry* gave it to *Walter*, the Son of *Thurstane de Cherlecote*, to whom King *Richard* I. and King *John* confirmed it. He was the younger Son of *Thurstane de Mont-*

fort. From *Walter* descended *William*, who assumed the Name of *Lucy*, as is supposed from *Cicely* his Mother, who was an Heiress of the *Lucy* Family."

If that be so, the four hundred years were hardly reached, when Sir William, who married Elizabeth, daughter of Richard Simpson and widow of George Catesby, of Easton Neston, Northants (note these names) sent, as the story runs, for John Foxe, afterwards the somewhat romantic martyrologist, to teach his boy Thomas, born in 1532. But Mrs. Stopes has pointed out that Foxe was only away from Oxford or London for eighteen months, and that both he and his pupil were married during that period, so we cannot lay very great stress on the tale. At any rate, Thomas Lucy was married on August 1, 1546, to Joyce, daughter and sole heiress of Thomas Acton, of Sutton, Worcestershire. He succeeded his father before a year was out. Sir Thomas does not seem to have been a very rigid Protestant at first; he obtained Hampton Lucy from Queen Mary, though no doubt he paid something for the grant. In 1558 he set about the rebuilding of the house, making it, after the polite fashion of the reign, in the shape of the letter E. The fine house we now see is that which he built, the only additions being a library and dining-room built in 1833.

To return to the Lucys. Sir Thomas, whose only son married Dorothy, daughter of Sir Nicholas Arnoll, in 1575, lived an active life as Justice of the Peace and Quorum, catching Romanists, entering into the affairs of Stratford (where his " players " performed in 1584), in Parliament active against papists and poachers. A certain John Shakespeare was one of the recusants presented by him, but this was not the father of the poet, but " another person of the same name." His son was knighted in 1593, and his wife died in 1596. His son-in-law, Sir Edward Aston, described her in far from polite language ; but it is difficult to think that the epitaph which the bereaved husband wrote, so beautiful in its simplicity, is not true. I quote it here :—

" Here lyeth the Lady Joyce Lucy wife of Sir Thomas Lucy of Charlecot in ye county of Warwick, Knight, Daughter and heir of Thomas Acton of Sutton in ye county of Worcester Esquire who departed out of this wretched world to her heavenly kingdom ye 10 day of February in the yeare of our Lord God 1595 and of her age 60 and three. All the time of her lyfe a true and faythful servant of her good God, never detected of any cryme or vice. In religion most sounde, in love to her husband most faythful and true. In friendship most constant ; to what in trust was committed unto her most secret. In wisdom excelling. In governing of her house, bringing up of youth in ye fear of God that did converse with her moste rare and singular. A great maintayner of hospitality. Greatly esteemed of her betters ; misliked of none unless the envyous. When all is spoken that can be saide a woman so garnished with virtue as not to be bettered and hardly to be equalled by any. As shee lived most virtuously so shee died most Godly. Set downe by him yt best did knowe what hath byn written to be true. THOMAS LUCYE."

Sir Thomas survived his wife no more than four years, dying in 1600. He received a magnificent funeral in Charlecote Church on August 7, when three heralds attended ; but he was never given an epitaph on his tomb. Sir Thomas the younger, who had married when only a child, died in 1605 at the age of fifty-four. He left a son of nineteen and of the same name, who was a friend of Lord Herbert of Cherbury. He was a man of more public eminence than his father or grandfather, and he actually did make a Star Chamber matter of a case of deer-stealing from his park in Worcestershire. Have we here the origin of the tale ? Not at all, for the reference occurs in " The Merry Wives of Windsor," which was printed in 1602, while the deer-stealing case did not happen till eight years later. It was he who purchased Fulbrooke park (see p. 209). He lived an active life, and in 1640 " placide dormivit in Christo." He, too, had a noble tomb, and he had a splendid epitaph, too long to quote, and a preacher at his wife's funeral (she was Alice, a Spencer of Claverdon) said, " It is true all that is said of him, everie word." He was succeeded by his son, Sir Richard, the first baronet (1618), who lived till 1667. With him ends the Lucy line which Shakespeare personally knew, but it was not until the nineteenth century that the male succession died out and the Lucy heiress affixed the equally famous name of Fairfax to her own. The present possessor is at least the lineal descendant of the Elizabethan owners.

And now for the house. In the fifteenth volume of " The Beauties of England and Wales," written by Mr. J. Norris Brewer in 1814, it is said, in the manner of a century 'ago, that

Charlecote.

" The mansion at Charlecote was rebuilt about the first year of Queen Elizabeth, by Sir Thomas Lucy ; and the edifice then constructed is yet standing. It is a noble specimen of the domestic style which obtained in the latter part of the sixteenth century. The material is brick, with stone coigns ; and, although too many freedoms have been taken, in the progress of various alterations, with its ancient character, the general effect of the structure is still venerable and impressive. The contiguous grounds are richly stocked with timber, among which are elms of unusual growth and vigour. It is impossible to walk through these grounds, and to view the mansion, without reflecting on the hour in which the great genius and boast of the island was (according to tradition) led through the humblest gate and condemned to bow in silence before folly in a ' furred gown.' " We do not now reflect on any such things, and I am not sure which the humblest gate may be. None look humble to-day. If you approach from Stratford you pass through a very fine gate indeed, go through a fine stretch of park, now tenanted by deer, up a fine avenue of limes, and cross a bridge where the Avon is joined by its tributary, the river Dene, which flows from Edge-hill and the borders of Northamptonshire. Then you come to the wall, and the beautiful iron gate, which connects the picturesque long, sloping-roofed stables with the house itself. Going through this, the garden gate, you come to the front of the house, from whence again runs a straight road, through a stretch of park, to the great gate-house. Between that splendid piece of Tudor building, so rich in its red colour with the white facings, and the house, is a garden court, terraced at each side. The gate-house is itself a house, with octagonal turrets at the corners, a big heavy mullioned window over the archway, and a large, long room, a " banquet-house " perhaps, on the first floor. Beyond the gate-house and the village is another stretch of park, ended by iron gates opening directly on the village.

You enter the house by a fine porch, which projects from the house (forming the central bar of the E). It has the royal arms and E.R. over the door, and T.L. below. Projecting wings extend at the ends, with many gables, and octagonal turrets. Your eye as you approach is struck by the many stacks of high chimneys and the single chimneys also, like minarets aspiring towards the sky. You enter at once upon the great hall, a splendid apartment with the fit chequered marble floor, an oak

Charlecote from the River.

panelling, and ribbed roof. On the panels are many coats, of Lucy and their alliances. Here, over the chimney-piece, is the magnificent family picture by Cornelius Janssen, which shows the third Sir Thomas, he who " peacefully fell asleep in Christ " in 1640, whom his wife so eulogised and loved. Washington Irving, when he saw the picture, seems to have been puzzled to date it ; satisfied it was not the first, he took it to be the second Sir Thomas. But he well describes it—

" Sir Thomas is dressed in ruff and doublet, white shoes with roses in them, and has a peaked yellow, or, as Master Slender would say, ' a cane-coloured beard.' His lady is seated on the opposite side of the picture, in wide ruff and long stomacher, and the children have a most venerable stiffness and formality of dress. Hounds and spaniels are mingled in the family group, a hawk is seated on his perch in the foreground, and one of the children holds a bow—all intimating the knight's skill in hunting, hawking, and archery, so indispensable to an accomplished gentleman in those days."

It is certainly a most delightful picture, belonging to that long school of composition which finds, perhaps, its earliest expression in England in the famous Holbein of the family of Sir Thomas More, and lingers on till almost the end of the seventeenth century—a great family group, showing the generations, wearing the very clothes they wore (not like the Lelys, often in some impossible garb, classical or angelic) and in the attitudes they may, at least for the painter's purposes and temporarily, have assumed. The rest of the hall seems to take its tone from this picture. There is a whole gallery of other Lucys, in picture or bust, by all the great artists in succession. Perhaps the most interesting of all are the two ovals on copper by Isaac Oliver (1556–1617) of Lord Herbert of Cherbury and Sir Thomas Lucy, his friend, a gentleman with a yellow beard, showing his bare neck in the fashion of smart young men of his time. Before leaving the hall, look at the wonderful table, which has in it " the largest piece of onyx ever found " set in many stones of various hues ; it was once at Fonthill, most wonderful of eighteenth century houses.

Now to the other rooms. In the library, which has delightful bookcases all round, not too high, and pictures above them, with a splendid embossed ceiling, there are some more fine pictures : Charles I. and Strafford, both by Stone ; a most charming Queen

The Gatehouse, Charlecote.

Henrietta Maria by Vandyke, given by the queen herself to one of her ladies ; a handsome George Lucy by Gainsborough ; and many other beautiful portraits. But above all you are to notice the two cabinets, sofa, armchair and eight chairs, of ebony and ivory, given by Queen Elizabeth to Leicester—I do not know how they came here. Then to the dining-room, where you again find yourself in the presence of the great Warwick carvers (Willcox this, not Kendall), a huge buffet, with fish and fowl standing out like life, and typical seventeenth century game pieces by Snyders and such. You see from the windows that lime avenue to the south, and to the west across the river to the Welcombe monument. The garden itself is a beautiful setting for the house —the formal flower-beds and the terrace above the river which here is broadened, for the nonce, almost into a small lake ; the fine trees of the park around and beyond—the elms which Nathaniel Hawthorne called " civilised trees, known to man and befriended by him for ages past." Charlecote, with all its changes, is still a typical Elizabethan house.

The last thought as you leave Charlecote is of the park. Shakespeare killed no deer in it, and Sir Thomas held no court in his house, in spite of the inimitable tale of Landor ; but no one can think of Charlecote now without its deer, at least since Washington Irving wrote of them thus :—

" By and by, among those refined and venerable trees, I saw a large herd of deer, mostly reclining, but some standing in picturesque groups, while the stags threw their large antlers aloft, as if they had been taught to make themselves tributary to the scenic effect. Some were running fleetly about, vanishing from light into shadow and glancing forth again, with here and there a little fawn careering at its mother's heels. These deer are almost in the same relation to the wild, natural state of their kind that the trees of an English park hold to the rugged growth of an American forest. They have held a certain intercourse with man for immemorial years ; and, most probably, the stag that Shakespeare killed was one of the progenitors of this very herd, and may himself have been a partly civilised and humanised deer, though in a less degree than these remote posterity. They are a little wilder than sheep, but they do not sniff the air at the approach of human beings, nor evince much alarm at their pretty close proximity ; although, if you continue to advance, they toss their heads and take to their heels in a kind of mimic

terror, or something akin to feminine skittishness, with a dim
remembrance of tradition, as it were, of their having come of a
wild stock."

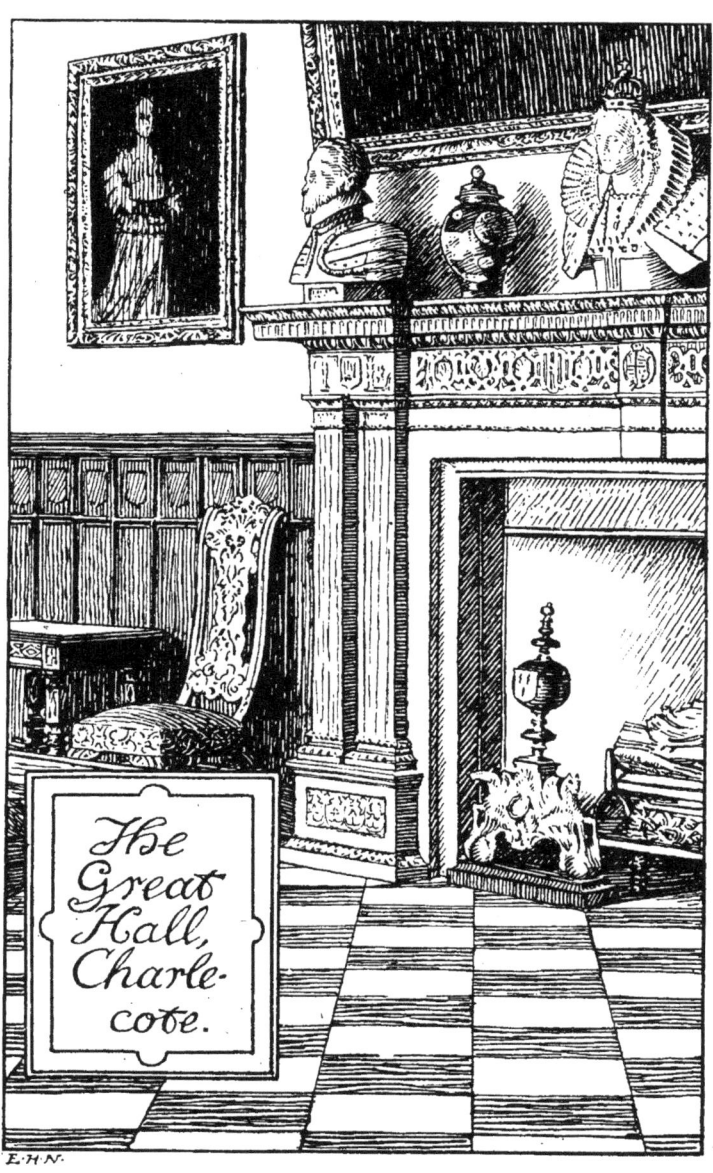

There is a pleasant round back by Hampton Lucy from Charlecote to Stratford. In order to take it you must pass through
the village—and there you will stay to see the church. It
is a bitter disappointment to find it of the Victorian-Decorated
style ; but the chapel at the north side of the chancel contains
the old Lucy monuments. A high tomb shows Sir Thomas
Lucy and Joyce his wife in alabaster, he in armour but without
any cap, she in a close gown and cap. Beneath in panels are
Thomas, their son, and Anne, their daughter (whose husband's
opinion of his mother-in-law, as well as the beautiful description of her, have been noted). On the other side of the chapel
is Sir Thomas, the son, who died in 1605, with his second wife,

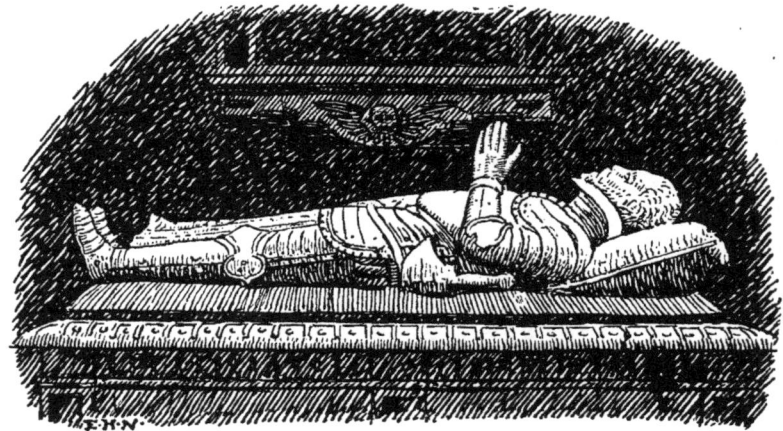

Effigy of Sir Thomas Lucy, Charlecote.

six sons and eight daughters. On the north side are the third
Sir Thomas and his wife. He was Member of Parliament for
Warwickshire in 1614, 1621, 1624, 1625, 1626, 1628, and 1640, in
which last year he died. This Sir Thomas is also in armour and
bareheaded. His wife, who died eight years later, lies beside him.
These figures are by Bernini, and on the tomb, besides the long
and exceedingly eulogistic Latin inscription, is a figure of Sir
Thomas on his horse, which no doubt seemed to his wife appropriate, as he was killed by a fall. The monuments are almost
the best of the great series of Tudor memorials in the county.
The church, if it were well decorated and always open, would
be a worthy partaker in the Shakespearean glory, for certainly
the poet knew these great neighbours of his who were buried

here, and often must have walked this way and, perhaps, worshipped with them.

Return, then, by the road from Hampton Lucy, and join the
upper road from Warwick (*see* p. 122) till you come, on the right,
to Welcombe Lodge, of 1860 building.   Here once was the house
of John Combe, who certainly left Shakespeare £5, though Aubrey
says that the poet wrote this of him—lines, says a writer of

Welcombe.

1618, "fastened upon a Tombe that he had Caused to be built
in his Life Time " :—

> " Ten-in-the-hundred the Devil allows ;
> But Combe will have twelve he sweares and he vowes ;
> If any man ask, who lies in this tomb,
> Oh ! ho ! quoth the Devil, 'tis my John-a-Combe."

The great landmark of Welcombe now is the obelisk of 120
feet high in Welsh granite, in memory of two brothers Philips,
1873 and 1890, the younger of whom, Robert, erected it in 1876
to commemorate his elder brother, Mark.   But behind the house

is a memorial more ancient and more durable. It is the deep ravine called " The Dingles," which may be an old river bed or perhaps an entrenchment. I do not propose to enter into the long and learned discussions which have been recently held about the Dingles. You may see them in Mr. New's character-istic drawing, as our ancestors saw them in that pleasing cut " the West View of Welcombe Hills," prefixed to " Welcombe Hills near Stratford-upon-Avon : a Poem, Historical and Des-criptive, by John Jordan of Stratford, Wheelwright," published for the Author in 1777. The author, a very pedestrian imitator of his fellow-countryman, Mr. Jago, says—I will quote only a few verses, for after the first sentence of four lines he goes on for eighteen more without a full stop :—

> " On Welcombe Hills I tune my willing verse,
> Point out their beauties, and their fame rehearse,
> Their ancient fame shall elevate my lays,
> A subject worthy of the Muse's praise.
> Upon these Hills one pleasing morn I stray'd
> To see what art and nature there display'd :
> The DINGLES first attract my wond'ring sight ;
> Their grandure gave astonishing delight :

He adds this footnote :—" The word Dingle, used by Milton in his Masque of Comus, is a compound, signifying double angle ; plainly observable in the sides of this great excavation. It is indeed a noble intrenchment, of a considerable length one way, and has a shorter branch shooting from it ; so that, take the whole work together, it appears not much unlike to the form of a Y."

The historic interest of the Dingles really belongs to the attempt, by William Combe, in 1614, to enclose the whole of the Welcombe Hills, on which the Stratford freemen undoubtedly had rights, and to the ambiguous statement of Thomas Greene, the diarist, as to Shakespeare's concern in the matter. The poet would give no aid to the Corporation in their successful attempt to save the fields. " The Dingles " is still unenclosed. Of all this Mr. Jordan knows nothing. His history, throughout the poem, is as shaky as his verse ; but he pleases himself by describing a fairy ring and the " cone-like hill," which is the smallest of the hills and stands between the Dingles and the house ; then he revels in etymology, deriving the name Combe from the Welcombe Hills, with other even more distressing sug-

gestions ; and ends with a lament for " the worthy and respectable John Lloyd, esq., late of Snitterfield, and proprietor of the
estate at Welcombe, the author's friend and patron, whose
death he particularly laments in these lines, which he has been
obliged to alter since the poem was written," and a glowing
eulogy of the " LADY whom he's left behind."

The Dingles.

A ramble in the Dingles is a very delightful thing, and it will
be none the worse for the reading of the wheelwright's poem.
Moreover, this will direct us to Clopton House. The property
in 1777 had passed from the Combes, who held it in Dugdale's
time, by marriage, to Edward Clopton, and again through his
granddaughter, Frances, to her husband. This lady " married

to John Partheriche, Esq.," and was "with him resident" (says Mr. Jordan) and " enjoying their extensive family manors and opulent possessions."

Clopton is a quite charming house. To reach it you may not only go from the Dingles but you may leave Stratford by Henley Street, follow Guild Street a little, and then turn up a road to the right, enter a charming wooded country, cross a little stream, and find yourself suddenly in front of a secluded and enchanting dwelling. The earlier history, for the house we see is almost the village, is summed up not uninterestingly by Mr. Cox :—

Clopton House.

" *Clopton,* originally a Member of *Stratford upon Avon,* and as such, belonging to the Bishops of *Worcester,* as seems plain from hence, that *S. Oswald,* Bishop of that See in King *Ethelred's* Time, by the Consent of the Convent of *Worcester,* did grant to one *Edric* his Servant three Messuages and an half, lying here, for three Lives, and afterward to return to the Church of *Worcester* ; but the Bishops soon lost them, for in the Conqueror's Survey, where 'tis said to contain five Hides, it appears to have been Part of the Possessions of *Robert de Stratford,* and that in the Confessor's Days, *Odo* and *Aileva* had the Inheritance thereof. In King *John's* Reign, *Anno* 13, it is reckoned as Part of the Barony of *Stafford*, but it was soon aliened from thence; for in King *Henry* III's Reign it was in the Family of the *Montforts*, and by *Peter de Montfort* granted to *James de Clopton*, and his Heirs, by the Name of the Manor of *Clopton*; excepting only some Parcels of Land and Meadow before granted by him to *Isabel de Norton* and her Son *Edmund*, and reserving to himself a Rent of Ten Shillings a Year, to be paid at *Michaelmas* and *Our Lady*, for all Services. The Family of *Clopton* take their Name from this Place, having been Inhabitants of it, before they became Owners."

Of these the most famous was the great merchant Sir Hugh, Lord Mayor of London in 1492. His brother Thomas was the owner of Clopton, a man of ecclesiastical sympathies who built him an oratory at the house and obtained the licence of Sixtus IV. for Mass to be said in the "fair chapel" which he built afterwards. Sir Hugh was he who built a typical Warwickshire half timber house at the corner of Chapel Lane in Stratford, which was afterwards the house of Shakespeare, and known as New Place; who rebuilt the Guild Chapel opposite; and gave to the town the splendid bridge, which still remains a "great and sumptuous bridge" indeed, with fourteen arches and a long causeway of stone, a noble gift remaining to-day as beautiful as of old. Of the Clopton tombs in the church sufficient is said elsewhere. Sir Hugh Clopton received Henry VII. in Clopton House, and died in 1496, a bachelor.

In 1580 Joyce Clopton, then owner, I think, of the house, married George Carew Earl of Tôtnes. She died in 1636, aged seventy-eight, and was buried in the Clopton chapel. In later times, after the succession of the Partheriche family, and its transmission to another line, the name of Clopton was assumed again by the owners in turn. In 1873 the late Sir Arthur Hodgson, K.C.M.G., to whom and his family Stratford owes so much, bought the property. The ancient line of Clopton, whether in Warwickshire or in Suffolk, is believed to be extinct, at least in England. Their house could be in the hands of none more worthy, or more careful, to preserve it than the present owner.

A portion of the old house, of Henry VII.'s time, survives at the back, and (I quote from Sir Arthur Hodgson's paper on the house) "was a porchway entrance across the ancient moat." He adds that "Shakespeare and his friends must have passed

Q

scores of times under its portal." In front of it rán the moat : when this was investigated in the middle of the nineteenth century three sack bottles of coarse glass with the Combe crest on them were found : they are still preserved in the house. The north and west sides of the house are ancient ; the east and south are of the very charming building of Charles II.'s time. Samuel Ireland, in 1795, thought nothing of the new court—so indifferent, he called it, as to be unworthy of notice. Happily our tastes have changed. In 1820 it was said to be full of crooked, half-lighted

Old Door, Clopton House.

passages. These are reformed, to say the least. A drawing-room and orangery were added in the nineteenth century. The interest of the house is considerable. First there is the attic story where was a chapel, " the entrance very low " in 1820, and only to be adventured " on hands and knees " ; the walls have inscriptions in black letter, two of them very wise advice to those who would plot against the Crown, and to those who would live a quiet and peaceable life in all godliness and honesty : "My son, feare thou the Lord and the King, and meddle not with them that are given to change," and—

" Whether you rise yearlye
Or go to bed late
Remember Jesus Christ
That died for your sake."

The house was in 1605 the resort, you will remember, of the Gunpowder Plotters. Ambrose Rookwood hired it to be not far from Catesby at Lapworth, and here Wright, Winter, Keyes, and Grant met the other two. At the discovery of the plot many " massing reliques " were seized there. There are several fine oak beams in the roof of the room opposite the old chapel, the priest's chamber, perhaps. One is reminded of Compton Winyates and of Baddesley Clinton.

The second interest is that of the later seventeenth century, the fine oak staircase, leading to charming panelled rooms, and a landing, from which you look out, over the front door, to a delightful formal garden. The dining-room, too, is an interesting room, with a square recess in it, and some good pictures ; and the large hall or sitting-room at the back of the house, looking upon a stretch of green turf, has a good collection of pictures, among them (it seems probable) Arabella Stewart by Vansomer, the Earl of Totnes ascribed to Zucchero, a very fine portrait of Ireton, and many excellent Clopton pictures.

Then there is the delightful garden, a succession of shady walks, walled treasuries of flower and fruit, summer-houses, terraces approached by stone stairways of dignity—with two great Italian jars, you will notice, at one place—and then a charming pond, almost a lake, fringed with tall trees, surrounded by a classic balustrade, and with stately statues looking down on the still water. Last of all there are the Shakespeare associations. There is the spring, at the far end of the garden, where Margaret Clopton is said to have drowned herself, and thus to have suggested to the poet the end of Ophelia. But there is no evidence at all to support this—nor any of the truth of that other legend, that Charlotte Clopton was buried during the plague in 1564 when she was not dead, awoke, and was found standing, but dead, by the gate of her tomb—and so suggested Juliet. There is a third, perhaps more plausible, tale. If the Wincot where Marian Hacket, the fat ale-wife, lived (*see* p. 248) was really close to Stratford, and it was there that Christopher Sly fell asleep, caring not for third, or fourth, or fifth borough, why, then, the Lord who came from hunting with his train may be the owner of Clopton—

says Halliwell-Phillips, "the only large private residence near the scene of Sly's intemperance; but, if so, not until 1605, in the May of which year Sir George became Baron Carew of Clopton." This is to be precise indeed ; but, still, one would like to think that here, in this place of most Shakespearean sympathy, it was that the tinker awoke and called for a pot of the smallest ale.   So we go away from Clopton with memories of him who must often have wandered in its gardens—and the thought leads us to one more Shakespearean hamlet, to complete the circle, the hallowed village, as so many think it, of Shottery.

There are two ways to the village of Shakespeare's wife.   The one is by Greenhill Street and a path to the left before you come to the railway bridge.   You then skirt the line for a hundred yards or more and afterwards cross it, coming into fields and across them straight to Shottery.   Or you can come from the church, up Old Town and Chestnut Walk and then by a stile into the field and eventually into the same path.   Shottery is a prosperous little village with one or two little industries and many substantial cottages.   At the end, on the outskirts, after you have crossed the Shottery brook, stand what look like two cottages, stretching east and west, the doors facing south.   These are really one house, once a large farmhouse (or part of it) of Elizabethan building.   There is no doubt that the house belonged to the Hathaways, but whether to those from whom Anne sprang cannot be certainly said.   But the tradition is very strong, perhaps continuous, that it was here the poet wooed his bride.   It is not very much changed since the sixteenth century and, since the Shakespeare Birthplace Trust bought it in 1892, it has been repaired and restored, very much as it must have been.   A stone chimney bears the date 1697, with the initials " I. H."   The same initials are repeated elsewhere.   The house is still a dwelling-place, but more of a museum too than it was when I first saw it in 1872.   Then Mrs. Hathaway Taylor, a descendant of the Hathaways, lived there; a delightful old woman who gossiped, without the slightest affectation of literary enthusiasm, but with a great deal of family feeling.   Then, I believe, the family who held it, also descendants, were named Baker, and one of them is still custodian. The low living-room with the large chimney, the parlour, the good bedroom, which they call Anne's, with sloping roof, and the Elizabethan bed, and the old linen, and the old pottery, and chairs, and tables, do something

Anne Hathaway's Cottage.

to recreate an atmosphere for the visitor. But our fortune to-day is not so good as that of the American man of letters, William Winter, who slept there with all sorts of pleasant dreams. The garden, with all old-fashioned herbs and plants, and great hedges sheltering them, is a perfect setting for the solid, unpretentious house. The walk over the fields to this pleasant old-world house, where the people are still kindly and simple, is one of the most delightful things in a visit to Stratford. And the identification is as good as one can expect, for Richard Hathaway, who made his will in 1581, bequeathed money to his daughter Agnes (a name interchangeable then with Anne) as though she were about to marry, and it was his friends who were both supervisors of his will and sureties of the bond for marriage given at Worcester in 1582. The seal " R. H." is on the bond too ; and Thomas Whittington of Shottery, Richard Hathaway's " sheepherd," at his death bequeathed to the poor of Stratford eleven shillings " that is in the hand of Anne Shaxpere, wyfe unto Mr. Wyllyam Shaxpere, and is debt due unto me." The Shottery association, indeed, is as close as any can be ; and the tradition has always fixed this as the house of Shakespeare's wife's father. It deserves the homage it receives. In the evening at sunset, in the hot summer afternoon when the sun shines on it, in the morning when the dew is still on the garden flowers, it has the same air of happy peace and brightness. The memory here of Stratford's great son is one wholly of happiness. You feel sure when you are here that the lovers were " handfasted " in true ancient form of betrothal, and knew it to be binding, long before they came together across the fields to Luddington Church, long destroyed, to be married, or he journeyed to Temple Grafton, if so it was, where Anne might be staying, for the wedding, or met with the priest in the old upper chamber chapel in Shottery Manor-house (for all these are suggestions as to when and where the marriage was solemnised).

Shottery has a charm like that of all these villages around. It is full of trees, quiet, rustic, unspoilt by all the crowds of trippers that descend on it daily. It belongs, the cottage of the Hathaways, like the house of the Cloptons and the great hall of the Lucys, to the days of great Elizabeth when life was spacious for poor and rich alike.

CHAPTER XI

ONE of those old stories which count for so much in Warwickshire has a scandal about Shakespeare (which indeed has quite as much general interest as, but perhaps less *vraisemblance* than, scandal about Queen Elizabeth). He is said to have joined a party of Stratford folk which set itself to outdrink a drinking-club at Bidford and, as a result of his labours in that regard, to have fallen asleep under the crab-tree, which in the person of its descendant is still called Shakespeare's crab-tree. When morning dawned his friends wished to renew the encounter but he wisely said : " No ; I have drunk with

" Piping Pebworth, Dancing Marston,
Haunted Hillborough, Hungry Grafton,
Dodging Exhall, Papist Wixford,
Beggarly Broom, and Drunken Bidford."

—and so, presumably, I will drink no more. The story is said to go back to the seventeenth century. But of its truth, or of the connection of any such story or such lines with Shakespeare, there is really no evidence at all. Yet I do not suppose that since some sixty years ago a crew of gossips began to waste other people's time by writing imaginatively about Shakespeare, it has ever been possible to dissociate the story from his memory.

Washington Irving introduces the tale with a few quips of his own, thus :—

" About seven miles from Stratford lies the thirsty little market-town of Bidford, famous for its ale. Two societies of the village yeomanry used to meet, under the appellation of the Bidford Topers, and to challenge the lovers of good ale of the neighbouring villages to a contest of drinking. Among others, the people of Stratford were called out to prove the strength of their heads; and in the number of the champions was Shakespeare, who, in spite of the proverb that " they who drink beer will think beer," was as true to his ale as Falstaff to his sack. The chivalry of Stratford was staggered at the first onset, and sounded a retreat while they had yet legs to carry them off the field. They had scarcely marched a mile, when, their legs failing them, they were forced to lie down under a crab-tree, where they passed the night. It is still standing, and goes by the name of Shakespeare's tree."

And he ends the story with the rhyme, after which he quotes the eighteenth century collector of gossip :—

" The villages here alluded to," says Ireland, " still bear the epithets thus given them ; the people of Pebworth are still famed for their skill on the pipe and tabor ; Hilborough is now called Haunted Hilborough, and Grafton is famous for the poverty of its soil."

True it is that the eight villages have come to be called the Shakespeare villages ; and it is a common custom to journey round them *in piam memoriam*. So let us do to-day. We leave Stratford over the level crossing, turn to the right, swiftly depart from the town, having the railway and the river to our left, and go on till we ascend the great hill of Bordon—a very steep tug. From the top a magnificent view spreads out—tree-crowned to the right, softly meadowed to the left, and away in the distance to the Cotswolds. There is no need to go under the line and visit Luddington, for there is nothing to see there, so we continue till a turn to the right takes us up the hill to Binton, where a modern church stands on a splendid elevation, with beautiful trees below it and westwards. Linger by the stile and let your eye follow the valley of the Avon, along which you well know Shakespeare must often have wandered. Then, just at the west of the church, the road again descends the hill, and you come to the two Binton bridges, across a very pretty bit of the Avon. You go under the railway and over the river, an island between the two bridges holding you, it may be, for a moment, and then you are at the " Four Alls " on the south bank, where perhaps you will not tarry, in spite of its quaintness. But, on the other hand, you *may* stop there. Many do, I have read, because it is a meeting-place for the men of two shires, who discuss the merits of Warwick and Gloucester, under the shadow of the great sign, which has on it the semblance of four men, and the lines which the talkers perhaps take to heart. Each man you see does something for all :—

> " A king who rules over all ; a parson who prays for all ;
> A soldier who fights for all ; a farmer who pays for all."

This may appear to the historian to be a relic of the time of that eighteenth century school of economists who made all wealth to come from land, and to the cynic to be a prophecy of a modern Chancellor of the Exchequer who would make land bear all the burdens.

The " Four Alls," Welford-on-Avon.

So, half a mile further, to Welford. This is a charming village, very like Stratford, with the same cottages of plain red brick and plain windows, very like those in Henley Street close to the " birthplace." Turn to the right, up a lane, and you come to the church, the churchyard standing a little above the street, with a low stone wall round it, and at the south a fine lychgate, which may go back to Shakespeare's time. It has seats in it and a tiled roof. The church itself has some good Norman work and a fine Norman font set on new bases, and some old glass. To the Norman building is affixed a late Decorated chancel. To the church belongs another " Tractarian " memory (*cf.* p. 247), that of James Davenport, who served here from his ordination in 1847 till his death in 1904, fifty-seven years, as curate and vicar. But the fame of Welford belongs to its Maypole, which is south-east of the church, in the main street, the road which leads to Marston and Gloucestershire. Indeed, you are now exactly on the border. The books seem a little doubtful as to where Warwickshire ends here; and the Ordnance Map, of course, does not help us. One would have thought that the river Avon was the divid-

Lych Gate, Welford.

ing line, but it is not so, for Barton, Marlcleve, Little Dorsington, and Bickmarsh are shown as in the shire of Warwick. But the Maypole, I think, may claim to be of Shakespeare's time. It is seventy-five feet high, painted ribbon-wise with red, white, and blue. It probably goes back for ancestry to Shakespeare's own day. You shall not try to dance about it, for it stands on a mound surrounded by a hedge. A local sceptic, or ignoramus, will doubt that it is a maypole. A rustic said to me on one of my visits in a tone of grave surprise, "Maypole, sir? Why,

I always thought it were a flag-staff." And he had certainly never seen a flag on it.

From Welford it is best to go out straight south and then turn eastwards, and make, by a road which turns once or twice, for Weston-on-Avon. Here there is a quite charming little church, buried away in the trees, quite close to the river, with a little lane at its south side. It has some fine heraldic tiles of the fifteenth century; glass, too, which is highly interesting to experts: a chapel of S. Anne at the south, with two narrow squints thence to the high altar; and in the north-west window is a curious device of a boat with what looks like a cover: this is described by Habington on its occurrence in Himbleton Church, Wor-

The Maypole at Welford.

cestershire, as " a table in a cockboat for Cokesey." It was perhaps a Wintour of Weston who had married the heiress of the Cookseys. It is a most interesting little church, by no means to be missed.

But we have not begun the Shakespeare villages yet, it seems, and so we must speedily rejoin the main road and come to Long Marston. Long it deserves to be called; there is a village street for more than half a mile, and at the end of it, by the cross-roads, stands the church. You see, then, that Long Marston has two objects of interest besides the pseudo-Shakespearean nickname. Its recently restored (happily

since the craze for destructive restoration) church of the
fourteenth century, still retains relics of the past: the east
window has fifteenth century glass, the B.V.M., and some
fourteenth century decorative fragments, with oak foliage; a
fine seventeenth century wall brass of a rector, 1634; and a
parish bier of 1641, most unusual to find preserved so long.
At the " King's Lodge," the ancestors of Mr. Tomes, its present
possessor, received Charles II. and gave the fugitive a
night's rest, when he was Jane Lane's servant, on his

Dancing Marston.

escape from Worcester. It is at the end of the village,
south-west of the church. Happily it has been hardly altered
at all; outside it is of little interest, but there are some
almost untouched rooms within. Charles's own account of
his escape, dictated to Pepys, shows that he " lay at Long-
Marston," he and Mrs. Lane, after they had been frighted near
Stratford-on-Avon by a troop of horse, and had parted from
Mrs. Lane's sister's husband. He speaks of it as " in the vale
of Esham." " Boscobel," the " Compleat History of his Sacred
Majesty's Most Miraculous Preservation " (1680), tells that in

Mr. Tomes's house, " Will Jackson, being in the kitchen, in pursuance of his disguise, and the cook maid busy in providing supper for her master's friends, she desired him to wind up the Jack. Will Jackson was obedient, and attempted it, but hit not the right way, which made the maid in some passion ask, ' What county man are you, that you know not how to wind up a Jack ? ' Will Jackson answered very satisfactorily : ' I am a poor tenant's son of Colonel Lane in Staffordshire. We seldom have roast meat, but when we have we don't make use of a Jack,' which in some measure assuaged the maid's indignation." Charles stayed there but one night and then " without any considerable accident rode by Cambden and arrived that night at an inn in Cirencester."

The Monks of Coventry and the Abbey of S. Evroult at Ouche held land in Marston in the early days. It was closely connected with its neighbouring Gloucestershire village, the Barell and Bushell families, of the late Middle Ages, living apparently in both.

Let us now go on to Pebworth. Turn back from Mr. Tomes's house by the road at the north of the church, which before long turns southwards again and you come to Pebworth.

The first thing you are to notice is the village street. And about this I will quote from the admirable " Evesham and Four Shires Notes and Queries," edited by Mr. E. A. B. Barnard, vol. i., p. 177 :—

" The Rev. Mr. Phillips, once of Pebworth, told me there is a local belief there that the reason the village street is called Friday Street is because it contained the only inn in Pebworth at the time Shakespeare was living ; and he was such a regular visitor there on that particular day of the week that the circumstance has been recorded in the naming of the street. There are probably many stories of witches having lived in this neighbourhood, if one only had time to search for them ; but this same village of Pebworth appears to have harboured a witch as recently as fifty years ago. She was supposed to have power to cure all sorts of diseases by muttering incantations over the patients, and I have heard of two cases of her miraculous cures by these means. One was that a young woman was completely cured of St. Vitus's dance, with which she had been afflicted from childhood. The other was a case of a very bad whitlow, which disappeared directly after some muttered words, and the application of a little saliva. Very strange things are said to have taken place in the old woman's cottage ; pieces of furniture travelled about from room to room without any visible hands touching them, and on one occasion a pot of broth deliberately removed itself from the fire, went into the adjoining room, and emptied itself into a basin waiting there to receive it.   Just outside this village, and upon Mr. Allen's property, there is a pond in which it is reported a woman was drowned long ago ; and the villagers even now will not go there at night, for they say it is still haunted by the ghost."

After this ghostliness we had better go to the church to recover our good spirits.

In Pebworth church the thing to observe is the wall painting which commemorates the Martin family, and is dated 1629.   The church itself has the usual Warwickshire tower, and has plenty of interest, Norman nave, and a clerestory of dormer windows.

But why in the world is it " piping " Pebworth ? For a similar reason, no doubt, to that which made Marston " dancing " : the one piped and the other danced.   One supposes they were Gloucestershire villages which always hung together and stood apart from the other six, which are all of Warwick.   An account of the early history of the parish can be obtained from Atkyns's " Gloucestershire " (1712) and Rudder's " New History " (1779). The story goes back to Domesday—then tells of Roger de Quiney Earl of Winchester, *tempore Hen. III.*   Rudder gives Sir Alan Bushel as lord of the manor in 1245, who was buried in the church.   But no one till a modern writer suggests the origin of the name of the village, which appears at least as early as 1396 : was it " the estate of one Pebba or Pebbe ? "[1]   William Grevil, that flower of merchants (*see* p. 145), possessed land there. Pebworth is closely connected with Broad Marston, where the Bnshells' mansion was, of which a part still remains, including what was once a private chapel, of seventeenth century date, and is now two cottages ; and the chapel was no doubt under the Pebworth church.

Of this there is not a little to be said.   It is set to the south of the village, on a hill ; of the fourteenth and fifteenth centuries as to tower and nave, with a " new aisle " (so described in 1528) at the south, which has niche and piscina.   From this aisle the rood loft was entered : one can still see several steps.   The

---

[1] W. St. Clair Baddeley, " Place Names of Gloucestershire " (Glos. 1913) p. 120, Pebworth, Pebeworthe (*c.* 848) ; Pebevorde (Domesday) ; Pebeorda (*c.* 1140), &c.   The prefix points to a proper name Pebba, A.S. worth, farm or homestead.

chancel is probably Early English : the nave has had dormer windows inserted in the roof on the south side.   There are many mural monuments, of Marten, Cooper, Howes, Eden, Shekell (originally Shakerley), Bonner (to be compared with a famous one at Mickleton).   In the church, and one may mention, by the north door of the chancel, is now the worn effigy of a priest, " Hic jacet dns' Thomas' Barell quonda' vicarius," who was appointed in 1458.   This (if I can trust the infallible Bristol and Gloucestershire Archaeological Society—" Transactions," vol. iv., p. 220) seems to have been moved out of the church since 1880. It ought to be moved back at once.   Or am I confusing this with what the learned writer therein terms a coffin lid ?   Mr. Bloom, also a learned man, has quite other views, and reads the name ' Viliett.'   At any rate, let us go back into the church and look at the east window.   It contains fragments of rather coarse fifteenth century glass, two female saints—S. Barbara, and S. Catherine or S. Margaret.   Then out into the sunshine again. Bear away the thought that there were Barells and Bushells here from the fifteenth to the eighteenth century.   And I cannot forbear to note that the last of the famous old Fettiplaces of Swinbrook, Oxon, and of Widford, an island of Gloucestershire close to it, was buried here in 1805.   I opine that the last Fettiplace but one married a Bushell.

Now we may turn backwards and follow a straight northern road to Dorsington : first the Great and then, crossing the brook, the Little.   You will go on to Bidford by Barton, where is an inn with a most delightful title, unique, I think, the " Cottage of Content."

At Dorsington, which is just on the Warwickshire border, and only two miles from Long Marston, is a quaint brick church of 1754, which could not do without the Warwickshire embattled tower.   Then the road winds and takes you across the bridge to Bidford.   The bridge itself reminds you of those on the stripling Thames—its buttresses stand out into the stream and their angles form convenient resting-places for the wayfarer who stays, as he crosses, to look up and down stream.   It was repaired in 1449 and again in 1482, and again in 1650, having been " broken down for the security of the country during the late wars " ; since when it looks, to your kindly eye, as if it had needed no restoration.   Close to the bridge is the White Lion, of which many good things are said, though one gathers from a local guide that its palmy days are over.   Go up the street which turns

to the left and broadens as it turns, and you will find in front of
you the church and what was once the Falcon inn. Take
the church first, and it will repay you. It, again, has an embattled
tower, but it is one unlike all others in the county, and you may
have the gravest doubts as to its date, though Mr. Bloom thinks
it of the fourteenth century. You may have none at all
as to that of the nave and aisles, which actually belong to that
rare period of church architecture, the reign of William IV. It
has no pretensions, and is quite content with a ceiling. The
Early English chancel, however, survives, and in it is the bust
of Dorothy Skipwith, first wife to Sir Fulwar Skipwith, Bart.,

Drunken Bidford.

who died in 1655. What you may not see perhaps is the fine
silver gilt communion plate, a gift, again, of that most generous
dame, the Duchess Dudley. From the church the graveyard
slopes down southwards to the river. To the north-west is the
fine Elizabethan house which was once the Falcon inn. And
there, they say, Master Shakespeare would make merry, and
somewhat more. One need not suppose there is a word of truth
in the tale.

Now as to the history of Bidford, Dugdale has a great deal to
say. It was of the crown demesne under Edward Confessor, and
William Conqueror retained it: it was not given away till John
gave it with his daughter Joan to Llewellyn Prince of Wales. It

was, of course, confiscated on Llewellyn's rebellion, and it came later on to the Wakes. One manor had been split off as early as Stephen's reign and given to the monks of Bordesley. But it is not worth while to tell the whole story. Interest to-day may be presumed, from a book I read recently, to centre in the public-houses. There are several, says the author, and the chief are the White Lion, the Mason's Arms, the Pleasure Boat, and the Fisherman's Rest. How attractive are the titles; and the writer implies that sobriety is the badge of them all. Only poor old Shakespeare was overcome at the Falcon, and

The Old Falcon, Bidford.

there is no Falcon now. One does not like the story of the Bidford drinking club, yet there is no doubt that people did drink in those days, but they were perhaps quite as sober as we are to-day, for certainly their liquors were less potent than those popular in England since the influence of the Scotch became predominant in our Church and State. But how did the story about these villages—it is " drunken " Bidford which sticks in one's gullet—originate? When was it first applied to Shake-speare? Why to Shakespeare at all? I cannot answer these ques-tions ; but I do think that the epithets must represent a common

R

idea of the reputation of each village. Happily they do so no longer. Before we turn away from the White Lion (for you will observe that we have gone back there again after the church), up the hill to look for the Falcon, we will note what the author of " The Idyllic Avon " says as to a night in August: " The romantic bridge, hundreds of years old, stands solid and still with the dark Avon flowing under. The backs of the houses, abutting on the river banks and the church beyond, show, in their elevated position, dimly above the rippling water. Silence.has succeeded the noise of the crowd of holiday makers ; all are now gone, except one couple who whisper together on the bridge."

Well, the Falcon—it has long ceased to be an inn. When it was an inn Shakespeare visited it; and, I think I have read somewhere, Charles I. Then it became a workhouse : the local historian does not know how or when. He adds (I am quoting from a highly pleasing " Souvenir of Bidford and Neighbour-hood," with twenty capital illustrations, published by Harry Collins, Post Office, Bidford, and sold for threepence—a booklet which every visitor should buy) the pleasant suggestion that Tennyson referred to it in the lines :—

> " The workhouse stands where was an inn !
> O earth, what changes hast thou seen ;
> Where now the pauper whines, have been
> The wines one keeps inside a bin ! "

But it is not a workhouse now, only a place where you may obtain outdoor relief. There is no doubt that it has been far, far too much restored ; but besides its solid strength it has still features which may be admired—its ribbed stone front, its two good gables, and its large mullioned windows. Altogether it is a good culmination to the hill top. But I wish it did not look so new.

So you may leave it, either turning at once, at the top of the hill, to Wixford, or going back again by the White Lion, on for a quarter of a mile by the Salford road, then turning north-wards to Broom. Beggarly Broom may soon be disposed of. There are some pretty houses of Shakespeare's time, not beggarly; but most things are new here, including a church. I am told by a local antiquary not to fancy that this is the Broom from which Miss Dolman wrote to Mr. Shenstone ; so I can find no pleasing memory of the past about the place. In truth, there are several

Broomes, or Brooms, in the district ; and even Dugdale confesses
that two of them he cannot distinguish.   So we will not tarry,
but go on at once into the Bidford-Alcester road and turn to the
left to Wixford.   Wixford is "papist" in the jingle, but I cannot
tell why.   Perhaps the church, hidden away from any road, up a
lane whose high banks remind one of Devonshire, seemed to have
something privy about it.   I know not.   But you will first see
the picturesque inn at the end of the village close by the bridge
over the diminutive Arrow, for you are quite sure to lose your
way.   My experience would rather transfer the Bidford epithet to
Wixford, for the man whom I questioned, as he sat outside the
inn door, knew nothing at all about the church, he said, but only
about the drink.   However, you must by no means fail to see
the church.   It has two Norman doorways (much restored), a
nave with thirteenth and fourteenth century work, a very good
roof, a chantry chapel with a fine fifteenth century east window
and two others at the south, all the architecture and glass
belonging to the same time and foundation.   This contains the
very fine tomb of its founders, Thomas Crewe and his wife, who
died in 1400 and 1411, about whom Dugdale has to tell you.
The man wears armour, the woman a rich gown, tied with
strings at the breast, and a long mantle.   It is a brass of quite
exceptional importance, a splendid example of its style, and
in almost perfect preservation.   On the west wall is the small
and very interesting brass of Rhys, fourth son of Rhys Griffin
of Broome, 1597.   The coat has twelve quarterings.   There is
the old parish chest with its three locks.   Outside there is the
base of the old cross and a quite magnificent yew tree, under
which very many folk could sit, and no doubt do.   They say the
branches are nine yards long.   In 1669 six parishioners com-
plained to the Registrar of the diocese that Mr. Kecke, the
Minister, desired to cut down "a certaine well growne yew
tree in our churchyard of Wixford, the like whereof is not to
be found in all the diocese," expressed their indignation that
he should desire to "deface ye churchyard of ys ornament,"
and desired "my Lord Bishop to putt a barr to his proceedings."   Mr. Kecke replied vigorously protesting against the
"false information of our papisticall parishioners."   The yew
is still the wonder that it was so long ago.   And so we leave
the church of papist Wixford in its beautiful solitude, far away
as it looks from the life and work of men.   Was there a papist

settlement here in the sixteenth or seventeenth century ?   It is curious that nothing is known about it.

Now back to the main road, then northwards and up the hill to the right to dodging Exhall; and here is a puzzle again. When did the village (I find what I think to be the only use of the word in Shakespeare) " dodge and palter in the shifts of lowness " ?   I cannot tell.   Its history goes far enough back. Thurkil held one and a half hides there (Ecleshelle) of the William-son of Corbucion (Corbison) in Domesday.   But I find no dodging then or in later times.   The church, I grieve to say, is exceeding hideous, having been carefully restored in 1863. There are beautiful views from the churchyard, all down the valley of the Avon and across to the Cotswolds.   Inside there have been spared the figures of John Walsingham, 1566, and Eleanor his wife, one of the daughters of Humphrey Ashfield of Heythrop, Oxon, her father an esquire like her husband ; but the tomb on which they once rested has gone.   There is also a good Jacobean chair in the chancel.   I do not think there is anything else, alas !   So we had better go on to Temple Grafton.   Now, about this journey, a word of caution.   You go along a delightful road, southwards, across a pretty little stream, and then you find yourself at the foot of what I believe to be the most abrupt hill in Warwickshire.   My adventures on it will interest nobody ; so I will only say to travellers, " Beware."   At the top you find some charming houses, and the disappointment of a quite modern church, in which only the windows are faintly reminiscent of what has gone.   The church (the old one) it is which claimed a Shakespearean interest.   Everyone knows that on November 27, 1582, a licence was granted by the Bishop of Worcester for the marriage of William Shakespeare to Anne Whateley of Temple Grafton.   Now, Sir Sidney Lee tells us that the diocese of Worcester was honeycombed with Shakespeares ; and it is quite certain that on November 28 two husbandmen of Stratford, Sandells and Richardson, bound themselves under surety of £40 to indemnify the Bishop against any proceedings if a pre-contract should be discovered to nullify the marriage of William Shakespeare and Anne Hathaway.   Mr. Charles Elton was of one mind with Sir Sidney in his scepticism.   Shakespeare was not married to a lady who lived at " hungry Grafton."   There is also the view already mentioned, a view that William, our William, was married in an oratory of the old manor-house at Shottery according to papist rites : there is no evidence at all of that. Others are so precise as to fix his wedding in Temple Grafton church on December 2, 1582. But Advent Sunday was December 1 in that year, and then marriages stopped ; so he was probably married on November 29. But where, we cannot tell. And why did his contemporaries call Grafton " hungry " ? It was an epithet attached to poor land, and is still, and has nothing to do with the people.

Leave Temple Grafton then, unsatisfied and hungry yourself, and go straight northwards, along a beautiful Warwickshire way, which crosses the main road from Stratford to Alcester, and come to Haselor, a place very well indeed worth seeing. The village itself may not long detain us, but there is an old house (Jacobean) and the old stocks are in the village street. But above the village, looking down upon it, and with a magnificent view north-west and south-east, is the fine Early English church, beautifully kept, and restored without ruin to its beauty. In the wooden porch, common in this district, is good old oak work, and on the footpath by which you ascend from Walcot (Haselor has two hamlets, Walcot and Upton) are the steps and the stump of the old village cross. From here you can go by a good road to Billesley (*see* p. 249). But now, before you go, you shall have the story attaching to it as given by Dugdale :

" Southward from Haselor," says he, " (but within the same Parish) is a Coppice Wood, and in it a notable Hill, which is of such steep and equall Ascent from every Side as if it had been artificially made, so that it is a very eminent Mark over all that Part of the Country and by the common people called Alcock's Arbour : Towards the foot thereof is a Hole, now almost filled up, having been the Entrance into a Cave, as the Inhabitants report : Of which Cave there is an old Wives story that passes for Current among the People of the adjacent Towns, *viz.*, that one Alcock, a great Robber, used to lodge therein, & having got much money by that course of Life, hid it in an Ironbound Chest, where unto were three Keys : which Chest, they say, is still there, but guarded by a Cock that continually sits upon it ; And that on a Time an Oxford Schollar came thither with a Key that opened two of the Locks, but as he was attempting to open the Third the Cock seized on him : To all whiche they adde, that if one Bone of the Partie who set the Cock there could be brought, he would yield up the Chest." There are those who trace this to a Celtic legend, and then rationalise that, but I confess I like it in its present form.

From Haselor you may go to Wilmcote, of which there may first be told a record, which has reached me, of the life of a modern parson, the squire of Alveston. (*See* pp. 206–8).

" In the thirties of the last century Mr. Knottesford turned his eyes towards Aston. He could not bear to send his last son to school, and desiring to keep him always near him, bought the Advowson of the living of Aston Cantlow. Belonging to this parish, about two and a half miles nearer Stratford, is the hamlet of Wilmcote. Here stone of rather uncertain quality had been quarried for some time ; and just now a successful attempt was made to utilise the bad building stone for cement. This more than doubled the population. The place was in a sad state. On a Saturday the quarry hands would get in a cask of ale and sit down to finish it, thus damning their souls and ruining their families at the same time. To remedy the deplorable state of things he freely spent his own and, no doubt, his friends' money. Mr. Knottesford and his son set about building a chapel-of-ease, hoping that in the end Wilmcote might form a separate parish, which it did in 1867. Land was given by the squire, Mr. Corbett, Mr. Butterfield was the architect ; the church was built and consecrated on S. Martin's Day, 1841. Next the school was added, and lastly the vicarage, forming a quad or three sides of one. Mr. E. B. Fortescue was the first priest-in-charge, while Mr. Knottesford's daughter's marriage, in 1843, to the Rev. G. F. Jackson, who also came to live in the old manor, provided a helper in both parishes, and also at Aston Cantlow, where, the old vicar having died, a Mr. Hill, also fresh from Oxford, had accepted the living and was using his money to restore the beautiful old church and build a ' Parish Hall,' still used as a school. Mr. Hill was called to rest before his work was done, dying at sea on his return from Madeira. Mr. E. B. Fortescue was also dangerously ill for some months at this time, and of the three zealous young men who were so eagerly striving to show the village folk what Christ's Church really is, only one, the Rev. G. F. Jackson, was left to cheer the fast ageing priest and keep the work going. In the end, mainly owing to the generosity of Mrs. Hill, widow of the late vicar, the work at Aston Cantlow was finished, though hardly as it had been hoped to be ; a vicar was appointed, and soon after

1850 Mr. E. B. Fortescue left Wilmcote to be provost of S. Ninian's Cathedral, Perth, and Mr. Sherard was placed in charge of Wilmcote. It is a doubtful point whether the ' vestments' were first used at Wilmcote or at S. Thomas's, Oxford. It is only a question of weeks. The first (?) attempt at a retreat for priests was made at Wilmcote in 1847 or 1848. About ten clergy attended. Many of the well-known men connected with the Oxford Movement used to come to see the first village church built on purpose to embody their ideas. The church is one of those gems of architecture produced by the first impassioned throes of the Oxford Movement. It was designed by Mr. Butterfield. The vicarage and schools were no doubt by the same hand, and the former was designed in the hope that it might be the home of one or two celibate clergy."

Wilmcote to-day, ecclesiastically, is a memorial of this good man. The place is well worth a visit, and still worthily upholds these holy associations. A traveller in the autumn of 1913 strayed into the church and found Evensong being said by a priest who might have come straight from the Tractarian workshop. The church was dim and the light which brightened it came from the candles lighted on the altar. The quiet restraint of the reader's voice and the reverent responses of the small congregation were in keeping with the simple severity of the architecture. The trees have grown up now in the little churchyard, and already an air of Victorian antiquity pervades it. It is not out of keeping with the memory of centuries earlier, when the village was the home of Shakespeare's mother. As you leave the village, north-eastwards from the church, you see three cottages (so they seem to be) which were once the farmhouse in which Mary Arden was born. They have dormer windows set in the roof, and the eastern end, with its old beams, is picturesque. Behind the house, too, are old buildings. But for the rest the house has no great claim to a visit. Shakespeare's mother lived there as a girl : that is all. Perhaps it is enough. The reputation of Christopher Sly, if really it belonged to Wincot where the fat ale-wife Marian Hacket lived (and if that be Wilmcote), has not survived, and probably the ale, which a seventeenth century poet asserts

> " —As Shakespeare fancies
> Did put this Sly into such lordly trances."

has hardly retained its reputation. Yet still the village wears its manner of placid content which befits the man who made it famous. "Let the world slip," it seems to say, " we shall ne'er be younger." And after all there were three " Wincots," one only a small hamlet (a single house, now) in the parish of Quinton, another (far away on the Staffordshire border), to which the ale poem really belongs. So Sir Sidney Lee thinks Sly's alehouse was not in Shakespeare's mother's village. I shake my head, but say nothing.

Mary Arden's Cottage, Wilmcote.

Let us return to Mr. Knottesford and eighty years ago, for we are on the way to another village with which he was connected. A sense of duty made him accept the cure of Billesley, a parish then consisting of five houses and a tiny Queen Anne church with enormously thick whitewashed walls, round headed windows, and west gallery at the end of the nave, an altar standing in the middle of the apse, and a small south transept which served as a vestry, and in which he and his wife, his second son, who died from scarlet fever caught at school, and a baby grand-child, are buried. Here he ministered till his death in 1859. The arrangement for the Sunday services was curious. On Sundays at Alveston the family coach came across to the front door. The clergy and the whole household found places in it or outside, and drove six miles to Billesley, where morning service took place at 11 o'clock : usually, no doubt, the curate took the service and the rector preached.

"After morning service" (says my kind informant) "my great grandfather and his family retired to one of the pews for dinner. The footman laid the cloth on a seat—the pew contained a firegrate—and the cold dinner, brought over in the coach, was set out. The rector, with the noble English tradition of observing the Sunday rest for his servants so far as possible, for a long time refused hospitality on Sunday. He would give no, or at least the minimum of, trouble to any servants on Sunday. He subsequently yielded so far as to accept the use of a parlour from a friend leading to an adjacent garden. After dinner the children retired to the churchyard to play, the rector rested in the pew, the servants elsewhere finished the dinner. At 3 o'clock came evening prayers and sermon, after which the whole family mounted the coach and drove six miles home.

"How well one can picture the old gentleman in old-fashioned black knee-breeches, black silk stockings, and silver-buckled shoes. Wigs by that time had gone out of fashion, but his wife said she had never seen the natural colour of his hair, as he wore powder. The old gentleman's surplice, no doubt, reached to his feet, and so he needed no cassock." So says his great-grandson, but probably he wore one.

At the time there was no church at Wilmcote or resident priest in the next parish when Mr. Knottesford was incumbent. Billesley church, therefore, was crammed and a large Sunday school was started and kept up in the old pigeon-house, lent and prepared for the purpose. "Several very old people now will ask me to read to them out of the Bible Mr. Knottesford gave me as a prize at Sunday school." So says one who remembers those days with affection. Such memories make the village well worth a visit. You may take it as you go from Stratford to Alcester. It is about half a mile from the main road and four miles from Stratford as you go westwards, or it will come in a very pretty winding way that you follow from Haselor. Here is another Shakespeare association : for Elizabeth Nash, then a widow and the poet's grand-daughter, was married here in 1649 to John Barnard, whom Charles II. knighted. It was by her that, before all was lost, Henrietta Maria had been received in the house where Shakespeare died. We cannot stand in the building where she was wedded a second time, for it no longer exists. The church is of the late seventeenth century rather than of Queen Anne's time, well built with very thick walls, and an apsidal east end. It contains good contemporary rails and chairs. But the churchyard is sorely neglected, the grass growing elbow high, the tombs covered, the walls falling down. The manor-house is, as I write, being restored and added to. There is a legend that Shakespeare used to visit there and wrote "As you like it" in the oak parlour;

Haunted Hillborough.

but a legend it is. It is a fine Elizabethan building with a good doorway facing south, towards the lawn with its large round basin and single fountain jet. There is a road thence to Wilmcote, but the ascent at one point is sudden and precipitous, and then you have many fields and many gates. Better go northwards, almost to Aston Cantlow and then turn east.

But you will observe that we have left out one of the villages —haunted Hillborough. I ought really to have taken you to it between Welford and Bidford, only we did not go that way. It is north of the Avon, about half way between the two villages, and south of the Stratford and Bidford road. But it is not a village at all. It is in the heart of the other villages. The local guide tells you that the best way is to cross to the

Avon at Binton bridges, if you come from the south, " turn to the left on reaching the Stratford and Bidford main road, and after the railway bridge, turn down a lane." Hillborough was once a much larger village than it is now, and it has a history, which Mr. Cox shall tell. Does any of it account for the haunting ? .

" *Hilborough*, a Lordship anciently given by [he leaves a blank] together with *Grafton*, to the Monks of *Evesham* ; but having been wrested from them by some potent Men in the *Saxon* Times, was soon after the *Norman* Conquest given to *Urso D'Abitot*, and *Osborn* Son of *Richard*, as appears by Domesday Book, wherein it is written, *Hildeborde*, and *Hildebereud*. What *Urso* held was then certify'd to contain one Hide and a Half, having been in the *Confessor's* Time, the Freehold of one *Ernvi* ; but *Osborn's* Proportion is not known. Whether the Monks of *Evesham* were ever after repossessed of it, is not known ; yet we find, that Abbot *Robert*, who liv'd in the Beginning of King *William Rufus's* Reign, made a grant thereof to *William de Sevecurte* ; but if he held it at all, 'twas not long ; for in King *Stephen's* Reign, *Peter de Stodleg*, the Progenitor of the Family of *Corbizon*, and *Henry Montfort*, were Owners of great Part of it ; and that immediately upon the Foundation of *Bordsley* Abby, the same *Peter* gave to that Monastry ten Acres of Land lying here, in whose Grant it was written *Hilburgworth*, Fishing in the River *Avon*, and free Passage thro' his Flood-gates here. *Peter Corbizon* and *William Cantilupe*, had some Interests in the Lordship, in King *John's* Reign ; but in the Reign of King *Henry* III. it was vested wholly in *Henry Hubaut*, tho' *Montfort* laid claim to some Part of it, and a Suit was commenced in the King's Court about it ; but it was recover'd by *Hubaut*. It was then accounted half a Knight's Fee, and was held of *Hastings* Earl of *Pembroke* by *John Hubard*, the Heir of *Henry*, whose Posterity have enjoy'd it ever since, unless they have lately aliened it."

After all this one feels that the village should have some size. Not so, as you see it to-day. There are very few houses there now ; one, with four tall chimneys (twins) and a high gable entirely covered with ivy, is the " haunted " house. It is to the left, by the way you came. And you can go on to Bidford by a footpath past Grange Mill, where the river's progress is stopped (you might well come by river). And no one can tell you why it is haunted, so people have taken to invention. Charles II.

stopped here in his flight with a large treasure chest, forsooth, from Worcester, there was a hot fight, and he escaped across the river to Marston ; all nonsense, of course. And so is the pseudo-Shakespeare rhyme. A much more genuine Shakespeare village than any of these is Charlecote, of which elsewhere (see above, p. 209).

Now at Hillborough you are not far from, or if you return from Alcester to Henley, leaving the Alne to your left, you will pass by, Kinwarton, a pretty little village, to your left, and reach Great Alne. Here the church is in a charming situation, back from the road and above it, approached by a pretty path, with a charming old farmhouse hard by. The church itself, enlarged in 1857, had a Sunday school joined on to it, and on the gallery is an inscription telling of the restoration and of the benefactions to the parish. So on by winding road you may pass through Little Alne without noticing it ; but if you wish to, you will know, where you are by the smithy.

Now at the smithy you can turn aside to the right, if you will, and go by the bridge over the river and the railway—or you may cross at a ford if you like—to Aston Cantlow or Cantilupe. Dugdale gives a long record of its history from the time of William Conqueror, when it belonged to Osbern Fitz-Richard, down to its possession by the Beauchamps, and then the Neviles, with a special reference to the Cantilupes, whose history is thus summarised by Thomas Cox :—

" In the Reign of K. *John, Anno* 6. it was given to *William de Cantelupe,* to whom the Sheriff, after he had had the Corn and Stock on it valu'd at a just Price, was commanded to deliver them ; and from his Descendents the Town had the Name of *Cantelupe* added to it to distinguish it from other *Astons* in this County. He by adhering to the Earl of *Chester* and the disaffected Barons against the King, was like to have lost this Manor upon the Claim of *Ralph Tankervile* ; but submitting in Time, the King confirm'd it to him during Pleasure. He procured a Market and a Fair here, by giving King *Henry* III. a Fine of 15 Marks ; and a little after, a Confirmation of it to him and his Heirs ; with a special Proviso, that if the King or his Heirs should ever think fit to restore it to the *Tankerviles,* he should have other Lands given him of equal value. His Son and Heir *William* was a martial Man, and in special Favour with the same King, but did nothing memorable relating to this Manor ; and so we pass to his Son and Successor *William*, who gave the Church of this Town to the Hospital built by his Grandfather at the Gates of the Monastery of *Studeley*."

There was not much more to tell of the lords of this place. The interest of the village has now all centred in Shakespeare, for Wilmcote, where his mother lived before her marriage, is a hamlet of Aston Cantlow. But the Ardens we may leave aside

The Guild House, Aston Cantlow.

for the moment, and look simply at Aston. There is no trace of the old castle of the Cantilupes remaining. Some book says there are signs of a moat, which fills when the river is high, but certainly it was not high in August, 1911, so I will not pretend to have discovered them. The church itself is very full of interest, and very beautifully cared for to-day. So well cared for, indeed, that the place where the key is hidden is sometimes searched in vain. But it has no air of being closed to men ; on the contrary, there is every sign of its being meet, and used, for daily and for private prayers. On the north porch door is an early stone representation of the Nativity. The tracery of the east window is of a rare and interesting design, suggesting that at Malmesbury. All the work within is good and mostly fifteenth century, though the church itself is earlier by a century or more. Especially you will notice the sedilia, the font, and the beautiful chapel in the north aisle. This last was the chapel of the guild of which Dugdale writes thus : " In this church there was antiently a certain Fraternity or Guild, consisting of the Parishioners only, being founded by them to the Honour of God and the Blessed Virgin ; but it had no lawful establishment till 9 E. 4, at which time, upon the humble petition of the inhabitants, license was granted to Sir Edward Nevill, Knight, then Lord of the Manor, that he should so settle and order the same, as that there might be a certain Priest maintained there, to celebrate Divine Service daily at the altar of the Blessed Virgin in the said Church, for the good estate of the said K. Edw. 4 and Eliz. his consort ; as also for the Brethren and Sisters of that Fraternitie during their life, and for their souls after their Departure hence, and the souls of all the faithful deceased ; which accordingly was effected, and lands disposed thereunto for that purpose." Who has those lands now ? They would be forfeited to the Crown under Edward VI., but not likely to remain in its possession. The guild chapel has two beautiful oak pews, with inscription, probably once belonging to the screen—" Thy dead shall live." And there are two ancient wooden candlesticks, with good pedestals of floral design. Another piece of the old woodwork is the faldstool of the fifteenth century. There is a little good fourteenth century glass ; and thus we find three centuries represented in this fine church, the late thirteenth its building, the fourteenth its glass, the fifteenth its woodwork. There still, in spite of restoration, lingers an air of medieval dignity and richness over the ancient and well-beloved church. And it was here at the end of 1557 that John Shakespeare married Mary Arden.

CHAPTER XII

JUST outside the range of the Shakespearean " villages," south of Wixford, south-west of Exhall and Bidford, on the road from Stratford-on-Avon to Evesham, is Salford. This contains the hamlets Abbot's Salford, Salford Priors, the two Bevingtons, Wood and Cock, and Dunnington. For the moment let us speak of the Salfords, through which we pass, before the Stratford road to Evesham joins the Alcester road which passes through the Bevingtons and Dunnington. The ecclesiastical designation of the two comes from their connection with the abbey of Evesham, to which they belonged of old. Priors Salford after the dissolution was royal property, and later it was held by the family of Clarke. There are good portraits of Sir Simon Clarke and his wife at Abbot's Salford Hall. This is a fine Elizabethan house. You may be confused by the date over the main doorway—it should be 1602 and was altered by a clumsy mason. It stands a little way from the road, and is approached through a gateway under a long rather low building, which within has a sharp gable in the middle, over the arch, and a little cord and plaster work. To the right, as you stand with your back to the house and look towards the porch—which has a high wood gate filling it—is a stairway to a barn or outhouse. In the gable is a sundial. A wall from this runs up to the house, dividing the garden from the court, with its flagged path betwixt large stretches of grass. The present house has taken the place of one which used to be to the east, surrounded by a moat, with an old walled garden, as now to the south. It is the most irregular of buildings ; nothing precise or symmetrical as the forecourt might have led you to expect. At the east is the tall Jacobean

Abbot's
Salford

E·H·N·

wing; at the west are low timbered plastered buildings of much earlier date. A smaller building behind, of modern erection, is used as a farmhouse, and most of the year the hall itself is in charge of a caretaker. But at times the ancient family of Eyston, one of the most ancient families in England, and the direct descendants of the great saint and hero of the sixteenth century, Sir Thomas More, come there, and the savour of old days is renewed. The great windows, bays and straight alike with large mullions, the projections and retreats, the different levels, the turns and twists of the building as you look at it from the front, prepare you for the strange alarums and excursions within. A most beautiful house it is, with fine rooms, panelled or plastered, high and low, upstairs and downstairs, with many staircases and many levels, built round a small court, but as you see from the back, with all sorts of surprising alterations and additions of different dates and different styles. From the hall you may pass into the chapel, on the ground floor (as is not common, and indeed it is hardly more than a century old, for two rooms were turned into one and made into this chapel by the nuns who occupied the house when they were exiled from France during the Revolution). This (Roman Catholic) has many modern decorations, and seems to have been made of two long rooms thrown together, out of the eastern-most of which is a comfortable little sacristy and drawing-room, for the clergyman. It would seem that, if not here, yet in this house, the Roman mass was said, at least intermittently, during the days of persecution. A relic of those times is the hiding-place upstairs, where an innocent cupboard with shelves, by a turn, reveals the way into a secret room, a " hole " indeed, below. There is a beautiful gallery at the top of the house, seventy-five feet long, with four-light transomed windows at each end. There is some good heraldic glass in the house, from which, as from documents, you can trace the history of the succession. At the dissolution of the monasteries the land of Abbot's Salford was given to Sir Philip Hoby. He sold it to Mr. Littleton, he to Mr. Alderford, and he left two co-heiresses, one the wife of Sir Simon Clarke, the other of Mr. Charles Stanford. The property continued with the Stanfords till the death of a possessor who left it to Robert Berkeley for his life, and then to his second son, and then in default of a second son to the family of Eyston of Hendred, Berks, to descend in the same way, which curious bequest is now

s

operative. Some have thought that it was Sir Simon Clarke (the son-in-law of Hobson, the Cambridge carrier of "Hobson's choice" and Milton's epitaph) who did the seventeenth century re-building here; but it is not unlikely that it was the work of one of the Stanfords who were owners when Dugdale wrote. It is a beautiful house, which should be but gradually restored and would make a most perfect Elizabethan picture were it restored to its first beauty. But as it is it has a strange mysterious charm, perhaps that of old loyalties or old plottings, certainly that of good building, original design, original work. You may wander about in it and easily lose yourself; and then you are back among the Tudors at once. Go up to the long

The Manor House, Cleeve Prior.

attic and the top of the house and look eastwards across the Avon and to Cleeve Hill which looks over you and shuts in your view with its rich verdure.

When you are at Salford it will be a very wise thing to take a walk of half a mile to the most beautiful Cleeve Mill, with its beautiful weir and plank bridge, whence you can look up stream towards Bidford. Cross the river and climb the hill and you come to the lovely hill of Cleeve, and the village of Cleeve Prior with its delightful manor-house and the wonderful clipped yews that Mr. New has shown so charmingly. Then there is the village green, and the church, with its two Norman doors, and its high tower, with battlements, of course, and everything handsome about it, including a modern brick transept. You will see all these things and take a cup of tea at the King's Arms, where certainly Shakespeare may have been, for they say that part of it is even of the fourteenth century ; but he left no record of it, as he did of Daventry, or Eastcheap, or that heath in Warwickshire (which was it ?) where Christopher Sly had his adventures. You might then perhaps go by the Worcestershire Littletons, villages on the south bank of the Avon, as you proceed towards Evesham. If you go thither, you must by all means see the great tithe-barn, which reminds you of the noble one at Coxwell, which William Morris so eulogised. But the prospect

Tythe Barn, Littleton.

from the hill is best, beautiful though the river way be; and this is what Michael Drayton has to say about it :—

" Shall every vale be heard to boast her wealth ? and I,
The needie Countries neere that with my Corne supply
As bravely as the best, shall onely I endure
The dull and beastly world my glories to obscure ;
Near way-lesse Ardens side, sith my rety'rd aboad
Stood quite out of the way from every common road ?
Great Evesham's fertile Gleabe, what tongue hath not estold ?
As though to her alone belonged the Garbe of Gold."

Which way shall we go ? I propose the main road. From Salford Hall a mile brings you to Harvington with its houses

of black and white and its modern church, and already you are
in the land of great orchards. Norton resembles it, and so you
come on to Evesham and mount the hill, the battlefield on your
right.

The battlefield of Evesham is notable, not only in itself, and
to the visitor because he can so easily trace it, but because it was
part of an extended and very important campaign. Though
we shall not follow this it will be worth while to get before us
that part of the localities of the campaign of July and August,
1265, which we ourselves may follow, going, as we shall, from
Evesham to Cropthorne, thence to Fladbury, Wyre, and
Pershore. All that ground, and much of Warwickshire, and
Shakespeare's country, was covered by the marching and counter-
marching. It was the summer of 1265. Henry III. was in the
custody of Simon de Montfort Earl of Leicester, and his son,
Edward, had escaped from his durance on the Welsh marches to
join de Clare Earl of Gloucester, and rescue him. The opposing
forces were on either side the Severn. Simon attempted to cross
somewhere between Worcester and Bridgnorth, but failed. His
son was gathering an army very slowly together, and brought
it at last to Kenilworth on July 31, where it lodged, partly in the
castle, partly in the town or in tents. Then it was thirty-two
miles from Worcester where Edward's army was stationed.
Edward instantly dashed by a forced march on Kenilworth and
destroyed almost the whole of the barons' army, only a few of
the leaders escaping into the castle where there was a small
garrison. This was accomplished on August 1. Simon, meanwhile, had determined to join his son, marching by Pershore,
Evesham, and Stratford-on-Avon. On the night of the 3rd he
encamped in Evesham. Edward determined to block his way,
by defending the roads that led to Stratford and Alcester.
Mortimer, it seems, came by Pershore and Bengeworth, Gloucester and Edward from the north. Simon's troops lay in the
town at night; he heard mass in the abbey, and then, when he set
out, found that troops had been seen on the green hill, by the
way along by which we have come from Harvington and
Norton. Simon's barber watched from the abbey bell-tower,
which Simon himself ascended ; not, of course, the present sole
remaining relic of the abbey, but one on the same site perhaps.
They saw Edward's troops northward, and Gloucester's—it is
the suggestion of our greatest authority, Professor Oman, whom

I am following in my account of all this—coming by the road from Wyre, while southwards was Mortimer's force approaching Bengeworth. " May God have mercy on our souls," cried Simon, " for our bodies are theirs." But he resisted all attempts to make him fly while there was yet time, and, forming his troops into column, he determined to strike sharply at Edward's force and endeavour to force his way through to Kenilworth. The Melrose chronicler, Simon's great admirer, says that King Henry was placed in the forefront because " the barons wished that the King should die with them, if it were their fate to die in the battle in which the King was engaged : their plan was that

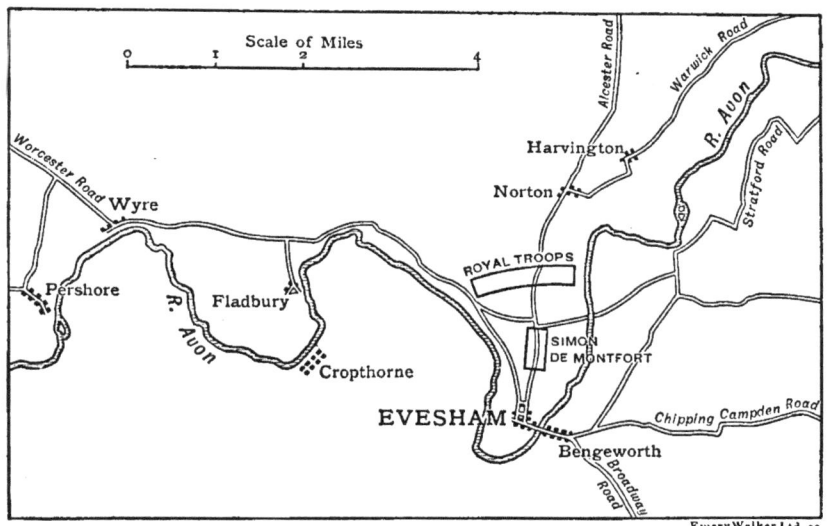

Plan of Battle of Evesham.

he should be unknown to his own adherents and should fall under the weight of their blows." So he was disguised like an ordinary horseman, and could only make himself known by his cries. This seems to me (though Professor Oman does not think so) to show that the barons really designed his death.

Up the hill then came de Montfort's cries, meeting those who were coming the way we have come from Warwickshire. They probably hardly extended in breadth beyond the road, and Welsh stragglers fell away from them as they marched, plunging into the town and trying to find their way home again by Crop-thorne or Fladbury. The column failed to break the Royalist line, and Edward's and Gloucester's men soon outflanked them, and after an hour's hard fighting they were split up and driven back down the hill to the meadow below where is a spring called Battlewell.   There, it is more likely than on the high ground where the monument to him now stands, fell " Earl Simon the Righteous."   And his son Henry fell before him, and most of his chief supporters died by his side.   So perished the gallant knight, skilled statesman, friend of good men, persecutor and intriguer and alien, but enemy of aliens and beloved by many throughout the land.

> " Simon of the mountain strong
> Flower of knightly chivalry,
> Thou who death and deadly wrong
> Barest, making England free.
> Not the holy ones of yore,
> They on earth who travailed sore,
> Came to such despite and scorn.

Meon Hill, from Evesham Battlefield.

Robert, the monk of Gloucester, who told in verse the sad tale of the wars, says :—

> " Such was the murder of Evesham, for battle none it was."

And all the while the battle raged a thick cloud covered the land, and a few drops of rain fell that did not assuage the heat.   "Grislier weather than it was might not on earth be," and the monk, thirty miles away, saw and trembled.   The day ended in a fierce storm.

As we descend the hill into the town there stretches before us the land that Drayton described :—

> " Great Evesham's fertile globe what tongue hath not extolled
> As though to her alone belonged the garb of gold,"

we say again.

Far away are Meon Hill and Bredon, the tower of Broadway, once the home of Burne-Jones, and the distant splendour of the Malvern Hills; and Evesham nestling below, out of the way of the old road which passed above it, lived apart from the main life and commerce of the nation, nor did it become important till the river was made navigable from where it joins the Severn up to Stratford. Up this is still a pleasant pilgrimage; but to-day we linger where once the abbey stood. The town has still many beautiful houses. Bridge Street, for example, contains some glorious gables and pent houses, and there is much later work of dignity and charm, such as Tower House in that street, or Dresden House in High Street, which Mr. Edmund New dates under William III., and says was built by a rich lawyer who came from the northern part of the shire to settle there. But, of course, the great fame of the town comes from the abbey that once was there, and its tower, and the two churches which still are. Back to the eighth century we go for the founding of the abbey, and century by century we trace its saints, beautifying the house by their lives and sometimes by their hands, one coming even from so far away as Crowland to build a chapel and a cell wherein he died. After the Normans came, the house grew in size and importance, and the mitred abbey of S. Mary and S. Egwin became one of the most famous in England. Of what it was at its greatest extent the gate-house and the almonry still survive, open to the green. In 1196 was written the wonderful vision of the monk of Evesham, himself a sort of prose Dante, and throughout the Middle Age great fame belonged to the house. It culminated in the days before the Dissolution when Clement Lichfield was abbat, who not only beautified the two parish churches, but built the magnificent bell-tower which is the finest relic of the monastic time.

To approach it you will pass from the market-place through Abbat Reginald's gateway (1122–1149) which is perhaps the only building still standing on which Earl Simon's eyes must have looked; and it, beautiful though it is, has been much restored, but still shows some of the fine old Norman work. Pass through it and you come to the parish church of All Saints. Enter by a small Norman door and look at the windows in the western wall which also belong to the earliest time. Then see the arches and north clerestory of the nave, much later; and lastly the beautiful outer porch with two doorways, battlements,

The Bell Tower, Evesham.

and fine carved roof, which are the work of Abbat Lichfield. And his, also, is the perfect Perpendicular chapel named after him, with its splendid roof. Then go out and enter the church of S. Laurence, not strictly a parish church, but built for the worship of the pilgrims who came to the abbey. It has suffered much from restoration, but enough of the work of Lichfield's times survives, notably the beautiful chapel now used as a baptistery, and the east window, to illustrate the best work of the fifteenth century. And here is one of those glorious fan tracery roofs, almost common among the churches of the Cotswolds, and marking the very end of the pre-Reformation time. So, too, does the bell-tower at the entrance to the meadow a short distance away, far the finest thing that remains of the abbey and the latest. Abbat Lichfield died before it was finished, but not before he had placed in it a great bell and a goodly clock. You may trace twelve tiers of arcading before you come to the battle-ments, each exquisite, broken by the lower single window and the double one above the clock, six pinnacles and two great buttresses, a thing of solid magnificence. And then go through to the meadow, and down, if it may be, to the river and look up at this splendid building from below, and you can guess how great was the glory of the town when the abbey was in its pride. Of its bells Evesham has always been proud; a traveller should read Mr. E. A. B. Barnard's excellent little book on them.

The churches and the tower survive from the Middle Ages; but the town itself bears not much of so distant a past. Leland said of it that it " is meetly large and well builded with timber. The market-place is fair and large. There be divers pretty streets in the town. The market is very celebrate." And so it is still. The single thoroughfare has its four streets. Port Street, that which brings you across the bridge; High Street, Bridge Street, and Vine Street, leading into the market-place. The Town Hall of 1586, and Booth Hall, in High Street, the charming house called "Almswood," as well as those houses we have already named, must be seen—and then, perhaps, one may imagine the marches and counter-marches through the streets in 1644 when Charles stayed two nights, was followed by Waller and the Parliamentary troops, returned again to fire the town heavily, and a year later, in May, 1645, Colonel Massey, Governor, " lost the strong garrisoned Evesham in a storm of fire and leaden balls ; the loss whereof did make the King shed tears." And so, rather hurriedly, you shall have seen all Evesham.

But before you go you will ask how this town comes into Shakespeare's country, and, instead of the usual answer, shall hear this tale. Robert Armin acted at the Globe when Shakespeare did, and a story comes from him which is used to explain the line :—

"The fool slides o'er the ice that you should break."

High Street, Evesham.

and is called "How Jack Miller the cleane foole ventred over the Severne on foot in great danger" (1605). It tells how Lord Chandos's players, of whom he was one, came to "Esam" (as it is still called by the learned) and Jack Miller, a local worthy and fool, fell in love with its clown, whom he called "Grumball." When the players must depart Jack would needs come too, for he "swore he would go all the world over with Grumball." But this the townfolk would not hear of, so they locked him up in the White Hart inn—(you must look for this). Thence could he see the players on the road to Pershore, and he determined to follow. He crossed on the thin ice, " some forty yards over,'' the ice cracking all the way, and a brickbat thrown at it instantly breaking it. It would bear a fool but not a brickbat. Armin, it is likely, was " a gentlewoman boy " : he tells later how one such pulled Jack Miller out of an oven by his heels. In 1603 a licence from the Privy Seal allows the Globe Players to act throughout the country and names Shakespeare, Burbage, Heminge, and Armin among them. So when we look out of window for the Pershore way we may bear Shakespeare in our minds, for it is very likely he was here before us.

Now let us follow the road that Mortimer came by and go uphill to Cropthorne. Nash says that Offa gave Cropthorne, in 780, to the church of Worcester, and that the grant was confirmed by Edgar. At Domesday it was still held by the same title. It was worth then six pounds; under Edward Confessor seven. The later history has no special interest. In 1779, says Nash, " the manor of Cropthorne now belongs to the Dean and Chapter of Worcester. The customs of the manor are for the tenant to have two lives in possession and three in reversion ; the widow to have her free bench, the best beast or in default thereof the best piece of furniture to be paid for a heriot upon the death of the tenant who dies seized ; the fines to be arbitrary, and the lords to hold court leet and court baron." But all that goes a very long way back. What does not go back so far is this amusing note :—

" In the Records of the County of Worcester, consisting of rolls of proceedings at quarter sessions, we find the following : 1633. Recognizance by James Fell, husbandman, William Roberts, labourer, Robert Beard, labourer, Richard Bideford, husbandman, Edward Nicholles and John Honnicome, all of Cropthorne, for their appearance at the next general sessions of the peace to abide such order as shall be enjoined them ' concerning the usage of the unlawful game of football contrary to the statutes of the land.' "

Most people when they come to Cropthorne think first of those who lived there. Nash's account of the Dingleys is that they obtained the estate of Charlton, a hamlet of Cropthorne, by marriage with the heiress of the Hondesacres, and leases to them from the bishops of their sporting rights are common from the fourteenth century. They " continued to flourish in great repute in this county," says Nash, " till the present century,

when they expired at Charleton in the person of Sir Edward
Dinely, Knight, sometime justice of the peace and deputy-
lieutenant for this county, who by Frances his wife, daughter of
Lewis Watson, Lord Rockingham, left an only surviving daughter
Eleanor, his heir, who was married to Edward Goodyere of
Burghope in Herefordshire, Esquire, which Edward was created
a baronet December 5, 1707, and was member of several parliaments for the borough of Evesham, and sometimes knight of
the shire for the county of Hereford.   He died at a great age,
March 29, 1739, and was succeeded by Sir John Dinely Goodyere, Bart., his eldest son.   Which Sir John assumed the name
of Dinely in respect of the large estate he inherited from his
mother, and was the last of the family who enjoyed it, for having
lived upon bad terms with his younger brother Samuel Dinely
Goodyere, captain of the Ruby man-of-war, and threatening
to disinherit him in favour of his sister's son, John Foot of Truro
in Cornwall, Esquire, it so alarmed and disgusted the said
Samuel that he came to the bloody resolution of murdering him,
which he executed on January 17, 1741.   A friend at Bristol
who knew their mortal antipathy had invited them both to dinner
in the hopes of reconciling them, and they parted in the evening
in seeming friendship, but the captain placed some of his crew
in the street near College Green, with orders to seize his brother,
and assisted in carrying him by violence to his ship, under pretence that he was disordered in his senses, where when they had
arrived he ordered him to be strangled in the cabin by White and
Mahoney, two ruffians of his crew, himself standing sentinel at the
door while the horrid deed was perpetrating.   It is sufficient to
say that the murder was immediately discovered and the captain
and his two accomplices, being tried at Bristol March 26 following,
were found guilty and there executed April 15."
     The estate then passed to John Foote, elder brother of the wit,
and was soon afterwards sold, Sir John's widow marrying again,
and purchasing the rights in the estate from the comedian to
whom they had come ; but the murderer left two sons, each of
whom _{was} baronet, and the younger was living when Nash
wrote in 1774.
     But now let us see what we have come to see, the church in
its fine yard at the top of the hill, a commanding site.   The
original church was Norman, and not a little of it survives—the
lowest stage of the tower, the windows pierced through the

pilasters to light the belfry, the arcades of the nave.   Then there was a thirteenth century English chancel ; this has been greatly restored, fifteen years ago.   But much more followed on.   I am tempted for once to quote a local paper, to show what people thought of the restoration, and then I will leave the visitor to judge.   The *Evesham Journal* (a most excellent paper) of July 30, 1910, thus rejoices :—

" As regards the work recently carried out the side aisles have been restored and cleaned, and the walls of these were found to be practically covered with frescoes.   Only one of these, however, has been retained, for the others were in a very bad state of pre-servation.   The columns have also been thoroughly cleaned, and the handsome runic cross and pre-Reformation altar slab have now found a more fitting place for such sacred relics.   The lath and plaster roof is now a thing of the past, and the old timber work, now laid bare, adds much to the beauty of the interior. Some time in the thirteenth century the church was partly burnt down, and while carrying out the present work some of the old charred and blackened stones were discovered in the porch.   A doorway to the old priest's chamber was found over the porch and this has been left exposed.   This chamber was probably demolished in the seventeenth century.   Many other interesting relics have been brought to light during the progress of restora-tion, which, although spread over a good number of years is now happily completed, and Cropthorne people can look with pride on their pretty little church, made all the more beautiful at the restorer's hands.   One thing it lacks, and that is a pulpit, but doubtless before long this will be provided."

After this one need not say much.   But the old altar slab re-mains, with its five consecration crosses, and it should be replaced— I will use the discreet words of the Bristol and Gloucestershire Archaeological Society—" on or before the present communion table."   There is, in the south aisle, the head of a beautiful cross, about which very much indeed is to be said.   With the curious delight people have in making everything " Anglo-Saxon," the cross has been given a very early date indeed.   On the west side of the cross are three griffins with knotted tails.   Mr. Francis Bond has given his opinion on the cross thus —:

" It shows a touch of Celtic influence, seen in many such, especially in the knots at the end of the arms.   The animals keep Norman type.   But the foliated ornament in the centre, and the trefoil curves in the exterior, show that the cross as a whole is of thirteenth century date, *c.* 1230."

About the Dingley monuments in the north aisle there is no dispute. On one are the recumbent figures of Francis (*ob.* 1624) and his wife Elizabeth. His shield above him shows him to have had twenty-four quarterings. The other monument of his son and his wife shows them kneeling facing each other with three male and three female children. The earlier monument, I think, shows eight sons living and two dead, seven daughters married, four unmarried and one dead. There is a good chair in the sanctuary, and the medieval pews remain. Outside one is struck by the fine fourteenth century completion of the tower.

Then on to Fladbury. Here the lower part of the tower is Norman, the upper part Decorated. The fine porch with its groined vaulting has lost (as has the one at Cropthorne) its parvise but retains a sundial. In the north-east chancel window are some good fragments of old glass, and in the vestry there is a most beautiful piece of thirteenth century glass showing the Madonna and Child. There is a good medieval door south of the chancel. And there are early fourteenth century tiles. A brass shows a priest (1507) in chasuble, stole, and alb. He is Thomas Morden, who was treasurer of S. Paul's and rector of Fladbury in 1458. There are brasses, too, I think, to William Pleume, rector, 1504, and Edward Peyton, 1488. The altar tomb of John Throckmorton, sub-treasurer of England, and Alianora his wife, bear date 1445. More interesting, historically, is the monument of Bishop William Lloyd, now, alas! divided into two—one part in the chancel, one in the vestry. The bust shows him in his rochet and surplice with gathered sleeves (but not full) and bands. Fladbury was, one supposes, the good bishop's favourite seat, and no wonder. After his gallant service with the Seven Bishops, and having been Bishop of S. Asaph for twenty-seven years, he was Bishop of Worcester from 1699 to 1717 ; and his son was rector of Fladbury, living in that quite beautiful house (or is it rather later?) which looks over the river, one of the finest rectories for what was, I suppose, one of the richest livings in England.

From Fladbury one should go to Wyre. Alas! the church is very much restored, so much so that, at first sight, you might think it was all new. The double bell-house on the east gable at once attracts attention, and the small semi-circular chancel arch is undoubtedly Norman. It has two huge " squints " in it. There is also a Norman font, and there is a good late Decorated window. And, of old glass, there is a curious portrait of our Lord with a divided beard. There is, indeed, a great deal of interest in the church in things both small and great. But it is so near Pershore that one must hurry on thither.

Pershore itself is a quite delightful town, with all sorts of charming houses, each with its beautiful garden—sometimes the garden better than the house, as in the case of that which is called the Abbey. Sometimes the house, if possible, better than the garden, as in that most perfect eighteenth century mansion (so indeed one may call it) with its beautiful rooms, and stairs, and ceilings, called Perrot's house. There are good wide streets, and

Pershore Bridge.

a good broad market-place. But, of course, most of all, there is the Benedictine Abbey of S. Mary, S. Peter, and S. Paul. Now, as to the date of its foundation, antiquarians differ, and it is not for us to decide between them. But in spite of the medieval passion for forged charters one may almost confidently place the date in the seventh century. William of Malmesbury is not always above suspicion, but he makes it to have been restored in 792. Then there is Odda, famous at Deerhurst, of whom it is said that the coffin was found in 1250 with an inscription which is distinctly suspicious : " Odda dux quondam, priscis temporibus Aldwinus vocatus in baptismo, cultor Dei qui monachus effectus fuit ante mortem, hic requiescit. Sit ei gaudium in pace cum Christo

Deo.   Amen.''   Now the work of the south transept of the great
abbey is attributed to him, and as that was the view of E. A.
Freeman it is not lightly to be gainsaid.   Part of the endowment
of the abbey was given by Edward Confessor to Westminster,
but the Benedictines were still able to hold their own and to build.
Introduced by Oswald here, as at Worcester, the "Worcester
Annals" give Foldbinth as their first abbat in 983.

Of the earliest building not much remains.   The chronicles
record continual fires ; no doubt much of it was of wood.   A
"new church" entered upon is recorded in 1020 and in 1102
another re-entry.   In 1223 the eastern part was entirely destroyed.   In 1239 the main part of the present structure was consecrated by Walter of Cantilupe, Bishop of Worcester.   Further
destruction was wrought by fire before the end of the century.
But the main monastic buildings seem to have endured till the
Dissolution, when they were demolished, with the nave of the
great church, the choir transepts and tower being suffered to
remain.   Little indeed is to be seen to-day of the old buildings,
though much of their position has been traced, including the
cloisters.   The abbat's lodging was no doubt on the site of, or
close to, the present "Abbey."*   But what remains is more than
enough to show how magnificent must have been the whole of
which the surviving portion of the church formed but a small
part.   In the transept, now the western portion of the church,
is much fine Norman work, notably the high arches at the crossing.
It is possible that the lower portion of the south is of Odda's time.
Above it is a good deal of Early English work, and the vaulting
is of the fifteenth century.   The splendid lantern tower was built
in the fourteenth century on the four great Norman arches which
were part of the original completed abbey and had once supported
the tower burnt in 1288 ; and 1335 is given by architects as the
date .when. it was finished.   From within it looks magnificent.
Outside it is spoiled by the pinnacles added by Mr. Scott in 1870.
It is worth noting that that eminent architect not only described
it as "with the single exception of Lincoln, probably the most
beautiful of its class to be found in any English church," but
added that he knew no lantern story so beautiful, and that it
stood alone in its design.   It was not allowed to remain as it was
built.   The remarkable similarity of the outside work to that
of the central tower at Salisbury has been pointed out ; it is
sufficient to prove the work to have been done by the same

architect. But the similarity belongs to the outside only. In the inside " that of Pershore," says Mr. F. B. Andrews (1901), " is far more beautiful than that of Salisbury, and no later vaulting exists to obscure it from view from the floor of the crossing : it forms, probably, the finest example of its kind in the kingdom : certainly there is no church of equal size in which anything comparable to it exists."

The choir was consecrated in 1239. It is certainly a most beautiful example of the very best Early English, and of unusual design. Four arches on north and south are terminated eastwards by one on each side turning inwards, and these are united by the larger and taller central arch which gives entrance to the comparatively small apsidal end. Above is a most graceful trifolium merged in the clerestory, and the vaulted roof is supported by triplet vaulting shafts which extend down to the corbels of the arcade below. Chapels radiate north and south from the choir aisles, one of them rebuilt half a century ago. Traces of chapels from the transept also remain. The monuments must have been rich. Most of them have perished, but three of those that remain are worth noting. They have been moved, in the craze for alteration which besets folk when they begin to " restore." One is the canopied marble tomb of a man in armour with civilian and a lady at his feet and head—of late Elizabethan date. (There is another less interesting one also of the Haslewoods.) Then there is a Templar of the thirteenth century, which Habington thus describes : " In the north side [it is now in the south transept] of the quyre, somewhat raysed from the ground, lyeth the portrature of a Knight of the holy voyage, armed all in mayle, saveing his face, and right hand upon a hunter's horne depending from his belt ; on his left arme his sheild, the extreame and lowest end whereof a serpent byteth ; over his armour a military coat gyrt, a sword by his side, the legges are crossed and at his feete a hare. It is a received tradition that his name was Hareley, sometyme lord of a place in this parish called Hareley.". This will not fit the Dean of Gloucester's identification with a knight who fought in the first crusade. And there is the very beautiful recumbent effigy of an abbat whose head rests on a mitre, supposed to be William of Harvington (1304–1340) who resigned. And so we depart. The outside view of the great church, particularly from a distance, is extremely striking, but the exquisite grace and delicacy within far surpasses it.   Before you leave Pershore you will see also the much rebuilt church of S. Andrew (fifteenth century) built for the tenants of the abbey of Westminster—a very good piece of work with a Norman nave and late Norman north aisle, to which a south aisle and west tower were added in the early fifteenth century.   It contains an architectural puzzle : how to account for the mouldings on the tower arch which do not belong there but exactly fit the width of the chancel.   Puzzle over that as you go homewards—no doubt to Evesham—over the high ground with the orchards and the river below you.

CHAPTER XIII

The delightful town of Henley-in-Arden, with its street a mile long, is an oasis on a hot summer day in the dusty road from Stratford to Birmingham. After you leave Wootton Wawen the road rises a little, and you descend into Henley by a pleasing slope. To your left is a park, ending in a brook, beside which is the pretty tree-fringed road which leads to Ullenhall and Tanworth and Oldberrow. To your right, by an inn, too rashly restored, or indeed an entirely new building, the road goes to Preston Bagot and Claverdon. In front the long street extends, with good brick cottages of the style made famous at Stratford-on-Avon when it was proposed to pull some of them down with Mr. Carnegie's money, and Miss Marie Corelli entered the fray, and with beautiful half-timbered houses too, some of them of exceeding quaintness. Everything in Henley has an air of kindly prosperity. The old fifteenth century market cross, covered by a shed for many years, and as late as 1815 bearing the Rood, the Holy Trinity and S. Peter, seems the centre of successful trading. There are good saddlers and good grocers and good stationers, and all that man may require. I read that the town was once more "vivacious" than it is now; but I do not know how to interpret the depressing suggestion. The writer who makes it quotes a presentment at the early Quarter Sessions of 1655 :—"that usually heretofore there have been at Henley-in-Arden several unlawful meetings of idle and vain persons about this time of the year, for erecting of May Poles and May Bushes, and for using of Morris Dances and other heathenish and unlawful customs, the observation whereof tendeth to draw together a great concourse of loose people." These customs, especially that of Morris dancing, have been revived in recent years: indeed at Stratford they seem to believe in the regeneration of the world by dancing, so that religion is to return t_0 what some anthropologists believe to be its most potent primitive element; but I do not see any signs of great concourse in Henley. And indeed the people there are most decorous folk, fearing God and honouring the king, though I have heard that there be Jacobites among them, though I think no Jacobins. As one walks the streets—or I should rather say the street—of Arden to-day, devastated as it is by motor cars, and only to be perambulated with caution by discreet ladies with dogs—you will observe that hardly anyone ever stands at his street door to gossip in Henley—one may recall a time when the streets rang with a different kind of tumult. I possess a very curious work, "composed and compiled by a friend to Truth and Peace," in 1651. This friend seems to have been Thomas Hall of King's Norton, whence the Latin dedicatory epistle, to John Trapp,[1] pastor of Beaudesert, is dated on Jan. 1, 1651 (*i.e.* 1652). It is garnished also with an address. "To my beloved Parishioners, the inhabitants of *King's Norton*," congratulating them upon having a succession of divines, "conformable nonconformists," through the influence of *Sir Richard Greavis*, who sheltered these Reverend Ministers from those Episcopal storms which otherwise had fallen upon them, and referring to the "lustre of years which I spent at *Moseley*, when I was threatened by the Episcopal party for Nonconformity ; since I came to you I have suffered deeply by the Cavaliering party ; oftentimes plundered, five times their prisoner, oft cursed, accused, threatened, etc." But the good man will not be content with this, and so writes "The Pulpit Guarded," to warn his people, by the awful example of Henley-in-Arden, "that Private persons (though they be gifted, yet) may not Preach in a constituted Church without a Call." He argues in presbyterian sort but will have no disparagement of bishops, and is sure that "we have our ordinations from Christ by bishops and presbyters." But, however, the point is what a fearful place Henley must have been when

---

[1] A learned friend tells me that "there is no John Trapp in the list of rectors of Beaudesert since 1550. Is this man the John Trapp of Christ Church, Oxon., Vicar for thirty years of Weston-on-Avon, who died 1669, and who was Head Master of Stratford-on-Avon Grammar School?"

it thought otherwise : so read Hall's title-page to see what was on the green then. It runs thus :—

" The Pulpit Guarded with XVII arguments proving the unlawfulness, sinfulness and danger of suffering private persons to take upon them publike preaching and expounding the Scriptures without a call ; as being contrary to the Word of God, contrary to the practice of all Reformed Churches, contrary to the three and twentieth Article of religion, contrary to two Ordinances of Parliament, and contrary to the judgment of a whole jury of learned, judicious, pious Divines, both forraign and domestick. Occasioned by a dispute at Henly-in-Arden in Warwickshire Aug. 20, 1650. Against Lawrence Williams, a Nailor-publike-preacher ; Tho. Palmer, a Baker-preacher ; Tho. Hinde, a Plough-wright-publike-preacher ; Henry Oakes, a Weaver-preacher ; Hum. Rogers (lately) a Bakers-boy-publike-preacher. Here you have all their arguments (never yet compiled in one tract) retelled and answered many Texts of Scripture cleared the quintessence and marrow of most of our modern authors (in reference to this controversie) collected, with references to such authors as clear any doubt more fully ; many incident cases resolved, the utmost extent of lay-mens using their gifts in eleven particulars demonstrated, and above thirty objections answered. In the close are added six arguments, to prove our ministers free from Antichristianism."

Probably this was a lesson to Henley-in-Arden. As we walk along the street to-day it does not seem to need any such to be repeated ; and we may go soberly and godly about our business. The only excitement we are like to see is what may happen if the lord of the manor still " holds his court here," as Mr. Hannett told us he did fifty years ago, " when an election of a new High Bailiff takes place, and High and Low Bailiffs, Affearors, Butter weighers, Beer Tasters, Brook Lookers, etc. are sworn in, whose duties are only preserved in the names which doubtless once gave the owners considerable power and importance."

And so we come to the church. Now this is still a chapelry of Wootton Wawen, though it has had its own building a long while. Dugdale says this :—

" The Chapell here (dedicated to *S. John Baptist*) was built about the 41, year of King *Edw*. 3. as appears by the confirmation thereof then made by *William Witlesey* Bishop of Worcester : in which is exprest, that it was erected at the sole charges of the Inhabitants, in regard of the large distance, the foul ways in Winter-time, betwixt this Village and the Parish Church of Wootton *Wawen*; and by the consent of *William de Senye* then Prior of Wotton (unto which Religious House the said mother Church of Wotton was appropriated) and *Will. de Perton* the then Vicar: which Inhabitants and their successors had authoritie then given them by the same Bishop to provide and maintain a fitting Priest at their own proper charges, for

Henley-in-Arden.

celebration of Divine service there, so that the Vicar of Wotton, for the time being, might wholly receive and take all Oblations, arising in the said Chapell, upon *Christmass* day, *Candlemass* day, *Easter* day, and *S. Peter's* day (being the day of the Dedication of that Church) and for Churching of Women, at any time, in the said Chapell: But of all other profits arising upon the said days, or any other throughout the year, the Vicar to have two parts only, and the Prior the third. And that the Priest belonging to this Chapell might have power, so often as occasion should be, to Church Women there, to administer the Sacrament to such old and decrepite people as could not go to the said Parish Church, and to perform all other parochiall rites therein, buriall for the dead only excepted. For the performance of all which, the Priest for the time being, at his first admission thereto, was to oblige himself by his corporall Oath, in the presence of the Prior of *Wawens*-Wotton and the Vicar, lest the said Church of *Wawens*-Wotton should be dampnified. And that all good people might be the more stirred up to contribute towards the charges for the fabrick hereof ; as also for the Bells, Books, Lights, Vestments, and other Ornaments belonging thereto, the said Bishop by that his publique Instrument, which bears date at Hertlebury, 5. *Cal. Aug. Anno* 1367. granted to every one that would be open-handed therein, an Indulgence of xl. days ; all which was confirm'd by the Prior and Monks of Worcester."

Things have changed, of course, and I do not know what Bells, Books, Lights and Vestments are now in use; but the people of Henley still appoint their minister and he has, strictly speaking, no parochial charge. At least this was so a few months ago, and may still be so. I do not know how it will be affected by the union of the benefice of Henley-in-Arden with that of Beaudesert. The contemplated change will no doubt be beneficial, but much ancient history will pass from connection with the twentieth century when it occurs.

The church itself is long and straight, the chancel a mere continuation of the nave. The whole was rebuilt in the fifteenth century. There is a good pulpit, with linen-fold carving. The corbels of the nave-arches have what may well be portraits of the burgesses, to whom the church or chapel owes its sustenance. The north aisle had apparently access to the house of the Guild. It contains on the north wall the excellent marble monument of Simon Kempson, son of William Kempson of Hilborough, 1719, and his wife Margaret, daughter of Wallaston Betham of Rowington 1699, with the words *Requiescant in pace.* This Simon planted in 1730 some yews which still beautify the street.

The Guild referred to was founded by Ralph Boteler Lord Sudeley, in the fifteenth century. The Certificate of Chantries, Guilds, &c., taken in 37th Hen. VIII. before the dissolution, states that the revenue was then £27. 3s. 3d., and the outgoings £26. 11s. 2d., and "that the seyde Gylde was ffoundyd by one Rauffe Butler for iiii prests to synge dyvyne servyce

within a Chapell of Saynt John Baptiste in the Towne of
Henley and to pray for the ffounders soules, how be yt there be
resydent at this present tyme but iii Prests. And in the seyd
Vyllage there ys a markett kepte wekely, and having D^c house-
lyng people. And no more Churches within the same Vyllage
but only the seyed Chappell whyche ys dystaunt ffrom the
parisshe Churche ii myles. Also between the same parisshe
Churche and the seyde Vyllage runnythe a Broke so that
dyvers tymes in the yere no man can escape withoute greate
joperdye."

At the south of the church runs a lane which, crossing the
tiny stream of the Alne, brings you within a quarter of a mile
to the Church of Beaudesert, which the people call Belser.
The history goes back a long way. Roman remains are said
to have been found there, and east of the church there can
still be traced the remnants of a castle, a mount with moat and
courtyards defended by a ditch. The mount is 300 feet above
the sea, and from it Malvern and Edgehill can be seen. The castle
itself had disappeared by Dugdale's day, and only its ditches,
almost filled as they were by the seventeenth century, can still
be traced here and there. The history of it belongs to the family
of the Montforts, whom some spell Montford to distinguish
them from Earl Simon the righteous. Righteous, indeed, by
the way, they were not. They would seem to have succeeded
to Roger of Meulan and Henry Earl of Warwick enfeoffed by
the latter. Their continuous history begins with Thurstan de
Montfort, *circa* 1120, who held *temp.* Henry I., and, under Henry II.,
was succeeded by his son Robert, and after by a younger son
John. John's son Peter, a minor when his father died, became
the ward of William de Cantilupe. The connection with the
Cantilupes led to his association with the Barons in their movement against the king. During his long minority it would seem
that his property was well guarded, for Peter was able to make
a contract for intermarriage of their sons and daughters with
William Beauchamp Earl of Warwick in 32 Henry III. Two
years later he was envoy to Castile, preparatory, no doubt, to
the marriage of the king's son Edward. From this time he became a prominent diplomatist : he was a warden of the Welsh
marches, he brought envoys from the Welsh princes to the
" Mad Parliament " of Oxford in 1258, and he was one of the
Council appointed under the Provisions. When war broke out

he was captured at Northampton, and after the barons' success he was one of the Council of nine, and from this time he was closely attached to Earl Simon, and fell fighting with him at the battle of Evesham. His lands were forfeited, but were restored after the Ban of Kenilworth to his son, also Peter. Meanwhile the castle had been burned, and much of Henley with it. If it was ever rebuilt it never regained .its grandeur. It was resumed, or acquired, by the Beauchamps : then the Botelers held its lands. The Crown held it, Edward IV. to Edward VI., who granted it to Dudley of Warwick and Northumberland, at whose attainder it again returned to the Crown. Elizabeth granted it to Ambrose Dudley : at his death it again reverted. "The site of the castle and park were subsequently purchased by Alderman Caldwell of London."

The castle, then, being no more, and the Montforts having passed away too, the interest of Beaudesert is centred in its church. This is a beautiful Norman survival—at least so much of it as has not been too greatly restored. The walls of the nave and the chancel are of Norman masonry ; the suggested date is about 1070 ; windows of the fourteenth century are inserted. The tower was added in the fifteenth century. Both the north and south doorways are fine Norman work, the south much restored. Within, you notice the curious irregularity of building, the west window being quite out of line from the east. The chancel roof, which at first strikes you as a fine and most unusual piece of Norman vaulting, is really an addition of the nineteenth century, certainly after 1846, probably in 1869 ; but it has an exceedingly good effect, and it replaces a plaster ceiling, so we may not protest too much. The windows in the nave are new ; they also replace what archæologists of the early nineteenth century wept at. Altogether it is a beautiful and well-kept church ; and the history of the parish, separate from the closely adjoining Henley, is curious and interesting. Henley has always kept its questionable independence, based upon its practical freedom from the mother church of Wootton Wawen, and had never, it seems, desired to amalgamate with the little parish on its borders ; at least till quite recent times, for it seems that amalgamation is now on the *tapis*. The list of vicars of Beaudesert since the Reformation has some interest. In the troublous days before the civil war the place seems to have had a strong Puritanical tinge. Here is a petition against the rector (from 1636), John

Henley-in-Arden *from* Beaudesert

E. H. NEW.

Doughty, who was also rector of Lapworth, and saw nothing to
except against in the Laudian canons of 1640 :—

" The said John Doughty is a common resorter to the houses of
Popish recusants, a favourer of them and their religion, and a
scoffer of goodness and good men.

" The said John Doughty preaching at Lapworth about Mich^s
last upon Matth. viii. 13. affirmed that it was not necessary for
the Minister to prove his doctrine by Scripture, but the people
ought to believe it on his authority ; and further said that there
is now a generation of men sprung up that will believe nothing
but what is proved by Scripture, insisting that turning and tossing
over the leaves of the Bible is a disturbance to the congregation,
with other words to that effect.

" The said John Doughty speaking of the new canons, said,
there was nothing in them to be disliked, and further that he did
verily believe in his conscience, that if S. Paul had been there
and made them, the Parliament would have condemned them,
or words to that effect."

I am bound to say that I incline to Mr. Doughty's opinion ;
though the Long Parliament might not have been averse from
finding S. Paul in error if he differed from them.

A later rector has some fame through his son—Richard
Jago, who held the living from 1709 to 1740, and married the
daughter of William Parker of Henley-in-Arden. On an
outside wall is a tablet to him. It ought to be brought in, for
it is almost obliterated. His son Richard was scribbling, as
clergymen's sons will, in the year before that last date,
when he was of University College, Oxford, a young poet
of twenty-four, and Lady Luxborough wrote him a most
polite letter, for that through his introduction to Mr. Shenstone
she owed " the pleasure of having enjoyed that gentleman's
conversation a few moments " and " the advantage of being
represented to him in the most flattering light " : compliments
to Mr. Jago, too, on his pastoral wherein he had " the art to
describe the most simple things with the nicest eloquence."
Young Jago was already in Holy Orders, since 1737, and curate
of Snitterfield, and "Ardenna," his pastoral, had received much
praise. The personification of the forest was regarded as in the
best possible taste. And Lady Luxborough was very ready
to applaud. So poetry brought the young man friends and
eventually benefices.

The White Swan, still quaint and beautiful as it must have been a century and more before Jago's day, may have been the resort of wits who came to see the literary and aristocratic personages of the neighbourhood. Boswell thought that it was there Shenstone wrote his famous lines about " the warmest welcome at an inn " ; but his friend Graves is the best authority upon that, and is quite explicit in his " Recollection," where he tells that it was written in a summer-house at Edgehill. The White Swan was built in 1353 and was part of the old Barrels property.

From Henley we may turn to the right, between the brook and a gentle ridge on which stands one of the few charming new houses you may see in these parts, a long, low, white house making for itself a lovely garden ; and then on under the railway bridge near the station, and out into the country again. And so we come to Oldberrow, or Oldborrow as Kitchin's map calls it.

Though Ullenhall seems to have been the church of which the Knights of Barrels regarded themselves as parishioners, Oldberrow, of which a view could be obtained from Lady Luxborough's gardens by one of the " vistas " which the gardeners of the time loved to create, was much nearer to their house. As you follow the road from Henley you have the park of Barrels, for a long way, on your right. You mount a hill and soon come to the church, which overlooks the park to the north. It has a pretty wooden porch which if it is not old has much of the charm of ancient style, a good short tower with a small spire. It was rebuilt in 1875, but there remain Norman and Early English windows and a Norman font. For the history of the parish you must not search the Warwickshire county books, for it belonged to Worcester, and thus shall you read of it in Habington's " Survey " of that county (Worcestershire Historical Society, 1899, vol. ii., p. 236). He calls it " Ullberge now called Owlbourge," which by no means exhausts the ways of spelling the name. Lady Luxborough, for example, writes it " Olborough," and her friend, Mr. Holyoake the curate, " Oldburrow." What Habington says is this :—

" Next Ombresley in S. Egwin's charter is Vlberge, a paryshe closed allmost with the woodland of Warwickshyre, whose trees and bushes (as the inhabitants saye) heeretofore so abounded with owles as they gave the place the name of Owleborough, and to confyrme it the more, John Owleborough dwellinge heere giuethe for his armes in this churche 3 owles ; yet nowe the woodes beeinge lessened the owles haue sought them other seates. But to returne to Owld Vlberge, it was by S. Egwin procured for his monastery of Euesham, under the Winges of which Abbey the family Owleboroughe sometymes flourished. . . . This name hathe synee leafte this place, and the Abbey by the dissolution lost this mannor, which was after, 4 & 5 Phil. & Marie, the landes of Valentine Knightley, in which name it hath synce continewed.

" In the east windowe of the chauncell of the church the armes of the Abbot of Euesham, the auncient Lord and Patron of this mannor, beinge Asure, a cheyne with a horslocke in cheueron betweene three bishop's mitres, which obteygnethe the highest place."

On either side were the kneeling figures of John Owleborough, his wife and his son John, with the arms, " Gulles a fesse between 3 owles argent." To this family also belonged, no doubt, the tomb " in the myddest of the chauncell "—a plain tombstone, Habington says, " robbed of the brasse which should discover the party." The new church has none of these things. It is only a pretty country church in a pretty situation. The parsonage house is a new one, and there is nothing to recall the good Mr. Holyoake who was so good a friend to poor Lady Luxborough, and ministered to her on her death-bed when she received the Holy Sacrament " with great devotion."

Barrels itself may next call us. It is not a " show-house," but its historical interest demands a word.

Barrels stands in a fine park. The house was originally built before 1580 and much added to, I think, by Robert Knight, son of the financier who made his fortune by the South Sea Company, but had to spend it abroad, living in Paris; and going once a year to Calais, according to Horace Walpole, that he might look across to the cliffs of Dover. A further portion was built about 1770, and joined by cloisters to part of the old house, still standing. The architect for this new part was Bonomi, who was the architect for Rosneath, built for the Duke of Argyll, and it is said that these are the only two houses built alike by him. The son returned to England and married Henrietta St. John, sister of the statesman Bolingbroke, in 1727. Twenty years later, or, rather, in 1746, he was created Lord Luxborough (the name of his property near Chigwell). Before that husband and wife had separated, it was said through her fault; and she was sent down to Barrels under engagement, it seems, not to come to London. There she lived, not very unhappily, for ten years more, dying in 1756. She devoted herself to the poets and the gardeners, admired her neighbour Mr. Somervile, the author of "The Chase"; made great friends with Mr. Shenstone of the Leasowes near Halesowen, visited him, and tried to imitate his style in prose and verse; was kind to young poets such as Mr. Jago, son of the rector of Beaudesert, and to poor clergymen and their children; and with her friend and steward, Mr. Outing, and her friend Mrs. Davies of Stratford-on-Avon (was she a daughter of the Mr. Davies whose death she deplores in a very kindly fashion, who may have been of kin to the tenant at the Moat Farm?) passed a quiet existence, occupied, when her health allowed, with her garden and her pen. Time, and changes of taste, have made her urns to disappear and her walks and vistas to be overgrown. No longer can you trace "the path in the coppice," which she "turned towards the Bank, where a seat is proposed above the Pit," or get that view she speaks of, from the Bank, of Skiltz (as she spells it); but the great double oak, under which she wished for Mr. Shenstone's and Mr. Whistler's company amid "the gay products of spring," still remains in much of its ancient grandeur. You may still wander in wildernesses not far from the house, and think what was there as Lady Luxborough planned it. The Ha! ha! is, presumably, that which she was proud of making. She preferred her garden, one tells, to her coal fire, of which she speaks disparagingly. The flowers gave her continual interest, the walks, and glades, and trees and urns; but these were less precious than society. None of the disagreeable events in life, she truly said, could make her unsociable, "but cities (no more than forests) do not afford society; it is the *conversation* of a chosen few that smooths the rugged road of life; such as *yours* [she wrote to Shenstone] strews it with *flowers*; but as *they* soon fade, so did *you* vanish, and all the company that surrounded my *hearth*," and so she must turn to planting the lane that adjoins the coppice with "abele, which in four years will grow to be a good shade."

The house itself has been largely rebuilt. Lord Luxborough, ten years after his wife's death, was created Earl of Catherlough : there is an indignant letter of George Selwyn's about it in 1768. His arms are over one wing, at the left of the present doorway, and show what are probably the only remaining rooms of his time. The rest of the house is much more modern, but bears a comfortable look of the period when people built plainly, solidly, and for dignity, not, as so often now, for affectation and show. Contrast Barrels, for example, with the modern house at Wroxall and you see the terrible descent of English architecture in some sixty or seventy years. Lord Catherlough built a mausoleum in his park, and thither were removed the coffins of his family. In 1830 it had fallen into decay and was pulled down : the coffins were taken to the old church of Ullenhall, where at last rests Lady Luxborough, with memorials of her kindred and of those who succeeded her at Barrels. There let us follow her through the little scattered village and by some twisting lanes. We are now north-east of the park, as Oldborrow is south-west.

Part of the old church of Ullenhall—the new one stands close to the village, just outside the gates of Barrels—still stands, and there are occasional services there ; but it has not many houses near it, and there is excuse, it may be, for its comparative neglect. It was, as I said, the Church of the Knights—then only a chapel of Wootton Wawen, and Lady Luxborough complains of the distance and the rough way : " I am certain the *rugged walk* to Ulenhall Chapel (however conducive to *health,* according to the Physician, or to *happiness,* according to the Divine) would never have inclined me to undertake it, had not the company I was with smoothed the road and levelled the ruts ; for such was the effect it had, at least upon my imagination. But the roads are as *rough* as ever, and I as *lazy,* which shows that we *hermits* are to blame, droning our time away in our cells." This was in August, 1748, when Mr. Shenstone had been staying with her and made her walk to church, one sees. It was a rough walk no doubt for my lady. But those who have seen the church will not forget its splendid position, high, like so many of the Warwickshire churches, overlooking a fine champaign country, southwards. And from a little way off in the valley can be seen the picturesque old house, the Moat House Farm, still belonging, with much of the land about here, and in Henley, to the family who owned it in the eighteenth century. The church itself, which Dugdale calls " a fair chapell (dedicated to the Blessed Virgin) wherein the Vicars of Wootton for the Time being, have of antient Time used to find a Priest, at their own proper Charge, to celebrate Divine Service "—Wootton Wawen was rich in chapelries— was built in the fourteenth century; only the chancel now remains, and all has been rebuilt, or, at least, very completely repaired. It retains, I think, its old bell, the work, there seems little doubt, of John Kingston, bell founder, who was living at Northgate, Warwick, in 1401. An inscription outside records the consecration of the burial ground by the Bishop of Worcester (Dr. Carr) in 1835. Restoration has robbed the church of much of its interest, but its memorials are worth noting. Dugdale figures the fine mural monument, flanked by Corinthian columns bearing the Throckmorton arms. Thus he gives the inscriptions :—

" Here lieth the body of Francis Throckmorton Esquire, borne in the Citie of Mantua, in Italy, son and heir unto Michael Throckmorton Esquire, and of Agnes Hide of Southamptonshire, which Michael was born at Coughton-Court in the Countie of Warwick, and youngest brother to Sir George Throckmorton of Coughton aforesaid Knight. And after that the said Michaell had lived a many years in Italy, in good and great reputation, with bountifull Hospitalitie, entertaining most of the Noblemen and gents of England that had occasion to come that way, and did returne into England in the beginning of the reigne of Q. Mary, and received of her gift the Manors of Honily, Blackwell, Packhurst, Winderton, Ullenhall in Ullenhall, and others, as appeareth in her Majesties Letters Patent, bearing date in the first year of her reign : and after went into Italy againe, where he departed this life, and lieth buried in S. Martin's Church in the said Citie of Mantua, under a fair Tombe. The said Michael married Judith Tracie, daughter of Richard Tracie of Stanway in the Countie of Gloucester Esquire, and of Barbara Lucy of Charlecote in the County of Warwick, and sister to Sir Paul Tracie Baronet, and had by her six Children, whereof three, that is to say Francis, Michael, and Judith here departed this life without issue, and the other three are living ; that is to say John, Michael, and Judith Anno Dom. 1617, and in the fifteenth year of the reign of our Lord James the 1st, King of England.

> Mors mihi lucrum, portus, & refugium.
> Sic transit gloria Mundi.
> Omnia vana vidi, solo mea XPŏ repono.
> Mors tua, Mors XPï, fraus Mundi, gloria Cœli,
> Et dolor inferni, sunt meditanda tibi."

I will add those of the memorial to the Knights of Barrels whose coffins were once in the fine south chapel at Wootton Wawen, and after vicissitudes now rest here at last—the coffins, an old inhabitant tells you, seen by her through the grating below the chancel not so long ago, but now not visible. Lord Catherlough, as I said before, had built for them a mausoleum in his park, but that was neglected and at length the coffins were moved. The two tablets summarise the history of the Knights and their connection with the St. Johns. The last descendant of Lady Luxborough was her grandson, the last of the list, who died in 1822. The tablet at the north has the arms, Knight Earl of Catherlough, surmounted by a Coronet, with this inscription :—

" In the vault under this Chapel lie the remains of Robert Knight, Earl of Catherlough, Viscount Barrells, Baron Luxborough, and Knight of the Bath. Born 17th Dec. 1702. Married 10th June, 1727, Henrietta St. John, sister to Viscount Bolinbroke, Secretary of State to Queen Anne, by whom he had one son, Henry, and one daughter, Henrietta. Died 30th March, 1772."

That on the south side of the east window bears the arms of Knight impaling St. John, and the inscription :—

" In the vault of this chancel lie the remains of—

Viscountess St. John, B. 25 Feb. 1723, D. 6 March, 1752
Josiah Russell, B. 1674, D. 7th May, 1755.
Baroness Luxborough, ᵉ B. 15th July, 1699, D. 26th March, 1756.
Honᵇˡᵉ Henry Knight, B. 25th December, 1728, D. 15th August, 1762. S. P.
Countess Doroure, B. 21st Nov. 1729, D. 1st March, 1763.
Elizabeth Powell, B. 7th Jan. 1692, D. 11th March, 1765.
Caroline Knight, B. 20th July, 1772, D. 22nd August, 1772
Henry Knight, B. 24th May, 1795, D. 14th Nov. 1800.
Count Duroure, B. 6th Feb. 1763, D. 24th Sept., 1822. S. P."

I conclude, as I have said, that this Count Duroure was the son of Lady Luxborough's daughter, whose unhappy marriage with Mr. Wymondesold was dissolved after her fault. She then married Josiah Childe, Lord Tilney's brother (according to a note of

Horace Walpole's in his copy of Lady Luxborough's letters) and
I suppose afterwards she married Count Duroure. But though
Lady Luxborough left no descendants the Knights remained
owners of Barrels till the middle of the last century, and still
continue to own property in the land of their ancestry.

From Ullenhall I think you will naturally go along shady lanes
to Tanworth, a village which connects the Knights with their old
friends the Archers.

Tanworth stands at the summit of a hill, a village with almost
a town-like air in its little square or market-place at the west end
of the church. It was, though so far away, as Dugdale tells us,
" antiently a member of Brailes." The church is the culmination
of the village. It stands high above the surrounding country,
approached by tortuous lanes. From the plain tower ascends a
lofty spire, graceful but with no special feature of interest. The
style is Decorated, but an observer some fifty years ago not unjustly remarked : " It is now mutilated and defaced to an extent
which can hardly be credited, and these sad disfigurements seem
to have been committed at no distant period." The eighteenth
century dealt severely with the church. In 1720 the steeple was
rebuilt—at least the upper part of it—and raised six feet. In
1789 a parish meeting agreed " that the church should be new
pewed in a regular way, so as to be fit and decent for divine
service." On this the work of restoration (or demolition) began.
I have heard the rage for " restoration " attributed to the Oxford
Movement. The history of the eighteenth century refutes the
view ; and nowhere better than at Tanworth. Here the north
and south porches were taken away, and the arches were used to
make doorways in the north and south aisles, a bay further westward than the existing doorways, which were turned into windows.
Then the arches and pillars of the north aisle were destroyed and
the ancient high roofs removed, the tower and east windows of the
aisles being divided from the church. " The windows of the north
aisle," says the same pathetic account, " originally large and fine,
have been completely despoiled of their mullions and once beautiful Decorated tracery." *Quid plura ?* It is only fair to say
that at the present day efforts have been made to undo, so far as
possible, the crimes of the past, and those who now have charge
of the church care for it and its history with intelligent zeal.
The restoration of the ancient roof in 1880 was a work of expiation. The organ case, easily recognisable as the work of the

Warwickshire genius, Mr. Kendall, is, with its splendid trumpeting angels, a noble ornament to the church. The interesting feature of the chancel are two fifteenth century brackets (once coloured) on the eastern wall, probably to receive statues, the B.V.M. and S. Gabriel, or there seems reason to believe, S. Catherine. On p. 13, Vol. II. of "The Churches of Warwickshire" there is an interesting reference to the thrice-repeated inscription to Richard Dolfry (ob. 1590) which was objected to in its original form as "importing praying for the dead." The monuments in the church are chiefly those of the Archer family, who bought the manor in the reign of James I. from the Throckmortons. The first, I think, is Edward Archer who died in 1592 ; then comes the brass of a kneeling lady with a ruff and head-dress, Margaret, daughter of Robert Ralegh of Farnborough and wife of Andrew Archer, who died in 1614 (*mitissima conjux* was she). The interest of this latter lies in the fine carved oak frame in which the brass is inserted. An adjacent one is to John Chambers of Woodend, 1650. The last of the Archers is the one who was kind to Lady Luxborough, almost the only friend of her own dignity that she had in the neighbourhood, and highly complimentary to the poet Shenstone and his *ferme ornée*. " It is the very thing one would choose," he said, " and what I have heard Lord Bolingbroke made Dawley." · I fancy it was his great politeness which is satirised by "The Abbey of Kilk-hampton " when it declares that he chose his companions " from the most wretched class of mortals " and accuses his conversation of " the boorish vulgarity which distinguished his associates." His monument on the north wall of the west end of the nave is in the most characteristic style of the eighteenth century. A lady leans on a pedestal on which stands the bust of Lord Archer. The Archer arms are Az. 3 arrows or. The motto, " Heu pietas, heu prisca fides." The inscription runs thus :—

　" Sacred to the memory of Andrew Lord Archer, Baron of Umberslade, who died April the 25th, 1778, ætatis forty one, and lies interr'd in the family vault beneath. He was the last male descendant of an ancient and honourable family that came over with William the Conqueror, and settled in the County of War-wick in the reign of King Henry the second, from whom his ancestors obtained the grants of lands in the said county. He married Sarah, the daughter of James West, Esq., of Alscot, by whom he has left issue four daughters. To perpetuate his fair fame this monument is erected, by her who knew and loved his virtues."

Andrew was the second lord, succeeding Thomas, his father, whose creation came from George II. There are also three Chambers brasses, one of which has interest :—

" M. S. Hic jacet Johannes Chambers, agri Varvicensis, generosus, tam pietate quam ævo obsitus, quo nemo magis religiosas domus frequentavit, cultor tam sincerus ut ipse pene templum præstabat ubicunq esset. Post plurimos annos sic totos Deo impensos, ut dubites an pertingant ad hanc vitam, ultimi an ad alteram primi, Obiit viii° A° D^{ni} 1670."

The name Fulwode also occurs twice, once on the brass of a man who was " excellentissime doctrinatus sive liberatus in communilege Angliæ." His date is 1531.

Turn down the steep hill at the north-east of the church and you soon come to the beautiful park of Umberslade, the property of the Archers from the time of Henry II. till after the death of the last Lord. A local antiquary traces its recent descent thus : " Umberslade came by marriage to the Earl of Plymouth, who disposed of it to Bolton King, who disposed of it to G. F. Muntz." The present owner is Mr. F. E. Muntz, whose skill and care have revived and added to the beauties the place possessed in the eighteenth century. The house was built by John Smith about 1680, but has received many additions at different dates, especially under the family to whom it now belongs. Horace Walpole in 1751 regarded it as " an odious place." In 1830 it was thus described :—" It is of square form, with two wings, slightly projecting from the main body. In the centre of the western and principal front, is a grand portico, supported by pillars of the Doric order, and surmounted by a bust of the Emperor Titus Vespasian. In the south front is a similar portico, above which are the family arms, surrounded by military trophies. The interior, long neglected, and now entirely unfurnished and forsaken, still retains the marks of its former grandeur. The hall, in particular, is a noble apartment ; and two excellent statues, placed in niches, on each side of the central door, one of Venus and the other of Apollo, are still to be seen. Stretching round the mansion in a wide circumference, is the park, now converted to the common purpose of agriculture." Great is the contrast to-day ! In the first place the house is inhabited, and by those who appreciate and add to its beauties. What was then the front entrance has now become the entrance to the garden, opening out of the fine large drawing-room. The present front looks upon the park and a wide expanse full of splendid trees and reclaimed from the " common purpose of agriculture." The busts and statues have disappeared, but they are replaced by many adornments which the original owners had not contemplated. Outside, the wings, generally a most mistaken addition to the plain dignity of an eighteenth century house, have certainly added to the dignity of the building. They have thrown out the central portico with its solid supporting wings, and though no one would mistake them to be parts of the original plan, they are not out of keeping with it. The gardens are a continually growing attraction, with their rare trees, their delightful surprises of arrangement, including the sloped garden down to a central basin and fountain, and the many lakes—I cannot count them. Inside, the great hall, now an entrance hall, has returned to its first splendour, and the drawing-room is as large without being exaggerated or uncomfortable. The skill with which an old ceiling, with its graceful decoration, has been imitated is one of the attractive features of the house. And not least beautiful is the wide and lofty but simple staircase, of the very best style of late eighteenth century ornamentation.

As you leave the beautiful grounds you recall perhaps the eulogies of Jago, the poet of Warwickshire, who mingled the charms of Umberslade (when Lord Archer was still living) with those of Hewel (now belonging to Lord Plymouth, but in the seventeenth century Lord Windsor's, and ransacked by the Gunpowder Plotters in their futile attempt to raise the country):—

> " See how the pillar'd isles [1] and stately dome
> Brighten the woodland shade ! while scatter'd hills,
> Airy, and light, in many a conic form,
> A theatre compose, grotesque and wild,
> And, with their shaggy sides, contract the vale
> Winding, in straiten'd circuit, round their base.
> Beneath their waving umbrage Flora spreads
> Her spotted couch, primrose, and hyacinth
> Profuse, with ev'ry simpler bud that blows
> On hill or dale.   Such too thy flow'ry pride
> O Hewel ! by thy master's lib'ral hand

[1] In the eighteenth century "isle" was often, confusedly, written for "aisle."

Advanc'd to rural fame !   Such Umberslade !
In the sweet labour join'd, with culture fair,
And splendid arl's, from Arden's woodland shades
The pois'nous damps, and savage gloom to chase."

We may complete our view of the woods and meads of Umberslade by ascending to the hill on which stands the large stone
column or obelisk, with a star at the head of it, of whose original
meaning it seems that man now knows nothing.   It is referred
to by Lady Luxborough in several of her letters to Shenstone.
In July, 1749, she was to dine at Umberslade and judge " how
it appears from the saloon it is seen from."   The old county
guide books pass it by with some such remark as that it " forms
a striking object from the windows of the house."

From Umberslade, passing by the obelisk to your right up
hill again, and crossing the main road to Birmingham, and with
a devious turn or two, you enter the parish of Packwood.   Dugdale thus introduces it to you : " Alne, having thus past that
large parish of Packwood, enters the hundred of Barlichway,
wherein, before it hath gone two miles, the access of a pretty
stream called Silesburne, which hath its beginning in the north
of Kineton hundred, before mentioned, about the edge of
Packwood, enlargeth its channel.   This place (Packwood)
lying in the utmost corner of Barlichway hundred, and bordering
upon Hemlingford, is reputed to be a member of Kineton
hundred, and as it hath in all taxes antiently payed therewith,
so doth it still ; the reason whereof I conceive to be because it
was originally a member of Wasperton, though it lye at so great
a distance from thence, and so consequently belonged to the
Monks of Coventre ; which was no strange thing, considering
what I have said in Tanworth relating to Brailes."   I quote
this as a good illustration of the extraordinary complexity of
local historical and geographical divisions.   One really cannot
go about Warwickshire without wanting to write a history of
the shire ; yet that is the last thing one would desire to do if
one wished to have an unconfused brain.   The manors of great
families or of great religious houses mixed in different counties,
attach themselves sometimes to the hundred, sometimes even
to the shire, of the lord's chief property, and those extraordinary
little islands arise in the maps which are the puzzle of the topographical investigator.

But here we are at Packwood, after leaving the Birmingham

road by an inn everybody will tell you of—the Nag's Head,
while further south is the Royal Oak—and wandering up a
road or two. If you turn to the left a little, pass the
pretty vicarage on the hill top, turn again to the right by
the smithy, you will descend a wooded lane and find yourself
quite suddenly in the grounds of Packwood house. The first
thing you will observe is the fine block of stables, said
to be where Elizabeth's horses were cared for on the way to
Kenilworth—and this, they tell, is one of the many houses
she stayed in. But there is no certainty about that, and the
stables may well be of a much later date. The house itself
is most attractive. There is no better instance in Warwickshire of how an ancient house can be adapted by skill and
patience, and restored to use as a home. The property has
often changed hands. It belonged once to the Abbey of
Coventry, then at the Dissolution to the Sheldons of Beoley.
William Sheldon made it over to Robert Burdet of Bramcote,
whose grandson sold it to Thomas Spencer of Claverdon—of
whom you see so much in that village—from whom it descended
to Sir William Spencer of Yarnton, Oxon, so Dugdale tells you.
The Yarnton monuments of the Spencers no one who has seen
them forgets; nor will they the monument and the stone house
at Claverdon. But now the Spencers are not recalled at
Packwood. Mr. West, in 1830, tells you that " the ancient
mansion and manor-house, designated Packwood house, has for
many years been in the highly respected family of the Fether-
stones." He goes on to give a delightful picture of the squire
of his day, who seems from it to have been inspired by the
example of Sir John Throckmorton (of whom under Coughton)
to " go one better," and dress always (and more completely)
as Sir John dressed once in his life. Thus Mr. West :—" Colonel
Fetherstone,[1] one of the family, still resides at the mansion
of Packwood-house, in the true style of an English gentleman,
who seems to feel a patriotic pride in being clad in the produce
of his own estate. His hat, coat, and under apparel, stockings,
etc., and even his shoes, are the produce from his own lands,
herds, etc., and are manufactured and made within his own walls.
A praiseworthy instance of national taste ! " But the family
did not find wealth in this praiseworthy way, and the beautiful
house, fallen almost into ruin, passed away from their hands.

[1] The family now spells the name Fetherston.

Now in the possession of those who have worked its regeneration with infinite zest and patience, the charming old manor-house is worthy to take its place again among the beauties of Warwickshire. You approach it through a forecourt, with the "domestic offices" to your right, and a wall, terminating in a gazebo, to your left. The house itself has been largely reconstructed within. It contains several rooms with beautiful oak panels, and a most ingeniously made hall and open gallery. The great merit of all that has been done is that the new work is not deceitfully confused with the old. The little dark room to the back, at the right, is a treasure from the past. The gallery with its fine French tapestry (Leda and the swan, David and the shewbread, and a French historical scene), and the Venetian marriage chest, is just what may legitimately be added within the four walls of the old house, increasing its dignity and interest without detracting from its antique charm. Coming out through the house you look on a long avenue stretching into meadows, with a lake to your left, and to your right a newly re-discovered and admirably restored open air bath, whose brick and stonework is of the very best style of the late seventeenth century. There can be little doubt that to the seventeenth century the main part of the house belongs. The fine sundial standing just in front of the door that opens on the park, dated 1660, probably marks the completion of the chief work. It bears the arms of Fetherston. The lead work of the house tells the same story, and it deserves attention. There is a fine pipehead in lead, with the arms on the bowl and twice below. Lead and iron here are alike at their best. Among the older treasures is a good iron latch, with fleur de lis above and below. There is a splendid vane on a turret. And there is a beautifully simple iron gate, of the late seventeenth century, and again another, more elaborate, at the end of the terrace, with fine steps leading to it. And the terrace takes you to the great feature of Packwood. A wall surrounds the garden, and the terrace runs with it, within, a gazebo standing at each corner. When you have passed through the gate you must notice on the south side of the terrace wall thirty small niches for beehives, two together beneath each pier—like the peacock nests (as they are said to be) at Riddlesden in Yorkshire. Then you enter the outer garden. It culminates in the fashion of the Tudor garden, brought from Italy, in a *monticello*. You may remember Ellis Heywood's memorial of Sir Thomas More, the charming Renaissance picture of a philosophic ideal (*Il Moro*, Firenze, 1556), which tells of the *animata tappezeria* which More made of his flowers and the centre of all in the mount where the friends sat and talked. But the Packwood mount is unique. The speech it recalls is the Sermon on the Mount itself. For the mount is approached by an avenue of tall yews, now happily relieved from the laurels which were killing them. Four tall yews, 20 feet high, stand for the Evangelists ; then six each side are for the Apostles. And you walk round the mount on a winding path amid clipped yews, to the arbour formed by a large yew, which represents the Lord looking upon the disciples and the multitude below. The quaint idea of the Tudor gardener seems likely long to continue to represent the past of this charming place. The yews, now well cared for, have still a long life before them. Mr. Ashe, the owner, deserves to be regarded as a benefactor to all Warwickshire, and a friend by all who study the social history of the past.

Before we go on to Lapworth we must see Packwood church. It is approached by a way which passes an old moated grange, where two red brick bridges give access to a house, one end of which at least, facing north, is old. The church itself has undergone many changes. In the porch is an ancient gravestone with foliated cross. There is work of the thirteenth, fifteenth, and eighteenth centuries. The tower, embattled, as is usual in this district, is said to have been built by Nicholas Brome, besides his additions to the church at Baddesley Clinton, in atonement for his murder of the priest whom he found " chokking " his wife under the chin. The south porch is a fine piece of medieval oak work. You may just trace on the chancel wall some fragments of medieval painting, representing the tale of the three living kings met by the three dead (as at Widford near Burford, or in another version in the famous Campo Santo of Pisa). And there are remains of glass of the first half of the fourteenth century. Another survival is the old oak parish chest, made out of one solid trunk. Before you leave the church you may recall one more memory. It was here that in 1706, as the register tells, " Mickell Johnsones of Lichfield and Sara Ford [were] married June ye 19th." Michael Johnson himself was a Derbyshire man, born in 1656 and baptised April 20. He was thus fifty when he married, and three years later, when his famous son was born (September 7, O.S. (16 N.S.), 1709), was sheriff of Lichfield.

And now before I leave Packwood I must add this. As I am writing this about Packwood at Burford, in Oxfordshire, in the hot August of 1911, this strikes me in the Burford town papers :—

" 1664, 24 March, 16 Charles II. Deed of sale by Thomas Greene the elder, late of Packwood, Warwickshire, and Thomas Greene the younger, to Ann Shackspeare, of Meriden, Warwickshire, widow, of a cottage granted to them 1 Dec. 1631 by Adrian Shackspeare, of Meriden, yeoman."

Now here is a name which brings Warwickshire and Burford and Shakespeare together ; also Packwood and Meriden, which as you know is five miles from Kenilworth, if you go out by the Birmingham road. But why does this Warwickshire document appear at Burford ? I do not know. And did anybody at Burford from 1664 to the twentieth century ever concern himself with the village of Packwood ?

From Packwood we may go north to Temple Balsall, or south to Baddesley Clinton and Wroxall. But Lapworth is much nearer, and to Lapworth, a large, straggling parish, not even now very densely populated, we will proceed. Let us go by the turning out of the road which passes through the park.

Of this pretty village, now filling with new houses built by Birmingham business men, a valuable history has recently been written by Mr. Robert Hudson, who resided at Lapworth for nearly forty years and died in 1910, " leaving the manuscript almost finished," so not much shall be said of it here. It is four miles from Henley, eight from Warwick ; and, in the heart of the country, it combines the characteristics, in one part, of a sort of suburb, with, in another, those of apparent isolation and solitude. In Domesday Book it is Lapeforde and has one hide, with woods two miles long and one broad. The woods are broken up now, but the character of the whole is still that of forest. The roads come, as it were, in unexpected places ; there are sudden turns ; and the railway running through the parish serves still further to confuse. There are two or three ways from the station, and from Baddesley Clinton, or Wroxall, or Packwood, to the church, and you are like enough to have taken one to find that it only brings you round to the one you left, little nearer to your destination. The village has always been a place of consideration. Like many other lands in these parts it was once the Montforts', later it belonged to Catesby, the cat of the rhyme about Richard III. Dugdale has a great deal to say of the history of its succession, and illustrates it by a fine series of coats, some of which survive or are reproduced in the church. The Catesby house became famous again in the time of the Powder Plot. Another interesting house in Lapworth is the red-brick farm with the fine chimney, not far from the station, which is all that remains of Brome Hall. This belonged to at least three John Bromes in succession, the first of whom appears in Lapworth deeds of 1361. It was the second John who became owner of Baddesley Clinton, and there the history of the family is to be looked for. The connection of the Bromes with Lapworth ceased in early Tudor times, for in the days of Henry VIII. Brome Hall was the residence of the Slyes. The church is of great interest. It occupies a splendid position on a wooded eminence. Its most remarkable feature is the chapel built over the western porch, of which the history is thus given in the "Churches of Warwickshire" :—

"A chantry was founded (47th Edward III.) in the chapel adjoining the west end of the church by Richard de Montfort and others, for the celebration of daily mass for the welfare of the founders and a long list of persons enumerated in the endowment. An indulgence of forty days was granted (Jan. 5, 1467) to all who should attend mass at the altar of St. Katherine in the parish church, daily to be celebrated for the good estate of William Catesby and others. There were endowments also for the maintenance of a light before the altar of St. James, and of the Blessed Virgin, the paschal and rood lights, and for the observance of several obits."

It is approached by two stone staircases from the porch. Another chantry chapel is at the north of the chancel, and probably belongs to the same date. The similarity of the windows to those of Wroxall has been pointed out. The clerestory is in three compartments, separated by buttresses, each containing a large window. The view from the south is very remarkable. The building looks as if it were a combination of church and castle, dominated by a tower, embattled like the nave. The tower has a watching turret.

There are many signs of restoration ; among them in the west windows the arms of the rector in 1807, H. Pye, as also those of

Heneage Legge and Thomas Fetherston with the same date. There is a good alabaster reredos which is strangely covered up by a green velvet hanging (August, 1911); but the Elizabethan altar-table with its fine carved legs still remains. A simple and dignified monument bears witness to the good work of a devoted benefactor to the church in Lapworth, Robert Hudson, church-warden under four rectors.

From the height of Lapworth then we descend to the beautiful lanes of the level land. Through them we may regain the main road at one point or another. Perhaps it is best to ascend and descend Liveridge Hill, which affords a fine view of the surrounding country, and so into Henley-in-Arden, under the railway bridge, and up the street, a mile long, leaving Beaudesert, and the church of Henley, to the left.

CHAPTER XIV

ALCESTER, RAGLEY, AND THE BANKS OF ALNE

THERE is a most lovely engraving of 1827 by W. Radclyffe, from a drawing by J. V. Barker of " Ragley and Alcester from the Ridgeway." Thither we will now make our way. Alcester you may reach by a good road from Stratford-on-Avon ; or, better, as I think, by the Roman road from Bourton-on-the-Water. This is the Rycknield Street, as Mr. Haverfield [1] calls it, which starts away from the Fosse at Bourton and goes on from Alcester to Birmingham and Lichfield. It would be a good journey to trace it through Warwickshire. We have been on it part of the way to Bidford ; and perhaps from Bidford to Wixford ; after that it is only a field track, an " interesting hollow way between the fields," Mr. Haverfield calls it. The road was early called Icknield Street, then, by a mistake of Higden's, Rycknield, and the two names occur in old charters, deeds, chronicles. It has also, as the maps show you, other names, and Mr. Haverfield puts them thus succinctly : " North of Alcester it is occasionally called Headon or Haydon Way, and also Eagle Street—perhaps a corruption of Ickle, that is, Icknield Street. South of Alcester, between Bidford and Weston Subedge, it is called Buckle Street, and this is probably

[1] *Victoria County History of Warwickshire*, Vol. i, p. 239. A portion of his footnote explains why he prefers Rycknield to Icknield. " No doubt, if antiquity of usage is to be considered, the road was called Icknield Street before it was called Rycknield Street. But . . . . I doubt whether the road has any real and original right to either name ; and if we style it Icknield Street, we risk confusion with the real Icknield Street in Berkshire and Oxfordshire. It seems best therefore to use the name Rycknield as being no less correct (or no more incorrect) than Icknield, and as having the advantage of being unmistakable."

its oldest existing appellation. It is the modern form of a name Bucgan or Buggilde Street, which appears in documents earlier than the Conquest, and which proves that the road was known in very early days, at least, between Bidford and Weston."

Alcester, however approached, is, I suppose, the most indubitably Roman town in Warwickshire (I cannot tarry for obvious contradictions of this), and so it has been known since Leland, one would think, certainly since Dugdale. Many remains of Roman times have been found there, and the cemetery was discovered at Grunt Hill, to the right of the road between Alcester and Arrow, just after the railway is crossed. The best memorial is the much decayed fragment of Romano-British Sculpture now on the wall by the rectory, at the west of the church, showing a man in a tunic with some drapery on the left shoulder. Mr. Haverfield refers us to the seventeenth century rector, Samuel (Clarke 1638), for a good account of a discovery, which indeed is typical of many discoveries there. Here is the passage :—

" [At Alcester] in plowing and digging, even until this day, are found many very ancient pieces of copper-money, some of which I have, and among them one of Vespasian with Judaea Capta upon it. When I was Rector there, about 1638, my next Neighbour, whose house joyned to the Churchyard, being about to sink a Seller, I lent him one of my men to assist him therein, and after they had digged about three or four Foot deep, they Encountered with two Urns not far asunder. In the one there was nothing but some ashes ; the other was full of Medals, set edgelong as full as it could be thrust : My man judging it only to be of that Copper-money which they find so oft about the Town, set it carelessly upon the ground by him : And the Town, consisting of Knitters, some of them coming to see the Work, picked out some pieces of this Money : At last one brought in a piece to me, which upon tryal I found to be Silver. and thereupon sent for the Pot into my House : . . . . In the midst whereof I found sixteen pieces of gold, as bright as if they had been lately put in, and about eight hundred pieces of Silver, and yet no two of them alike, and the latest of them above fourteen hundred years old : They contained the whole History of the Roman Empire from Julius Cæsar till after Constantine the Great's time : Each of the Silver pieces weighed about sevenpence, and each of the Gold, about fifteen or sixteen shillings " [Geographical Description of all the Countries in the known World, by Samuel Clarke (London 1671), p. 167].

It is to be noticed that " Alauna " is a modern invention for the Roman name of the town. While Rome thus continually asserts its power here, the remains of the Middle Age seem quite to have passed away. Leland said Alcester was " a praty market town." So it still is, and " the market kept there on the Twesday." But of the thirteen parish churches " some say " were there, there is but one left. The Benedictine priory, founded by Ralph

Alcester Town Hall.

Boteler, has vanished, and the church was practically rebuilt between 1727 and 1734. It is by no means uninteresting. The tower surely is old, not very good, but still of the late fourteenth century; and the taste for what antiquaries now call " debased Gothic " may return. Why should we not enjoy the " Doric columns " in the nave, or the little apse for the altar ? But I may as well quote what the severe authors of " The Churches of Warwickshire " say about it, in those days when nothing would serve but what was medieval, and in consequence many horrors of restoration were perpetrated :—

"The Body of the Church, comprising the nave and aisles, is built in a kind of debased, or *Batty Langley*, gothic. At the west end of the south aisle is an ogee-canopied doorway. There is no external division between the nave and aisles. The south wall is pierced with five four-centered arched windows of two lights each, which have no foliations, with lozenge shaped openings between the heads of the principal lights. The windows have hoods over them. Between the windows are pinnacled buttresses rising above the parapet, which is embattled. There is a shallow base moulding. The north aisle presents, externally, a similar appearance to the south aisle. The altar recess, for it is nothing more, is lighted by a single window in the east wall, this is of three lights comprised within an obtusely-pointed arch. The vestry is on the north side of the Altar recess, and is entered through a square-headed doorway. The whole design of the modern work is poor, and meagre in execution."

Much of this severity, but not all, is deserved. A good Tudor screen fences off the •organ : it came from Warwick Castle, they say. The splendid brass chandelier (how often these things are neglected: I saw a beautiful one the other day still hanging in a church but covered with verdigris) was given by the great and good Dr. Hough, revered of all Magdalen men, and bears the words, "The gift of ye Rt. Revd. Father in God, Dr. John Hough, Ld. Bp. of Worcester, 1733." There is also a curious seventeenth century triptych, which commemorates the gifts to poor tradesmen : "Behold within this table all the names with the memorial acts of those who have most liberally extended their bountie to help Tradesmen and releave poore and aged people dwelling within the Towne and parish of Alcester." The date is 1683. The altar was one of those gifts common till meddlesome persons in the nineteenth century began to protest against them. It was a slab of marble supported by iron scroll-work brackets fixed into and projecting from the east wall. On a tablet in the church was the account of the gift, stated thus :—"The communion table was, in 1733, gave by William Somervile, Esq., Richard Brandis, Gent., &c. The brackets to support the same, in 1733, were given by Samuel Barnett of London, Gent." 1733 we see was the date of the

" re-edifying " of the building, within and without. But the chief interest of the church lies in the chapel at the north-west, which contains the Greville tombs. There are the recumbent effigies of Sir Fulke and the Lady Elizabeth his wife, who died within a year of each other, on November 10, 1559, and November 9, 1560. These are rich with paint and gold, he in ceremonial armour, she in gown and ruff, with pomander and lapdog complete. But the smaller figures at the south and north, intended perhaps for offspring, are equally interesting ; they include the sign of a child who died in infancy. The inscription reads thus :—

Here lyeth the body of foulke Grebill knight and lady Elizabeth his wife the daughter and heire of Edward Willoughby Esquier the sone and heire of Robert Willoughby knight Lord of Broke and lady Elizabeth one of the daughters and coheires of the lord Beauchampe of Powyk wch foulke dyed the Xth day of Nobember Anno dni. MDLIX and the saide ladye Elizabeth his Wife departed the IX day of Nob. in the yeare of our lord God MDLX of Whose soules god habe mercy Amen.

I will add for the benefit of ladies the very careful description of Lady Greville's dress, from " The Churches of Warwickshire." I certainly cannot improve upon it.

" The lady is represented with her hair combed back, close, and parted in front, with a close coif, or ornamental caul on the head, with a black frontlet hanging down behind like a tippet, and the head reposes on a double cushion. Her dress consists of a gown, open in front, and tied with strings, a short ruff round the neck, a falling collar to the outer robe, and short sleeves gathered in full at the shoulders, from whence loose demi-canon hanging sleeves depend, or hang. Beneath is a stiff under gown, or petticoat without folds or plaits, the sleeves of which are close fitting. Under this are seen, at the feet, the plaits or folds of an inner robe, or under petticoat, and on the feet are worn broad-toed shoes. Hanging down by a chain in front of the body is a circular pendulet or pomander box, with a double rose. The mantle appears at the back of the effigy, and is fastened across the breast by cordons, the tasselled extremities of which hang down. Ruffles and gilt armlets encircle the wrists, and on the fingers of each hand are five rings. Round the neck a gold chain is worn. At the skirts of the robes, on the left side, is a small lap dog. The robes are red, black and gilt, and the hands are joined on the breast in prayer."

At the east end of the south aisle is a Chantrey figure of the second Marquis of Hertford, Francis Ingram Conway, lying on a sofa with a book in his hand. The inscription reads thus :—

" To the memory of her justly and deeply lamented husband, Francis Ingram Seymour Conway, Marquis and Earl of Hertford, Earl of Yarmouth, Viscount Beauchamp, Baron Conway of Ragley and Killultagh, Knight of the most noble Order of the Garter, and Lord Lieutenant of the County of Warwick. Isabella Anne Ingram, Marchioness of Hertford, has dedicated this monument. He was born, February, 1743, and died, June, 1822."

The coat is : quartered 1 and 4, Conway ; 2, Seymour ; 3, Ingram. For the Marquis, see Creevey's " Memoirs." There is no memorial here of his more famous son, the Monmouth of Disraeli and Steyne of Thackeray (as is commonly asserted).

We leave Alcester on our way to the house of the Conways and Seymours, not without a look at the Town Hall, towards the north of the church, which has a good timber roof.

Now leave the town to the south-west, by a very pretty road, crossing the river to the church of Arrow which has a charming eighteenth century tower, which Horace Walpole is said to have designed. An inscription says it was " built at the expense of the Right Honourable the Earl of Hertford, 1767." The church itself has a Norman doorway and a very fine Decorated door. It was restored in 1863. The stone coffin is that of Gerard de Camville—" cî git Gerard de Canvill " may still be read on it—1303, of that famous line of lawyers whom we know in Plantagenet days. There are several monuments to the Hertfords. The family has had an extremely chequered career, as may be said indeed of all those famous in English history. It includes Secretary Conway of Charles I.'s reign, the Duchess of Somerset of Lady Luxborough's day, and the nineteenth century personages, the bad and the good, of whom history speaks. We go on to Ragley, their residence. But before we do so we pass the mill whereby hangs much history. The story may be read in Dugdale, who gives the records of Arrow most fully, with an elucidatory pedigree. The exciting tale attached to the mill is that of King Edward IV.'s hunting there, in 1477, when Thomas Burdet was lord of the manor. Thus Dugdale tells it :—

"In 17 E. 4, having incurred the King's Displeasure for his good Affections to the D. of Clarence, so strict were the Eyes and Ears that were set over him, that an Advantage was soon taken to cut off his Head; for hearing that the King had killed a White Buck in his Park here at Arrow, which Buck he set much store by, passionately wishing the Hornes in his Belly, that moved the K. so to do, being Arraigned and Convicted of High Treason for those Words, upon Inference made this his Meaning was mischievous to the King himself, his lost his Life for the same."

The pedigree shows how the Burdet property passed by marriage to the Conways, as it did again to the Seymours in 1683. In the time of "the Warwickshire Coterie" the property belonged to that Earl of Hertford, whom the Dictionary of National Biography ignores, who became Duke of Somerset in 1750 and had for wife the excellent lady whom Shenstone and Jago courted and sang. With these personages in mind we go on to the park of Ragley, a most delightful place, large, well timbered, with splendid views, and a classic mansion built in 1758. Earlier than that of the famous Henry More, a Cambridge Platonist (1614–1687), who placidly lived through times so dangerous, found there a congenial resting-place. Says one of those who have written of him :—

"Ragley retired from the ordinary haunts of men, with its woods and shady walks, was an ideal retreat for one of More's highly imaginative temperament; and in its recesses, he tells us, 'the choicest theories' of one of his most noteworthy treatises, that entitled 'The Immortality of the Soul,' were conceived. Lady Conway also became his pupil, of whom his biographer gives the following account : 'She was of incomparable parts and endowments. . . . and between this excellent person and the Doctor there was, from first to last, a very high friendship ; and I have heard him say that he scarce ever met with any person (man or woman) of better natural parts than the lady Conway. She was mistress of the highest theories, whether of philosophy or religion, and had, on all accounts, an extraordinary value and respect for the Doctor,—I have seen abundance of letters that are testimony of it. . . . And as she always wrote a very clear style, so would she argue sometimes, or put to him the deepest and noblest queries imaginable.' "

The aspect of the place is very different now. The straight front with its "offices"—in all senses of the word—below, and the two upper rows of fine tall windows—broken by the huge portico with its four great pillars—is really impressive, and its fine entrance hall though Horace Walpole mocked at it, and at Sanderson Miller who was concerned in its creation, is dignified. Among the pictures are some good family portraits of each century, and a fine Lely of Van Helmont. About him, and indeed about More, everybody knows who has at least read " John Inglesant." It is said he caused the body of Anne Viscountess Conway, who died in 1678 in Ireland, " to be preserved in her

Ragley, from the Ridgeway.

coffin above ground with spirits of wine, having a glass over her face, that he might see her, before her interment " on April 17, 1679. From the house you look upon a beautiful Italian garden, and down innumerable paths through the woods. One of these leads you, as does the broad road through the park and out at the Evesham lodge, to the villages of Bevington which have an interesting history. We are here on the verge of Salford (*see* p. 256) and indeed both Wood-Bevington and Cock-Bevington, the "two pretty Hamlets" named by Dugdale, were "members of Salford Priors" in the time of Domesday and were granted to the canons of Kenilworth. Later we find in 1531 that there is a grant of the village or hamlet of Wood-Bevington in the parish of Salford, Warwickshire, with all messuages, lands, tithes, etc., by the abbat and convent of the monastery of Kenilworth to William Grey and his heirs male, with remainder to Elizabeth Grey, daughter of William, and to her heirs male, and then remainder to Anne Grey, another daughter of William [20 Dec., 23 H. VIII.]. This family transferred to the Randolphs in 1548. The Randolph property increased by their obtaining certain lands in Wood-Bevington and Cock-Bevington, formerly belonging to the monastery of Evesham, which were sold to the Randolphs in 1609. The lease of these properties was continually transferred by the Randolphs, and in 1636 Ferrers Randolph, son and heir of Thomas Randolph, sold the Bevington property to S. John's College, Oxford. On March 10, 1636, the college obtained a licence in mortmain to purchase and hold "the township of Wood-Bevington and certain lands in Wood-Bevington, Cock-Bevington, Dannington and Salford, co. Warwick," provision being made that the lands are not to be held *in capite* or by knight's service. The lands were then let to Mr. Secretary Conway and his heirs, for 300 years ; provision being made that when the college sent down their representatives to inspect, they were to be entertained at the manor-house. The college made the purchase with the money left by Sir William Paddy, physician to James I., and certain moneys added to it, for the maintenance of daily choral service according to the use of the Church of England in the college chapel, a trust which still remains. It seems that the Conways leased some parts of the property to the old family of Randolph, for in 1657 a Romanist representative of that family began a confraternity of tertiaries of S. Francis in the old manor-house ; and later the house is found belonging to the Archers, who altered the old house much. There was a chapel in it from 1339 (license) till after the Reformation, used by the Romanists in the seventeenth century, but this has been so altered that it is not recognisable in the present parlour and study, to the right of the porch as you enter. Mr. H. S. Gunn, in a very interesting, privately printed "History of the Old Manor House, Wood-Bevington" (1911), prints the inventory *post mortem* of the goods of Edward Ferrers, 1578, which gives a list of the furniture in the hall, " ploure " (parlour), " chappell chamber " (already turned into a bedroom) and the other rooms, down to the meanest detail. It was a large and well-furnished house. The later history, during the time of the Archers, is not without interest, too; and thus Mr. Gunn gives a passage of it: "The Archer family chariot, with its pair of long-tailed black horses, might often have been seen wending its way to Cookhill" [where resided Captain Fortescue, the friend of the Archer ladies, who lived so long at Bevington in solitary and somewhat impoverished stateliness]. "When they went far from home a man on horseback usually attended the carriage, carrying pistols in the holsters, and they have been known to have two mounted men, one preceding the carriage and the other bringing up the rear." The Archers died out in 1791 ; the Ferrers passed into the Randolphs, the Randolphs (I think) into the Conways. So branches of good old Warwickshire families passed away. The present family have been in the manor for over a century. Land tenure in these parts is a long-lived business. The one lease which connects to-day with the time of Archbishop Laud has still twenty-three years to run. What will happen then ? The old manor-house happily survives, and one trusts is in no danger of further defacement. The heath, the woods, the solitary roads, remain as the centuries pass, and the families at the great house and the lesser houses decay. The colony of Romanists exists no longer. The Church foundation survives.

At the Bevingtons we may end our survey of this corner of the shire. One wonders if Shakespeare passed this way when he went towards Berkeley or " the Hill," or to see Justice Shallow's greyhound outrun on Cotsall.

CHAPTER XV

CLAVERDON is reached by a side round, past Preston Bagot, east-wards from Henley-in-Arden. Here the Count of Meulan held land in Domesday Book, and the manor passed through many hands including those of the Hospitallers till the Dissolution. The church of Preston Bagot stands high on a hill above the fields, and is one long unbroken building originally Norman and with Norman and Early English work and fourteenth century enlargement. It has a pleasing brass of a lady, headless now, well dressed with a falling collar, a stomacher, and a short petticoat, whose inscription reads thus, much better than the conventional ones :—

" Dormitorium Elizabethæ Randoll Richi Knightley De Burge Hall in Cōm. Stāff. Armīg. Filiæ secundæ, Coniugis Willi Randoll legis Consiliarii, quæ per breves aliquot in hac parochia menses devotissima Deo, amicissima populo, præcharissima marito suo, feliciter vixit, et dein cum optima apud pios memoria non sine plurima lamentatione spiritus ejus rediit Deo illius Datori 12° die Decembris A° Dni 1637 ; Cujus tamen caro viva sub spe hic secure requiescit, ac plena integræ per Iesum suum redemptionis adventu suo proximo ad optimam resurrectionem."

So on to another church, Claverdon, at the top of another hill, but surrounded by houses. The church is at first sight a dis-appointment ; it has been so much restored—rebuilt, indeed, they say, in 1875. The admired authors of " The Churches of Warwickshire " had in 1847 some very hard things to say about it and its neglect ; but the Oxford Movement did some good here. Among modern things is a very good screen to the belfry, and there is a charming window by Mr. Kempe; but the best things after all are the old, and here is a very good thing indeed—the tomb of Thomas Spencer, of whose fame Warwickshire history is always telling :—

"Here lyeth the body of Thomas Spencer of Claveydon in ye County of Warwicke Esquier second sone of Sir John Spencer of Althroppe in the county of Northampton Knight who deceased the 8th daie of November in the yeare of our Lord God 1586. This Thomas Spencer married Mary Cheeke the eldest daughter of Henry Cheeke Esquier, and had issue by her one only daughter Alice Spencer married unto Sir Thomas Lucy of Charlecott in the saide County of Warwicke Knight. ' All the daies of my appointed time will I wait till my change come.' Job xiv., 14."

What was once a good monument to this eminent person's steward—and Sir Thomas Spencer in his house, of which hereafter, "for the great hospitality which he kept thereat was the mirrour of this county," says Dugdale—by name Christopher Flecknoe, is now on the outside south wall of the chancel, and has almost perished; nor could you make anything of the rhyming epitaph of John Matthews, a benefactor, if it had not been repaired, for it also is exposed to the weather.

When you leave the church and descend the hill again and take some difficult turnings, as to which a map must be your only guide, you will come to the solitary remains of Sir Thomas Spencer's great house, now called "the Stone Building," which is three stories high, but of disproportionately small breadth, each of the upper stories having only two rooms, the ground floor an entrance-hall. It looks very much like a "hunting lodge" such as the early seventeenth century delighted to build, comparatively simple and with no provision for a long stay; but there seems sufficient evidence that it is only part of a large house, which had a tilting yard, a bowling-green, and terraced gardens. *Sed transit gloria horti.*

To Claverdon, Rowington is the next parish. Perhaps the way is easier to find than that which I have taken when, diverging from the Leamington to Birmingham road some way after leaving Hatton, I have been lost in the mazes of lanes among woods and hills, where the landmarks to the stranger's eye are few and hard to find. Really we are not far away from any of the notable places here, but we seem buried in the heart of a forest, now we are in Arden. Nowhere, indeed, does the forest of Arden,

which yet never really was a forest, look more like a forest than
here.   Rowington, I repeat, is not easy to find.   One of the landmarks is the Elephant inn, with such a nice portrait of him.
Somehow you may wander round and round the village from this
notable house (I mean even if you have never been inside, as
I have not), and be a very long time before you come to the church.
When you do you will find it set on a hill, embedded on one side
in trees, but on the other, the east, affording an extensive view.

The Stone Building, Claverdon.

Archæologists, and even architects, profess to be puzzled by the
shape of the church, and to wonder as to its original ground plan ;
I cannot elucidate the matter.   But it is sufficient to say that
at the west is a splendid window with five large lights over the
great west door.   Above the window is a blank shield.   The nave
has aisles north and south, the former with a plain pointed doorway.   From the east of the nave rises the embattled tower, with
shields on two of the battlements, the northern one of which bears
a horseshoe over a pair of pincers between two hammers.   There

is a north chantry chapel, a chancel with a late Decorated east window. A very shallow transept is south of the tower. The ancient screen separates the chancel from the north chapel. The roofs appear to have been restored in the original colours and are very good. The altar is like that at Lapworth, with fine carved legs. From the seventeenth to the nineteenth century a marble-topped table (still remaining in the church) was used as an altar. It is described as " an immovable slab of marble fixed on iron scroll work projecting from the wall." There is a fine fourteenth century carved stone pulpit, and the red sandstone font is a hundred years older. On the north of the altar is the monument of John Woollaston, whose son-in-law, Thomas Betham of Rowington, erected it in 1615, and on the floor a slab of alabaster with man in gown and ruff, and woman in hat as well, who cannot with certainty be identified ; though the inscription appears to commemorate " John Oldnall and Isbell his wife late bayliff of Rownton a worthy man to be hadd in memory," but how about the date ? John Oldnall flourished at the beginning of the seventeenth century. A great deal may be read about him and his contemporaries in Mr. J. W. Ryland's Records of Rowington based on the deeds of the Feoffees of Rowington (1896). Outside is the fine monument of Robert Pett and Margaret his wife, 1720, decayed, of course, by exposure. Altogether Rowington is a highly interesting church, worthy of a village which has an interesting history. The village was an early clearing in the forest land, and Dugdale thinks it had its name in Domesday, Rochintone, from the rocky ground on which it stood, which is not very likely. It was a parish in late Saxon days. Under Henry I. was founded the small priory of Cistercian nuns within this parish, fragments of whose buildings may still be seen between Claverdon and Hatton. The house seems to have been well conducted, save for a mention in the Register of Bishop Thoresby of Worcester, 1350, when certain secular persons are ordered to be removed from the house on account of the ill-fame attaching to the nuns from this residence. In 1536 there were only four nuns with the prioress, with eight dependants. The last abbess was Margaret Wigston, and it is to be observed that the king sold the site and lands to one William Wigston. He was the son of the last high steward of the priory. Those parts of the buildings which remain belonged to the chapel, and are partly of Norman work. In the main village itself there are some charming houses, such as the Horse Shoe Inn and Mouseley End, both half timbered, as well as the fine brick Holywell farm with its splendid chimney stacks. But the most interesting house is that on the green, called Shakespeare Hall, half timbered and with good gables, with at least one oak-panelled room. Its history is rather uncertain. Mr. Haliwell-Phillips thought for certain that the poet " was in no way connected with the family " of Rowington, while Mr. _{T.} W. Ryland claims that Thomas Shakespeare, who lived in the house, was of the elder branch of the poet's family. It is worth noticing that this Thomas's son John was apprenticed to William Jaggard, " a well-known pirate publisher," Sir Sidney Lee calls him, who published " The Passionate Pilgrim," and later on the First Folio likewise. Rowington is only twelve miles from Stratford, and there are known to have been four William Shakespeares there between 1560 and 1614. But I think what Mr. Ryland says is worth quoting as an illustration of the history which enthusiasts have made out of a possible association. He tells us that the late John Fetherston, F.S.A., believed that " Shakespeare visited his relations at Rowington, worshipped at Baddesley Clinton church, and roamed in the fine old wood (Haywood), both of which almost joined the house above mentioned, meditating on the play of ' As You Like It,' which Mr. Fetherston believed was written in the same house."

Let us leave these speculations and go to Wroxhall. To this most interesting place, the house and church with the ruins of the priory, approached by a delightful avenue, much after the manner of Maxstoke Castle, Thomas Cox's summary of Dugdale —omitting all that they both say about the interesting but not specially relevant subject of the dedication of churches—is an excellent introduction. So here it shall be quoted :—

" *Wroxhall*, a Village, not mention'd in the Conqueror's Survey, because it was a Member of *Hatton juxta Haseley*, and so included in that Manor. It was the Estate of *Henry de Newburgh*, the first Earl of *Warwick* after the Conquest, and holding of him with *Hatton*, by one *Richard*, whose son *Hugh*, being a Person of great Stature, went in the Expedition into the *Holy Land*, and was there taken Prisoner, in which Condition he remained seven Years, and underwent great Hardships ; but at length, calling to Mind that their Parish Church was dedicated to *S. Leonard*, he made his Prayers to him for Deliverance, which he attain'd upon his Vow to build a Nunnery of the Order of St. *Benedict*, in this Place, (but of that afterwards). To this his Nunnery, thus built, he gave this whole Manor, the Church of *Hatton*, and no inconsiderable Part of his Royalty there. To it at first there was doubtless a Church erected ; but being afterwards rebuilt, was consecrated by *Walter de Maidenstone*, Bishop of *Worcester*."

This was Walter of Maidstone, bishop from 1313 to 1317. And the story of S. Leonard and Hugh, son of Henry, Earl of Warwick, is more interesting than Mr. Cox tells, for it was a matter of many dreams, and at last the identification of the site at Wroxhall as the one seen. The priory thus founded went through the usual vicissitudes, was not always found perfect at visitations, and, indeed, was occasionally the scene of considerable strife ; and in 1339 at a visitation of the Prior of Worcester, *sede vacante*, was found to be in a very lax state indeed. The last prioress was Agnes Little, and the house was reported to be in a very good state, at the time of the Dissolution.

" After the Dissolution of the Nunnery, this Manor, with the Church, and Site of the Nunnery, as also the Rectory and Tithes of the Place, were granted, 36 *H. 8.* to *Robert Burgoigne*, and *John Scudamore*, and their Heirs ; to the former of which, Sir *John Burgoigne* of *Sutton* in *Bedfordshire*, Bart. was Heir, and his Descendents are, or lately were, Possessors of it."

This was so when Mr. Cox obtained his information, but in 1713 the property was sold to Sir Christopher Wren, in the possession of whose family it remained till 1863, when it was bought by Mr. James Dugdale, who erected a new house, pulling down the Elizabethan building which had been attached to the remains of the priory. An engraving in Hannett's charming book, " The Forest of Arden," (1863) shows a delicious composite building which it was a vandalism to destroy. The history may be completed by pointing out the peculiar position of the church, which is thus given, accurately, in " The Churches of Warwickshire." The constitutional position of Wroxhall is not, of course, unique, though it is, at the present day, unusual. The chaplains, as they strictly are, are not found in the bishop's registers.

" No Parish Church appears to have ever been founded at Wroxhall : which may readily be accounted for on the supposition, that as the whole lordship was granted to the Priory, the tenants probably attended the service of the Conventual Church. Since the Reformation this sacred edifice has supplied the place of the Parish Church ; the Parishioners have attended its public ordinances, and the dead have been buried within its Church-yard : Parish Registers have been regularly kept, and Church-wardens have been appointed. From the absolute grant of the Priory and the comprehensive terms in which the buildings were conveyed, it appears that the Church is the absolute property of those who derive their title, under that instrument ; and the appointment of the Minister, and his salary, rests wholly in the hands of those to whom the possessions of the suppressed Priory belong."

The church is the most conspicuous part of the remains of the priory. It consists of continuous nave and chancel, and at the south probably was entered from the cloisters. The five Decor-ated windows on the north are curious, and the third has a story attaching to the blocked-up door beneath ; it demands insertion :—

"'Dame Alice Craft, somtime nunne and lady of this place, poore of worldly goods, but riche of vertues, desired heartily of God and our Lady that she in her dayes might see here a Chapell of our Lady. To that intent she prayed oft time : and on a night time there came a voice to her, and bad her, in the name of God and our Lady, beginn and performe a chapell of our Lady. She remembred her thereof, and thought it but a dreme, and toke noe heede thereof. But not long to, another night following, came the same voice to her againe, and gave her the same charge more sharplye.' Still delaying to execute the work she was visited by our Lady who reprimanded her for her neglect : on which going to the Prioress, and stating that she had only the sum of fifteen pence to commence with, she was encouraged to undertake the work in trust that our Lady would encrease her store. 'Then this dame Alice Craft gave her to prayers, and besought our Lady to give her knowledge where she should build it, and how much she should make it. Then she had by revela-tion to make it on the north side her churche, and there she should finde markyd the quantity. This was in harvest betwene the two feasts of our Lady : and on the morrow earlye she went unto the place assigned her, and there she found a certeyne ground covered with snow, and all the Churchyard else bare without snow ; and there the snow abidde from foure of the clocke in the morning untill noone. She glad of this had masons ready and marked out the ground, and built the chapell and performed it up. And every Satturday whilst it was in building she would say her prayers in the allyes of the church-yard, and in the playne pathe she should and did finde weekely sylver suficient to pay her workmen, and all that behoofull to her worke, and no more. This good lady, dame Alice Craft, died the vii calends of Feverell, on the morrow after the Conversion of Saint Paul : and she is buried under a stone in the same chapell afore the doore, entring into the quire. She, as beseming of her bones, was a woman of grete stature. There was a young lady buryed in the same grave, and there we see her bones.' "

The church has undergone restoration or alteration from Reformation times. The eastern window on the north side was thus treated in the sixteenth century, and the tower, embattled as usual, is of the seventeenth. The initials " R.B." and the date 1663 on a leaden spout direct attention to the work which Sir Roger Burgoyne did on the church. It was he, probably, who built the tower, and probably in 1664. His relict Anne was buried here in 1694. Some of the ancient glass (fourteenth century) still remaining on the north side is very interesting : we have the four Evangelists, the Crucifix with S. Mary and S. John, and a large number of angels holding shields, as well as donors, a black nun, and S. Benedict himself in a green apparelled alb, with red dalmatic and gold chasuble. The monuments, too, are interesting. Among the Wrens is the Rev. Philip Wren, rector of Ipsley and vicar of Tanworth, who died in 1829. The last was Christopher, who died in 1842.

Before we leave the church we should notice the beautiful old wood worked up into the pulpit, and the brass on the south wall of a lady of the early fifteenth century.

Outside in the sunlight are the beautiful ruins of the priory. There is the chapter-house, with its lovely doorway, a small building only about sixteen feet square, with the slender shafts, with bell-shaped capitals, intended to support a groined roof. A few other arches there are, a few crumbling walls over which stray creeping plants; but little indeed remains of what was still standing sixty years ago. The garden, with its fine pillars and the huge shells at their feet, is charming on a summer day. Wroxhall is a memory rather than a memorial of the past.

The next house we visit is both. We may get to it (if we are allowed) north-westwards by Hay Wood, without coming out again on to any public road ; or, rejoining the Birmingham road, up to Priest's Park, and, turning to the left, west and south. But, however we come to it, the position, the strange out-of-the-world air that belongs to it, the air of unchangedness, make the place unique.

One of the most beautiful houses in Warwickshire, Baddesley Clinton, is, like many of the others, secluded from the eye of man as he traverses the highways. The roads hard by, little more than lanes most of them, are shaded in summer by the leafy screen of close planted trees. The house itself, though it stands, as they tell you, on high ground and receives the fresh winds unchecked from the Ural Mountains—a not uncommon boast on the part of geographers in central England—cannot be seen as you descend the hill (only a moderate one) from the park above it, till you come quite close, and see the fine gate beyond the bridge which crosses the moat. The common approach is from Lapworth station—near which the line from Henley-in-Arden meets the main line to Birmingham. Leaving the station yard you turn to the left, by a wooded lane, then to the right, on across the Warwick and Birmingham canal, up a slight rise, and through the lodge gates to the right. So across the park to the hall. First, perhaps, you take the path by a copse to the church. There is a charming view of it from the south-west. Restoration in 1872 may confuse the archæologist, but the nave is probably of the earlier fourteenth century. There is a Decorated south doorway ; indeed, most of the building is Decorated. But the tower was added in 1517 ; the walls of the nave were raised ten feet, and the clerestory windows put in by the same person, all " in the raigne of King Henry the Seaventh " as an inscription on the south wall says. He was Nicholas Brome, Esquire, Lord of Baddesley, who died in October, 1517, and is buried " under ye blew marble stone at ye entrance into the church at ye door." About this personage there is much to say, which Dugdale tells with evident enjoyment. John Brome, a lawyer, and, one sees, a very acute one, " did descend from a familie of that name which for several descents were tanners and resided in that suburbe of Warwick, south of the bridge." They were of the household of the Beauchamps, John serving in Parliament 8 Henry IV. as burgess for Warwick ; and also they owned Brome Hall, of which remains may still be seen near Lapworth station. John Brome obtained Baddesley from the Catesbys. He was an energetic, busy fellow, and came to the end which so many of his kind did, in the late

Baddesley-Clinton.

fifteenth century, which were not the safest days for busy-bodies. So Dugdale : " At the beginning of Edward IV.'s reign he was set aside as to any Publique employment." Clearly, he was a Lancastrian. " And at length had the hard fate to be slain by John Herthill, steward to Richard Nevill, the great Earl of Warwick, who, sending for him out of the Whitefriars Church in London, where he was then at Mass, upon some words which happen'd between them, killed him in the Porch." It was a dispute about lands, and the redemption of the manor of Wood-low. About real property people were exceeding fierce in the days of the Roses, and when the Pastons wrote their immortal letters, and even lawyers fought. So John Brome died ; but not before he had made his will—like so many lawyers he left it till the very last—wherein he " used this Expression : *scil.* that he forgave his son Thomas who smiled when he saw him run through by Herthill in the Whitefriars Church Porch." His wife was a Shirley, of that famous Warwickshire family. Their son Nicholas (who doubtless had not smiled) succeeded him and made a blood feud of the murder. " About three years after " he waylaid John Herthill " in Longbridge field, in his passage towards Barford to keep the Earl of Warwick's court, and there, after a short encounter, slew him." Then the Herthill widow came on the scene, and there was arbitrament, and Nicholas Brome had to pay fifty pounds to S. Mary's church at Warwick for a priest for one whole year to say mass for the souls of John Brome and John Herthill, and for two years for another priest to do the like at Baddesley Clinton. This was the earlier history of Nicholas, who now comes before us as he who so enlarged this church ; and now again it was his violence, justifiable it may be, that brings him forward. Of him, said Sir William Dugdale, " I have further seen that coming on a time into his parlour here at Badsley, he found the parish priest chokking his wife under the chin, whereat he was so enraged that he presently killed him ; for which offence, obtaining the King's pardon and the Pope's, he was enjoined to do something towards the expiation thereof ; whereupon he new built the tower steeple here at Badsley from the ground, and bought three bells for it ; and raised the body of the Church ten feet higher." The nave thus beautified, the chancel waited another century for enrichment, and it was not till after the repudiation of Roman supremacy, and the reigning

Y

of a new family at Baddesley Clinton, that this was done. A tablet records this thus : " Edward Ferrers, Esquire, sonne and beire of Henry Ferrers and Jane White his wife did new builde and re-edify this channcell at his owne prope costes and charges. Año Dom. 1634. This Church is dedicated to Saint James." In this chancel is the fine coloured tomb of Sir Edward Ferrers, 1535, and his wife, Dame Constance, 1551, daughter and heiress of Nicholas Brome, by whom the property came to the Ferrers family. With them is their son, Henry Ferrers, who died in 1526, · before his parents, leaving a son who lived till 1564. The pedigree is in Dugdale. The memorials of other members of the family which he mentions have disappeared ; and are represented by a large marble slab in the floor inserted by the last Mr. Ferrers, recording how Edward Ferrers in 1830 united by his marriage " the Chartley, Tamworth and Baddesley lines of the family." The most famous of the older Ferrers was Henry, the antiquary, who died on October 10, 1633, in the eighty-fourth year of his age, having been lord of the manor for seventy years. " May they rest in peace " : so Marmion Ferrers, of whom all who knew him speak with affectionate respect, concludes his record. He was a staunch supporter of the Papal supremacy, and the Ferrers family had long, perhaps without break, been so likewise. But as lay rectors of the parish they took a continuous interest in the preservation of the chancel of the parish church, whether or not they received its ministrations. Thus the quaint oak screen (unhappily removed at the restoration in 1872 to the west end under the arch of the tower) was set up between nave and chancel in 1634 by Edward Ferrers (the lord of the manor when Dugdale wrote). The inscription runs : " Memor esto brevis aevi : hic querite regna Dei : procul hine, procul este prophani. 1634." As to the Ferrers' monument in the chancel, one word more. Dugdale drew it for the engraver " with great curiosity." Yet it does not appear in his work, as is thus explained : " But so frugall a Person is the present Heir of the Family, he now residing here, as that, he refusing to contribute any Thing towards the Charge Thereof, and it being not proper for one to undergo it totally, they are omitted."

The most beautiful thing in the church is the east window, a collection, for the most part, of sixteenth century glass : the Crucifix in the midst, before which Sir Edward Ferrers and his wife Constance, with her father, Nicholas Brome, kneel in adoration, the label proceeding from Sir Edward's lips : " Amor meus crucifixus est." Above the couple kneel again, with their children, now before S. George, the legend, " Sancte Georgi, ora pro nobis." Shields of the ancient families surround them and fill the rest of the window. That of Sir Edward and his wife has thirty-two quarterings.

And now we may go, along the charming woodland path at the copse's edge, to the house itself. There is a wide moat round it, with flowers and fish and swans therein, spanned by a strong bridge. This we cross, and we enter under a stout tower, the upper part of which is adorned with battlements, which are at least not earlier than the eighteenth century ; they, and the admirably designed front of the opposite side of the court—added a few years ago for enlargement, the work of local builders under the guidance of the lady of the manor herself, and already having the tone of age befitting its position—are, one may say at once, the only modern parts of this beautiful house. The bridge, one is told, replaced in Queen Anne's reign the medieval drawbridge. Above the archway of this tower is what is now called the Banqueting Hall, hung with fine tapestry, and oak panelled— a splendid room, marred hardly at all by the low ceiling which covers what was no doubt the open timbered roof. This room was undoubtedly of old the chapel, as in other houses of similar design. It was changed, one supposes, when the penal laws made the open profession of Roman Catholicism impossible. As you go under the tower archway you see the loopholes for defence, the stone for steadying the drawbridge, the ancient oak door with its wicket. Through the door to the left, in the midst of the house, looking across a lovely court with old beds of flowers, on to the moat, you enter the house. Soon you are in the hall—a fine room of dark oak with a carved fireplace of 1634 :—Edward Ferrers preferred rather to spend his money on adorning his house than to give it to Dugdale for the figuring of his ancestors' tomb. The windows have the most delicious shields commemorating the family alliances, from which the succession of the Ferrers may be traced from the Norman Conquest down to this day. The Ferrers arms, of Baddesley Clinton, are—it must be noted, for they are so often seen here—Gules, seven mascles conjoined, or, 3, 3, 1, a canton ermine. Among their marriages are those

Y 2

with Jane White, grand-daughter of Sir Thomas White of South Warnborough, Hants, the brother of John White, Bishop of Winchester, who preached the funeral sermon for Queen Mary, in which he made so unfortunate an allusion to Queen Elizabeth —a family not to be confused (their arms prevent it) with that of Sir Thomas White, Lord Mayor of London and founder of S. John's College in Oxford, who preserved the city for Mary from Northumberland's attempt to win it for " Jane the Queen " ; and with Katherine Hampden, of the family of the rebel, who married Henry, the antiquary. In the hall, among other delights, is the famous waxen medal copied with legends from a well-known medal of Charles Edward and Henry Benedict, but by some curious family tradition said to be quite a different thing. It is believed at Baddesley that this is a bit of Jacobite work, of which one side showed the true King James (James III.) with the motto " Micat inter omnes," and the other, with the words " Alter ab illo," the false King George, as the Ferrers would say two hundred years ago. The hall has also a portrait of James III. as a boy, in semi-classical dress with a white shaved poodle ; and a fine oak table, twenty-one feet long by two feet eight inches wide ; and—yes, surely it is, we have all read of them in Elizabeth's days—a unicorn's horn. This last is said to have been given in 1400 by a French ambassador to the Ferrers of Henry IV.'s days. At the left of the hall is the quiet drawing-room, filled with beautiful furniture and ancient pictures ; at the right is the dining-room, also most charming, and with the same heraldic glass. So you go above, round the gallery, now enclosed, through room after room, decorated for the most part with rich oak carving, up stairs and down stairs, by the chapel now used, with the little sacristy and confessional behind it, down a stairway again into the room below the tower, or up again through rooms which have strange tales and strange memories attaching to them ; room after room, beautiful, homely, rich in interest. Nor will you forget the secret staircase, and the priests' holes, the memorials of the penal days. The great characteristic of the house is its panelling ; some of this is ancient, some still retains the paint of the eighteenth century, but most has been cleaned, and has the rich dark tone of age ; and most, in the words of the late Father Norris, who wrote a valuable book on Baddesley Clinton in 1897, " of the panelling and most of the handsome carved oak mantels to be found in the majority of the rooms was set up in " Henry Ferrers's " days, since in one of the upper rooms in the north wing, now the library, a mantel-piece, similar in style and design to the rest, bears in a panel the date 1634." So back again to the courtyard, which gives you the most perfect example of late medieval domestic architecture ; or round the moat, where every view of the house is exquisite ; or below to the pools covered with water-lilies, where the great trout, and many lesser ones, lie hid. And then, alack ! back to the modern world.

CHAPTER XVI

ON THE OUTSKIRTS OF ARDEN: BEARLEY AND SNITTERFIELD, EDSTONE AND WOOTTON WAWEN

THE country between Stratford and Henley must have been well known to Shakespeare. Names of his kindred occur constantly in it, and allusions to it in his plays may readily be traced. It is the beginning of the well-wooded country which deserved, whether strictly or not, its name of the Forest of Arden:—

> " Muse, first of Arden tell whose footsteps yet are found
> In her rough woodlands more than any other ground,"

says Drayton. It is of the southern part of this, or the road which goes from Henley to Warwick, that we may now speak; Bearley and Snitterfield, Edstone and Wootton Wawen, all of them places of interest, lying on the edge of the forest land, lying east of the Alne. To visit these villages one may make Henley the starting-point, or Warwick. In either case we shall have to go down dale and up hill. To Drayton, certainly it was the heart of England, for thus he begins to tell of the shire in which it nestles:—

> " Upon the Mid-lands now the industrious Muse doth fall,
> That shire which wee the hart of England well may call.
> As she herselfe extends (the midst which is decreed)
> Betwixt S. Michaels Mount, and Berwick-bord'ring Tweed,
> Brave Warwick ; that abroad as long advanc't her Beare,
> By her illustrious Earles renowned every where ;
> Above her neighbouring shire which alwaies bore her head.
> My native Country then which so brave spirits hast bred,
> If there be vertue yet remaining in thy earth,
> Or any good of thine thou breathd'st into my birth,
> Accept it as thine owne whilst now I sing of thee ;
> Of all thy later Brood th' unworthiest though I bee.

326

> Muse, first of Arden tell, whose foot-steps yet are found
> In her rough wood-lands more then any other ground
> That mighty Arden held even in her height of pride ;
> Her one hand touching Trent, the other, Severns side.''

I do not know that it is possible to make any strict limits for the " forest of Arden," any more than it is for the " Cotswolds." I should recommend everyone who can to procure, or at the least to read, in the first edition (for the second rather confuses than improves the matter), " The Forest of Arden : Its Towns, Villages and Hamlets," by John Hannett, published in 1863. It would be well worth while to urge a local antiquary to re-edit it. But, failing that, you should take its enthusiastic gossip as it is, for it preserves a great deal that had else been quite forgotten and that is well worthy even now of remembrance. Mr. Hannett rightly doubts if Arden ever were strictly a forest ; and he will draw no exact boundaries. At first he says Arden very likely meant the whole of Warwickshire ; then in the course of time it became restricted to " the locality including the towns of Henley and Hampton, together with the neighbourhood of those places." And his map extends northwards to Acock's Green and Diddington, westwards to the Roman Road, eastwards to Temple Balsall and Wroxhall and south to Aston Cantlow and Bearley Bushes. And so to Drayton Arden is the centre of Warwick, and thus he fits it into his scheme :—

> " This song our shire of Warwick sounds ;
> Reviues old Ardens ancient bounds.
> Through many shapes the Muse heere roves ;
> Now sporting in those shady groves,
> The tunes of Birds oft staies to heare;
> Then, finding Herds of lustie Deare,
> She Huntresse-like the Hart pursues ;
> And like a Hermit walks to chuse
> The Simples everywhere that growe ;
> Comes Ancors glory next to showe ;
> Tells Guy of Warwicks famous deeds ;
> To th' Vale of Red-horse then proceeds,
> To play her part the rest among ;
> There shutteth up her thirteenth song."

It is not our thirteenth song yet, and the Red Horse is far away from our journey to-day. It is the heart of the forest we aim at, where one fancies one's self with Rosalind and Celia and Touch-stone, not far from the banished duke, among those shepherds who made the Warwickshire poets think of nothing else but shepherdesses for two centuries or more, and seeing many an Audrey and thick-headed William, and not altogether out of hearing of Sir Oliver Martext. Let us plunge into it at Bearley. Bearley is on the hill, its quaint little old church looking down on you. So with woods to the right, then a common, then woods both sides of you, you take your way towards Snitterfield. Snitterfield begins in a valley, where they are building many new red-brick houses. Then a rising hill, and again above the church fields rising still, from which you get a view over a great valley, the Welcombe monument to your right, and the Malvern Hills in the distance. Let us linger in these villages.

If we have started from Warwick by the upper or western road we shall turn aside, to the right, at Sherborne, and follow the long wall beside the park (if we have not turned earlier at Longbridge—famed in the history of the Ferrers family), and so by an exceeding pretty way, mounting Sherborne hill, we shall come (at 348 feet above sea level) to nigh Snitterfield, and be ready to miss it if we do not turn, at a first or second chance, sharply to the right. It is from this point that we can see the Welcombe monument and the Malvern hills. Now turn into Snitterfield, and come to the church. It is Decorated, as regards chancel, nave, and aisles ; Perpendicular as regards clerestory, nave, roof, and tower. But the great glory of the church is the ancient woodwork. The description in the " Churches of Warwickshire " is the best I know. They are two standards " with large carved finials ; one of these standards is entirely covered with panel work ; the other, besides panel work, contains within a kind of quatrefoil compartment, a shield quartering the arms of France and England, the supporters to which are a Greyhound and Dragon ; these are surmounted by the bowed crown introduced in the reign of Henry the Seventh. At the end of this standard is the carved figure of a Bishop, represented in his alb, dalmatic, and cope, with the mitre on his head, the *infulæ* or pendant laminæ of which hang down behind. This is placed on a kind of nondescript baluster of renaissance or semiclassic design. Near to this, under a canopy, is the nude full length figure of a boy with wings. In the buttresses which divide the panels are, or have been, small figures of angels clad in albs, with caps on their heads of a fashion prevalent in the reign of Henry the Seventh. One of these bears a shield, another a scroll, and on one is the

nude figure of a boy with wings.   The heads of the compartments,
five in number, are filled with panel work.   On the opposite
standard is a figure in long hair and loose drapery, not unlike a
representation of St. John, carrying apparently three loaves.

Snitterfield Church.

In a spandrill are represented two mermaids supporting a hand
holding an entwined knot.   This woodwork is very curious and
interesting, being of the early period in this country of the introduction of the renaissance school, and intermixture of Gothic
with semiclassic design, of which particular period few specimens

of carved woodwork exist in our churches. The figure of a Bishop was probably intended to represent Thomas de Cantilupe, Bishop of Hereford, from A.D. 1275, to A.D. 1282."

I am by no means sure of the last point. Why should it not be a contemporary bishop ? The work is clearly late fifteenth century. There is other good woodwork in the church, two centuries younger, in altar rails and pulpit.

The village has two memories of Warwickshire poets, the great and the small. Shakespeare's grandfather held property there, and his father after him, selling it when he was in low water. Richard Jago was vicar for twenty years, and there is a slab to his memory at the west end of the church, on which the date of his death (May 8, 1781) has never been inserted. As you leave the church you will linger by the great double yew, and the three limes, one huge indeed for such a tree. In the vicarage garden hard by you will see the three silver birches which Jago's three daughters planted. Not far from the church was Shakespeare's uncle's house, and near it are Burman's field and Red hill, both mentioned as his in 1596. Through Snitterfield, resting at Norbrook, some of the Gunpowder Plotters rushed in their vain attempt to escape. It was John Grant who lived at Norbrook, and he sheltered the traitors on December 6, 1605, as they fled westwards ; and Digby sent Bates, Catesby's servant, to Coughton with the news of the failure of the plot to Father Greenway. Turn aside there for a moment, thus as you go by the upper road to Stratford from Warwick, after you have taken the right of the two roads and come up on the road to Snitterfield, there is a road, where you have descended a little, to your right again, going due northwards ; follow this, and to your right, at about half a mile, in the valley is Norbrook. There is now a modern farmhouse, but in 1604 there was an ancient moated grange, where lived John Grant, a Warwickshire Papist gentleman of some wealth, but of a settled melancholy. He had joined in Essex's brief tumult and suffered for it, and he had married the sister of Thomas Wright. Catesby had sold his property at Lapworth and Bushwood to the Grevilles, and Grant was ready to allow his house at Norbrook to be used as a store for arms and powder in view of the contemplated insurrection. The Wrights moved to Lapworth, near which was Bushwood, once the property of Catesby. Sir Everard Digby was at Coughton, and Rokewood, another conspirator, at Clopton

house. Norbrook was convenient for them all. The whole
district, one feels, is full of history. But also you are not likely
to forget that it is one of sport. After you have come down the
hill from the village, passed the cross road which runs through
it, and mounted another hill on your way to Bearley, you will
pass through a deer wood which has fame for centuries, called
Snitterfield bushes. The delightful Mr. John Hannett in his work
of love, " The Forest of Arden," aptly quotes Somervile's lines
in " The Chase " :—

> " Hark ! what loud shouts
> Re-echo through the groves ! he breaks away—
> Shrill horns proclaim his flight ! each struggling hound
> Strains o'er the lawn to reach the distant pack."

So he might well have done when he was outside Snitterfield
bushes, running southwards by the road perhaps towards Bearley,
but not inside the wood.

Bearley I have already said something about, and there is not
much else to say, unless we remember that Charles II. passed
by the cross, with Mistress Lane on the pillion, when he was
flying from Worcester, and passed but a short way from a troop
of horse that was probably on the look-out for him. Bearley
Cross is just by the Hatton and Stratford branch of the Great
Western Railway. We pass under the bridge and come almost
at once to Edstone Park. You may turn aside to the left for
half a mile to see the very pretty half-timbered Sillesbourne
farm, but back again to the Henley road, and let us look at the
park, the distant house with the lake, and the quite delightful
eighteenth century lodge which leads to them both, at Edstone.
Mr. Hannett grew enthusiastic about the house, which no doubt
has " everything handsome about " it, but nothing so specially
beautiful ; and most of all because " the cellars are remarkable
for their loftiness and as running throughout the whole extent
of the building." But the interest of Edstone, its best friends
will admit, goes far back, and the cellars of Somervile would have
been more interesting than those " built by H. Mills, Esq., and
finished by the late John Phillips, Esq." In the old house,
pulled down by Mr. Mills, Somervile lived, as I suppose,
but he was born at Rugeley in 1682. He became all
sorts of useful things, such as a Fellow of New College and
a Justice of the Peace. He also ran through his money, it
seems, in the service of sport ; and he was not only, not an abste-

mious person, but delighted in a most unpleasing and dangerous
drink of rum and blackcurrant jelly with a little water. He was a
writer of verse rather than a poet. His early volume of poems
has some good but several very unpleasant things in it. His
" Hobbinol " is a rough piece of rusticity, worth reading for the
picture of Midland manners in the eighteenth century. He wrote
a burlesque poem called " The Wicker Chair," which nobody
(except the writer of these pages, who is therefore highly con-
ceited) seems to know anything about. It was probably written
at Evesham (for Somervile is a link between the two shires,
and his friend and cousin, Lord Somervile, lived, I think, even
before the poet left the property to him, at Aston Somerville) in
the winter of 1708, and he describes its origin in the house of a
" dry, drolling, subtle old fellow," a farmer with whom he stayed
when he went every winter to hunt in Gloucestershire. It is a
" study " for " Hobbinol." But his great work is " The Chase,"
1735, which my sporting friends tell me is the best poem
ever written about sport. Somervile was not a poet who tried
to write about sport, but a sportsman who set down his advice
and opinion in verse. The " squire well born and six foot high "
was a sportsman to the last. He lived till 1742, and it is recorded
that in the last year of his life, when two hundred like-minded
folk entertained him (and themselves) at dinner, he bet £50 that
he " would kill his hares, and pick them up too, before any of the
young bloods present would accomplish it (provided they would
let him hunt the hounds) " ; and he won his bet. But he was
not a sportsman only. He was a friend of Shenstone, who
certainly did not enjoy hunting, and of Lady Luxborough, whom
one cannot imagine to have felt the smallest interest in any so
rough and rapid an amusement. Both most genuinely lamented
his death, though they commemorated him, after their fashion,
by urns in their gardens.

It is but a couple of miles from Edstone to Wootton Wawen.
There as you came from Snitterfield, just at Edstone lodge, you
join the main road from Stratford to Birmingham. You pass
another wood, Anstey Wood, on your right, and then descend a
hill, going under the canal, into the village of Wootton Wawen.
At your right, on a bank, are some good red houses of the true
Warwickshire character ; and then you come to the park, and
cross the river Alne. I do not know any more charming view of
a fine house than that you come upon as you get to the bottom of

the little hill. The river is crossed, in the park, by a fine classical bridge, where two cascades meet, and then the house, part of which at least was built in the seventeenth century by Lord Carrington (of Charles I.'s, not Pitt's, creation). The house is the most attractive place I know near here : not too large or too small, not too dignified, but quite dignified enough ; and it deserves all the praise we can give it, because it is in such a position that the poorest passer-by can see it and have his ideas of build-ing enlarged. Near it, Mr. Hannett said in 1865, is a Roman Catholic chapel, very costly and complete ; but that I have not

Wootton Wawen Church.

seen ; indeed I believe it is now a music room. It was built in 1813, so it cannot compare with the ancient church of the parish, in the patronage of King's College, Cambridge. That is a very famous church, well known to many visitors in many shires, yet not always easy of access. It stands high up, surrounded by grass fields, above the village. The ground plan is unusual : a nave and south aisle, and east of the nave a square tower ; beyond that the narrow chancel arch—and at the south of the chancel, as wide as the chancel and extending as far eastwards as the chancel, and westwards to the south aisle, a chantry chapel. It is said that the lower parts—the two lower stages—of the tower are

Saxon ; they are certainly Early Norman ; the upper part with
the battlements is, as usual, of the fifteenth century.   The east
window of the chancel (externally Decorated) has a curious
decoration—a series of crockets in a hollow moulding.   Within,
the nave has clerestory windows which are above the height of the
original building.   The heads at the west window may be Edward
II. and Queen Philippa.   The nave is separated from the north
aisle by stone Decorated arches ; and the north wall of the church
has one Decorated and one Norman window.   The whole church
is a puzzle of many pieces : some Saxon perhaps, certainly some
Norman, some Decorated, and wood-work of the Perpendicular
time.   The altar is at the end under the tower, and behind it you

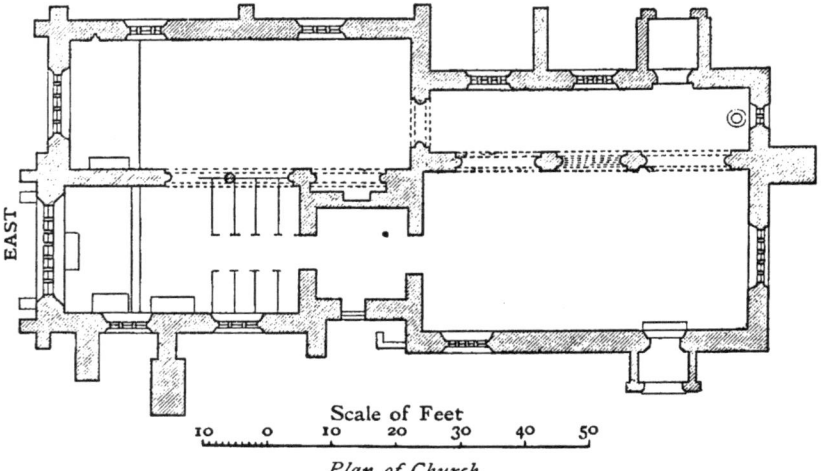

EAST

Scale of Feet

10   o   10   20   30   40   50

Plan of Church.

come to the chancel, like a separate chapel, which contains the
fifteenth century pews, the good Laudian altar rails, and two fine
sixteenth century brasses.   At the north wall is the fifteenth
century tomb, with the recumbent alabaster effigy, in armour,
of (probably) John Harewell, 1428, his feet resting on a dog ;
and within the altar rails the very beautiful tomb of John
Harewell and his wife, he in armour, she in a most elaborate
costume.   The inscription is :—

" Ḣic iacet Joḣes Ḣarewell armig' et ḋna Anna qonḋam
uror eius ac nup' uror Edwarḋi Grep militis qui quiḋem
Joḣes obiit X° ḋie aprilis anno ḋni MVᶜᵛ et que quiḋem
Anna obiit ḋie a° ḋni MVᶜ quorum aiabȝ ppitietur ḋeus."

In Dugdale this tomb is shown with ornamental panelling and shields. On the south is an inscription written by Dr. Parr, a good specimen of his style :—

"Danieli Gaches A.M. Collegii Regalis in Academia Canta-brigiensi quondam Socio, Ecclesiæ hujusce per ann. 38 mens. 9 Ministro, Irenarchæ de Comitatu Varvicensi optime merito ; Siquidem æqui et boni peritissimus fuit, et ad nodos legum solvendos quam maxime expeditus ; Viro non solum litteris Græcis atque Latinis apprime docto, sed etiam vi quadam ingenii, quæ ad excogitandum acuta et ad memoriam firma atque diuturna erat, egregie predito. Qui vixit ann. 72 mens. 6. Decessit 4 Id. Sept. Anno Sacro 1805. Maria Gaches conjux ejus superstes H.M.P.S.P.C."

Now enter the south chapel on the north side is the good seventeenth century tomb of Francis Smith, 1626. But the memorials which give its character to the chapel are those of the Knights and the Somerviles. The north and south sides belonging to the owners of Wootton Hall, and Edstone, within this parish. By an award made by the Bishop of Worcester, 11 April, 1609, it appeared that the late Sir W. Somervile " had a particular right to the south side of a certain Isle or Oratory in the parish Church of Wootton Wawen and Sir Francis Smith deceased had also a particular right to the north side." And on February 16, 1738, these rights were confirmed, and the privilege of " burying their dead bodies therein for ever " was secured to the owners of these two estates, a privilege which did not last very long. Besides the memorials of various kindred to the families, you will notice on the floor the slab on which are the words Somervile wrote for himself, and for his wife :—

" H.S.E. Gulielmus Somervile Armig. Obiit 17° Julü, 1742. Si quid in me boni compertum habeas imitare. Si quid mali totis viribus evita. Christo confide. Et scias te quoque fragilem esse et mortalem.

" H.S.E. Maria Guilielmi Somervile Armi^g: uxor dilectissima, Hugonis Bethel de Ryse in Com Ebor : Arm : Filia. Pie Vixit. Intrepide Obiit, Nonis Septembris, A.D. 1731."

The arms are : Somervile impaling quarterly, 1st and 4th a chevron between 3 boars' heads, 2nd and 3rd a lion rampant.

On the south you enter the chapel, of late date, with a huge, ugly east window, which architects describe as " five lofty ogee-headed principal lights trefoiled within, with some small portion of tracery within." The whole chapel (was it ever a lady chapel ?) is bare and uninteresting and ill cared for; but the interest of its memorials is very great.

In the south-west corner was the grave of Somervile's huntsman, with this inscription, also the poet's (is it there still?):—

"H.S.E. Jacobus Boeter, Gulielmo Somervile Armigero Promus et canibus venaticis Præpositus ; domi forisq fidelis : Equo inter venandum corruente, et intestinis graviter collisis, post triduum deplorandus obiit, 28° die Jan. Anno Dni. 1719."

The memorials to the Knights commemorate the mother of Lord Luxborough, his two children, his sister-in-law, his grandfather, and his cousin. The inscriptions were all written by Lord Luxborough, so I will quote them. At the east end, in front of the east window and on the site of the ancient chantry altar, is a plain plinth of dove-coloured marble, with an urn. On it is the following inscription :—

"M.S. Marthæ filiæ et cohæredis Jeremie Powell de Edenhope e Salopiæ comitatu Armigeri, itemq mariti ejus Roberti Knight Armigeri ab antiqua de Barrels in Varvicensi Comitatu familia oriundi : Illa filiarum conjugum et matrum optima Obiit 6 Kalendas Augusti MDCCXVIII, Ætatis XXXVII. Hic facilis benevolus animoque in omnes propinquitate sibi conjunctos paterno memorabilis decessit 6 Id Novembris MDCCXLIV, Ætatis Suæ LXIX. Parentibus optime de se meritis Honoratiss. Robertus Baro Luxborough De Shannon apud Hibernos hoc Monumentum Pietatis causa S.S.P.C."

On the south wall is a large mural pedimental-headed monument of veined marble, with fluted Corinthian columns at the sides ; a centre, with a wing of similar design on each side, with the following inscription :—

"To the memory of the Honourable Henry Knight, who was born the 25 of December, 1728 ; married in June 1750 Frances the daughter of Thomas Heath, of Stansted Mount Fitchet, in the County of Essex, Esquire, and died without issue the 15th of August, 1762. Also to the memory of the honourable Henrietta Knight, who was born the 21st of November, 1729, and married in April, 1754, to the honourable Josiah Child, second son to Richard Earl Tylney, by whom she had issue one son. This lady was likewise married in May, 1762, to Lewis Alexander

Count Durore in the kingdom of France, by whom she had issue one son. She died at Marseilles in France the 1 of March, 1763. These Henry and Henrietta were the only children of Robert Earl of Catherlough, Viscount Barrels and Baron Luxborough of Shannon in the kingdom of Ireland by his wife the honourable Henrietta St. John and sister of Henry Viscount Bolingbroke, Principal Secretary of State to Queen Anne, in the year 1710. Jussu Roberti Comitis de Catherlough. 1764."

Near it a marble monument with arms nearly effaced :—

" To the memory of Jeremiah Powell of Edenhope, in the County of Salop, Esquire, and of his wife Martha, eldest daughter and coheir to Robert Barrington of Stalsfield, in the County of Kent, Esquire, by whom he had five daughters. The eldest, Martha, was married to Robert Knight, of Luxborough in the County of Essex, Esquire, father to Robert Earl of Catherlough. The second, Catherine, was married to Benjamin Collyer of Ruckholt, Esq., member of Parliament in the reign of George the 1st for Grimsby, in Lincolnshire. The third, Margaret, was married to Michael Impey, of Richmond in the county of Surrey, Esq. The fourth, Elizabeth, was married to John Weaver, of Morvill, Esq. member of Parliament in the reign of George the 1st, for Bridgnorth in Shropshire, and the fifth, Mary, was married to Rowland Aynsworth, Esquire, third son to Sir Rowland Aynsworth, Knight. H.P.C. Robertus Comes de Catherlough, 1765."

Another marble monument, with arms, ar. on a chief gu. 2 mullets or. impaling az. a chevron between 3 swans arg. :—

" To the memory of Hester Viscountess St. John and eldest daughter to James Clarke, of Wharton, in the County of Hereford, Esquire. This lady was born on the 9th of Feb. 1725, was married the 19th of June, 1748, died the 8th of March, 1752. This monument was erected by the order of her ladyship's brother-in-law and executor, Robert Earl of Catherlough, 1765."

Another marble monument, with arms, gu. a chevron between 3 mallets or. :—

" To the memory of Jane Sarah Soame, daughter to Sir Peter Soame of Heydon in the County of Essex, Baronet, and niece to Henry Viscount St. John. This lady was born the 12th of February 1703, and died unmarried the 7th of November 1744. This monumental inscription was directed by the Lady's executor and relation Robert Earl of Catherlough, 1765."

There is also on the floor, with the arms of Knight impaling Rawlins, the memorial of John Knight of Barrels and Joan, his wife—his death in 1681, hers 1664—erected by his son William (grandfather, I suppose, of Lord Luxborough). In the chapel should also be noticed the old parish chest with its three locks, and the desk with eight chained books of spiritual reading ranging from 1570 to 1646. The whole church is of singular interest, in some ways the greatest in the county.

As you come out of the quiet porch, when you go and look for the grave of the huntsman whose epitaph Somervile wrote, you may search also, at the north-east of the chancel, for another, who survived Boeter nearly a hundred years. He was commemorated by Mr. Gaches, vicar from 1766 to 1806, in these lines :—

> " Here Hoitt, all his sports and labours past.
> Joins his loved master Somervile at last ;
> Together went they echoing fields to try,
> Together now in silent dust they lie.
> Servant and lord, when once we yield our breath,
> Huntsman and poet, are alike in death.
> Life's motley drama calls for powers, and men,
> Of different casts, to fill its changeful scene ;
> But all the merit that we justly prize,
> Not in the part, but in the acting lies.
> And as the lyre, so may the huntsman's horn
> Fame's trumpet rival, and his name adorn."

The churchyard also contains at its north end six plain slabs under which rest six vicars.

The history of Wootton Wawen has points of interest— Dugdale traces the addition Wawen to one who had the land before the Conquest. " But he, as great as he was, was the more liable to the *Normans* Depredations, when they became Masters of all, as were all the wealthy *Saxons* ; and so this *Waga* (for so his Name is written in Domesday-Book) or *Wagen*, was outed of all his fair Lordships in this and other Counties ; and they were bestow'd by the Conqueror on *Robert de Stadford*, who, with several other noble *Normans*, attended Duke *William* into *England*, and by their valour, seated him on the Throne ; for which he rewarded him with Possessions of a vast Extent." In his family the lands remained till the attainder of Buckingham in Henry VIII.'s day. In Elizabeth's time the Smythes bought it—of whom somewhat has been said. The priory here was a cell of Conches, and after the Dissolution of the alien houses came to King's College, Cambridge, who are patrons of the benefice. And so on to Henley.

Descend the hillock again and rejoin the road, turning to the right, and as you go out of the village you will see a beautiful house, small and cosy, with a scallop filled with flowers almost worthy of a Della Robbia over the door. And so with Wootton Park to the right, and Anstey Wood, beloved of the fox and those who hunt him, and Mays Wood, on the left, till we come among the trees, and down a little hill, across the stream into Henley-in-Arden.

CHAPTER XVII

A BYWAY TO HATTON

THERE is a pleasant way from Bearley, or, rather, from the road which leads from Stratford to Henley, if you turn to the right in front of Bearley Cross Inn, just as you approach Edstone park, the home of the Somerviles. Turn to the right, that is, north-eastwards, and you skirt the park, an uneven ground, the very place for " The Chase," the kind of chase, that is, which the poet described, when there were no very great runs nor very swift ones. You catch a glimpse of the house to your left as you go by. The road is sandy and up-hill. You may turn aside, perhaps, to Langley, where there is not much to see ; but, more likely, you will go on, passing under the railway, up a hill, and then turning sharp to the right, to Wolverton. This is a pretty village on a hill, and the church is on a smaller hill west of the village street. A path leads up from the very pretty parsonage and garden to the east end of the church. This is partly Early English—the high altar consecrated in 1316 —with some Perpendicular additions, including the much restored chancel screen. At the north of the chancel is an arch, now leading to a modern vestry, but perhaps once covering an earlier sepulchre ; at the south the remains of the three-staged sedilia. The Elizabethan table stands now in the choir ; it looks as though folk might lay their hats on it, as when Laud was moved to wrath. There are tablets in the chancel to the families of Stanton and Roberts. But the main interest of the church lies in the ancient glass. In the east window is the angel of the Resurrection : in the south-east of the chancel is some early Morris glass. In the nave is some fifteenth century glass, very like that at Malvern, one window showing in its fragments the donor and his wife, the former having the name, Johannes de Wolford [ton] ; an angel and a saint, who is almost certainly not S. Peter (as the guide-books think). The same good books tell of a custom here that on the Sunday after a funeral when the kinsfolk attend the service the women remain sitting while the hymn is sung. Outside, in the churchyard, is an iron tomb-stone, 1795, with a *requiescat in pace* on it.

Now from Wolverton one may go easily to Norton Lindsey, turning to the right again from the main Warwick road to which you have returned from Wolverton. It is well worth a visit. The church, on an eminence to the east of the village street, has a lovely view southwards over meadows and hills, reminding one of the view from the old church of Ullenhall. The building is mainly Early English, with four of the original windows left in the chancel. There is some Decorated work, and there is a curious little font, the bowl much smaller than the shaft on which it stands. As one goes through these byways of Warwickshire, how few churches there are that have *not* some special interest in them, ancient or modern ; and the great houses, too, even if they are not very old, preserve the memories, and the portraits, of old families.

Here is one, a mile or so north of Norton Lindsey, from which we may go by an easy road to Hatton, also of an almost modern fame. Besides this way, there are other approaches. If you go out of Warwick by Hampton-on-the-Hill, or if you turn aside from Hatton by a side way you come, perhaps by a difficult and private way, to Grove Park. This is a modern house, finished in 1832, but it has the attraction of a splendid view over the surrounding country. From the drawing-room and dining-room you see the tower of S. Mary's, Warwick. The park is large and beautifully wooded. The treasures of the house are its pictures, of which the most famous is that of Jane Dormer Duchess of Feria, wife of the Spanish ambassador at the court of Elizabeth, as a widow, in what looks to the uninstructed eye like a monastic dress. There is another portrait of her earlier in life. There is a good portrait of Ann Sophia Countess of Carnarvon, by Mrs. Beale, one of the rather neglected school of English painters of the time of Charles I., in the hall, and scattered about the house and on the stairs which ascend round an open space to the top of the house are many eighteenth century portraits of persons connected with the Dormer family.

Now go northwards, crossing the Great Western line, and here is a place of modern fame. Less than three miles from Warwick, on the Birmingham road, is Hatton church. Of the old one alas! only the tower—a fine fifteenth century, plain, with battlement—remains. The new church is large, plain, and without interest, and was finished in 1880. It may be worth recording what it replaced, for fear that we should seem to think all modern building worse than what it supersedes.

"The nave, which was rebuilt and widened on each side to the extent of four feet six inches, under the supervision of the late learned Dr. Parr, presents anything but an Ecclesiastical appearance, and in architectural design is most miserable and poverty-stricken. The walls, probably of brick, are, externally, covered with stucco ; and the south wall is pierced with five round-headed Palladian windows, disposed three below and two above. The north wall of the nave has a similar arrangement. These windows, for many years, had dwelling-house shutters, opening outwardly, to protect the painted glass with which they are filled.

The south wall is covered with stucco and the buttresses are of brick. This wall is pierced with a single Palladian round-headed window. Two windows of similar design appear in the north wall of the chancel. The east window contains three modern lancet lights with cement mullions, and the gable above is surmounted by a large stone cross. The chancel is part of the ancient structure, but the windows are of modern insertion. Annexed to the chancel on the north side is a wretched brick vestry."

So we are better off than in 1847. But still we may look sadly back to the days before Dr. Parr. In past times the chief bene-factors were Mrs. Jane Norcliffe (1745) and her husband, whose monuments are in the church. There is also the monument of Dr. Bree, who married a Dormer, and died in 1749. "His great knowledge in the several branches of Physick was equal to his generous and friendly manner of applying the benefits of that to the necessities of mankind, for which reason his death was greatly lamented and may be esteemed a Publick Loss." But these were the days before Agamemnon. Dr. Parr is the great name at Hatton. One rubs one's eyes to think it is less than a hundred years ago since he died. Here is his epitaph, and those he wrote for his family :—

" On the north side of this chancel lieth the body
Of Mrs. Jane Parr
Who died at Tinemouth, Devon, April 9, in the year 1810
Aged 63.

And next are deposited the remains of her husband
The Rev. Samuel Parr, L.L.D.
Who for 39 years was resident and officiating minister of this
Parish
And who died on the 6th of March, in the year 1825
Aged 78.

Christian reader
What doth the Lord require of you but to do justice
to love mercy, & to be in charity with your neighbours
reverence your holy Redeemer & to walk humbly
with your God.

Marble tablet.   Catherine Jane Parr, youngest daughter of S. and
J. Parr, died Nov. 22, 1805

Quæ templo Catharina in hoc sepulta est,
' Prudens, casta, decens, severa, dulcis,
' Discordantia quæ solent putari
' Morum Commoditate copulavit.
' Nam Vitæ comites bonæ fuerunt
' Libertas gravis et Pudor facetus'
His est junctus Amor pius suorum,
Et Cura ex Animo Deum colendi.

Mrs. Sarah Anne Wynne, daughter of S. and J. Parr,
died July 8, 1810.

Madalina Wynne, who died May 26, 1810,
2 years 8 months 9 days."

One turns over the eight volumes of his works, with Dr. John
Johnstone's " Memoirs and Selections from his Correspondence,"
to discover what manner of man he was, this Radical Dr.
Johnson, this disappointed ecclesiastic, this petulant and
assertive pedant.   There emerges a kindly gentleman, a
good tutor, a hospitable neighbour, a politician of vehemence, a practical parish priest.   There can be no doubt
that Dr. Parr loved the society of great people.   There
can be no doubt he ate a great deal.   I remember an old

man who kept a curiosity shop thirty years ago in the High
Street of Warwick, who told me he had been Dr. Parr's page-
boy, and that when the doctor went out to dinner, two plates
of all his favourite dishes were always given to him when others
were content to begin with one. His oddities were the theme
for many a scribbler. Let us take an example. Who wrote
" Guy's Porridge Pot " (London, 1808) ? It is very much in
the style of the Reverend Richard Graves, but he was just then
passed out of this world. It is a satirical poem in twenty-four
books, of which, happily, only five saw the light ; and the unfortunate hero is Dr. Parr, who is pursued through hundreds of
verses of now obscure scurrility into a refuge at Guy's Cliff, where
Mr. Greatheed " resented " his behaviour and absented himself
from his sermon. No doubt the fuss is all about that most famous
source of quarrels, the election ; when even Warwick loses its
equanimity. But Warwick, says the satirist, does not satisfy
the critic of manners or literature (the blanks are filled up in my
copy by a neat-handed scribe " who knew ") :—

> " And thus with [Warwick] in the smoke
> Dwell civil, quiet, decent folk,
> But all the learned, wise, and bright
> Live further off, live out of sight."

And the chief of them lives at Hatton, where

> " News flies fast as fame can carry
> That Fox is chosen secretary !
> Post-office, shambles, bank, and fish-shop
> Resound prophetic of a bishop.
> Happy the man who first arrives
> To tell the doctor how he thrives,
> What people say, how sure they are
> That none stand half the chance of [Parr]
> So firm a friend, so fine a writer,
> His wig so suited to a mitre,
> And many pretty things beside,
> Feigned just as fast as he could ride."

So the doctor orders a good dinner and his oldest port, and
everybody " arrived in gigs, on foot, or horses " to congratulate
him, but all in vain, for nothing comes of it except his picture.
Parr was never a bishop, and " Della Cruscan Greatheed " received the sharpest of his criticism.

Everybody laughed at, and a good many with, the learned

doctor. His well-known portrait, of which a mezzotint hangs in the vestry, shows such a face and figure as one would expect. Under it is a letter to a neighbour in which he shows his joy in his new church, which was really a mangling of the ancient. It is worth printing here. Thus it runs. The writing, flowing but somewhat tremulous, is easy to read, though it was written when the infirmities of age had begun to be felt :—

" Mr. Samuel Cotton, Gent., Kenilworth.

" Dear & much esteemed Namesake.—If you wish to see my new Church, come over on Sunday morning. Bring your wife, or possibly a sister, or all of them, with you, and be sure to take your dinner at the parsonage. I wish you all well and am truly yours,   S. PARR.

" *Oct.* 15, 1823."

In spite of his sympathy with the French Revolution, which made him no longer regarded, as when first he came into Warwickshire, as belonging to " the High Church party," and his strenuous opposition to the influence of Warwick Castle, he had friends among Tories as well as Whigs, the Greatheeds of Guy's Cliff, the Knights of Barrels, the Ferrers of Baddesley, the Wises of Warwick and Leamington, Lord Dormer, Earl Ferrers and others among them. The very affectionate memoir of his friend and physician, introductory to the seven volumes of his classical annotations, his ceremonial sermons, his historical essays, his letters, and all the rest of the mass of printed matter which the world was never willing to buy, paints him best in two aspects ; the first as a man fond of excessive hospitality, the second as a very sensible and straightforward parish priest. In the first character the recurring glory of his life was his birthday dinner, held sometimes in friends' houses, latterly in his own. Dr. Johnstone writes of this with a curious glow of enjoyment. "The feast was sumptuous, the wines were rich and various, and the master was always in his glory." Sometimes he appeared at great risk to his life and spite of the protests of his physicians. So in 1821 " He did appear. He was dressed out in his best apparel—his fullest wig, his velvet coat, with the scarf bound in the frogs, his hands were muffled and enveloped in ferment, and one of the servants attended to feed him. In this apparel he conversed as usual with gaiety ; nor was it obvious, except to a few who knew him best, that the tone of his mind was more sober and more grave." The worthy doctor dilates upon the "game and provisions and delicacies" from Holkham, from Hartlebury (whence the venison came with a letter in elegant Latin), from the Royal Duke of Sussex and the Whig Duke of Bedford. There were pleasant times, no doubt, at Dr. Parr's table. He was a warm-hearted friend though he was too fond of boasting of his sincerity, and he had a harsh tongue, which he used far too freely on his intellectual inferiors. But he was much better as a parish priest than in the character which his admirers loved best to depict him. In 1786 he wrote from Hatton : " I have an excellent house, good neighbours, and a Poor, ignorant, dissolute, insolent, and ungrateful beyond all example. I like Warwickshire very much. I have made great regulations, viz., bells chime three times as long; Athanasian Creed ; Communion service at the altar ; Swearing Act ; children catechised every first Sunday in the month ; private baptisms discouraged ; public performed after second lesson ; recovered £100 a year left to the poor, with interest amounting to £115, all of which I am to put out and settle a trust in the spring ; examining all the charities." He certainly took the keenest interest in the social as well as the spiritual well-being of his people. " Parr," says his biographer, " was the father of his parish. His manner of instructing them was affectionate and familiar, and well adapted to the meanest capacity. He explained as he went along ; and if any particular occurrence in regard to morals or discipline had taken place during the week, he was sure to notice it." Something like the old discipline survived in his hands. He is said to have never let any guilt escape public notice: " from the desk or the pulpit, in the more atrocious cases he even mentioned the parties by name, and always designated them and the fault that had been committed, in such a way that the picture could not fail of being recognised." Perhaps this was one of the reasons why his church was so often filled with visitors to Leamington. No doubt he sometimes preached above the head of his congregation ; he often " flew off from the text " ; he had a lisp ; he was too emphatic. But these are minor matters. Hatton may honour him because " in his attendance on the poor he was unwearied and humane. The sick were fed from his table, and the necessitous relieved by his bounty." So best the friend of Fox and the tutor of Landor may be remembered to-day.

The rectory, of red brick, standing away from the road, is a

little farther than the church along the Birmingham road :
I think it is the one Parr lived in. From it he would set out in
that " coach and four with all the proper appointments and
state " which was the joy and pride of his last years.

At Hatton you are on the main road to Wroxhall, and you are
not far, by a very winding way indeed, from Rowington, of which
another chapter tells. So here we may pause and take breath
after a talk with Dr. Parr. Such an event generally left a
stranger gasping. Such, no doubt, was the fate of the young
clergyman who said to him, " Dr. Parr, let you and me write a
book," and received the reply, " Yes, sir ; and if we put in it all
that I know and all that you don't know, we'll make a big one."
It is unfortunate that Dr. Parr's assistance cannot now be
obtained by those who write books on Shakespeare's country.

CHAPTER XVIII

STUDLEY AND COUGHTON

LET us start from Alcester, on the straight road called the Haydon Way. It will lead us to Birmingham or to Redditch. Or let us take journey the reverse way, from Birmingham and visit two places of some special note, Studley and Coughton.

Studley is more than a village. Its history dates, I suppose, from the priory which was founded by Peter (*Petrus filius Willelmi*, or *Petrus Corbezon*, or *Petrus de Studley*, Dugdale finds him described as), or rather transferred from the House of Austin canons he had already founded at Wicton, Worcestershire. This was in the reign of Henry II. He richly endowed it, but it was never very prosperous, in spite of later endowments from the generous family of Cantilupe. It was not till the fourteenth century that the church was built. It was consecrated in 1309. The small remains of the priory that still exist are embedded in a XVIth century farmhouse, which has some good rooms, an eighteenth century porch, and some stones in the yard from the monastic buildings, but is most conspicuous for the fine brick chimney—a tall stack in three divisions which, though an evident piece of sixteenth century building, is worthy of the priory itself. The house stands back from the road in a field to the right as you go northwards. To the left is the old inn, wood and rough cast, which was no doubt part of the priory buildings, perhaps the guest-house. The priory, as I said, never became wealthy. Its income in 1536 was but £141 4s. 9½d., while its stocks and goods were covered by its debts. John Yardley, the last prior, became vicar of Morton Bagot. The church of S. Mary, standing some way to the east of the main street, has a good deal of interest. It has a fine

Norman doorway with spurred ornamentation, and an Early English doorway at the south. Within is a stone coffin removed from the priory. Without, a large mausoleum at the east end, for the Goodricke family, with only one occupant, and already falling into decay. There is also a good Fortescue tomb outside, and within, the monuments of Chambers and Dewes. The good ceiling is dated 1723, but has been restored. By the chancel arch is a fine stone Agnus Dei, recently removed for safety from the north porch. There are good iron-work brackets, and good late seventeenth century altar rails. In the aisle lurks a Chippendale table with marble top, once used as the altar.

For houses, Studley looks rather on utility than beauty. But there is one that is called the manor-house, of Queen Anne's day, in which the parapet stands up high and conceals the chimneys, and there are rows of plain, oblong windows, but a lovely doorway, with a beautiful iron-work gate, more elaborate at the top than that at Packwood, and as fine. The castle, which you see in the distance as you go towards Coughton, is an erection of the year 1854, and now a Horticultural College. It is by its grounds, Camden says, that " the river Arrow maketh haste to join himself in society with Avon " ; but that does not really happen till a good way southwards, and on its banks before the junction you will come to Spernall, of which Dr. Thomas Cox shall speak first :—

" The Church here was formerly a Chapel unto *Coughton*, which belonged to the Canons of *Studley* ; to whom therefore, *Henry* Bishop of *Worcester* order'd, that the Profits of the Burials of such of the Inhabitants as were not of a free Condition, should accrue, and shortly after happen'd a violent Pestilence, which swept away most of the Tenants which held by Bond Service ; so that the Lords were forced to supply their Places with others of another Quality. In the mean Time, the Nuns of *Cokehull* had obtain'd the Advowson of the Chapel ; and when it became presentable, there arose a Controversy between the Nuns, and Canons of *Studley*, touching the Right of Sepulture, 11 *Henry* III. which lasted some Years ; but at last, *Reginald Brian*, Bishop of *Worcester*, composed the Difference, by ordering, that the Canons of *Studley*, in the Right of the Church of *Coughton*, should have the Burials of such Inhabitants as dwelt on the Lands held in Villanage, and the Nuns of *Cokehull* the rest. In 19 *Edw.* 1. It was certify'd concerning this Church, that the Portion that the

Canons of *Studley* had out of it was 25*s.* a Year, and that of the Nuns of *Cokehull* 20*s.* a Year; but the Nuns having yet some Pretensions to part of the Tithes, *William Wittlesey,* Bishop of *Worcester,* was forced to take the Controversy between them and the Parson into his Hands ; but how he determin'd it, we find not. In the Church is · a Marble Monument for one' *William Parsons, Vir quondam magnæ honestatis,* as is said in the Inscription, who dy'd *December* 28, 1482, and *Joan* his Wife, and in the Windows of it are the Arms of the old Earls of *Warwick, viz.* The *Newburghs* and the *Throkmortons,* empaling those of Family of *Spine."*

There are also several Chambers monuments in the church, which has suffered a good deal from restorers, indeed, rebuilders ; the chancel, *par exemple,* having been re-erected " in the Norman style." The chief historical interest of Spernall belongs, I fancy, to the career of Henry Teonge, rector from 1670 to 1690, who was for four years of that period a chaplain in the Royal Navy, and kept a diary of humorous quaintness, published at last in 1825. He was a poet and a wit quite as much as a parson. His son was his contemporary in the neighbouring church of Coughton. The registers only date from 1663 ; they are full, like so many registers, of reference to the egregious " urchins " which are the despair of those who want to keep churches clean.

To Coughton at length we come, a pretty village. It stands at the south-west entrance, as it once was, of the forest of Arden, that woody district, not strictly a forest, which stretched from the Avon over most of North Warwickshire. Warwickshire, one may here interject with the late Mr. Charles Elton, is the most wooded of shires, and " a squirrel might leap from tree to tree for nearly the whole length of the county." But pleasant though the little village is, Coughton has its history written most boldly in its court and its church. The lordship of Coughton is one given in Domesday to Thurkil, William (probably as Mr. Round says, William de Corbucion, whose heir gave the church to Studley priory) held four hides there from him. Also " there is land there for six ploughs. There are 2 free men and 7 bordars and 4 serfs with 3 ploughs. There is a mill worth 32 pence, and in Warwick one house paying a rent 8 pence. There are 10 acres of meadow ; wood 6 furlongs long and 4 furlongs broad. Pasture for 50 swine." But Thurkil did not hold it long. It was given to Henry of Newburgh, and so passed under the Earl of Warwick

to one family after another till an heiress of the Spines carried
it into the family of Throckmorton, who still hold it.   On them
thus speaks the Rev. Thomas Cox ; and the early history of the
family is so interesting that I will quote what he says, which is
practically an abridgment of Dugdale :—

   " This Family of *Throkmorton* is ancient, having taken their
Name from their Original Seat in *Throkmorton* in the Parish of
Flatbury in *Worcestershire* ; but since this Manor came not into this
Family but by *John* the Son of *Thomas's* Marriage with *Eleanor
de la Spine,* we must begin our Account of the Family from him,
yet mentioning them no more than particularly concerns this
Place.   He was bred up in the Study of the Law, and was not
only entrusted in many important Affairs by the Earls of *Warwick*
but was in the Commission of the Peace, and one of the Chamber-
lains of the Exchequer to the King, *i.e.* Under Treasurer, *&c.* in
which Station he dy'd 23 *Hen.* 6. leaving *Thomas* his Son and Heir,
and *John* a younger Son.   'Till the Time of this *Thomas,* this
Family was not wholly possessed of *Coughton,* because the *Traceys*
who married *Alice* the eldest Sister, had a Moiety, which *John
Tracey* her Heir granted by Deed to this *Thomas.*   He was
Sheriff of this County and *Leicestershire,* and dying 12 *Edw.* 4.
left *Robert* his Son and Heir.   He was a Justice of the Peace the
greatest Part of his Life ; made a Park at *Coughton,* inclosing
therein a Common called *Wikewood, &c.*   He was a Person of
great Devotion, and according to the Custom of the Zealots of
his Time, went on a Pilgrimage to the Holy Land about 10 *Hen.* 8.
and therein dy'd.   By his Will (which he made before he went)
he order'd his Burial to be in the Church of *Coughton,* if he dy'd
any where in this Realm ; the East Window of the Chancel to be
glazed by his Executors, with the Story of the Dome, and twenty
Shillings to be given towards the glazing of the East Window in
the North Isle, with a Representation of the seven Sacraments,
and as much to that in the South Isle, with a Draught of the seven
Works of Mercy ; that his Feoffees to pray for his Soul, and the
Souls of his Ancestors, perpetually in the said North Isle, should
give a Priest 8*l. per Ann.* and his Chamber, and 8*l. per Ann.*
more to five poor People dwelling in the Alms-House here, at 7*d.*
a Week, and House-Room for ever, and the other 8*s.* and 8*d.* to
be spent on the Reparation of the said Alms-House.   *George* his
Son and Heir succeeded him in his Estate : He was a Knight,
and built the stately Castle-like Gatehouse of Free-Stone before

his House here, and had made the House suitable if he had liv'd, but he dy'd before it was begun, 1 *Phil.* and *Mar.* 1. and was buried under a Monument he had erected for himself in his Lifetime towards the North Side of the Chancel here.   He had seven Sons, but none proved of Notice but the Youngest, *John,* who in Queen *Mary's* Reign, was her Master of Requests, Justice of *Chester,* Vice President of *Wales, &c.*   He was knighted by Queen *Elizabeth,* and left *Francis* his Son and Heir, who being attainted for High Treason for corresponding with the Queen of *Scots,* was executed for the same, and so this line came to an End ; but the eldest Son of Sir *George's* Line named *Robert,* who was also a Knight, continued ; for his Son and Heir *Thomas* succeeded him, as did also his Son *John* him, whose Son *Robert* was created a Baronet by King *Charles* I. and succeeded by his Son *Francis,* who was living near the Restoration of King *Charles* II."

Of several of these personages we shall see and hear more as we visit the house and the church.   The family has remained Roman Catholic.   It succeeded by marriage to the Yates, of Buckland in Berkshire, a property only sold the other day, and the Packingtons of Harvington.   Coughton is one of the houses which is • connected with the Gunpowder Plot.   A map of the centre of England from Dudley and Nuneaton to Worcester and Stratford-on-Avon shows how near, as we judge distances now-a-days, were the houses with which the plotters were connected.   From Shelford House, John Littleton's, past Combe Abbey, where the Princess Elizabeth, who was to have been seized and made queen, to Ashby St. Ledgers, where was Lady Catesby, one passed through Dunchurch, where a great Romanist hunting party was to be held on the day of the opening of Parliament.   Thither the conspirators fled from London, and thence they separated to meet their doom, separately and in different ways.   Catesby had a house at Lapworth, John Grant at Norbrook, further south, while Clopton House was hired by Rokewood.

.Another Romanist house was that of Hindlip, south of Droitwich, out of the range of " Shakespeare's country," I should say, but to be mentioned here as it was a frequent resort of Romanist clergy.   Its owner, Mr. Abington, refused to take any part in plots, though he was quite willing to shelter any clergy, as the house was designed to do.   The house, says Dr. S. R. Gardiner (" Hist. Engl. 1603–1642 " vol. i., p. 270), " was amply provided with means for secreting fugitives. There was scarcely a room which did not contain some secret mode of egress to a hiding place constructed in the thickness of the walls. Even the chimneys led to rooms, the doors of which were covered with a lining of bricks, which, blackened as it was with smoke, was usually sufficient to prevent detection." And it was there that Father Garnet and Father Oldcorne were ultimately concealed and surrendered themselves. But the plot was very much the concern of the country round Stratford-on-Avon, and must have been the continual talk of Shakespeare's fellow townsmen. And most conspicuous of all the houses concerned was Coughton. There, while it was hired by Sir Everard Digby, was Father Garnet, from whom "equivocation" became classic in " Macbeth." At Huddington was Robert Winter. When the plot failed it was at Coughton that Bates found Garnet and Greenway, the last "a gentleman who would live and die with them," said Catesby. At Coughton the party of traitors, now reduced to thirty-six, heard mass before they made their last desperate flight to Holbeche, Stephen Littleton's house in Staffordshire, where the leaders met their death, all save those who lived to perish on the scaffold. Happily the Throck- mortons were not mixed up in the treason. When one notices how closely the plotters were connected with Warwickshire, it is perhaps worth noticing that Garnet, in his famous " Treatise on Equivocation," the book which made his execution certain, and gave him literary immortality through the mouth of the porter in " Macbeth," when he gives a critical instance of his theory, brings Warwickshire into his illustration : " A man cometh unto Coventry in time of a suspicion of plague. At the gates the officers meet him, and upon his oath examine him whether he come from London or no, where they think certainly the plague to be. This man, knowing for certain the plague not to be in London, or at least knowing that the air is not there infectious, and that he only rid through some secure place of London, not staying there, may safely swear that he came not from London, answering to their final intention in their demand, that is, whether he came so from London that he may endanger their city of the plague, although their immediate intention were to know whether he came from London or no. This man the very light of nature would clear from perjury." What Shake- speare thought of this argument, used no doubt often among

A A

Coughton Court.

his many Romanist neighbours, all men may read without mistake.

The more recent history of Coughton is diversified by an incident which had great fame a hundred years ago. Sir John Throckmorton in 1811 determined to show what could be made of British sheep, and how rapidly. On the 25th of June in that year he had two Southdowns shorn, and the whole process, from that action till a coat " of the admired dark Wellington colour" was produced, was gone through in the day, under the superintendence of Mr. Coxeter, a weaver from Newbury, whose descendants in 1911 came from America to Coughton to see the coat, still preserved there in a glass case. The noble deed accomplished, some five thousand people were fed at Buckland, and they consumed one hundred and twenty gallons of beer, while Sir John Throckmorton dined in the inn at Speenhamland, to the admiration of the county, wearing his new coat. This event belongs rather to the history of the Throckmortons than to that of Warwickshire, but the memorials of it, the authentic description framed, a large oil painting depicting the whole proceedings, and the coat itself, have found a home now at Coughton.

Before we leave the history of the family we may observe that the pictures in the house illustrate in a very interesting manner the family history, and the family alliances with the Giffards, the Actons, and other Roman Catholic houses. There are excellent portraits by Rigaud of Sir Robert Throckmorton, and of his wife by Battoni, and an interesting series of pictures representing different aspects of the work of Sir John Acton when he was the practical ruler of Naples. Now let us look at the house. Some part of it is said to have been built by the Spines, Spineys, or Spinetti, from whom it passed to the Throckmortons. Sir George Throckmorton, temp. Hen. VIII., built the main part, or, rather, the most impressive part, the " stately, castle-like gatehouse of freestone," as Dugdale calls it, which is one of the finest pieces of Tudor domestic work even in this county. For a long time this remained as a gateway, which gave access to a quadrangle, and the whole was surrounded by a moat. But the Civil Wars subjected the house to grievous damage, and it was set on fire in January, 1644, by the Parliament's troops. Sir Francis restored it under Charles II. Under James II. it was stormed by a Protestant mob on the eve of the

Revolution, and the chapel, which then stood at the east, opposite to the gateway, was pillaged. Sir Robert in 1780 made it what it is to-day. He disliked the quadrangular form, he had no very great affection for the chapel, he admired the new Gothic style which Mr. Sanderson Miller and Horace Walpole had made popular, and he acted accordingly. "This venerable seat," says "The Beauties of England and Wales" (1814), "was originally of a quadrangular form, but such a mode of construction being found gloomy and inconvenient, one side of the building was taken down some few years back, and a prospect is now obtained of the windings of the river Arrow, and the diversified country beyond." The gateway was enclosed and the lower part made into an entrance hall, to which on either side were added new wings in the most approved "Gothick" manner of the eighteenth century. These contain some excellent rooms, including the beautiful dining-room panelled in dark oak, which has a splendid chimney-piece (arms of Yate and Packington) and a chair " made from the wood of the bed occupied by Richard III. the night before Bosworth field." Richard III. seems very popular, so far as memorials of him go, in Warwickshire, perhaps because he married the last survivor of the children of Richard Nevile, Earl of Warwick, the king-maker. But let us look first at the outside. The great door bears the motto above it, with the Throckmorton arms, "Nisi dominus edificaverit domum, in vanum laboraverunt qui edificant eam," and, within the court, the door has "Nisi dominus custodierit domum, frustra vigilat qui custodit eam." Horace Walpole vastly admired the gateway ; " very handsome " he called it in 1751, but added that " there is nothing else tolerable but twenty-two coats of the matches of the family in painted glass." When you pass through the gateway, still more of a gateway than a hall, for the birds have an ancient tradition of finding their way in and take much trouble to eject, you come into the grass court, with the garden in front of you, and to your left the bedrooms and kitchens (the dinner is still carried across the court, in fine weather, to the dining-room), Tudor work, wood and rough cast, and to your right under the dining-room the pantries, etc., with, beyond, the splendid Jacobean hall, which extends the whole height of the house and is approached from the upper floor by a double staircase, and from the ground by a fine doorway opening on the court. Let us enter by the great gateway, and ascend by the stairs to our right. The tower itself ends in a large room with a large fireplace, and a turret at the east corner, hollow, which led down to a priest's hole, wherein was a stone *mensa*, now in the Roman Catholic chapel built in the Victorian age. Other relics of old time are plentiful in the house. There is the shutter, or portion of a bread box, which bears the name of Elizabeth Throckmorton, last abbess of Dennye, Cambridgeshire, who is buried in the church; there is a glove of James III. (James Edward, son of James II.); some of his hair and his son's, Henry IX.; a chemise of Mary Queen of Scots; and other memorials of the Stewarts. And there is some important tapestry of scenes from the Æneid. But the most interesting thing in the whole house has only recently been rediscovered. It is the large painted cloth, now preserved in the hall. It is dated 1596. A full description is to be found in the " Proceedings of the Society of Antiquaries " (second series, xxiii., 1909–10, pp. 255 *seq.*) by Mr. St. John Hope. Father Pollen regards it as possibly commemorative of the negotiations entered upon by James VI. of Scotland in that year with the Romanists, and as alluding also to the rising of Essex, and treats the representation of the Resurrection at the top as giving the clue. Below this is a view of Ely Cathedral, and below again are rows of medallions with heads of English kings and queens, abbats, bishops, priors, and deans of Ely down to Elizabeth and Bishop Richard Cox (who is mitred and bearded). Below these are a series of seven panels with names and arms of " yᵉ knyghtes and gentlemen commytted prisoners " to various places (such as the Palace of Ely, castles of Broughton and Banbury) at various dates under Elizabeth, followed by notices of their release. Thos. Throckmorton of Coughton is among them. " The Cloth commemorates in some way those recusants who were imprisoned (as above) . . . but the immediate connection between them and the church and monastery of Ely is not apparent." [*Cf.* " Acts of the Privy Council of England," N.S. xviii., p. 415.] It is apparently by the same painter as the author of the copy of the famous Tabula Eliensis now in the Bishop's Palace at Ely, which contains some of the early historical heads given to the Coughton cloth. The explanation of Father Pollen needs support, but is, at least, not impossible.

When we pass from the court to the church, of which we have a delightful view from the great south window of the hall, we are brought into still closer connection with the past history of this ancient family. The church is a very fine and late example of the late Perpendicular style, at a time when that style had lost, it is true, its most conspicuous merits, but when it had still dignity, strength, and the merit of being admirably lighted. It has a western tower, with a modern embattled top, nave with north and south aisles, each with an eastern chapel. It was probably erected by Sir Robert Throckmorton, lord of the manor from 1486 to 1518, who left benefactions for it in his will. The " Churches of Warwickshire " describes his work thus :—

" Presuming Sir Robert Throckmorton, lord of this manor, who flourished at this period, to have been, as is most probable, the builder of the present Church, it appears not to have been entirely finished internally during his life time, for by his will, made A.D. 1518, he bequeathed his body to be buried under a tomb in the midst of this church, which, it would appear, he had prepared for that purpose. He also willed that the east window of the chancel should be glazed with the story of the *Doom* (the last judgment) at the charge of his executors, and that xxs. should be given to the glazing of the east window of the north aisle with the representation of the *Seven Sacraments*, and the same sum to the glazing of the east window of the south aisle with the representation of the *Seven Works of Mercy*. He also willed that the image of our Lady should be set on the north side at the end of the altar, in the south aisle, and the image of the angel Gabriel on the same side of the aisle, at the pillar between the aisle and the chancel, with a roll in his hand of greeting looking towards our Lady ; and at the south end of the same altar the image of *St. Raphael*, painted and gilded ; and that in the north aisle, at the north end of the altar, the image of the *Trinity* was to be ; and at the south end the image of *St. Michael ;* all which images were to be richly painted and gilt. He further willed that certain lands should be put into the hands of feoffees to the use of a priest to sing perpetually in the north aisle of Coughton church, for his soul and the souls of his ancestors ; and that thenceforth the said aisle should be called the Trinity Chapel. This Sir Robert Throckmorton, described by Sir William Dugdale who gives the substance of his will at length in the ' Antiquities of Warwickshire ' as ' a man of singular piety,' died in a pilgrimage to the Holy Land, A.D. 1519–20. No traces of his bequests are now apparent, but the Trinity Chapel has a parclose to screen it from the chancel and north aisle, part of which it is described to be."

Leland speaks of the tomb of Sir Robert as already erected though he died on a pilgrimage to the Holy Land, and of the church " as very fair, exceedingly well glazed, partly by Sir George Throckmorton, partly by his father." I may quote also the excellent description of the nave from the book already named :—

" This is divided from the aisles by obtuse-pointed four-centered arches, double faced, with plain soffits and hollowed chamfers, the piers are angular-edged, and elongated in section. The clerestory above the arches on each side contains four square-headed windows, each containing three cinque-foiled lights, with hollow jambs, and labels over. The nave and aisles have wooden roofs of modern construction. The body of the church and aisles are mostly fitted with the original low open sittings, panelled at the sides, and presents a favourable contrast, in that respect, to the manner in which many of our Churches have, during the last century, been refitted. Some of the linen-pattern panel work, much in use in the reign of Henry the eighth, appears in front of the sittings under the gallery at the west end of the nave. The gallery contains a small organ. The pulpit and reading pew are placed at the north-east corner of the nave."

Further changes have altered the church since this was written, but the details referred to are easily recognisable in spite of the disappearance of the gallery. Other interesting features are the fine octagonal font and the ancient glass. The east window contains the Sybils— Sybilla Europea, Sybilla Persica, Sybilla Samia. Are they copies of the old ? There are fragments of the old glass above. You will notice also among the inscriptions : " Nascetur puer de paupercula. Bestie terre adorabunt Eum." The windows of the Trinity Chapel, at the north, have the family subject of the Apostles with their verses of the Creed Thus : —

S. PETER, with the key . . . . . *Credo in Deum*
S. ANDREW, with the cross saltire . . *Et in Jesum Christum*
S. JAMES the greater, represented in pilgrim's garb, and in a hat with a cockle shell in front, bearing a boton-ated bourdon or staff, with a bottle tied to the top . . . . *Qui conceptus est*

S. JOHN, with the poisoned chalice containing a serpent	*Qui passus est*
S. PHILIP, with the cross staff and bag or purse .. .. ˙ ..	*(Descendit) ad infernum*
S. THOMAS, with a spear	*Ascendit ad cœlos*
S. BARTHOLOMEW, with a butcher's knife	*Inde venturus est*
S. MATTHEW, with a halbert and book and, in the south-east window of the south chapel	*Credo in* [the rest destroyed]
S. JAMES the less, with fuller's club	*S'tam ecclesiam Catholicam*
S. SIMON, with saw	*Resurrectionem Carnis*

S. Jude and S. Matthias are lost. These most interesting figures are probably German of the early sixteenth century. But the historical interest of the church centres chiefly in the tombs of the Throckmortons. The most important is that fine central one of the builder of the church, already referred to, which was intended to contain his body, but, as he died in 1520 on pilgrimage, was left vacant ˙till the late eighteenth century, when Sir Robert Throckmorton, who died 1791, was interred therein. The inscription recording the latter's virtues, his devotion to study and philanthropy as a solace for his enforced abstention, as a Romanist, from public life, occupies the fine marble slab which covers the tomb, which records also the interment of Sir John, 1819, and Mary his wife (*née* Giffard), 1821.

Under the arch which separates the chancel from the north chantry is the tomb of Sir George Throckmorton, Knight, the builder of the great gatehouse, the father of eight sons, present at the coronation of Anne Bullen, Keeper of the Household of Queen Anne of Cleves, High Sheriff, 35 Hen. VIII., and husband of Katheryn, "one of the daughters of Syr Nycholas Vause, Knight, Lord Harroden," who lies beside him—if indeed they were ever buried in the tomb, which must have been erected while they were still alive, since the space for the dates of death has never been filled in. The brass on the top gives the figures of the knight in armour, with his eight sons, and, on his right, his wife in a high bodied gown with full skirt, eleven daughters depending from her. His arms (*gules on a chevron argent 5 bars gemels sable*) are given, and hers (*chequy or and gules, on a chevron azure* 3 *roses or*). In the north chantry the chapel once contained the brass of " Dame Elizabeth Throkmorton, the last abbas of Dennye and aunte to Sir George Throkmorton," with the date 1547. When the tomb was opened some time ago her skull and those of the two nuns who retired with her to Coughton were found.

On the south side, within the rails, is the fine tomb with recumbent marble figures of Sir John Throckmorton and Margery his wife, of which the detailed description well deserves to be quoted :—

"The Knight, whose effigy lies on the right of the tomb, is represented as bare-headed with mustachios and a beard, and with his head resting on a tilting helme, whilst round his neck is worn a short ruff. His body dress consists of a doublet or jerkin buttoned from the neck downwards, the sleeves of which fit close down to the wrists, round which are cuffs. A chain crosses the breast diagonally from right to left. Over the doublet is worn a long side gown open in front and purfled with fûr ; the sleeves cover the shoulders only ; the right hand lies on the stomach, whilst the left touches that of the lady. The lady is represented in a puckered gown, arranged in parallel folds, and tied round the waist with a short and narrow sash or scarf ; the sleeves of the gown are close fitting ; round the neck is worn a ruff, and on the head is a close fitting cap, coif or caul, over which is a French hood which covers both the head and shoulders. The head of this lady reposes on a square tasselled cushion ; her right hand is holding that of the knight, whilst her left is placed on her breast. Both of these effigies recline on a mattress or mat. At the head or west end of the tomb, sculptured in low relief, are the small kneeling figures of five children ; one, a male, appears in a doublet and puffled side gown ; another, a male also, in armour ; a third, that of a female, in a bodiced gown, buttoned in front to the waist ; the fourth and fifth are those of males, represented as clad in tight hose, doublets, and short cloaks ; these and the figure in armour have swords, and all have neck ruffs. On the north side of the tomb are two compartments, formed by the projecting plinths, which are covered with lozenge panel work, which support the columns of the tester. In one of these is the small kneeling figure in relief of a female in a gown and sash with demi cannon hanging sleeves and a hood over the head, and the figure of an infant in swathing bands. The other compartment contains two kneeling figures of females in the same dress as the former. At the foot of this monument, against the wall, is the following inscription :—

Here liethe interrid ye bodie of Sir John Throkmorton knight of Feckenham the fibethe sonne of Sir George Throkmorton Knight of Coughton sometime master of ye Requests bnto queene marie of hap pie memorie who in respecte of his faithful serbice bestowed upon him ye office of Justice of Chester & of hir cobnsaile in ye marrches of Wales in wch rome he continewed xxiij yeares & supplied wth in ye same time ye place of bice president ye space of iii yeare, he had to wife margerie Puttenham daughter of Robert Puttenham Esquire by whom he had Issue 6 sonnes & iiij daughters, he departed this life ye 22 off may Ao 1580 his wife surbibinge who libed & died widowye . . . . and is here also interred
on whos soules God take merce.   B."

Here again the wife seems never to have been buried in the tomb, and the date of her death was not even recorded. The same is the case with the great tomb, between the chancel and the south chapel, of Sir Robert Throckmorton, who died in 1580, but whose time of " departure for happier estate " is omitted. There are a number of other interesting memorials to the chief family, going down to the present day, and to those of their religion, notably one which shows how happy were the relations between those of different opinions in the early nineteenth century. " Here lies the Rev. Thomas Barr, O.S.B., who officiated as pastor to the Roman Catholic congregation of this place, during thirty-eight years. He died May 20, 1823, aged 83 years. R.I.P." It is a pleasant footnote to this that in the year of grace 1911 relations are reported to be equally friendly, in the cricket field *par exemple*. On the floor of the south chancel aisle is the inscription which records the death of " Mistress Vallantine Grevil," 1648, " A Maide." And there are several memorials of the family of Dewes, the most important of whom appears to have been William Dewes, born 1637 and died 1717, a great benefactor to the parish.

One leaves the church with regret. It is a splendid memorial to a family which has served England through many troublous generations. The history is one which may be read in the State papers, in Tudor manuscripts, in pictures of noble men and women, as well as on the walls of churches. Some of the family served the sovereigns well, some plotted. One was executed as a traitor, one as a highwayman ; and even to Nicholas the great ambassador of Queen Elizabeth, to whom that suggestion that the Pope would recognise the English Prayer-book was made, things were not always pleasant. He was not himself a Papist, but he suffered at one time with the rest. So in a quaint contemporary poem he is made to describe his state :—

> " Our sun eclipsed a long time did not shine
>   No joys approached near unto Coughton House ;
> My sisters they did nothing else but whine
>   My mother looked much like a drowned mouse.
> No butter then would stick upon our bread,
>   We all did fear the loss of father's head."

Happily, Sir George, the father, lived to die in his bed, perhaps, as the poem suggests, by the intercession of Queen Catherine Parr. But one could find interest for ever in the story of the Throckmortons, and it is time to hurry on to Alcester, southwards, or if you will to Henley-in-Arden, that pleasant harbour of refuge to the north-west of our road.

CHAPTER XIX

BETWEEN Henley and Redditch—I despair to describe the way, and yet you pass a private road to it if you go from Old-berrow to Mappleborough—is Skilts; or, I ought to say, are Skilts: there is Lower and Upper. They belong to the old parish of Studley. The Lower is said to have been at one time a monastery; if so, it can only have been a small cell of Studley. You are told that the paved.way round the farmyard was once the cloister, and the entrance gate where are now the wooden doors. Even the site of a chapel is suggested opposite to this gate, and there is a good deal of old stone work there. But the main house as it now stands, a great height, with a most curious inlet in the midst of the wall—suggesting perhaps that the rest of the wall, with the windows, is comparatively modern—is of Tudor, or even later date. This side is a floor lower than the other, if I remember right. It is a fine red-brick building with a good pediment and a high roof. It stands very high above the surrounding country, giving magnificent views in the direction of Alcester and even (I think) to Malvern. It is built on the edge of a steep incline, and many steps descend from the garden, walled in with an ancient wall, to the field below, where is a well with picturesque wooden shelter. Inside, the farmhouse is as comfortable as it is solid; there is a pleasant room with deep recessed fireplace, and there are splendid cool dairies and larders. The house and its position are indeed unique. Certainly one must turn aside and ascend the hill to see them. And from Lower Skilts it is only a few fields and one comes upon Upper Skilts. This, I take it, is the residence—much altered now, and indeed rebuilt, by Sir William Jaffray—which Lady

Luxborough mentions in her letters; but whether this, or Lower Skilts, was the home of Captain John Smith (*see* p. 28), I know not. It has a lovely garden with a very fine gateway of red brick with decorative stone facings and two beasts comfortably seated on the top. From the garden is a most magnificent view westwards over the plain and Redditch, one of the finest views in a county of vistas and expanse. This, I suppose, is the Skilts, and not the Lower—but I will not be sure—which Dugdale speaks of as having been a grange to the priory of Studley, and, concerning it, of a petition " to the Bishop of Worcester, *temp.* Hen. vi., by Thomas Atwode, right Heir of Blood (as he there styles himself) to Peter Corbicon, the Founder of that religious House, wherein he complains against Thomas Bedull the then Prior [this Bedull, I may interject, was Prior from 1450 to 1454, but Dr. Cox, in the ' Victoria County History ' seemingly knows nothing of him] for keeping a Paramour here, *viz.*, Joane, wife to one John Greene, by the connivance of her husband, to which Joane he sundry times resorted in secular Apparrell, allowing her Wheate, Malt, Wooll, and other things, whereby the Monastery was much impoverished." Before the Dissolution, Prior John Yardley wrote that the chief possession of the Studley house was this farm of Skilts (or Skillus) which was never let, and that if this (which Cromwell wanted for a friend of his) were taken they would starve. What then should it profit them to have the Lord Cromwell for their visitor, and to have taken the king (so the prior reminded him that they had done) for their supreme head ? Mr. Cox, of 1700, who copies Dugdale very closely, continues the history of Skilts thus :—

" After the Dissolution of the Monasteries, one *Knightly* was Owner of it ; and leaving only Daughters for his Heirs, it upon the Partition fell to *James Duffield*, in Right of *Frances* his Wife, one of them. *James* sold it to *William East*, and others, who 2 *Eliz.* sold it to *William Sheldon*, Esq., by the Name of two Messuages, 600 Acres of Land, 60 Acres of Meadow, 600 Acres of Pasture, 120 Acres of Wood, and 100 Acres of Heath and Furs ; all which he imparked for Deer, and on the South Side of it built a very fair Brick House, of which his Posterity are, or lately were possessed."

This brick house, I confess, looks very like that at Lower Skilts ; but what, then, is the history of Upper ? I believe that the researches of the present owner leave the difficulties unsolved.

From Upper Skilts, by wood and park, it is but a short way to the beautiful old house of Gorcott. It stands just above the high road to Studley, in the midst of a steep hill. Through a gate with two balls (signs of magistracy, so the historian Edward Augustus Freeman would always say) you approach the mansion, half brick, half plaster and wood. It belonged for centuries to the Chambers family, whose memorials may be seen at Tanworth. Great among them was an admiral of Queen Elizabeth's day. It may have been from him that there came the beautiful Chinese design painted on wood that you see over the fireplace in one of the rooms. And no doubt it was he who set up the arms of Queen Elizabeth in the glass of a fine window of three hundred and sixty-five panes, such as you see often in Yorkshire houses, a compliment to the reigning sovereign which was no doubt manufactured by a good London firm and supplied to the loyal. Perhaps, too, the queen may really have stayed here, as they say, on her way to Kenilworth. The Chambers family could show possession since Edward VI., but no " title " could be found when the property was sold to Sir William Jaffray. There is in another window of coloured glass a curious spider dial, through which the sun, when it shone on the room, would tell you the hour, and the design suggested the web in which the rash fly is imprisoned. The house is full of old oak, in panels and furniture, and there did I see, suspended from the ceiling, a most quaint oaken object like a huge bed, in which all sorts of unconsidered trifles could be, and were, stored, out of the way of children and .dogs.

We may turn out of the way here, if you will, soon after we begin the long, straggling village of Mappleborough, and have passed its modern church, to the village of Morton Bagot, secluded between Spernall and Oldberrow. The name is taken from William Bagot of Edward I.'s day, who held the manor, but the family soon sold it to the Coningesbys. It remained with the " Coningesby family for many generations : when their portion was ultimately sold to Mr. Holyoake, who afterwards disposed of it to Mr. Horseley, of Henley-in-Arden. The manor is now the property of Sir F. L. H. Goodricke, Bart., who also owns the principal part of the parish." So wrote the authors of " The Churches of Warwickshire " fifty years ago. The patronage of the church was at one time belonging to the canons of Kenilworth ; and in later times—Edward II.'s day—there was a contest between the rector and the all-snatching canons of Wootton Wawen as to mortuary fees. Wherever you go you find Wootton asserting itself. The church again is on high ground " with undulating scenery of hill and dale, wood and pasture, around it ; Studley Castle is seen in the distance ; a few farm houses and labourers' cottages lie scattered about in the vicinity of the Church. It consists of a nave and chancel only. At the west end of the nave, and issuing out of the roof, is a timber-framed belfry, pierced for lights, with a pack-saddle roof."

It has a wooden bell-turret ; perhaps the original church was of wood. Inside it has considerable interest ; the chancel unfortunately ceiled, but with remains of the fifteenth century roodscreen, and with a low side window which has been maintained to be for confession [so *Gentleman's Magazine*, October, 1846, p. 380]. Thus Bedyll, reporting to Cromwell in his hunt for iniquities to justify a dissolution :—

" We think it best that the place wher thes freres have been wont to here *outward confession of all commers* at certen times of the yere *be walled up*, and that use to be fordoen for ever."

The memorials include the names of Chambers and of Holyoake, the first important at Gorcott and Tanworth, the second the kindred of that Mr. Holyoake who, with his son, " Master Franky Holyoake," apprenticed in Birmingham, occurs so often in Lady Luxborough's letters as a trusted adviser and friend.

We will turn back from Morton Bagot towards Studley, but first pass Mappleborough on the way thence, leaving Studley for another day. We can go by Ipsley to Redditch.

Mapleborough (or Mappleborough) Green is a pretty village that you pass between Gorcott and Studley. Dugdale tells that in his time it was a waste, and " the only place that now retaineth anything of that antient Name, but was heretofore called the ' Hay-Wood.' " The manor-house in the eighteenth century belonged to the Dewes family (whose memorials are seen in many neighbouring churches), and there is a note of it in Lady Luxborough's Letter (August 31, 1750) : " I have had the pleasure of seeing Mrs. Dewes three times lately, who is now at Mapleborough Green for change of air for her children. It only serves to make me regret her not continuing at that house of her husband's, for Wellsbourn is almost too far for a visit. She is very agreeable in conversation, and shows all that politeness, delicacy, softness, and grace, which one distinguishes in her uncle, Lord Lansdown's, Poems, and which I have so often observed in him, having been personally acquainted with him." As to Lansdown (George Granville), by the way, Dr. Johnson speaks with courtly civility but very mild praise indeed : " His works do not show him to have had much comprehension from nature, or illumination from learning," and some of his verses are dismissed as " commonly feeble and unaffecting, or forced and extravagant."

If you turn to the right as you come to Mappleborough from Gorcott hill, before you get to the Green, you will come, going due westwards, to Ipsley, which is about six miles from Alcester and two or three from Redditch. Its history goes back far. The chief landowner in Domesday was one Hugh. The authors of " The Churches of Warwickshire " continue the story of the manor thus :—

" From this Hugh the possession appears to have descended in direct male descent for nearly seven centuries, the family first taking the name of Hubold, or Hubald, which, subsequently, became changed into Hubaud. About the middle of the last century the heirs male of this ancient family became extinct, and the inheritance divided among several coheiresses. The estates were then sold, and the manor purchased by Charles Savage, Esq., of Tachbrook, from whose family it afterwards passed by marriage into that of the present possessor, Walter Savage Landor, Esq., the well-known and highly talented author, who is the present lord of the manor."

To his family it still belongs. The manor-house, to speak of that first, to the north of the church, and divided only by a hedge from the churchyard, is called Ipsley Court, and is a long, quaint building, with high-pitched roof and the characteristic chimneys of the period. It runs on two sides only, now, of a courtyard, and (I think) is for the most part only one room deep. Near by is a very good old stable and barn, and from it there is a great view—or from the churchyard—over all the valleys of Avon and Alne and Arrow, to Edgehill, and, nearer, across to Skilts. The church is of the fifteenth century, very much restored. There were once north and south aisles, but these have been pulled down, and the Decorated arches now stand, filled up with masonry, in the walls. The chancel is raised one step above the nave, then the sanctuary one, and the altar one. " It is difficult," said the author of " The Churches of Warwickshire,"

" to imagine a more complete subversion of the original character and proportion of the structure than this Church exhibits in its present melancholy condition." This is true, alas! and chiefly so, perhaps, in regard to the disappearance of the splendid Hubaud monuments described by Dugdale. There remain two beautiful marble (or alabaster) slabs, north and south in the chancel—one of which used to be in the north aisle and the other in the south of the chancel, both then raised on plain stone. Part of the inscription on the first of these still remains :—

✠Here lyeth the bodyes of nycolas Hubaude [and Doro]the hys wyfe whych nycolas deceased the seco[nd day of] maye in the yere of oure lorde ✠ m° [D°] liii and the sayd dorothe deceased the xbi ✠ daye of maye in the yere of oure lorde m° D° lbiii [upon] whose soles god habe mercy Ame ✠

The letters in italics have disappeared. The slab represents an esquire and his lady, with sixteen children, he in beautiful armour of the early sixteenth century, she in an open gown, tied in front half way down and then opening again. The inscription of the other tomb, which shows a knight and his lady, has entirely disappeared. The date was 1557. At the west end stands a very fine classic monument of seventeenth century classical order, with Corinthian columns, which has the inscription :—
" Domus Viventium."
" Here lyeth the body of Anne Hvbaud davghter and cohæress of Gervase Tevery of Stapleford in the covnty of Nottingham, Esq., the wife and relict of her deare hvsband Ralph Hvbaud Lord of this Manovr a person rather to be admired then imitated for her piety towards God her charity towards her neighbours and her incessant care of her sons and being only married to them and the family sleighted all matches that she might restore and leave a fair and free estate to them and their posterity she departed this life ye 23 of March 1672 in the yeare of her age 59. To whose memory her afflicted sons erected this monument as a grateful and lasting testimony of their never dieing love and duty.
John Hvbaud Baronet
Tevery Hvbaud Natv Minor
Quos Vita Seperaret Tumulus Sociaret "
You will notice among details a quaint face on the capital of a pier on the south side of the church, and a good chair of 1618.
Down below, eastwards, you will find the charming vicarage,

B B

with tower and clock, a weather cock, a stucco front, a decorative winged lion, and several other cheerful and handsome things about it.

Half a mile south of the church, is Forge Meadow, and by it are the remains of a Roman camp, on Riknield way. From the hill on which the church stands, after looking at the splendid view, you descend westwards, and by a very pretty and winding road, over the little stream of Arrow, to Redditch. Redditch is not quite in the Shakespeare country ; or at least it seems not to be, for it is, as one sees it to-day, so many centuries beyond his time. A large modern, red-brick town has grown up beside the one good street, of various dates, in which stands the large early Victorian church, not at all undignified, possessing a good southern chapel. Evidently from an earlier church is the brass of Nathaniel Mugg, 1712, who retired and gave a perpetual benefaction to "This Chappel." This is explained in Mr. Woodward's "History of Bordesley Abbey," whence I learn that until 1805 there stood between Redditch and the Abbey Meadows what was known locally as Bordesley Chapel. It was really the Gatehouse Chapel of the Abbey. In 1805 an Act of Parliament was obtained for "pulling down the last relic of old Redditch and building a new Chapel on the site of the present Church. So eager were all men to destroy this temple that a reward of 5s. was given to the man who threw off the first stone." Mugg's memorial alone escaped destruction. There was "an earlier Church" (chapel) on the site of the present Church, but not the one referred to on the tablet, which was on a different site.

From Redditch is a good and very pretty road, due south, to Alcester.

CHAPTER XX

BEYOND Guy's Cliff and Blacklow hill the road goes, as straight as though it were Roman, towards Kenilworth. The only village you pass is Leek Wootton, of which there is not very much to be said. In 1830 the church was described as "a handsome modern structure, standing on an eminence," which is sufficient. The value of the benefice, then stated to be £5 12s. 1d., has, one is happy to note, increased to £300 net. and house. The population has slightly decreased. A privately printed index to the parochial registers, 1685–1742, " printed at the private press of Frederick Arthur Crisp," is sought for by collectors. Then, further on, to the left, some way from the road, are the kennels of the North Warwickshire ; not far away again the modern house which has replaced the old " Good Rest Lodge," where, according to Dugdale, countesses of Warwick used to retire for the birth of their children, " to avoid much concourse of people " ; and again, not far away, we go by Bannerhill farm, an old " Gospel Oak," twenty-seven feet in girth, says the guide-book.

As we approach near to Kenilworth the road from Leamington comes in on our right, and we pass through a good deal of modern, unpleasant building, and by a modern, uninteresting church. Then we come to the brow of the hill. From this we look down upon a valley through which runs a brook. On the hill opposite is the church, and round it the older part of the town. We may now go to the castle either by the left, more directly, or to the right and then left into the village (I suppose it is a town now) and round. The first way is the prettier, for it is all country— a shady lane, which a big brook runs across at one point, where

Kenilworth
Castle

E.H.N.

carts must go by a ford, and the castle is seen through the trees, then, rising in a solid block of ruins ; so one draws near through the old tilt-yard.

But the more usual way from the top of the hill is to turn to the right, passing by the corner house of the King's Arms, which is to be noted because here stayed Sir Walter Scott, in 1815, not 1820, as the guide-books tell, for he himself says in his diary that he was not at Kenilworth between 1815 and 1828. And all modern Kenilworth is due to Scott ! In 1828 he says of the castle : " The relentless rain only allowed us a glimpse of this memorable ruin. Well, the last time I was here, in 1815, these trophies of time were quite neglected. Now they approach so much nearer the splendour of Thunder-ten-tronckh as to have a door at least, if not windows. They are, in short, preserved and protected. So much for the novels." *The* novel was published in 1821. When Scott saw the castle in 1815—it was remembered some five and twenty years later—he looked at the carving, no doubt the chimney-piece in the gate-house, and then stayed alone in the ruins some two hours. It is with Scott for guide that one must visit Kenilworth.

We pass by an old house of Elizabeth's day, a very good example of Warwickshire Tudor building, with its rough-cast and wooden partitions, the bear and ragged staff carved over the door and the initials " R. L." When we come to the main street, the Coventry road, there is much of interest : good houses, good shops ; but we pass on, and descend slightly, at the left, to visit the ancient parish church. This has a western tower with spire, a large nave with aisles and transepts, and a chancel with lady chapel to the south. It is built in the rich red stone of the neighbourhood. In the west of the tower is a Norman door, which no doubt was rebuilt here from the priory. It is of three arches within each other, the innermost fluted, the next with beakheads, and the third embattled ; and outside all a richly ornamented square. Within one has a feeling (from the archaeologist) of distress : all has been restored, too, too much, scraped and spoiled, and the roof would be described by a sensitive person as dreadful. The font is of 1664 and interesting. So are some monuments. The Birds, John, an alderman, and Joan, two tablets ; Gulielmus Phipps, advocatus, 1727 ; Bayes Cotton, 1827 ; Elizabeth, wife of Edmund Hector, 1741, with the inscription :—

" O fida et amabilis
O dulcis et nimis placens uxor
Olim deliciae
Sponsi nunc inconsolabilis.
Vale.   Vale."

And lastly, Westmacott's fine figures in marble of Mrs. Caroline Gresley, herself on a bed watched by her husband and child,

Kenilworth Church.

who died in 1817, and is said by the inscription to be " now receiving her merited reward."

There is a list of charities which is worth reading.   Let us, by the way, do all we can to prevent iconoclastic if well-meaning clergymen and architects removing these ancient lists—which are of such great importance for local and family history—on the plea that they are not beautiful, or devotional.   To the well-instructed mind they are both.   As to what Dugdale figures in the church it has long ago disappeared. Let the charities at least survive.

Just below the church, partly in the church and partly in the meadow, are the remains of the priory founded in Henry I.'s time by Geoffrey de Clinton. These are the beautiful arch of the gate-house with its four doorways—called in Ireland's time "Tan-tarra," and he adds, "I know not why"—and the porter's lodge, in most glorious red sandstone, and the old granary, now a barn. The foundations of the church can be traced, but the rest of the buildings have disappeared ; the stones were no doubt used to build up the later parts of the castle, as well as many private houses.

E·H·N·

Priory Ruins, Kenilworth.

One of these, perhaps, is the charming eighteenth century Gothic dwelling at the north-east of the church.

Then return to the street. We approach the castle now at the north, where an open space, at the foot of one hill and on the brow of another, is outside the gate-house, by the side of which we have access to the ruins. The first thing to remember, when one visits the castle with an eye to its history, is that it is quite different now from its position in the time of its greatness. By this I do not mean only that it is in ruins, but that what was once one of its main defences has disappeared. The south and west, now a meadow, were in the time of the castle's strength a great lake.   The stream that runs along the valley was dammed up, and what should have been the easiest approach was thus entirely blocked.   From the lake a moat ran round the castle. The keep was placed at the highest point of the enclosure. The outer walls were at some distance from it, and the eastern one had two curtain towers to defend it.

Kenilworth was one of the largest castles of the Norman period, even before its enlargement.   The mound of the original conqueror was early in the twelfth century surmounted by the huge

The Gate House, Kenilworth Castle.

keep.   It will be best to sketch the history of the building, briefly, as we go round it.

At the left, as we enter the little door overgrown with ivy, by which is the porter's cottage, is the gate-house, the dated chimney-piece whereof, 1571, with the bear and ragged staff and the initials "R. L.," help to fix the age of the building. It is now used as a private house ; and a good deal of the decoration of the principal rooms, no doubt, comes from the castle itself.   Leaving the gate-house, which is the only part of the castle that remains habitable, to our left, we enter what was once the base court, and almost the whole range of ruins is before us. Facing them, and looking westwards, we have the great Norman keep, dated about 1170, to the right. It still stands about eighty feet high and nearly fourteen feet thick. As early as Elizabeth's time it was called "Cæsar's tower," like its neighbour at Warwick, and it resembles its contemporaries at Rochester and Castle Rising, though it is but a ruin. It had originally only one story, the first floor being larger than the ground floor through the walls being two feet less in thickness. The big mullions show where Robert Dudley cut Tudor windows in the huge walls. At the south you will see the well. Beyond the keep is a smaller building which moderns call "the annexe," and from it there was access to the garden at the north. The south wall bears the date 1570, which marks Dudley's alterations. The garden, whose glories are described by Laneham (whose record was of such use to Scott when he wrote his novel), is now fallen indeed from its high estate; but we do not enter it.

Here the Norman part of the castle ends, and we come to the fourteenth century buildings, which are called Lancaster's buildings, and extend all round the inner court. They were built by John of Gaunt. The kitchen has entirely disappeared; so has the buttery next to it. The outer wall, however, remains, and following it, and mounting the uneven ground, we come to the strong north-west corner tower which Scott, without reason, dubbed "Mervyn's Bower," and described as the refuge of Amy Robsart (who probably never saw Kenilworth in her life). From its tower, the staircase still remaining, you can see exactly where was, to the right, the pleasance, and in front the great lake, beyond the outer walls, its extent now marked by hedges. Coming down from Mervyn's Bower, and turning round by the wall to the south, you enter, through a fine arch, the great hall, probably John of Gaunt's work. The roof, of course, has long gone, and the floor too; but you must note that the hall itself stood over the cellar, in which you stand, and had for floor the vaulted roof, springing from ten piers from which the vaulting stretched to the half pillars in the walls and at the angles. The splendid windows of the hall—four west, three east—remain, and also two large fireplaces, a charming oriel at the south-east, and a small recess, in a tower, at the south-west. You may spend a long time in the great hall, and gradually notice how much of this splendid Perpendicular building, in spite of its destruction, is still left standing ; and how you can, with a little stretch of imagination, see Elizabeth sitting here in state upon her throne. And you see how what began as a castle, with its huge Norman keep, changed gradually into a palace. We have now come, at the oriel, to the south of the castle ; and there is a gap, where once the white hall stood, from which was entered the Presence Chamber—whose fine oriel window remains, looking northward on to the court—and again from it the Privy Chamber, a smaller hall of audience, whose fireplace is said to be the place whence came the chimney-piece now in the gate-house.

Beyond this, at the southern part of the main building, and nearest of all the edifice to the outer wall of the castle, is the fine Tudor building which completes our circuit. It extends along the south side, and has a large projection southwards ; it then turns east and goes forward till it reaches, or till it once reached —the gap was filled by what were called Henry VIII.'s lodgings and Dudley's lobby—the gateway which connected it with the clock-tower and the great Norman keep. It is called Leicester's buildings, and, ruinous though it is, its fine mullioned windows and its lofty rooms well illustrate the magnificence of Elizabethan domestic architecture.

Thus we finish the circuit of the inner ward. But this was but a small part of the great castle. You walk eastwards now, still within the ramparts, and over grass-grown mounds where trees are growing. You go to the south-east limit of the outer wall, and find yourself in the ruins of Mortimer's tower. You will now be in a position to observe, with Mr. Hamilton Thompson in his book on " Military Architecture in England during the Middle Ages," that the approach to the outer ward, across the lake, had three lines of defence. First there was an earthwork with stone bastions and a gatehouse ; then a long causeway, or dam, with a wall at the east of it ; and, lastly, Mortimer's tower with two portcullises. Modern writers suggest that this was built in Henry III.'s time, but Dugdale is most likely right who says that Robert Dudley erected not only Leicester's build-ings, but " did he raise from the ground two goodly Towers at the Head of the Pool,[1] viz., the Floud-Gate or Gallery-Tower, standing at one end of the Tilt-Yard, in which was a spacious and noble room for Ladies to see the exercises of Tilting and Barriers ; and at the other end Mortimer's Tower, whereupon the Arms of

[1] i.e. The point where the stream entered the great lake, I suppose.

Mortimer were cut in Stone; which doubtless was so named by the E. of Leicester, in Memory of one more Antient that stood there formerly, wherein, as I guess, either the Lord Mortimer . . . did lodge, or else because Sir John Mortimer Kt., Prisoner here in H. 5 Time, was detain'd there." The tilt-yard is just in front of you as you look south-east, and there was held, not only much sport in Leicester's welcome of Elizabeth, but also " that great and solemn Tilting " which Dugdale tells us was held in the seventh year of King Edward the First when " there was a great and famous concourse of noble Persons here at Kenilworth called the Round-Table, consisting of an hundred Knights and as many Ladies ; whereunto divers repaired from foreign Parts for the Exercise of Arms, viz., Tilting and martial Tournaments ; and the Ladies Dancing ; who were clad in silken mantles Rog. Mortimer E. of March being the chief and the occasion thereof." About this famous tournament Dugdale adds the delightful comment that it was called the Round Table " to avoyd contention touching Precedency, a Custome of great Antiquity, and used by the antient *Gauls*, as Mr. *Cambden* in *Hantsh*, from Athenaeus (an approved Author) observes.'" The incursion into history is so attractive that one is tempted to hurry over the remains of walls and buildings facing east. They extend by the water tower, the picturesque stables, a beautiful rich red with black timber, and Lunn's tower (an early building) till they join in the gate-house, and the outer circle is complete.

 Not only are the ruins of Kenilworth perhaps the most extensive, as ruins, of any castle in England, and certainly not the least picturesque, but there can be none which call up memories richer or more intimately connected with the great names of English history. Scott, who called Warwick the " fairest monument of ancient splendour which yet remains uninjured by time," spoke of Kenilworth as that " lordly palace where princes feasted and heroes fought, now in the bloody earnest of storm and siege and now in the games of chivalry, where beauty dealt the prize which valour won." It is a long record indeed which might be recalled by one who looked upon the ruined walls. After its first building, on the lands of a manor named in Domesday, by Geoffry de Clinton, it saw changes and vicissitudes, often being in the king's hands and then restored to a tenant. John acquired it as his own, and was often there, and built at considerable expense. So was, and so did, Henry III.: new walls were built and towers repaired and the chapel was enriched. Then Henry gave it to his sister Eleanor and her husband, Simon de Montfort, Earl of Leicester. "About which time," says Dugdale, "the woods belonging to it, lying neer the Road betwixt Coventre and Warwicke, were very thick (which now are all gone). Wherefore in 34 Hen. 3 the Constable hereof had command to cut down six Acres, in Breadth, of the Under-Wood there growing, for the security of Passengers." In the Barons' Wars it became Earl Simon's chief fortress. Thence raiders marched to Warwick and sacked it; and there at last the remnants of Earl Simon's men held out till the very end of 1266, and the terms on which they yielded, the Ban of Kenilworth, became a famous pledge of constitutional liberty. The castle, now in the king's hands, was given to his son Edmund Earl of Lancaster, and it was there in the time of Edmund's son Thomas, the leader of the barons, that Edward II. yielded up his crown. When it came by succession to John of Gaunt he made large additions to the buildings, and every king, when the Lancastrian house was on the throne, paid visits to it. In 1563 Elizabeth granted it to Robert Dudley, Earl of Leicester, and it was there that he received her four times, in 1566, 1568, 1572, and 1575. Leicester was a magnificent lord of the castle. "I have heard some who were his servants," says Dugdale, "say that the charge he bestowed on this castle, with the Parks and Chase thereto belonging was no less than 60 Thousand Pounds." And then he tells of the culmination of all this grandeur, the greatest entertainment of the great Queen. Before we quote his account, which is really the best there is in a small place, we may note that from the Pepys MSS. (Magdalene College, Cambridge) are to be obtained several pleasing details as to the preparations for the queen's progress to Kenilworth in 1575. On a paper of "remembrance for the Progress" three alternative routes are given from Windsor : one by Chenies, Rycott, Oxford, Woodstock, Banbury, Coventry, and Warwick—a curious route, taking Kenilworth on a return from Warwick. This plan was followed, evidently by direction, in the two other routes, which both go to Coventry first, the one by Bisham, Ewelme, Bicester, and Banbury ; the other by Missenden, Aylesbury, Buckingham, and Daventry. "Carriage" was to be appointed for all the nobility and officials of the queen and her household. Letters were to be sent to the sheriffs of Oxford and Warwick to levy 300 quarters of wheat in each shire,

" besides the privy bakehouse," or to say whether they can serve baked bread ; and to the commissioners of peace in both shires to show how the queen could be " served of beeves, muttons, veales, and lambs, herons, shovelards, biltors of any kind of fowl or freshwater fish, rabbits, etc., and what may be served by the day " at the resting-places of Woodstock, Coventry, Warwick, and Kenilworth, and the price.   It is noted that the brewing of Oxford and Coventry may serve for the other places, but the wines of all sorts must come from London.   Yet " if the ale of the country will not please the Queen, then it must come from London or else a brewer to brew the same in the towns near."

The provision of fireworks at Kenilworth was of a most entertaining kind.   A contractor undertook for £50 to give a most varied entertainment in fire—the first night in the meadow, with serpents of fire and " eight or ten pots of wonderful and pleasing things," birds flying and cats and dogs fighting ; the second, in the courtyard a fountain throwing wine, water, and fire for seven or eight hours continuously, and other things ; the third in the river (moat), " a dragon as big as an ox which will fly twice or thrice as high as the tower of S. Paul's, and at that height will burn away, and suddenly will issue from its whole body dogs cats and birds which will scatter fire on all sides."   This was the project of an Italian artist.

On Saturday, July 9, the Queen arrived, in one of those scenes of mingled pomp and fancy which were her delight.   Leicester received her with ostentatious devotion, and entertained her for seventeen days, " with excessive cost," says Dugdale, " and Variety of delightfull Shows as may be seen at large in a special Discourse thereof then printed and entituled ' The Princely Pleasures of Kenilworth Castle,' having at her first entrance a floating stand upon the Pool, bright blazing with Torches, upon which were, clad in Silks, the Lady of the Lake and two Nymphs waiting on her, who made a Speech to the Q. in Meeter of the Antiquity & Owners of that Castle, which was closed with Cornets, & other loud Musick.   Within the Base-Court was there a very goodly Bridge set up of xx Foot wide, & lxx Foot long, over which the Queen did pass, on each side whereof were Posts erected, with Presents upon them unto her, by the Gods, viz., a Cage of Wild-Fowl, by Silvanus ; sundry Sorts of rare Fruits, by Pomona ; of Corn, by Ceres ; of Wine, by Bacchus ; of Sea-Fish, by Neptune ; of all Habiliments of War, by Mars ; & of

Musical Instruments, by Phœbus. And for the several Dayes of her Stay, various and rare Shews & Sports were there exercised, *viz.*, in the CHASE a Savage Man, with Satyrs ; Bear-Baitings, Fire-Works, Italian Tumblers, a Country Brideale, with running at the Quintin, & Morrice-Dancing. And, that there might be nothing wanting that these Parts could afford, hither came the Coventre-Men, & acted the antient Play, long since used in that City, called HOCKS-TUESDAY, setting forth the Destruction of the Danes in King Ethelred's Time ; with which the Queen was so pleased, that she gave them a Brace of Bucks, & five Marks in Money to bear the Charges of a Feast.

" Besides all this, he had upon the Pool a Triton riding on a Mermaid 18 Foot long ; as also Arion on a Dolphin, with rare Musick. And to honour this Entertainment the more, there were then Knighted here, Sir Thomas Cecill, Son and Heir to the Lord Treasurer ; Sir Henry Cobham, Brother to the Lord Cobham ; Sir Francis Stanhope, & Sir Tho. Tresham. The Cost & Expense whereof may be guest at by the Quantity of Beer then drunk, which amounted to 320 Hogsheads of the ordinary Sort, as I have credibly heard. Shortly after which, *viz.*, the next ensuing Year he obtained, by the Grants of the said Q. a weekly MERCATE here upon the Wednesday, with a FAIRE yearly on Midsummer-Day."

Of the dramatic entertainments charming memorials remain in those " Masques performed before Queen Elizabeth, from a coeval copy, in a volume of manuscript collections, by Henry Ferrers, Esquire, of Baddesley Clinton, in the County of Warwick," and printed in 1820, for though they are largely concerned with Sir Harry Lee, it seems likely from their association with the great Warwickshire antiquary that they had been played in this county too. The motto for them which Mr. Hamper who published them chose is the very fit one from Oxford's commemorative verses when the great Queen died—" Sol mundi Borealis erat, dum vixit, Eliza."

So, indeed, she was in the Kenilworth firmament. And after her going the glory of the castle insensibly melted away. Robert Dudley had some more years of bravery and fame. His wife Amy had been made away with in 1560 ; in 1573 he had married Lady Sheffield and " pretending a fear of the Queen's indignation in case it should come to her knowledge, made her vow not to reveal it till he gave Leave,"and in 1578 he married Lettice

Knollys, Countess of Essex. After campaigns and intrigues he died, with every suspicion of poison, at Cornbury—you may still see the room he died in—in 1588. His brother Ambrose succeeded him, and was eventfully good. He died in 1590. Then came Sir Robert Dudley, the son of the famous Earl and Lady Sheffield, who was never publicly acknowledged as legitimate, yet claimed the title. His father's widow made a Star Chamber matter of it; her proceedings were stopped, and he had to travel abroad. He left his wife, Alice Leigh (whose praise is in nearly all the churches of Warwick and some of London), repudiated her in 1605, took to himself another lady, became a Duke of the Holy Roman Empire, wrote on naval

Kenilworth Castle in 1656.   [E. H. N. after Hollar.

architecture, and died in 1649, a ruffian and a clever rogue. Prince Henry, James I.'s son, had bought his rights in Kenilworth, and Charles paid again for them to his widow. James stayed there in 1617, Charles in 1643 and 1644. In the Civil War it was destroyed, dismantled, disparked, drained, and a ruin it has remained to this day. The ownership was granted by Charles II. to Lawrence Hyde, Earl of Rochester. His son succeeded to the title of Clarendon, and the property has followed that title to this day. But for the Wizard of the North it might well have been forgotten. But the revival of English enthusiasm for the heart of England has caught it up into fame again, and we may even link it with Shakespeare. He may well have seen Elizabeth there in 1575, as a boy of eleven, for all the

county was gathered together to do her honour and to gape at
the fine shows. May be the water pageant and the other
fantasies were in his mind when he made Oberon see

" Flying between the cold moon and the earth
Cupid all arm'd,"

and his fiery shaft

" Quench'd in the chaste beams of the watery moon."

It is only an idle fancy that links his thoughts of the imperial
votaries with this Warwickshire castle. Kenilworth has certain
memories enough, but Shakespeare is not one of them.

Now from Kenilworth I propose to take you to Stoneleigh.
The way is not a very easy one, and I do not propose to describe
it. You must use your map and your ears, and it is quite
possible that both will deceive you. But somehow you will get
there, and before that you will have turned to your great
Warwickshire book to read all about this ancient famous place.

Of Stoneleigh Dugdale says that it is " situat on the north
bank of the Sow, a little below the joyning of Kenilworth water
therewith," and that it is " a very spacious parish and con-
taineth many pretty hamlets and places of note." These places
one may now ignore, unless it be to hunt for them upon the map ;
let us confine ourselves to the Abbey, the Church, and the Village.
The manor was of the royal demesne, and it had interesting
customs and tenants, of which there is much interesting record
at the time of the Dissolution of the Monasteries. It had " within
the Precincts of it two Houses, and several Tenants called *Soke-*
manns, who paid their Suit at his three Weeks Court, kept upon
Motstow-hill, each Tenant holding a Yard-Land, and paying
yearly thirty Pence." And there were four bondmen who held
their land by the service of making the gallows and hanging of
thieves, " every one of which bondmen was to wear a red clout
betwixt his shoulders and upon his upper garment," besides his
ordinary duty to plough and reap.

The foundation of the abbey, Dugdale tells, came from Queen
Matilda (once Roman Empress) who gave to a number of would-
be Cistercians land and a settlement at Redmore in Staffordshire, where he tells " what molestation they had by the Foresters, who, riding frequently that way, much disturbed their
Devotions," and were " not only troublesome but by their
frequent visits somewhat burthensome also." Henry II., at

their petition, transferred them to Stoneleigh, where the first
stone of their church was laid in the very year of his accession.
It was consecrated by Walter, Bishop of Coventry, on the express
condition that the Abbey should not interfere with the parochial rights. With the King's foresters in Arden the monks
had many a disagreement, but benefactions flowed in to them,
from royal officials like Stephen Segrave, and evil men like
Robert de Broc (whose name be abhorred by all who read of
S. Thomas of Canterbury), as well as those who stole from
neither lay folk nor clerks, and the Abbey grew rich. The

In Stoneleigh Deer Park.

history of the house was chequered like that of any other monastery. It had an abbat who was given legatine authority in
Wales, but accused in that " he countenanced a shepherd belonging to the monastery to fight a Duell and to hang a thief that
had privately taken away some cattle." He was William of
Guildford. Robert of Hockley was one who greatly enriched
the abbey buildings. Thomas de Pipe, though he kept records
so well as to delight Dugdale, was charged, in the time of King
Edward III., with the support of a lady named Isabel Benshall,
and of his and her children " which were more in number than

the monks then in the Convent." At the Dissolution its revenues were £200 a year, and it was more in debt than any other religious house in the Shire. Its lands were given to Charles Brandon, Duke of Suffolk, and passed before long to the Leighs, to whom they still belong. The Gatehouse of the Abbey still remains, deserving Dugdale's description as a "fair and strong building." Most of the other buildings have been destroyed, but the south aisle of the chapel and part of the south transept

Stoneleigh Abbey Gatehouse.

remained, translated to secular and domestic use, while the chapter house and the abbat's lodging " are converted into domestic offices." The south aisle has become a fine corridor, extending from the north door (and several of the old Norman doorways remain) to the entrance hall of the fine eighteenth century building which forms the greater part of the modern residence. This was built in 1720. It is a house at once charming and impressive. If one can forgive the destruction of so much of the old abbey and the transmogrifying of the rest, the turning of the chapter house into a servant's room, the gabled roofs and mullioned windows which in James I.'s day were added to the old buildings, one may be happy in the lofty rooms and among the beautiful pictures and the delightful china, which belong *par excellence* to the Leighs. Not that the family who now own Stoneleigh are of mushroom growth. Very far from it. Not many houses, even in Warwickshire, have been held continuously by the same family since Elizabeth's day, and that is what has happened here. Sir Thomas Leigh, who was Lord Mayor of London in the year of Queen Elizabeth's accession, was of the great Cheshire family of High Leigh, which has its ramifications in so many parts of England (as in Gloucestershire, at the charming manor house of Broadwell near Moreton-in-the-Marsh, just beyond the other end of our Shakespeare country). Dugdale tells the story of his success, and the extension of his family's estates with a note of cheerful satisfaction. Sir Thomas himself, knighted by Queen Elizabeth, was "bred up" under Sir Rowland Hill, "an opulent merchant of London," and "became at length, for his Skill and Diligence, his Factor beyond sea," and so like all industrious apprentices married his master's daughter—in this case, for there was no daughter, his niece. He died in good age and fame and wealth, and his second son, Thomas, knighted by Queen Elizabeth, "and honoured with the Title of Baronet at the first creation of that Order," married Jane, daughter of Sir John Spencer, of Wormleighton. He survived his son, Sir John; "and having lived to a great Age in much Reputation, being Custos Rotulorum for this County, and, in all publique employments of his time, one of the Superior Rank," died in 1626. His grandson, Sir Thomas, his immediate successor, was knighted by James I., "and firmly adhering to the late King Charles, in his greatest Distresses, was, in Testimony of his stedfast Loyalty, advanced to the Degree and Title of a Baron of this Realm." So Dugdale. The history of the family since then is equally interesting and honourable, and it is very happily presented to us in portraits by Lely and Kneller, as in those fine pictures, once attributed to Holbein (1497–1543), of Sir Thomas Leigh aged seventy (he died in 1572) and his wife, and in the faces of many great personages with whom the family has been connected—the Wentworths and Watsons, the Egertons, the Turners (Sir Edward Turner, of Ambrosden, 1719–66, was a notable patron and friend

C C 2

Stoneleigh Abbey.

of the Warwickshire antiquary and architect, Sanderson Miller), Alice Duchess Dudley, and the first Lord Leigh himself " who entertained King Charles I. when his rebellious subjects of Coventry refused to open their gates to him." It is a long, loyal, and honourable record. And the splendid library, famous so long for the four Folio Shakespeare's, and the portrait and relics of Byron, show that literature, as well as public service, has formed the characters of the Leighs.

The park, in which Stoneleigh Abbey is situated, is a charming one, with its fine trees and the Avon flowing through it. In front of the house the river becomes a lake, and then contracts again, falls down a weir and makes rapids for itself over the shallows. The road crosses a very fine medieval bridge, of red sandstone, no doubt the work of the Cistercians. If you make the circuit of the park and return from the village having the house and park to the right, you will see to your left another park—for Stoneleigh has two—in which the deer live ; and this bridge it is that stands betwixt the two. It is here, when you have left Bubbenhall, with its old mill below, that the Avon becomes at last a river. The deer come down to drink in the stream, accustomed to men, though thus in Arden they are " exempt from public haunt," and you forget how near you are to the crowded centres of England's life. You forget it, too, in the village itself. Here is one of the most beautiful of all Warwickshire's smaller houses, of brick and rough cast and black wood, with stone buildings at the west end, fine chimneys, three gables, which perhaps Mr. Metters will show you, and within the beautiful oak-panelled room looking on the road. There you may see a relic of the time of alarm a century ago when Warwickshire had its yeomanry ready to fight against the French, for they preserve the shako with the badge " Loyal Stoneleigh." The house looks across a narrow road on to meads that slope down to the river Sowe, and from the churchyard it shows its best front beautifully. Till a few years ago it was smothered (as they would say here) in ivy, and its exquisite decoration was unseen ; now only roses cover part of the front with delicate, fragrant tracery.

Now we are close to the beautiful church of Stoneleigh. It has a good western tower, nave with south aisle and vestry, and a mortuary chapel for the Leighs at the north. The original church was Norman, and of it the north door, the lower

part of the tower, and the chancel remain, a good deal restored ;
the most interesting relic of these early times are the tympanum
of the north door, with its fishes and strange beasts, and the
font with the twelve apostles under " Lombardic " arches,
a very fine piece of early sculpture.   The rest of the church is
good Decorated work, but all has been tremendously destroyed,

Stoneleigh Church.

the penalty of belonging to a parish where the landowners are
rich and generous. You might take the church nowadays for
a mere memorial to the great, were your unkindly thoughts not
rebuked by the standing witness of this inscription.   " To the
memory of Humphrey How, Porter to the Rt. Honble. the
Lord Leigh, ob : 6 : ffebr : An. Dom. 1688, aetat 63.

" Here lyes a Faithful Friend unto the Poore
Who dealt Large Almes out of his Lord'ps Stor
Weep not Poore People tho ye Seruants Dead
The Lord himself will give you Dayly Breade.
If Markets Rise Raile not against theire Rates
The Price is still the same at Stoneleigh Gates."

The great tomb, and the most interesting historical memorial
in the church, is that to the north of the altar, where the only
English woman ever created a duchess in her own right lies as
on a bed with her daughter lying a tier below her.

The Duchess Dudley was perhaps the most famous, certainly
the most generous, woman in England in the ninety years of her
long life. She was the daughter of Sir Thomas Leigh and (I
suppose) great aunt of the first Lord. Her husband was that
Robert Dudley, son of the famous Earl of Leicester whose
matrimonial proceedings were a scandal to the world, but made
no difference to his Italian career, when he was made Earl of
Warwick and Duke of Northumberland in the Holy Roman
Empire. He repudiated her in 1605, to live with Elizabeth
Southwell, and she devoted herself to good works and the support
of the cause of Charles I., by whom she was created a duchess
in 1645. She is a lady whose biography ought certainly to be
written. And her tomb is worthy of her. She is represented,
in white marble, wearing what I suppose to be her shroud, but
with her long serious face uncovered. A tier below her lies
her daughter, who died forty-eight years before her. Alice
herself survived to the age of ninety, and died January 22, 1669.
The sarcophagi, on which the bodies rest, are of black marble ;
and over all depends, from Ionic columns, the decent drapery
of a tester bed. It is very impressive and edifying, and was
erected, it seems, some while before the great lady herself died,
by Nicholas Stone, that great master of the art of tomb-making,
who died as early as 1649. When Dugdale drew the tomb
there was no inscription on it. Other monuments in the
church are good ; and there is a large Leigh mausoleum ; but
nothing equals the glory of Duchess Dudley. A fourteenth
century tomb has an effigy in grey stone of a priest in chasuble
and alb. And the alabaster monument to Chandos, Lord Leigh,
1850, should be observed. And so out into the air, and
remember that Stoneleigh has never ceased to send forth its
sons into the great world, and that Sir Henry Parkes, maker of
Empire, will not be the last of them.

CHAPTER XXI

FROM KENILWORTH TO COVENTRY, AND FROM COVENTRY TO COMBE ABBEY

THE road from Kenilworth to Coventry, which is five miles away, is one of the most beautiful in Warwickshire. About two miles from Kenilworth is Gibbet Hill, on the left, where of old the criminals hung in chains. It is a hundred feet higher here, but again you drop fifty feet or more ; and all the way it is a most delightful avenue, with a broad sweep of grass on either side. From here the road is so straight that you can see the next mile stone, and the distance looks but half what it is—and yet, says a writer at the beginning of the nineteenth century, " on approaching Coventry, so much does the same road wind about, that the spires of that ancient city are seen at one moment on the right, and at another on the left." He adds—and the passage is worth quoting for its resemblance and contrast to-day as well as for its information—" The road from Stoneleigh and Bagington falls into this, at the Toll-gate, beyond which, from the summit of a gentle rise, Coventry appears to view, with its crowded buildings and numerous spires and towers, displayed in nearly its whole extent from east to west. The last four miles of this road are shaded, on each side, by a fine plantation of young and flourishing trees, forming an avenue, much in the style, it has been remarked, of those of France, Flanders, and Germany." So those trees, which are at their perfection to-day, are not much more than a century old. They certainly do not remind one of the poplars of the modern French roads. But still there is something that reminds one of France in this way-faring, if it be but of the very fine saying of a French writer, which I think of when I wonder how Shakespeare went along

that Coventry road, where his mind's eye saw Sir John Falstaff ;
a very different manner of voyaging from that which we affect
in our hasty foolishness by the motor car or even the bicycle :—
"Je ne conçois qu'une manière de voyager plus agréable que
d'aller à cheval, c'est d'aller à pied. On part à son moment, on
s'arrête à sa volonté, on fait tant et si peu d'exercice qu'on veut.
Quand on ne veut qu'arriver, on peut courir en chaise de poste ;
mais quand on veut voyager, il faut aller à pied."

That is the very truth about the road from Kenilworth to
Coventry. It has beauties all the way and you do not see them
unless you loiter on your legs. There are fascinating byways
you may take at every half mile. You may turn to the right
and go backwards to Stoneleigh, or look at Bagington (and
remember that Richard II.'s Bagot is buried in this church, even
if you forget its notoriety in Stewart times), or Einham Park ;
or a little further on go into Stivichall, and think how it is altered
since Mr. West wrote of it in 1830, "the ancient church (a
member of S. Michael's, Coventry) was taken down and a
handsome one has recently been built under the auspices of
Mr. Gregory, who has a fine mansion very near it. This
substantial-stone building was erected by Francis Gregory, Esq.,
father of the present owner, who has lately improved it with an
additional wing. An anchorite fixed his melancholy abode
at Stivichall, in the time of Henry VI." There would be no
home for an anchorite now, and little melancholy either, I hope.
But Stivichall is not alone in this respect.

Among the hamlets round Coventry, "pretty villages and
places of note that environ it," named by Dugdale, which the
encroaching city has long swallowed up, was one, to the south
it seems, named Olney, of which already in his time was there,
"no memorial now left but a double moat which beareth the
name." It is there very likely, as Mr. Laurence Stratford in
his fascinating Life of Edward IV. argues, that the Yorkist king
was captured by the Earl of Warwick in July 1469. So Waurin
and the Crowland monk seem to suggest, but indeed the place
may have been Honiley, between Warwick and Coventry,
though I do not find Honiley called Olney. The historical
associations of the whole district seem to come to a focus when
one nears Coventry. It is difficult to begin early enough or
end late enough to satisfy the antiquary's enthusiasm here.

We cannot however go back, with Drayton, to the eleven

thousand virgins of Cologne for colonists of Coventry, or find much history in the fragments of Roman pavement that have not long ago been discovered. Dugdale tells us of a sack by the Northmen of Cnut in 1016. Later in the eleventh century the continuous history of the town—a city, surely, for once it was a bishopric and may be again—begins with the foundation, by Leofric, Earl of Mercia, and his wife Godgifu, of a house for an abbat and twenty-four monks under the Benedictine rule, in 1043. They had the usual grant of sac and soc, tol and theam, and the rest, with liberty for the monks to elect their own abbat; privileges confirmed by William Conqueror. Of the fine conventual church, later a cathedral, not a stone remains. The only thing which pretends to survive from that day is the legend of Godgifu's ride, and that does not appear before the thirteenth century. Leofric, it is said, was always heavily taxing his folk of Coventry, and one day he told his wife (now Latinised into Godiva) that he would take off a heavy exaction if she would ride naked through the streets. She did so, covered only by her flowing hair; all the people shut their shutters up till she had gone by; only one " peeping Tom " (a later addition to the legend—late itself) looked and was struck blind. You may see his figure looking out of a window at the north of the King's Head; but it is only a soldier of Henry VII.'s time in fantastic armour. The legend preserved the fame of Coventry when foolish people forgot its great history; so we may forgive it. The seventeenth century gave it much embellishment, and Tennyson in the nineteenth made poetry of it. So it may rest.

More authentic history is to follow. The growth of the abbey, its riches, its disputes with the bishop. From 1095, for a century, there were Bishops of Coventry; then the See was united to Lichfield, and so remained till 1836. Hugh of Nunant (1188–98) had mighty fights with his monks, and they eventually conquered him. Then the abbey flourished, and we need not concern ourselves with its history. Fragments of its buildings remain by S. Michael's Churchyard, and of its woodwork in an inn called the Palmer's Rest in Ironmonger Row. Two other features of the medieval life of the city must be remembered, the overlordship of the Earls of Chester (of which part of the old Cheylesmore Manor house, in the south-east, contains some relics in stone) and the great trading period, when the Guilds of Coventry were among the foremost in the kingdom. By the end of the thirteenth century the Gild Merchant had won victories over both the lay and ecclesiastical lords, and in the Parliament of 1295 two of its burghers attended. The story, in fact, is too long and too important to summarise. It must be read in the history of England. Its visible presentment remains in the grand hall of S. Mary, the possession of the Guild of S. Mary (founded

Peeping Tom.

in 1340). Here, as so often elsewhere, the guilds and the corporation became practically identical. S. Mary's Hall from 1388 was the " hôtel de ville." Eventually the government became a sort of Venetian oligarchy. The mayor and his council of forty-eight, from 1423, ruled supreme. But the crown, in the person of the queens, as owners of the manor of Cheylesmore from 1327, kept a watchful eye on the city, and paid it many

S. Mary's Hall, Coventry.

a visit. The most memorable sojourn, perhaps, was that of Richard II. in 1397, when the combat between Henry of Lan_caster and Mowbray took place on Gosford Green. It is one of the strongest links between the new and the old Coventry that Gosford Green still exists and has not been built over. You might have a combat there to-day. There are two special memories of the Middle Age which must be mentioned. The first is the persistence of Wycliffe's influence—Lutterworth is not far off—and the number of Lollards who crop up in the annals of Coventry from time to time; the other the story, almost certainly apocryphal, that Prince Hal, afterwards Henry V., was arrested by John Hornby, mayor in 1412; what did happen is that in that same year the citizens of Coventry lent that prince £100. What a fine story you can make out of that; only you must make it up yourself, and you must not say that the prince was ever arrested or that he dismissed Gascoigne, C. J. when he came to the throne, for both statements are untrue. The Gascoignes lived at Oversley (under Arrow) and Henry V. was popular in Coventry, where he had a magnificent reception, in 1421, with his French queen, each receiving £100 and a cup of gold. During the Wars of the Roses this attachment remained still the perquisite of the Lancastrian house. Henry VI.'s wife made Coventry her chief resort, her " secret harbour " ; but the citizens did not hesitate, as citizens will, to turn a favourable eye later to the winning side. The Leet book shows that in the time of his prosperity Henry VI. was most loyally welcomed by " Richard Boys and his worthy brethren arrayed in scarlet, and all the commonalty clad in green gowns and red hoods." He stayed till Michaelmas, when he departed to Kenilworth, having told the citizens that they were the best ruled people within his realm. For years Coventry was the centre of public life. There Henry and his wife were greeted with pageants and plays; there York and Warwick swore to keep the King's peace which yet they were plotting to destroy ; there a great Council was held in 1457 ; there the queen saw the mystery plays performed ; and then very swiftly you find the town has turned its coat, is thanked by Edward IV. for its loyalty to him, and sends a hundred men with him " to the felde yn the north." When Edward was king he came often to the town, notably at Christmas, 1467 ; yet two years later when their neighbour Warwick the kingmaker was of Henry VI.'s side they turned over with him. Edward was captured at Honiley, and Lord Rivers, his father-in-law, with his son John Wydville, were beheaded on Gosford Green. Again they turned, and refused Edward, King Henry's son, aid, because they saw that Edward of York would win ; and so he did, and they were forgiven. Poor little Edward V., when four years old, as Prince of Wales, spent S. George's Day, 1474, in the city, and was received to the strains of the harp, the dulcimer, and the lute, and in 1478 he stayed some weeks at Cheylesmore, and became a member of the Guild of Holy Trinity and Corpus Christi. Richard III. visited the town in 1485, and so did Henry VII. after Bosworth field. Under Henry VIII. the city was heavily taxed, and the destruction of the great religious house, followed by the dissolution of the Guilds reduced the citizens almost to ruin. Dugdale says, from the letter of Protector Somerset, that when this had been accomplished there were " not more than three thousand inhabitants, whereas within memory there had been fifteen thousand." Miss Mary Dormer Harris has rightly pointed out that it was the destruction of the gilds which was the chief cause of this depopulation. The old system of insurance was utterly destroyed. At last the citizens were allowed to buy back the gild lands, and the town started again on a career of less abundant prosperity. It was now disturbed by the religious troubles of the time.

It had long been a home of religious bigotry. Sir Thomas More's record of his visit to Coventry, and the religious squabble there, is well known. It reminds one of the *Epistolae Obscurorum Virorum* in its picture of obscurantism. He had occasion, he tells, to go to the city, to see a sister of his there, and had scarce alighted from his horse when one proposed to him the question " whether he that said over the Psalter of the Blessed Virgin daily can possibly be damned " He laughed at the silly question, but it pursued him throughout his visit. A holy friar, it seemed, and one most learned, had preached that such could not be damned ; and before More had sat down to supper he came, with great tomes carried for him by a boy, to prove it. The argument continued all supper time, the friar barking out matter enough for two sermons ; and More was forced to argue at length that no books, nor miracles either, could prove such an absurdity. " For though you may easily find a prince, who, at the entreaties of his mother, may sometimes forgive his enemies somewhat ; yet there is no prince so foolish as to make a law promising impunity to traitors that shall perform some certain offices to his mother, thereby to make them the more audacious against him." Truly, the Rosary had no miraculous effect; and those who were so foolish in disturbing all Coventry by such an absurdity, in spite of all the bishop could do to stop them, were such as made Erasmus justly attack the danger of ignorance in the Church. No more to blame was Erasmus for such plain speaking than was S. Jerome for his. It is an interesting letter ; but perhaps what it most makes us inquire to-day is, where did More's sister—probably Mistress Stafferton—reside ? To that there is no answer.

No doubt the exaggerations of obscurantist friars give fuel to the Lollardy which revived under Edward VI. and Mary. Among the insurrections at the accession of Queen Mary not the least formidable was that of the Duke of Suffolk, the father of " Queen Jane." He believed that the citizens of Coventry, always a stronghold of Lollardy, would help him. But his agent Rampton could not win support, and one Burdet (a familiar Warwickshire name) was with him ; but they failed utterly. The citizens shut the gates upon him ; and the whole attempt proved but a pretence. Says Dr. Gairdner, in the last volume of his *Lollardy and the Reformation* (iv. 255) :—

" A pretence it certainly was, as Rampton called it ; for it was not an ill-founded fear of foreigners, but a deep seated hatred of the Mass to which the Duke trusted for his chief support in Coventry ; and it was because he sympathised with that feeling that ' Protestants ' in Coventry found that ' only my lord's grace did cleave and stick to God's truth.' That was an enviable distinction for the harsh father of Lady Jane Grey—a man with as little parental feeling as loyalty to his sovereign. He tried to raise civil war by a ' pretence,' to be financed by a religious faction ; but his attempt had proved a failure."

Suffolk himself was found in a hollow tree at Astley, his park near Arbury, betrayed, it was said, by one of his men, and he suffered as a traitor. Then the burnings began, and in 1556 Laurence Saunders and Robert Groves suffered for their Protestantism in the Little Park.

Queen Elizabeth visited the city in 1565, " being lodged at Mr. Hales's in the Whitefriars "—of which the east wing of the cloister, and a window, still called hers, remain. Mary of Scots was a prisoner for a few days in 1569, first at the Bull Inn, then in S. Mary's Hall. In 1605 the Princess Elizabeth, James I.'s daughter, was brought from Combe Abbey, at the time of the powder plot, to Coventry for safety, and the beautiful house in which she stayed still exists in Earl Street. Coventry indeed was ever anti-Romanist. It was also, for a time at least, anti-Royalist, for it refused entrance to Charles I. just before the Civil War began, an act for which Charles II. took vengeance by levelling its ancient walls. The last royal visits was one of James II. who touched for the King's evil in S. Michael's Church, and one of William III. in 1690. In 1798 George, Prince of Wales, sold the Manor of Cheylesmore to Lord Hertford, and its park was soon sold for building. The revival of Coventry, owing to the cycle and motor trade, and its immense increase, belongs to quite modern days. Long may its prosperity endure.

We may now enter the city, full of ancient memories. There are few towns which at the centre of modern business retain so much of what is ancient. One custom, as I learnt so long ago as 1883, indeed survives, which shows that it is not only old churches and houses and halls which recall an unbroken history. " To this day animals are slaughtered in the open street known as Butcher Row, and that thoroughfare, with the ancient channel in the middle of the roadway, still runs with blood every Thursday, during the hours allotted to slaughter by old Charter, not yet superseded by Acts of Parliament." (I quote from the *Oxford Times* account of our expedition on June 2, 1883. Is it still true ?) It is an idle and foolish form of praise, which one so often hears, that such or such an English city is " quite like a foreign town." Yet there is a certain truth in the thought at Coventry. Not that the buildings are not thoroughly English, whether they be domestic or ecclesiastical, but that to find in the very centre of a busy working town what one finds at Coventry is rare in England. The narrow streets, twisting every way, yet converging on the great open space where stand the two magnificent churches, and, again, the great wide street westwards of the churches where all the business of the town seems to converge, have an unusual appearance. It is not often that in a modern English town so much has been allowed to survive that is good.

The town has changed enormously within the last twenty years, since the rise of the cycle industry ; or it might be more true to say has increased enormously without the core of it being much touched. In 1815 " W. F. " wrote, in his book on Warwick, that its general appearance was " that of an old, irregular, ill-built town ; with houses so crowded, as almost to exclude the light and the air ; and with streets so narrow as scarcely to be passed with safety. Yet, to the lover of architectural antiquities, a walk through the city will be highly interesting. In every direction he will see houses stampt with the venerable marks of age, exhibiting specimens of the different styles that prevailed in different past eras ; and in the religious, and other edifices, he will find objects to excite, in a high degree, and to gratify his curiosity. It must be added that the modern houses are many of them spacious and handsome ; that the spirit of public improvement, long dead or dormant, in this city, has lately been aroused into life and action ; and that an important and extensive plan of opening and widening some of the streets has been already, in part, carried into execution."

The language sounds still and quaint to us now but the facts it sets forth have repeated themselves and the description might be employed for Coventry to-day. It is through one of these broad openings that we now approach the city. It may well be that we go with Drayton's lines in our mind :—

> " Now flourishing with fanes and proud pyramides,
> Her walls in good repair, her ports so bravely built,
> Her halls in good estate, her cross so richly gilt,
> As scorning all the Towns that stand within her view."

Coventry has abated no whit of her pride in these long centuries, and still the " pyramides " remain. Dugdale's record of her cannot be obliterated. She is " remarkable for antiquity, charters, rights and privileges, and favours shown by monarchs." Let us see the city as she stands to-day.

Most travellers, the wise ones certainly, arrive by the Warwick road, that is, the road from Kenilworth which we have traversed. And if they travel humbly by train they come at once into the same wide street, one of the main arteries of the city. At once you will see the three tall spires, the city's glory. Reserve them for a moment, and look at the site and remains of Cheylesmore manor-house. (Remember, if you cannot find it, to ask for " Chylesmore," for that is how it is pronounced.) Then go (if

D D

from the station, along Eaton road) left till you come to the
Greyfriars' Green.   Here is the statue of Sir Thomas White,
the Lord Mayor who did so much to preserve London for Queen
Mary, who founded S. John Baptist College at Oxford and
endowed it with scholarships for boys from Coventry school.
The College still retains a little property in the city from his
gift.   Here on the Greyfriars Green was for long held the city
fair, under charter of Henry III., 1218, which was only abolished
in 1858, at the meddlesome and grandmotherly period of English

Coventry Spires.

history.   A little farther on is the first of the three tall spires.
It is all that remains of the Franciscan convent, built, in the
fourteenth century, from the quarry at Cheylesmore.   The
convent stood, as always with the settlements of the mendi-
cants, just outside the city walls, where sprang up the wooden
huts of the poor settlers who came to benefit by the neighbourhood of the towns without falling under the power of their
strict regulations.   The earlier edifice made way for the stately
tower and spire built with stone from the grant of Edward the
Black Prince, who gave them also " liberty to have a postern

into the park to carry out any of their convent that should be diseased." Nothing of the ancient house survives beyond this fine spire, 204 feet high, and even that, with its tower, has largely suffered from the restoration by Rickman in 1832. It was here that the most famous of the Coventry plays were acted, "with mighty State and Reverence," says Dugdale, "by the Friars of this House," and "had Theatres for the several scenes, very large and high, placed upon wheels and drawn to all the eminent parts of the City, for the better advantage of the spectators." Henry VII. and Elizabeth of York saw the Greyfriars act their plays in 1452. Attached to the ancient tower and spire is the modern church, which was built on what had long been a vacant site where pigs had been kept, in "the tallest pig stye in Europe." It is a curious example of how the architects of William IV.'s day thought they could copy the builders of the Middle Age.

You may now go up Warwick Lane, one of the old streets, and pass the Grapes inn, a charming building of black and white, spotlessly clean as an inn should be, with a beautiful court inside. Then you come to Ford's Hospital, another and more splendid building of black and white timber, founded in 1529 by the will of William Ford, a merchant of the city. It is a beautiful and elaborate piece of Tudor building, not to be surpassed in its kind anywhere in England, I think. Therein dwell seventeen poor old women, and, indeed, they have fine windows to look out upon their neighbours from. Each has nine lights, divided into triplets, with headpieces most exquisitely carved. The courtyard is a haven of repose indeed, where nothing brings one nearer to to-day than the time of Harry Eighth. Now follow straight on and you find yourself at the corner of High Street, whence if you go right, that is east, again, you come to Earl Street (*see* p. 416), and eventually to Gosford Street and Green. But you may here cross the street, going onwards down Pepper Lane, modern in its houses but ancient in its crookedness, till you come to S. Michael's Churchyard, and you see before you the finest part of ancient Coventry. It may be best before you go in, to walk to the south, where at the corner you will find a very pleasant little antique shop, which looks as if it were still in Elizabeth's time, or earlier, kept by the very pleasant verger of S. Michael's, till you see the entrance to the great S. Mary's Hall. One soon begins to

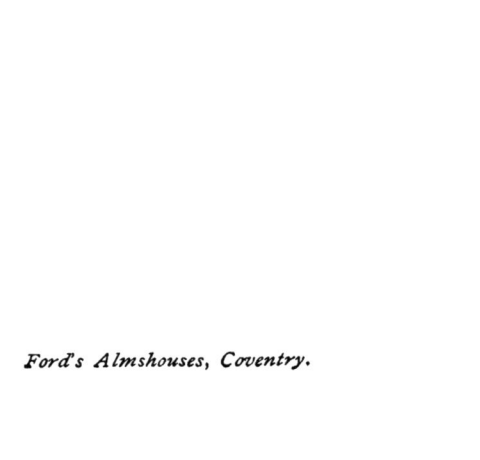

Ford's Almshouses, Coventry.

exhaust the terms of eulogy in regard to the domestic architecture of Coventry, so let this fine hall take rank at once among the finest municipal buildings of the fifteenth century. It was the hall of the Guilds of the Holy Trinity and our Lady, in which were merged those of S. John Baptist and S. Catherine. The first thing you notice, to the right of the large late Early English or Decorated doorway, is the magnificent north window of nine lights, the lower part filled with masonry, the upper very richly decorated. Leaving this to your right you enter into the fine courtyard, where the tall buildings crowd round you, and the sun must only find full entrance at midday. Leaving the porch you turn back to see the carving of the Coronation of the B.V.M. on the keystone, and on the impost of the inner arch, projecting, the Annunciation. At the east of the porch is a large room once a chapel. Then on the south is the kitchen, still used, originally the hall of the Gild Merchant. It has four huge chimneys and a louvre, and a statue said to be of Henry VI. It is of the mid-fourteenth century, and the initials ɪ. P. belong to John Percy, a benefactor of that period. Go then to the muniment room where the ancient charters are admirably kept, and you may see Elizabeth's letter ordering the safe keeping of Mary of Scots.

Next you ascend the fine, broad stairs to the Mayoress's parlour, which has a noble ribbed ceiling, and a fine stone fireplace. Here is kept the ancient chair, in which the Mayor still sits on great occasions, ornamented with the arms of the city (the familiar Elephant and Castle). Of the pictures you may note one of the many of Sir Thomas White, painted for the cities to which he bequeathed educational endowments, after his death, and by a tradition among the chief heirs of his bounty said to be taken from his sister, a lady of severe countenance; whose authentic portrait remains at S. John's College in Oxford, one of John Hales, the founder of the Grammar School; and a very fine portrait, said to be, but most certainly not, of Queen Mary I, and dated 1573. Now to the great hall, approached at the north from the Mayoress's parlour on to the daïs, or at the south by a flight of steps from the kitchen below. This is the scene of much of the history of the city.[1] It contains a fine

[1] See, for an excellent account of the city, M. D. Harris' *Coventry* (*Medieval Towns*), which I have had constantly at hand and found most useful.

collection of armour, mostly Elizabethan, but including a helmet
of the late fifteenth century with a slit for air and vision.   Look
now, if not before, at the details of the splendid dark oak roof,
the beams decorated with fine figures of angels.   And then
rejoice in the great north window with its glass of the fifteenth
century.   Henry VI. is in the middle, and around him are the
sovereigns who seemed to the artist (probably John Thornton)
to be the heroes of English history, Constantine the Emperor
(born at York), Arthur, the perfect kingly knight, William
Conqueror, Richard Lion-heart, Henry III., giver of Coventry's
charter, Edward III., Henry IV., Henry V., the near ancestor
of the reigning sovereign.   Fine though all this is, and extremely
interesting, the great treasure of the hall is the great piece of
tapestry which hangs over the daïs at the north end of the hall,
under the great window.   It is of the early fifteenth century, and
reminds one at once of the great piece of the same date at Hampton Court.   The design is said to be Flemish, the execution
English, and the object to commemorate the visit of Henry VI.
and Margaret of Anjou to the city in 1457, on perhaps the
admission of Henry VII. and his wife into the Guild of the Holy
Trinity.   At the centre was undoubtedly, at the original making,
a representation of the Holy Trinity, the Father holding our
Lord upon the Cross with the Dove over Him, surrounded (and
this remains) by the emblems of the Passion.   The centre is now
occupied by a figure of Justice. no doubt substituted at the time
of the Reformation.   Below is the Assumption of the B.V.M.,
her feet on the moon, adored by Apostles.   Among the kneeling
figures in the lowest part of the design are, apparently, Henry
VI. and Margaret of Anjou, with Lancaster roses, perhaps
Cardinal Beaufort and Humphrey of Gloucester or (if the portrait
be of Henry VII. and Elizabeth, whom they do not much resemble), Cardinal Morton and Arthur Prince of Wales.   Other
figures may be Margaret Countess of Richmond and the Queen's
children.   The Saints above are the patrons of the Guild, S. John
and S. Catherine, with other saints who may be identified by their
emblems.   Notable is S. Gertrude, patroness of travellers within
that country from whose bourn no traveller returns.   The whole
is worth most attentive examination and comparison with the
glass of the period.   The other glass in the hall, by the way,
belongs to 1826, a curiosity in its way; and the walls have
portraits of royal personages of varying merit.   Other rooms

have still the ancient flavour, in spite of some modern adornments.

After you leave this splendid relic of medieval craftsmanship and city life, you may look for a moment at the Draper's Hall, next beyond S. Mary's, with its large ballroom. And then you will turn to S. Michael's Church, and first you will walk round that masterpiece of the Perpendicular architecture, built in the century following 1371. The tower is about 300 feet high, and no doubt looks higher (as it certainly does) because it springs immediately from the ground without being a necessary part of the adjoining church, which is much broader. The chief decoration of the spire is low down, where it can be seen ; as your eye ascends, it is the size and the grace which attract you, and the four flying buttresses which attach the second tower, from which the spire springs, to the four pinnacles at the corners of the great tower. The steeple itself has undergone very much restoration, and still looks new in consequence. The south porch is the only portion which remains of the Early English thirteenth century church, except some of the lower portions of the walls and the south-west doorway. As for the church, we see tradition gives the name of its munificent builders as Botoner, and adds that a brass plate once recorded their generosity thus :—

> " William and Adam built the tower,
> Ann and Mary built the spire,
> William and Adam built the church,
> Ann and Mary built the quire."

Fine though the outside is—and this can only be appreciated when it is seen from an elevation, such as the top of a house hard by or the roof of the Holy Trinity church to the north-west—the inside, as with all Perpendicular churches, is the real glory of the building ; its size, unbroken by any chancel arch, and width, its light—all one uninterrupted whole, unbroken by transepts, undistracted by side chapels interfering with the main design. Only on each side of the south porch are two excrescences, the Dyers' chapel (now a baptistery) and the Cappers' chapel, east and west of the door ; and at the north the larger chapels of S. Andrew and the Girdlers (the latter now to be specially set apart for the use of the Church of England Men's Society), also not essential parts of the main building in design, yet not detracting from it, though of later date. The east end terminates in an octagonal apse, the sacristy, behind the presbytery. The choir, where the arches are much more pointed, is older than the nave, which no doubt was not long completed when Henry VI. made his much commemorated visit ; and the chancel is much the finer, the space below the windows adding dignity and an appearance of height, while the nave, which is not really so large as it looks from the west end, is not a good specimen of the Perpendicular style, having too much of the less interesting Decorated work about it.   The whole idea of the church, how-ever, is of the rich period of the fifteenth century, the thought one of dignity and splendour, not mystery or severity.   It is the church of the great merchant folk of a rich city.

The nave has six bays ; then comes the step which is the chief separation between nave and chancel.   The chancel is ninety-three feet long, and a few feet less broad than the nave, and it gradually diminishes as you go eastward as well as inclines slightly to the north.   The decoration of the chancel is weak and uninter-esting.   Is it Victorian ?   There is some fine old glass, but jumbled in the northern of the five great east windows.   Thus one insensibly wanders off into detail, when speaking of a church of such huge size.   But detail is just what one should not observe, and is not intended to observe.   The art of the architect was concentrated on the broad effect, the width, length, dignity, the grace of the lofty and comparatively slender pillars which support the clerestory, more decorated in the nave than in the choir ; the rich ribbed roof ; the tie beams supported by carved brackets.   Yet details there are, too, to observe when once the main idea has sunk into your mind.   The tombs, it seems, have all been dis-placed, but much of their beauty remains.   Let us look at the different chapels.   The Lady chapel or Drapers' chapel, the latter name dating from the sixteenth century, has remains of the stair-cases leading to the rood loft.   The screen is an ingenious manu-facture from different parts of the church, and the stalls (with misereres) are excellent work of the fifteenth century.   The brass to the memory of Mr. Thomas Bond Draper, 1506, founder of the Bablake Hospital (p. 414), is now almost illegible.   It is the only pre-Reformation brass left.   There is a small eighteenth century font now kept in the Lady chapel.   Turn then eastwards and look at the good seventeenth century altar, the top resting on pillars, then a broad piece and four legs—a curious construction. Westwards of the Lady chapel is the chapel of S. Laurence, which contains some bad glass and some good monuments, a very charming Latin one of 1648 to a child of nine, and another to Mrs. Bathona Frodsham, the daughter of the (to Coventry "ever-memorable ") John Hales, of whom we have already twice spoken. Then, beyond the main line of the aisle, are the Girdlers' and S. Andrew's chapels—with the black marble altar tomb (with a large mitre—but why ?) of Sir Thomas Berkeley, 1611, and William Stanley, a Coventry man who became Master of the Merchant Taylors' Company, 1640 ; and then, passing by the good fifteenth century chest, we come, in the main north aisle, at the west end, close to the font, to the beautiful sculptured tomb of Julian Nethermyl : " pannarius, quondam maior hujus civitatis, qui obiit xi die mensis Aprilis anno Domini MDXXXIX. et Johanna uxor eius quorum animabus propitietur Deus. Amen." It is a beautiful Renaissance tomb, with charming domestic figures (the Crucifix is, alas, defaced), especially graceful being the group of the merchant's sons. There can be little doubt that there was a school of marble workers at Coventry at this time, from which such fine work came.   There is some work suggestive of it, but rougher, at Fawsley in Northamptonshire.   On the wall is the brass of Mary Hinton (a vicar's wife, 1594) kneeling at a faldstool in a high crowned hat (like that at Ufton, p. 59) with her four dead babies at her feet.   Now cross to the south aisle, and go eastwards to the fine Mercers' chapel, which contains the fine sixteenth century altar tomb of Elizabeth Swillington, erected before her death, for the date has never been filled in, with her two husbands, Ralph Swillington, Attorney-General to Henry VIII., and Recorder of Coventry, and his predecessor, Thomas Essex, Esquire, the former in his robe with chain of office, the latter in armour, with a beard.   Near it is a tomb, much less graceful, of about a hundred years later, and then what is known as Wayd's tomb, which shows nine figures in relief, very good, but much defaced, of the early sixteenth century. Above the Wayd tomb is a brass to a Lady Skeffington, whose husband describes himself as a " true moaneing turtle."   On the wall near the south porch is a brass to Captain Gervase Scrope, 1705, who, in the course of a very long inscription, written in the agony of gout by himself, is described as " an old toss'd Tennis Ball," and says he " was never at quiet till quite dead."   The details of the church are, after all, full of interest.   But the history, which they illustrate, is more interesting still—the rich life of religious citizenship. And that is not over, for now the collegiate church of S. Michael has its staff of canons, with the Bishop of Worcester as dean, and looks forward to be ere long the cathedral church of a new diocese.

If we have hurried over this great church it is because we feel unconsciously the call of the other great church beside it—which in its origin is earlier, and in its interior more beautiful—the Church of the Holy and Undivided Trinity. It has a complete list of Vicars from 1298. The north porch is a little earlier than that; and we know that in 1391 the chancel, being " ruinated and decayed," had to be rebuilt. It is clear that the nave arches were rebuilt before that date; but the actual history of building and rebuilding must be largely conjectural. Everyone will notice resemblances with S. John's Church in this city, and experts assign both to " within the second and third quarters of the fifteenth century." If the architectural history of the church cannot be derived from records, the personal history is to be found in many documents, which tell of the foundation of chantries, the endowment of obits, the clergy employed, and the like. These endowments were very rich, and the amount confiscated must have been very large. The church seems at one time to have contained fifteen altars. There are records also of great havoc in the destruction, and the sale of beautiful things for pitiful sums. In the Civil Wars, again, the church suffered, for the materials of several houses that were pulled down were stored within its walls. In Charles II.'s time the spire was blown down. It was restored five years later. A passage through the south transept led at one time to the " Butchery." The adjoining Jesus Hall was destroyed in 1742. The later history of the church contains one fact of interest at least. It was there that Sarah Kemble, who had lived at Guy's Cliff, was married to William Siddons on November 25, 1773.

Let us first examine the outside of the church. No doubt it suffers from its nearness to its larger neighbour : as Dugdale says, " the Archangel eclipseth the Trinity." But it is not less beautiful. The plan is quite different ; cruciform, with a long chancel and short nave, and a central tower. The spire is at least seventy feet less high than S. Michael's, but it is quite as graceful, though it is without the flying buttresses of its neighbour. The details of the tower are interesting, but in many respects the spire seems to have been copied, perhaps at its

S. Michael's Church, Coventry

rebuilding, from S. Michael's. The bells are now hung in a wooden campanile, as the tower is not strong enough for them. Outside, the whole church has greatly suffered from restoration, the old red sandstone having often been patched with grey.

Within, the fine proportions and the grace of the arrangement strike us at once. We pass in by the north porch, which has a fine groined roof, and a fine door—now unused—into S. Thomas's chapel, eastwards. The nave is of the early fourteenth century, earlier than the chancel, which was built when the city was growing richer, but its four bays, with their fine arcading, are as rich as the best work of the time. The clerestory is stronger and more solid in design than that of S. Michael's, the space below the windows being less. The low pitched roofs, divided panel wise and again into quarters by mouldings, richly coloured (it is said according to the old colours), are an impressive feature ; the nave roof has large angels on the spandrels, carrying shields with the emblems of the Passion. At the chancel arch was once a fresco of the Last Judgment ; it has practically disappeared within the last fifty years. The pulpit is a fine late medieval stone one, and, it may be added, a very pleasant one to preach from ; and the beautiful eagle is also of the days before destruction. Of the chapels that remain the first and most noticeable, but the only ugly thing in the church, is what is called Marler's chapel, a mid-sixteenth century work very poor in style. Very different is the charming S. Thomas's chapel, west of the north aisle, with a beautiful early decorated double arch between it and the porch. It was founded in Edward I.'s day, and the architects who place it earlier must surely be dreaming, though some of the chancel work is no doubt antique in character for that date. After all, Edward I. began to reign in 1272, when Early English had not entirely died. On the other side of the porch is the Archdeacon's chapel, or Consistory Court, used as such at least from 1588, a most beautiful piece of early fourteenth century work, with many interesting monuments, among them that of the great translator Philemon Holland (under whom Dugdale was at school), who kneels facing the spectator with a prayer desk in front of him and a wife at each side of it. Fragments of the old glass are in the middle window on the north side, among them fragments of the " Godiva window," which existed as a whole till the nineteenth century restorations.

Dugdale dates the window *tempore* Richard II. and describes the Leofric (whose head survives) as holding a charter in his hand with the words :—

> " I Luriche for the love of thee
> Doe make Coventree tol-free."

The church has other good features—a good reredos (a bad east window), good stalls, with hardly any heads remaining. You will observe where John Sheepshanks cut his name. There is a good medieval font on nine steps ; a good Elizabethan alms box. The south transept has been spoilt ; but what is now the clergy vestry is a beautiful room with a rich dark oak roof, and the royal arms of Charles I. over the fireplace. But details such as these, though they must be remembered, do not help to recall the grace and beauty of the church of the Holy Trinity, which belong to its harmony of design and richness of effect, uniting with something of the merchant's utilitarianism the mystery of an older and more devotional age. Coventry is rich indeed in two such fine churches as stand close together.

When you leave the church, at the north side you will see the bases of the pillars which once stood at the west front of the destroyed cathedral, the priory of Leofric's great foundation. Then go down some of the beautiful old streets of the city— the Butchery (the old houses hanging their upper storeys far into the street), Broadgate, by Peeping Tom (*see* p. 395) and the site of the old Cross ; down Cross Cheaping to the old Grammar School where Hales Street begins. This was once the Church of the Hospital of S. John Baptist, founded by the Prior Laurence (happy name !) in the twelfth century for the infirm and poor. The old stalls of the Hospitallers still remain, cut, alack, by the schoolboys who have often sat in them, since Dugdale was a scholar and felt the birch of Holland. It is now used as a parish room for Holy Trinity—and it seems (1912) as if a new window was to be put in, though there is a fine east window of late medieval type.

Thence visit the site of Swine Cross and see the little remains of the city walls, with Swanswell or the Priory Gate, part of the walls begun in 1355, the archway now blocked up as part of a house. In Cook Street, hard by, is another gate, without its battlements, only a wreck. Look at the beautiful houses in

Well Street, timber-framed, note the site of the Well Street Gate, and the remains of the walls here.

So to another of the glories of Coventry, the Bablake Hospital, founded by Thomas Bond in 1506. It forms three sides of a quadrangle, the fourth being the north of S. John's Church. On the east is a cloister with a good brick doorway and barge board. The other side of the quadrangle has the old school, built by Thomas Wheatley in 1560 ; a beautiful staircase within, the roof supported by huge beams stretching across the stairway and the open space. There is a great deal of interest in the rooms within, both in the school and the hospital, fine oak, ancient settees and chairs. The hospital still serves its ancient use of a refuge for " poore men, so long as the world shall endure, with a woman to look to them." All has been recently, but not badly, restored, and indeed looks first as the pious founders would have it look. From the Bablake Hospital you pass to the church of S. John Baptist, which stands on a broad open space at the junction of the Birmingham road with other ways into the city. Outside it has been restored out of all whooping. Within it is deliciously rich, quiet, solemn.

The church is believed to have been built in 1357, and is regarded as a commemoration of the battle of Sluys, as well as (absorbing an earlier and smaller church) an atonement for the murder of the " dear lord Edward " the second, whose wicked widow Isabel gave the site. The south aisle is the work of her *vadlettus* (valet) William Walscheman, and Christiana his wife. It has a large central tower, in two stages, a large lantern and a smaller upper storey with small windows (spoilt by the clock now there), and battlements. The top of the tower has a distinctly military air, and it may well indeed have been an important part of the city's defence at this point, close to the Spon Gate. Within you notice at once the difference between the north clerestory—the most ancient—and the south with its high, long, narrow windows divided by arches ; the smallness of the church, the nave having only three bays ; its height and dignity ; the two side altars ; the good marble reredos at the high altar ; the modern screen with its good rood but poor woodwork of the screen itself and really bad gilt gates below. " The south aisle of the nave," says Mr. Woodhouse, in his excellent book on *The Churches of Coventry*, " including the lower part of the transept, is doubtless the aisle erected for the gild by

William Walshemann in 1357. The two windows are not central with the nave arches, and the third is not in the centre of the transept. Their tracery is somewhat peculiar in design, and has the transitional character one would expect from its date. There are designs on the face of each western tower pier of the altars which once stood there, probably those of the Trinity and S. Katherine, which are known to have existed." Partly, perhaps, from the contrast of its size to the vastness of S. Michael's and Holy Trinity, and certainly from the exquisite grace and solemnity of the central portion, S. John's leaves a very special impression on the visitor to Coventry. Mr. Woodhouse reports Sir Gilbert Scott as saying " that he knew of no interior more beautiful than S. John's."

There is much more to be seen in Coventry. Some things at least must be noticed. Going along Smithford Street from S. John's, that is to say, back again into the heart of the city, we come to the Barracks, which were built in 1793. They stand on the site of the Black Bull inn, where Henry VII. was given a triumphal banquet after the victory of Bosworth by the Mayor, and where Mary of Scots was kept for months in 1569. This brings us again to the centre of the town, the good solid eighteenth and nineteenth century Hertford Street with its extremely solid and well-built houses, to the Corn Exchange of 1858, not so bad for its date. Little Park Street, too, which goes southwards from the junction of High Street and Earl Street, contains many good houses, Jacobean, Classical, Medieval. At the end are remains of the city walls, and in the gardens, called Park Hollows, many heretics were burnt just before the Reformation and during its progress. Among these should especially be mentioned the two Coventry men, Lawrence Saunders and Cornelius Bungey, and the companion of the latter, Robert Glover of Mancetter, the nephew by marriage of Latimer. Mr. Richings's little book on *the Mancetter Martyrs* (4th edition, 1860) says that " the Hollows " owed their origin to a grant of Richard II., 1385, to the Corporation, to get stone out of his park to complete the walls and build two of the city gates. The ground was levelled, he adds, in 1821, and the ancient appearance of the spot destroyed. The Little Park was taken out of the Great Park in 1547 and separated by a wall. Going along Much Park Street you come to the Workhouse, in which are incorporated the remains of the Whitefriars, or Carmelites, house. Their house was finished in 1348, and after the Dissolution it passed into the hands of Sir Ralph Sadleir the most prominent of the English diplomatists employed in the tangle of Scottish politics. He died in 1587, but had sold the house more than twenty years before to John Hales, and it was here that Queen Elizabeth was entertained by him in 1565. Of the ancient convent, the outer gate, the east cloister, fragments of the chapter house, the inner gate, and the dormitory are still in use. The remains are considerable. Then let us go on to the Charter house, and lastly to the old Palace Yard. The Charterhouse is on the east side of the beautiful cemetery, laid out by Sir Joseph Paxton. It is now a private house, but an enthusiast might beg entrance. The wall which surrounded the old Carthusian dwelling still exists ; and the dwelling-house is what was the Prior's Lodging. It contains a most striking fresco of the Crucifixion, of which, unfortunately, only the lower part is preserved ; it is of great beauty in idea, the Sacred limbs covered with lilies, angels receiving the Holy Blood. Another room has a Renaissance decoration with inscription— " A mā oughte to be the same to his frēde as he wold be to hymselfe. Loue and feare God." •

Travelling eastwards with a northerly twist one comes to Gosford Green, the place where Mowbray and Bolingbroke fought, still happily an open space. Return then from there, up Gosford Street (look at such wonderful survivals as 24, 34, 36, 40, and 91, houses that might have sheltered Sir John Falstaff at his famous visit), to Earl Street, and, again in the heart of the city, you find an archway to the left, almost opposite where S. Mary's Street diverges to the right, and you come into Palace Yard, where of old lived the Hopkins family, where Princess Elizabeth stayed with Mr. Hopkins in 1605, James II. held court in 1687, and the Princess Anne, afterwards Queen, and her husband were lodged. It is a quite charming seventeenth century house, with everything handsome about it that a merchant liked in those days—good lead work, and a beautiful plaster ceiling which only needs skilful restoration.

As you go away, the memories not only of the great churches and halls will abide with you, but also those of streets which England nowhere can surpass, since Oxford did its best to destroy every old house, and Chester to change them into new imitations —Priory Row, Smithford Street, High Street, New Street,

Palace Yard
Coventry

E. H. N.

85

Butcher Row, and Gosford Street itself, which seems to have felt no harsher hand than that of time.

But the last house we visited, that in Palace Yard, tells us by what way we should leave Coventry. It is by the Hinckley or Lutterworth Road, through Stoke, with its fine church, tower and nave of the fourteenth century, past Caludon Castle, now a farm-house, through Walsgrave-on-Sowe, with a fifteenth century church—notice its fine oak south door and the old lock —and the road bids farewell to all signs of man's gregariousness, and you come to the long wall of the splendid park of Combe Abbey. The ancient history of the abbey, one of the earliest Cistercian houses, endowed by one of the Camvilles, under Stephen, is less interesting that it's modern. It was after the Dissolution the property of the evil Northumberland—and at his attainder it was granted to Robert Kelway, a Crown official, whose daughter married Sir John Harington and came into possession of Combe Abbey in 1580. The Haringtons were of kin to the Bruces and so to the Stewarts, and James VI. and I. was received by Sir John Harington at his house in the county of Rutland when he came to claim the English throne. In the same year Princess Elizabeth, the king's daughter, stayed at Combe Abbey, where, a little while later, she was placed under the charge of the owners. There she dwelt till she was hastily moved to Coventry for fear of the Powder Plot. The charge was not profitable to the Haringtons, and Sir John died in 1613 a ruined man. His sister, to whom Combe Abbey passed, sold it to a rich London merchant, Sir William Craven, in whose family it still remains. The second William, the first peer, was the devoted servant and loyal helper of the Princess Elizabeth, who had spent her childhood in his Warwickshire house. Electress Palatine and, for a winter, Queen of Bohemia, she died in exile at Lord Craven's house in London. From her came the splendid Vandykes and Honthorsts at Combe, and the Bohemian glass and other pictures at Ashdown in Berkshire.

Now look, if you are so fortunate as to be allowed, at the house itself, set in most beautiful gardens—formal, Italian, aquatic and of still more varieties, set themselves in the great park with its fine trees. The house without shows the work of century after century from the first days of the Cistercians. There is a fine archway with the cloister (if such it be) beside it, much restored, indeed, but still beautiful, of late Norman as it begins to turn

into Early English work.   Other cloister windows north and west
show the last work of the religious.   Then comes the Palladian
front, built by Captain Wynne for the first lord, and dated 1684,
but never finished.   And then there is the building by William
Eden Nesfield in the clever late Gothic of the Victorian age.   One
may regret that this is there at all, yet one cannot but admire
much of it—the east side notably, and the moat, and the western
garden with its lawn and terraces, and the canal which the moat
eventually merges into.   An eminent modern authority speaks
of Nesfield's ": Anglo-Franco Victorian medievalism," a barbarous
phrase, coined, no doubt, to describe a somewhat barbarous architecture.   But there is an undoubted charm in the mingling of
national ideas—English, French, and Dutch—and of well-marked
periods—medieval, Caroline, and Victorian—which are the
characteristics of Combe Abbey to-day.

The setting of garden and water is an exquisite one, but it is
the riches within which chiefly fascinate the visitor.   The entrance
hall, with its armour and beautiful tapestry, its Tudor chairs,
and Italian chests and lanterns ; the oak of the " old pantry ;
the beds and their rich hangings : the chimney-pieces, Tudor in
the Griffin room, Adam in Lady Craven's room, Grinling Gibbons
in the Brown Parlour ; the graceful glasses ; the exquisite Palladian staircase, the almost successful medievalism of the library ;
and, above all, the wonderful collection of pictures which throngs
every room."   Of this a word at least must be said.   It " belongs
to the house " in a sense which is not very often true of collections
even in great houses nowadays.   The house has been continuously occupied, and the pictures belonged to those who lived
there.   And the same, one may interject, is true of much of the
furniture, among which one notices especially the fine beds,
notably that in which it is said that Elizabeth, Queen of Bohemia,
died at Lord Craven's house in London.   With Elizabeth, and
the respectful and romantic devotion of Lord Craven to her, is
associated the most interesting part of the pictures.   The writer
I have already quoted (*Country Life*, December 11, 1909) says :
" Portraits of the Queen are plentiful at Combe, and especially in
the Bohemian room.   That over the mantelpiece represents her
in black, standing on a formal terrace, with a landscape back-
ground.   It is one of several by her favourite artist, Hondhorst,
who was also her teacher, for she and her daughters had artistic
training, and one of the portraits of Lord Craven at Combe is by

the Princess Louisa." The collection of Stewart pictures, left to the first lord by the queen, is indeed a magnificent treasure. In the dining-room, for example, are six full-length portraits, of Charles I., the King-Elector, Elizabeth his wife, their sons Rupert and Maurice, and Lord Craven in armour. In the Brown Parlour are portraits of James I., Anne of Denmark, and their children—belonging to the same collection. You will notice Prince Henry and the charming one of Elizabeth herself; and Barbara Palmer, Duchess of Cleveland. Earlier is the portrait, now in the Gilt Parlour, of the Countess of Bedford, for a short time the owner of Combe, who was daughter of Sir John Harington. But one could linger long indeed over the beauties of this place, within and without. We must return, for it is the limit of our survey. Back, it may be, by the banks of the beautiful lake, round the park, and into the Coventry road again, or across that and by the woods, New Close or Birchley or Brandon or Binley, and so southward by the devious ways of Dunsmore— even on to the "straight mile," to Princethorpe and back to Leamington. Either way is interesting with the true Warwickshire interest of rich pasture and fine trees.

CHAPTER XXII

SOLIHULL, KNOWLE, AND TEMPLE BALSALL

AMONG the villages that have changed, grown into towns themselves or become absorbed by towns, Solihull must claim an almost primary place. A century ago it lay deep in the lanes of Arden, which seem to be the survival of mere forest path, and it is said that " even the inhabitants found it hard to be found "—strange phrase —" a mile or two away, so similar and numberless are the thickly-hedged, tiny roads." Now it is a dusty resting place on the highway to Birmingham. But something of the old charm lingers ; the new red brick houses have not yet eaten up the old; and some elms in the street remain to show where men used to sit out with their pipes in the evening when the nineteenth century was young. The church is a fine one, large, and with a splendid chancel. There is no clerestory and the nave arches are consequently high. The east end of the south aisle has a reredos, stone, of fourteen niches, but with no remaining figures. The Malvern Chapel has the remains of a reredos. Malvern Hall, once the house of the Greswoldes, part built by Inigo Jones, the wings by Sir John Soane, and the statues on the gates by Caius Gabriel Cibber, the German sculptor, who made the phœnix over the south door of S. Paul's, is a mile or so nearer Warwick, on the Birmingham road. The south transept has a good screen with carvings of fruit and vines on the bosses, which were taken from the roofs of the north and south aisles. There is a good rood screen, chiefly modern, but with ancient figures and Georgian gates. Other screens also very good are before the organ and to the Malvern chapel. The chancel is over fifty feet long, and has a two-storeyed chapel at the north, the upper S. Alphege's, recently well restored, and having a new window of S. Edith of Wilton, the Blessed Virgin and S. Elizabeth of Hungary, while below is a mortuary chapel, with the ancient stone altar, and a fine groined roof. Very good early Georgian rails, happily allowed to remain, protect a good modern high altar. On the south wall of the chancel is the brass of William Hyll and his wives, 1549 ; other brasses deserve inspection. A brass plate of 1746 copies the rough distich on Shakespeare's grave, an early instance of interest in the memorials of the man apart from his work. Till last is left what one sees most conspicuously, the beautiful grey spire, rising from the red sandstone of the church to a conspicuous height : it is seen a long way off as one comes from the south, most graceful above the houses and the trees.

At Solihull, too, we reach the School which Jago tried to immortalise, for he was there with Shenstone when they were boys, and the walls seemed " awful " to him. The building they were taught in, where Dr. Johnson tried in vain to be appointed master, and was refused because he had the character of " being a very haughty, ill-natured gent," has been replaced by a new rosy edifice. So one may leave Solihull, but not without one word about an Oxford memory attached to it. Sixty years ago " Tommy Short " was a famous Oxford personage, Fellow and Tutor of Trinity, described by an affectionate writer of a short biography as " a high and dry Tory Churchman, who could see nothing specially incongruous in a Bishop discussing the breed of sheep during the pauses of a Confirmation service caused by a broken window being mended " ; and yet a friend, as he had been the tutor, of J. H. Newman till his death. He was born at Solihull, descended from the ancient Warwickshire family of Holbeche on the mother's side, his father a surgeon who set up a sign-board before his door, but also kept a pack of hounds and lost most of his and his wife's money. The family was a large one, and it clung to the home of its youth, its members, such as Colonel Short, of the East India Company's service, and the Rev. Thomas himself, returning there for the last years of their lives. The Colonel became Lord of the Manor and bought the manor cottage with " the largest horse-chestnut tree in Warwickshire." An old-fashioned hospitality was kept up, among old-fashioned surroundings, and the glass and furniture of old days. And it was there that Thomas Short ended his long life. He had just failed to be Head master of Rugby, just failed to be President of Trinity. Stubbs, afterwards Bishop, had belonged to a party which dreaded " a tyranny of port," perhaps because it rhymed with Short. Anyhow, Short was not elected ; and he felt that though College rooms were a good place to live in, they were not a good place to die in, and so he returned to the old village and the old church where he had himself written inscriptions for the tombs of his ancestors. Solihull is the heart of a district of old houses. Solihull Hall itself is ancient, half timber, but has been rebuilt or added to till almost all the old front is hidden. The ground floor is modernised, but the upper part remains as in the sixteenth or even fifteenth century. Southwards is Hillfield Hall, also sixteenth century, but covered with ivy so that you can see little of the good work. It has the charming motto—" Hic hospites : in caelo cives. W. V. H. 1576." This was the residence of the Greswoldes, after the Hawes who built it. The great room, on up a newel staircase, extending over the whole front, is the most notable feature of the house. Then, eastwards of Solihull, is Berry Hall, which has still its moat round three sides. It has been a good deal altered and reconstructed, but there is still a great deal of charming work in it. It has the motto, on two brackets, " I.H.S. Amor est meus," and a monogram, perhaps of the Waring family. More remarkable, and more in need of immediate treatment, is Grimshaw Hall, about half a mile to your left as you enter Knowle from Solihull.

It is only a yard or two from the road, but the trees in front of it have grown up so much that you can hardly see it, or at least if you were driving by rapidly—on your way to nowhere, for I do not know where you would get by this wriggling road—you might well not notice that there was anything. It is a " timber and plaster house with projecting porch, shallow bay windows supported by brackets, and brick clustered chimneys," and parts of the house too of red brick. It has elaborate framework on the gables, richly ornamented, suggestive of the work of the quite early seventeenth century, if indeed it be not earlier still. At present the view from the back is even more interesting, for it is less blocked by trees. The ends stand out more than in front ; the chimneys are better seen in their effective simplicity ; but a great yew tree in the midst obscures the view of the centre of the house. There are remains of what was an old walled garden with a good dovecot at the end. Inside there are oak-panelled rooms with old doors and a stately staircase. This is a house—I write of August, 1911—which cries out for treatment at once, and a conservative restoration. It is one of the most beautiful places in a district of beautiful houses; it would be an irreparable loss if it should perish.

And while I am mentioning this old house let me name others not so far away from it. On the estate of Berkswell Hall is a charming old Warwickshire farm house called Ram Hall, with a row of elms beside it. It has a fine moat in front, and a long wall; two gables and a large quadruple chimney stack, and fine mullions in the windows. Or again there is Bott's Green House, not easy to find, but not far from Shustoke Station, a long, low, restful-looking place, half timbered. Of it I speak elsewhere (p. 431). Or again, nearer still, the house with a name famous among Warwickshire worthies, Sheldon Hall is a noticeable house five miles from Birmingham, with a splendid chimney-piece in one beautiful panelled room. This has three pilasters at each end, two in the middle, and between them two arches, with a fine pediment along the top—suggestive of that in the house of the President of S. John's at Oxford, traditionally said to have been put in by Laud. It has a stone opening. A staircase also attracts by its fine newels, and the very elaborate panels at the top. There are six stairs and then a landing; and all the panelling is somewhat elaborate. None of these are precisely within the ways I am taking, so I set them down here.

So much for these houses. We will now think ourselves back at Solihill; and then? Northwards, to Birmingham, we will not go. The task of following the highways and byways of that great city is too large for us. Shakespeare's land is the land of country villages and old cities, old houses and quiet streams. Our line must cross the shire before it touches Birmingham. Solihull we will fancy to be still as it was when Shenstone went to school. And Aston Hall, beautiful though it is, with its splendid treatment of red brick, must be beyond us, for it is now the possession of Birmingham itself. Reluctantly, too, must we pass by Castle Bromwich, that wonderful Jacobean mansion set in gardens only five miles from the heart of the capital of the Midlands, with only a word. It has its formal garden, its forecourt, and its general plan is early Jacobean with the chief additions of the Restoration period; its beautiful ceilings, rich carving, fine tapestry, a noble long gallery with delightful bookcases, and in the garden an open-air bath, concerning which I must quote this letter of Sir John Bridgman, because it reminds one of Pack-wood and the similar provision there. " I am making in my garden House," says the rich beautifier of the house who reigned from 1710 to 1747, writing in 1733 " (in the Back garden) a Cold Bath, and adjoining to it have a Room with a fireplace in it, not only for my grand children but will prove any Grown Person, and recommend you to ask the Dr. and Surgeon theyr thoughts of your making up of such an appreciation, when it please God you may use it with safety." But here we go not, into the bath or out of it.

It is difficult not to ramble, one sees, with pen if not in travel-ling. Let us steadily turn our faces southwards now, from Solihull to Knowle.

Knowle is an interesting place and has an interesting history. At Domesday it was a part of Hampton-in-Arden, and Dugdale tells that he found no reference to it before the time of King John, when William de Arden of Hampton settled it on his wife. Eventually it became the property of Eleanor of Castile, and with much of the rest of her lands passed at her death to the abbey of Westminster " upon condition that the abbot, prior, and covent of that house, or the Prior and Covent, if the abbot should be out of the way, upon the eve of S. Andrew the Apostle, on which day the said Queen's Anniversary had used to be kept, being solemnly revested in the Quire of that Monasterie, should sing a *Placebo* and *Dirige*, with nine Lessons, C Wax Candles, weighing xii lb. a Piece, being then burning about her Tombe, and every Yeare new ones made for that purpose. And furthermore, that those Wax-Candles should be lighted at the *Placebo* and *Dirige*, on the eve of the same Anniversarie, and burn on the Day thereof till High Masse were ended ; and that all the Bells, both great and small, then ringing, they should sing solemnly for her Soul's Health. And moreover, that on the Day of her said Anni-versary, the Abbot himself in case he were present, or the Prior in his stead, if he could not procure a more eminent Prelate, should sing Masse at the High Altar, the Candles then burning, and Bells ringing ; and every single Monk of that Abby a private Masse, the inferior monks their whole Psalter, and the Friars Converts of that House the Lord's Prayer, Creed, and Aves, as many as the Abbot and Covent should appoint, for her Soul and the Souls of all the Faithfull deceased. And that likewise the said Prior and Covent, to distribute unto every poor Body repairing to that Monasterie, one Penny Sterling, or Money to that Value ; staying till Three of the Clock, expecting their coming, before they should begin the Dole, which was to be unto seven Score poor People."

More likewise about candles, as that there should always be two burning at the tomb of the beloved Queen ; and that after the cost of all these ceremonies the revenues should belong to the Abbey. And there is a touching fact you see when you read it all, which Dugdale does not note, that it was in the last year of his life, on his last expedition to Scotland, that the great King Edward, at Berwick-on-Tweed, gave this charter of grant in memory .of his dear wife, who, as we still would believe, thirty years before had sucked the poison from his wound. But all this memory passed away. Westminster was made a bishopric, then displaced and turned into a college of canons. And the property of Knowle, under Queen Elizabeth, found its way into the full pockets, for ever emptying, of Robert Dudley Earl of Leicester. Back again it came, by exchange, to the Crown, and so at last to Fulke Greville of Warwick, and Lord Brooke, of whom so much more has been said. Thus, mixed with things ecclesiastical, the civil history of Knowle. But the ecclesiastical history is likewise mixed with secularity. At the end of the fourteenth century there arose a much endowed clergyman, Walter Cook, who had more canonries than I can easily recall, who " bore a special affection to this place." Knowle was till then only a chapelry of Hampton, and it was far for the people to go to be baptized and buried. So he procured a bull and a licence and erected a church which was consecrated on February 24, 1402. Eventually a college of chantry priests was founded to look after the church, but they were not adequately endowed, for by the time of Henry VIII. there were but two of them with the rector. The guild was richer ; it had still six priests. But of lay associates there was a mighty following. Says Dugdale : " a multitude of Persons, whereof most of good Qualitie, nay some of the great Nobility in those days, had admittance to be of this Gild." The gild of S. Anne must not be confused with the chantry foundation ; it was in 1413 that it was founded, whereas the college of priests, from the same founders, bears

date three years later. Edward VI.'s survey urged the maintenance of the guild, since it has been used " to minister all sacraments and sacramentals within the chapel of Knowle for the ease
of the inhabitants in the same town," and repeated the original
statement of need for separate provision because Knowle was
divided from Hampton by a great and dangerous water which
in winter neither man nor beast might pass without danger of
perishing. Dugdale's account of the popularity of the guild is
borne out by the register, which proves that the numbers at one
time were 3,000, in the early years of the sixteenth century
many names of dukes and abbats and knights and priests being
included. This guild accounts for the beautiful half-timbered
house at the south-west of the church, whose arch at the junction
eaves with wall, with curved ribs, you notice from without,
notable also for its large hall with carved oak pillars. It has
recently been purchased by a generous neighbour, restored, and
presented to the parish.

The church also has been in the restorers' hands. The western
tower is like many a Warwickshire one. The long nave and aisles
with chancel and chantry chapel have all interesting features.
In the changes the floor of the chancel has been much lowered.
The north chantry chapel, built by Walter Cook, is now filled by
the organ, and .here is a new vestry north of it. But though
much harm has been done, the oak stalls removed from the
chancel, and the beautiful Perpendicular rood screen taken from
its place, there is still much of the original beauty of the church
surviving. There is one of those fat-legged Elizabethan altar
tables, and there are two fine oak chests, each made from a solid
trunk. And on the floor is a circular stone, robbed of its brasses,
which is said to mark the resting-place of Walter Cook, to whom
the town owes its first prosperity in Church and State. And so
we pass on towards Balsall.

The excellent Mr. Jago introduced Temple Balsall in manner
most characteristic of his century, after moralising on Kenilworth's departed pomp—

> " Thee too, tho' boasting not a royal train,
> The Muse, of Balshal, in her faithful page
> Shall celebrate : for long beneath thy roof
> A band of warriors bold, of high renown,
> To martial deeds and hazardous emprize
> Sworn, for defence of Salem's sacred walls,
> From Paynim-foes and holy pilgrimage

Now other guests thou entertain'st
A female band, by female charity
Sustained."

He added the explanatory note that Balsall was " formerly a seat of the Knights Templars, now an Almshouse for poor widows, founded by the Lady Catherine Levison, a descendant of Robert Dudley Earl of Leicester." And so Temple Balsall is certainly a place to see. Now I warn you that you will find it a place rather difficult to discover. The turns from Knowle are very perplexing, but after all not more perplexing than those in many another part of leafy Warwickshire in summer, when you can never see far enough before you or else see much too far. When eventually you find your way, you see the splendid church standing on a hill, across the meadows in a valley. You turn sharply to the right, mount a short steep ascent, and see a narrow path before you. Beyond it is a fine eighteenth century red house, no doubt the rectory, eminently comfortable and beneficent in aspect. Then up this well-kept path, with its clipt hedges on either hand and you see the collegiate buildings, and then the magnificent church. But first you shall hear the history, from Mr. Cox, who so bravely epitomises Dugdale :—

" *Balshall,* a Place included in the Manor of *Hampton in Arden,* and so not mention'd in the Conqueror's Survey, but with it came to *Nigel de Albani.* To this *Nigel,* succeeded *Roger* his Son and Heir, who took upon him the Sirname of *Mowbrey.* He being a very devout Man, among other his pious Works, gave all this his Lordship of *Balshall,* to the Knights *Templars ;* and to render it a fit Habitation for them, he built a Church for God's Service, and an House ; whereupon the *Templars,* whose chief Seat was in the *Temple* at *London,* made a Preceptory or Cell to their House, and sent divers of their Fraternity to dwell here (but of this we must speak more in our History of Monasteries.)

" While this Lordship remain'd in the Possession of the *Templars,* they obtain'd, 32 *Hen.* 3. a Charter of Free-Warren for all the Demesne Lands here, and afterward in the same Reign, *Anno* 52, procured a weekly Market on *Thursday,* and two Fairs every Year, the one on the Eve, Day, and Morrow of the Feast of St. *Gregory* the Martyr, and the other on the Eve Day and Morrow of the Feast of S. *Matthias* the Apostle ; and for a surer Enjoyment of their Interest here, they procured a full Confirmation fron *Roger* the Son and Heir, of the first Donor. The Order of the *Templars* for Heresy, Idolatry, and Blasphemy (charged on them but not proved) being abolished, and their great Estate seized into the King's Hands, 4 *Edw.* 2. this Lordship and many others returned to the Heirs of the first Donors, 'till by a Decree of the Council of *Vienna*, under Pope *Clement* V. they (and this among others) were annex'd to the Knights Hospitallers of St. *John of Jerusalem*, so called from their first Seat at *Jerusalem*, and dedicated to St. *John Baptist*. While the Hospitallers had this Lordship they had no Preceptory here, as the *Templers* had, but one *John de Beausik*, Esq; farm'd the House call'd the Preceptory, in which he liv'd, and the Lands thereunto belonging, the Tenants, to secure their Privileges, setting Crosses upon their Doors."

Temple Balsall, after the dissolution of the religious houses, became part of property of the third Catherine among Henry VIII.'s wives, and the only Catherine among his widows. After her death Edward VI. gave it first to Somerset and then to Dudley first Earl of Warwick, then Duke of Northumberland. Mary wanted to give it back to the Hospitallers ; but their day was past, and Elizabeth gave it back to the Dudleys in the person of her admired Leicester. Then it came to the dear Duchess Alice, whose "many instances of signal piety " infected her daughter the Lady Katherine Levison, " who rebuilt," you will notice—" at her own charge the church of this place, and beautify'd it very much for the Use of the Inhabitants there, and those of the Neighbouring Hamlets, which lye at a distance from their Parish Church, assigning 50 *l.* a Year for the Support of a perpetual Incumbent therein, and in Augmentation of the Vicarage of *Long Itchington*, gave 50 *l.* a Year out of this Manor of *Balshall*. She also, by her Will, appointed, That out of the Revenues of this her Manor of *Balshall*, an Hospital should be erected for twenty poor Widows, to be chosen out of the poor Inhabitants of this Place, or if so many could not be found there, then out of *Long Itchington, &c.* each of them to have 8 *l. per Annum*, and a Gown of Grey Cloth ; and 20 *l.* a Year to a Minister to read Prayers every Day in the Hospital, and teach 20 Children. She also gave to the Poor of *Balshall*, 50 *l.* for a Dole, to be paid out of the first Rents of her Estate due, after her decease. In the Church are the Arms of the King, *Peache, Revel*, and *Weston* the Prior, and divers others in a Chamber of the House."

Now first to the Hospital, a " quad." of three sides, two sides for the ladies, one for the Master. I discover that the Master is the Vicar of the parish, so that I must be wrong in calling that beautiful house a rectory, unless there is both a rector and a vicar.   But these matters I have not investigated. I leave that to my readers.   But the Hospital is a delightful building, shady in the hot sun of a summer day, warm and sheltered in the winter's storms—for it is open only to the south and yet not so as to let the sun visit the widows' faces too roughly. So on to the most beautiful church, which began with the thirteenth century and went on till the fifteenth.   It is one long straight building, the nave rising by four separate divisions, up to the chancel.   Outside there was once a south porch but it has gone, and there is a curious turret at the south-west. Within you observe at once that the windows are all different, except two at the north ; but all have been much restored. The bosses are heads of Templars.   The east window is a splendid thing : so are the beautiful sedilia, exquisite Early English work.   The finest thing at first you think is the splendid west front, the lovely early English door with the great Decorated window over it : then you go within, and the grace and dignity of the beautiful expanse before you are more than equal to what you saw outside.

CHAPTER XXIII

FROM WHITACRE TO MAXSTOKE AND COLESHILL AND SHUSTOKE

AMONG the castles of Warwickshire Maxstoke stands out. A good way to visit it is to take the road from Whitacre station, having on your right, after a while, Blithe Hall, which should ever be regarded with respect because it was the home of Sir William Dugdale, greatest of all Warwickshire antiquaries, who tells the early history of the manor, and of the persons (not always creditable) to whom it belonged till Sir Walter Aston (whom James I. made Lord Aston of Forfar) " by his Deed of Bargain and Sale, dated 14 Nov. 1 Car., conveyed it to me, William Dugdale, it being the Place of my Residence, and where I compiled this present Work." He died there in 1686. Hard by is the Blithe stream, over which is a beautiful medieval bridge.

You might, perhaps, turn to your left and wander away towards Shustoke, where you should find Bott's Green House. Hard to find it is. I think, perhaps, I had best give the advice which a local expert gave me : " Go to Shustoke railway station and inquire." When you get there you find it long, **low**, restful, half-timbered, with three chimneys, a gable over **the** door, and large gables at each end, more buildings **to** the right. It has **a** low wall in front and a gate with balls on the posts **each** side, and some good timbered out-houses. Of itself let me quote Mr. P. H. Ditchfield :—

" Its curved and slanting braces and its fine porch and entrance gate are charming features. It stands completely away from the busy haunts of men in an unspoilt country. The **fleur** de **lis** of the Digby family is very conspicuously inserted in the front. Within there is a carved stone mantelpiece carefully painted and grained to imitate wood, and upstairs a small panelled room of plain design."

You may, I say, turn aside to Shustoke. But on to Maxstoke, and turn aside to the right, from a well-wooded road, up a narrow avenue, till you come to the gate-house, and then pause to consider.

The castle was begun by William de Clinton, Admiral, Warden of the Cinque Ports, and many other things, in 1345 ; but his nephew seems to have changed it with Humphrey Earl of Stafford, afterwards Duke of Buckingham, two years later. It has passed through many hands, and now is inhabited by the Tangye family. A paper written some half a century ago by Mr. George Robinson compares its position with that of Kenilworth, and says that, unlike the latter, here " the beauty of the situation alone directed its locality," and adds that " domestic comfort takes the prior place and military architecture plays only a secondary part in its construction." The plan is a hollow quadrangle with one side occupied by the living house of the lord, two other sides formerly occupied by the wooden houses or huts in which the retainers dwelt, under the shadow of the great wall, the fourth side being occupied by the gate-house with the walls from which it projects. " Its military condition is confined to an embattled wall, 26 feet high, flanked by large octagonal towers at each angle, rising a story, and, in one instance two stories, above the curtain. Outside there is a broad terrace of earth, once defended by a stockade, and beyond this a wide moat," said to be sixteen feet deep and forty yards wide. The gate-house is rectangular, with two octagonal flanking towers both commanding the drawbridge. You may still see the openings in the archway from which hot liquids could be poured upon besiegers ; and also " two fine old massive oaken doors, now covered with iron plates répoussée, that is, beaten up into a pattern, forming as it were the first rudiments of the knowledge that corrugated iron. presented more resistance than if flat ; these iron plates, however, were not a part of the original work, but were added by the Duke of Buckingham in the reign of Henry VI., though from the circumstance of the massive hinges beneath them bearing the cross-crosslets, the distinctive arms of the founder of the castle [Clinton] it is probable that the doors upon which they were placed are the original ones ; these open into a large and

beautiful groined archway, lead without the intervention of any
other barrier into the courtyard." [1]

There are two small guard chambers on each side the archway,
one of which has a staircase leading to two rooms above. One
of these rooms communicates with the ramparts, and above the
second is a flat leaded roof from which a fine view can be obtained.
I should like to add what Mr. Robinson says about the battlements of this tower and their relation to the excellence of
English archery at the period. " If we examine these battlements we shall see that the sections of their coping is exactly
that shape which will prevent the ricochet from any arrows that
might fall upon them reaching the garrison on the ramparts or
within the court-yard ; fall where or how the arrows might, it
was always opposed by some projection of the moulding, which,
whilst it added a beauty, served a valuable purpose. For as
Rufus fell by the glancing of an arrow in the New Forest, so the
ricochet of missiles often proved as dangerous as direct aim.
Nor were the archers blind to avail themselves of a fact each
day presented to them, but where a direct shot was impossible,
seized upon the chance of the rebound to attempt their object,
but they could not ensure it, and the science of the architect
stepped in to frustrate them. Another fact worthy of notice is,
that all the embrasures which face outwards, whatever may be
their position or height from the ground, are precisely the same
width. In each of the coping stones of the merlons before
reverted to, is cut a deep slanting chase, terminating in a round
hole. This explains the reason of such exactitude, for to each
of these embrasures was attached in the time of war, a wooden
shutter or mantlet suspended from a wooden roller, and the chase
in the merlon served to slide this hinge into its place, so by thus
making each of them the same size, all that was required was to
bring the mantlets from their store when needed, and slide them
into the embrasures without any trouble of selection or fitting.
These mantlets protected the whole alure, and by being of equal
height with the merlon, not only shielded the defenders from the
arrows of the assailants, but also hid their movements from them.
One man in his sheltered nook on the summit of the gate-house
could thus see the tactics of the attack, and direct the movements of the defence, without those outside being able to discern
the number or position of the garrison ; who, when they required

to discharge their missiles at the foe, had simply to raise their wooden shield to such an angle as would best reveal the enemy and least expose themselves." The castle, in fact, was not built to resist a long siege or powerful engines ; it was only meant for defence against sudden attack, till aid should come from outside. And that need has happily long passed away.

Maxstoke Castle is a delightful example of the adaptation of an ancient stronghold to a modern dwelling-house. The charming garden between the moat and the walls gives an air of calm and happiness to the grim and stately structure which overlooks it. The house itself is not very large, but it has some large rooms on the first floor. The arms of the Dilkes are in many places, notably on the great chimney-piece in what is called the hall, which bears the inscription :—

WHER NO WOOD IS	NO TALE BEARERS
Y^E FIRE GOETH OUT	STRIFE CEASETH

There is a splendid oak table, like that at Baddesley Clinton, a suit of armour, an impressive pair of jack boots, and the coat in which (as Sir William Dugdale's diary tells) Mr. Fetherston was slain by a trooper at Kensington, September 2, 1682. There is likewise an oak chair which claims to be that in which Henry VII. sat for his crowning on the field of Bosworth. A charming little turret-room (which has a bedroom above it) shows the thickness of the huge walls, and gives charming views of the moat ; but the hall and the drawing-room are the two best survivals of old days, though there are many more rooms which have interest, and the passage within the battlements is characteristic.

From Maxstoke Castle it is not far, along wooded lanes, to what remains of the priory. This was founded by Sir William de Clinton first as a college of chantry priests in 1331, then five years later as a priory of Austin canons. It was given for endowment the churches of Long Itchington, Maxstoke, Fillongley and Shustoke, and it received a charter of incorporation in 1337. A prior and twelve canons were provided, who were to wear the black *cappa* and cowl, with linen vesture within befitting their order. William de Clinton, who became Earl of Huntingdon, considered the distance from his castle too far for wet weather, and petitioned in 1350 for the Pope's leave to build a chapel at his castle and provide chaplains. On this I can do no better than quote Dr. Thomas Cox, his " Topographical, Ecclesiastical and

Natural History " (London, 1700), which tells us the history, incorporating that of the religious foundations, thus :—

" The Church here, is dedicated to St. *Michael*, and was, by Sir *William Clinton*, Knt. given to the Chantry, which he founded in it, with divers other Lands, for five Priests, (one of them to be the Warden to celebrate Divine Service daily in the said Church, where his Ancestors lay interr'd, for the good Estate of the Souls of himself, Wife, Father, and Mother, as also of King *Edward* III. all the Lords *Hastings, &c.*) This Chantry was afterwards by him dissolv'd, and incorporated with the Monastry, which he built in this Place, of which we shall speak in its Place. The Advowson of the Church being at first appropriated to the Chantry abovemention'd, and afterwards to the Priory, a Vicar-age was appointed ; but it being done in a peculiar Manner, we shall set it down as we find it given in by the Parishioners, to the Visitors in the Beginning of Queen *Elizabeth's* Reign, *viz.* That the Vicar should have for his Support, 1. Meat and Drink for himself and a Child to wait upon him. 2. Every Year a Gown. 3. Every Week three Casts of Bread and two Gallons of Ale. 4. His Barber, Launder, Candle, and Fire-Wood as much as he would spend, with 40s. Wages yearly, and all at the Cost of the Convent. In the Chancel are these Grave-stones, for *Richard Slade*, Esq ; and *Margaret* his Wife, dated in 1480 ; *Thomas Slade*, Esq ; and *Elizabeth* his Wife, dated 1530 ; *Edward Pyes*, Esq ; and *Margery* his Wife, dated 1500 ; and *Thomas Dilke*, Esq ; Lord of this Castle, dated 1632 ; and in the East Window, the Arms of the *Beauchamps* Earls of *Warwick*, and *Clintons* Earls of *Huntingdon*, and *Maxtoke*. The Vicarage, 26 *Hen.* 8. was valued at 5l. 6s. 8d. *per Annum*."

Leaving the church we turn to the conventual buildings, of which not a little remains, though much has been destroyed or " translated." The chapel was built, but it is no longer a distinct room. The canons seem to have been rather riotous persons, in the early years of this house. Complaints of assault and marauding were made against them in 1440, and in 1399 one canon killed another. Records show also how cheerful was their manner of living ; jesters, play actors, singers, were continually entertained in the fifteenth century, from ordinary mimes to a " necromancer with his fellows playing in the painted chamber." In 1536, when the commission reported, there were but seven canons with the prior, but twenty-six servants of different kinds, including two priests and three women ; the house being described as " a very stately and goodly house in most part builded in hard stone and in good repair." Of the seven canons two were suspect, the others virtuous. The property was granted to Charles Brandon, King Henry's brother-in-law. There remains now the parish church, separate and completely restored. The gate-house is a fine red brick building, with vaulted passage of entry, from which stairway leads to the upper room. Opening on what was the court are two doors, one for foot passengers, the other for the knights who rode in. Within the farm buildings and the Tudor house built from the remains of what is called the Middle Gatehouse make a pleasing picture. There is little which belongs as it is to the old time, save the great central tower of the conventual church, the only piece that is now left standing. It is a lofty structure with two arches, and suggests the size of the great church of which it is the survivor. Pass through it, and past many rebuilt walls and fragments, round by the vicarage garden where is a picturesque arcade ; and so westwards, gradually mounting till you come to the comfortable town of Coleshill.

Coleshill to-day has some really beautiful eighteenth century houses. It must be a delightful town to live in, and is certainly a very Tory one. It is not precisely a stirring place. It has an omnibus which goes to the station some two miles away, but I do not advise you to depend upon its catching the train ; if you do you will very likely have to walk, to run, to miss the train, to see the omnibus arrive still later than yourself, and to wait an hour or two, with such patience as you can command, as I have done. When I say this I do not mean Coleshill's own station, for that has but one train a day each way, and they are before nine in the morning. I mean Forge Mills, from which you can see Hams Hall, Lord Norton's place, among the woods in the distance. Your walk, when you try to catch the train, will not be an unpleasant one, for you will pass over a fine bridge at the foot of the town, over a shallow pretty river, and by some, I think, prosperous mills. But of Coleshill itself in its beginning I may tell what Dugdale says and what Dr. Cox. The former thought there was a castle once there by a " Quercus Castelli," and that it went back to Roman days. Domesday Book shows that King William held the land, in succession to King Edward.

Cox then begins the story—I do not vouch for the accuracy of it—of the property, which I will quote till its details become tedious :

" *Coleshill,* so called from its Situation upon an Hill on the South side of the River *Cole.* It was one of those Towns which we call *Ancient Demesne,* because *Edward* the Confessor, and King *William* the Conqueror held it in their own Hands at the Time that Domesday-Book was made, wherein it is rated at three Hides, with a Church and Mill, ten Burgesses in *Tamworth,* and Woods three Miles in Length and two in Breadth. How it was alienated from the Crown, we find not ; but that it was so, appears in this, That it was bought by *Jeffrey Clinton,* of some Person to whom it was given. His Son *Jeffrey* left it to *Osbert* his Kinsman, in whose Family it continu'd from King *Henry* II's Time to King *Edward* III's. This *Osbert,* who is sometimes called *Osbert de Colshill,* left it to *Osbert* his Son, who obtained a Charter of King *John, Reg.* 9. for a weekly Market on Sunday, and a Fair yearly for two Days, *viz.* on the Eve and Feast of St. *Peter* and St. *Paul, June* 29. He was in Arms against King *John,* but returning to his Loyalty, 1 *Hen.* 3. had his Lands restor'd to him. His Heir was *Thomas de Clinton,* a Man of fair Possessions, and of great Reputation in his Country, for he was Justice of Assize and Gaol-delivery in this County, Escheator, *&c.* He obtained a Charter of Free-Warren in all his Demesne Lands here, 38 *Hen.* 3. His Son *John* inherited this Lordship after him. He adher'd to the rebellious Barons against King *Henry,* and held out the Castle of *Kenilworth* against him, for which his Lands were seized ; but soon recover'd by the Statute called *Dictum de Kenilworth,* and afterward was in such Esteem for his Fidelity, that he was put in Commission for Gaol-delivery at *Warwick, &c.* 20 *Edw.* 1. He was entomb'd in an Arch of the Wall in *Colshil* Church, of which he had the Advowson, and there lieth cross Legg'd, because he had taken upon him the Cross to serve in the *Holy Land.* His Successor in this Manor, was his Son *John,* who was afterwards made a Knight, and was constituted one of the Conservators of the Peace in this County, and was more than once in the *Scotch* Wars with King *Edward* I. He left *John* his Son and Heir, who was also knighted ; but dying, left only one Daughter and Heir *Joan,* who was within Age at her Father's Death, and after marry'd to Sir John Mont-

fort." He was a distinguished bastard of the family of Beaudesert. In his family, with some vicissitudes, it mostly remained till Henry VII.'s day, when it was forfeited for its lord's
support of Perkin Warbeck. Thence to the Digbys, notable
persons in their way, but some of them such as to be briefly
described by Dr. Thomas Cox that they " have nothing peculiar
in them to be taken Notice of but that being Gentlemen of a
superior Rank in this County, they bore the publick Employments of Sheriffs, Justice of Peace, and Commissioners upon
great Occasions," which, a county family will remark, might
be said of any of us. But the end of the matter is that we come
to the great and loyal Earl of Bristol, the Ambassador at Madrid,
the honest man who might have saved James I.'s throne for all
the days of Charles, if Charles had not been a believer in Buckingham's wisdom. Of Coleshill Park, now belonging to Mr.
Wingfield Digby, it shall only be said that the house was built
in 1873. Of the church, much more. You approach from the
market place where you shall see a very rare sight—I indeed have
never seen another like it—an engine of punishment which is,
like Cerberus, three gentlemen at once—namely, the stocks, a
whipping post, and a pillory. Now you may observe what the
pillory really was ; how exceeding uncomfortable was the
punished one's position and how unpleasantly near he was to his
enemies in the crowd. And it may not have occurred to you
that he would probably be whipped before he was thus lifted
up, and that when he was tired of standing he could be accommodated with a seat in the stocks, the whole process with no
undue call upon the official's time, and with no sacrifice of a
suitable publicity. It is said that the stocks at least were used
as late as 1863, but (as the lady's maid in Sir William Gilbert's
play says of kissing) stocks are nothing : I have myself seen
vagrants sitting quite comfortably in them on the roadside at
Lea in Lincolnshire, and I have a shrewd suspicion that it was
my father, as a magistrate, who placed them there ; but then
that too is a good many years ago. At Coleshill it is quite close
from the stocks to the church ; but the stocks are not used and
the church is locked up. Perhaps this last is due to the fact
that the sacred edifice is of so delicate a nature that it is always
being restored. Mr. George Miller, in his volume on the parishes
of Warwickshire ("The Parishes of the Diocese of Worcester,"

vol. i) remarks, in 1889, that "the tower and spire are now undergoing restoration," though he tells us that the church was restored in 1854. But it is still a beautiful church. The tower and spire are exquisite, the spire almost the finest in all Warwickshire. Earliest memorial in the church is the splendid Norman font. The chancel is assigned to the time of William de Montfort, under Henry VI. You can still see where the nave was lengthened at this same time, by the height of the newer piers. The curious clerestory is lighted only at the east. The roof is the old one, splendid in its decoration, though restored. There are some most interesting monuments of the Clintons, which are shown in Dugdale. The best perhaps is that of John de Clinton, at the end of the thirteenth century, in chain mail, with a shield bearing two fleur de lis. The most interesting, historically, as illustrating both the dress and the theology of the Elizabethan clergy, is the brass in the midst of the chancel. The figure is habited in cassock, and the inscription runs thus :— " Here lyeth the body of Syr John Fenton, Prest, Bachelor of Law, sometyme Vicar of this Church and offishall of Coventree, who deceassed the xvii daye of Maye 1566 whose soule Jhesus pardon Amen." There are also Grevilles, Blyths, and Riddels of Blyth. But more ·important than these are the splendid Digby monuments. The grandest is that in the south-east of the chancel of Sir George Digby and his wife Abigail, the parents of the great Earl of Bristol, he in armour, she in a stiff gown with ruff. On the other side of the chancel is the tomb of Simon Digby, who it seems betrayed his master Sir Simon de Montfort, who was executed for supporting the attempt of Perkin Warbeck. His wife Alice is delightfully dressed and has all the adornments of a fashionable lady, including two lapdogs. Also there are the tombs of John Digby and his wife, of William Abel, priest, of Sir Robert Digby, of Reginald Digby, and his wife. Time fails one to tell of them, for each is worth studying for its dress and its heraldry ; and that the thirty-two coats in the chancel windows, which Dugdale gives, have gone the way of old things. All the doings of the mighty persons who have held Coleshill, their sufferings and their quarrels, may be read in Dugdale ; the tale is too long to quote, but like all Dugdale writes, it is often diverting as well as tragic. William Hutton, the historian of Birmingham, ends his account by telling you that he knew several of the descendants of the Montforts, "well known to poverty and the hammer" in his city, and he sums up the story by recording that their old hall was pulled down at the beginning of the nineteenth century.

This is, let us note before we leave it, the very district of Dugdale; and let us add a word on a place with which he was particularly connected. Alas that the beautiful glass shown in his book has entirely gone from it! Nothing is as when he wrote of the church and worshipped there.

Shustoke Church, dedicated to S. Cuthbert, might be passed by during this generation, till the year 1886 becomes of respectable antiquity, for it was burnt down in that year and rebuilt—were it not for a few features such as one early Norman window, and a chest carved out of a solid tree, and most of all the monument of Sir William Dugdale, the father of all those who love the legends and memorials of this noble shire. But there is another monument, now cruelly placed outside the church, which has a curious interest. It is the tablet to the memory of Thomas Huntbach and Margaret his wife, who died in 1712, It has these lines :—

" When Death Shall Cut the threads of Life
Both of me and my Louing Wife
When pleaseth God our Change shall be
Here is A Tombe for me and Shee
Wee Freely shall Resigne up all
To him woh gaue and us doth Call
Sleep here wee must both in the dust
Till Resurrection of the just
Good freind within these railes forbear
To Dig the dust inclosed here
Blest be the man that spares these stones
And Curst be him that moues our bones
Whilst liueing here learne thou to die
This benefit thoult reape thereby
Neither thy Life or Death will be
Greiuiouse or sad but Joy to thee
Watch thou and pray, thy time well spend
UnKnowns the houer of thy last end
As thou art so once were wee
As wee are so must thou be

THOMAS HUNTBACH GENT AND
MARGARET HIS WIFE
Dum spiramus speramus."

Local Shakespearians are said to have puzzled much over this ; the simple explanation is probably the true one, that Mr. Huntbach was a Shakespearian himself, and ordered the four lines to be copied from his hero's tomb.

And so let us leave Shakespeare's Country, its churches and castles, its forests and its river banks, its memories of poetry and prayer ; and the name of Shakespeare shall be the last upon our lips.

INDEX

A

Abington, Mr., 352
Alcester, 302–306
Alderminster, 40, 41
Alscot, 42
Alveston, 206–209, 246
Archer family, 291, 292, 309, 310
Arches, Court of, 40
Arden, forest of, 326, 327, 350
Arden, Mary, 247, 254
Arlescote, 25
Armin, Robert, 266
Arrow Church, 306
Arrow River, 349, 370
Ashbee, Mr. C. R., 145
Ashby, Mr. A. W., 16, 18–20
Asheton, Nicholas, 9
Aston Cantlow 252–254
Aston Hall, 424
Atherstone, 41, 43, 158
Avon Dassett, 21, 22, 23

B

Baddesley Clinton, 319, 323–325
Badsey, 142
Bagington, 393
Balliol College, 10, 59, 61
Barcheston, 43
Barford, 122
Barnard, Mr. E. A. B., 152, 237
Barnard, Sir John, 165, 250
Barrels, 285–287, 289, 338
Barton-on-the-Heath, 2, 3, 151
Bascote, 64
Bathurst, Allen Earl, 49
Bearley, 326, 328, 331
Bearley Cross, 331, 340
Beaudesert, 280–283
Belknap, Sir Edward, 23
Bengeworth, 141
Bennett, Richard, brass of, 69
Benson, F. R., 199, 201
Beoley, 5, 295

Berry Hall, 423
Bevington, Cock, 255, 308, 309
  , Wood, 255, 308
Bidford, 231, 239–242, 251
Bigg, Dr. Charles, 130
Billesley, 248–50
Binton, 232
Bishop's Tachbrook, 68, 115
Blackford, Daniel, brass of, 39
Blacklow Hill, 80, 120, 371
Bloom, Rev. J. Harvey, 41, 185, 239
Blore, Mr., 6
Blithe Hall, 431
Boeter, 336
Bott's Green House, 424, 431
Boteler, Ralph, 279
Brailes, 6, 7, 8, 9, 20
Bretforton, 141, 142–4
Bristol Waters, 137
Broad Marston, 238
Broadway, 141, 145
Brome, John, 299, 319, 321, 322
Brome, Nicholas, 122, 297, 319, 321
Broom, 242
Bubbenhall, 389
Buckle Street, 301
Burbage, Richard, 190
Burford, 15, 298
Burton Dassett, 21, 23, 34
Bury, Elizabeth, 2
Butler's Marston, 37

C

Camperdown, Earl of, 6, 7
Carrington, Lord, 333
Cassy, Richard, brass of, 46
Castle Ashby, 14, 15, 42
Castle Bromwich, 424
Castle Hill, 8
Catherlough, Earl of, 287, 289, 337
Chamberlayne family, 61
Chambers family, 349, 350, 366, 367
Charlecote, 126, 205, 209–219
  Church, 220

443

INDEX

R. CLAY AND SONS, LTD., BRUNSWICK ST., STAMFORD ST., S.E.

THE HIGHWAYS & BYWAYS SERIES.

Extra crown 8vo, gilt tops, **5s.** net each.

London. By Mrs. E. T. COOK. With Illus-
trations by HUGH THOMSON and FREDERICK L. GRIGGS.

GRAPHIC.—"Mrs. Cook is an admirable guide; she knows her London in and out; she is equally at home in writing of Mayfair and of City courts, and she has a wealth of knowledge relating to literary and historical associations. This, taken together with the fact that she is a writer who could not be dull if she tried, makes her book very delightful reading."

Middlesex. By WALTER JERROLD. With
Illustrations by HUGH THOMSON.

EVENING STANDARD.—"Every Londoner who wishes to multiply fourfold the interest of his roamings and excursions should beg, borrow, or buy it without a day's delay."

DAILY TELEGRAPH.—"A model of its class, for it is difficult to see how descriptive work of the kind could be performed with a more sympathetic and humane touch."

Hertfordshire. By HERBERT W. TOMPKINS,
F.R.Hist.S. With Illustrations by FREDERICK L. GRIGGS.

WESTMINSTER GAZETTE.—"A very charming book. . . . Will delight equally the artistic and the poetic, the historical and the antiquarian, the picturesque and the sentimental kinds of tourist."

ST. JAMES'S GAZETTE.—"Cram full of interest and entertainment. The county is singularly rich in material for gossip and comment, and Mr. Tompkins has made a very charming book from it. Nothing more can well remain to be said, yet all that is said in these pages is to the point."

Buckinghamshire. By CLEMENT SHORTER.
With Illustrations by FREDERICK L. GRIGGS.

WORLD.—"A thoroughly delightful little volume. Mr. Frederick L. Griggs contributes a copious series of delicately graceful illustrations."

OBSERVER.—"A very full, pleasant, and informing book. . . . Mr. Griggs again gives us of his best."

Surrey. By ERIC PARKER. With Illustrations
by HUGH THOMSON.

DAILY TELEGRAPH.—"Author and artist have combined to give us one of the very best books on the most variedly beautiful of the home counties."

SPECTATOR.—"A very charming book, both to dip into and to read . . . Every page is sown with something rare and curious."

Kent. By WALTER JERROLD. With Illustrations by HUGH THOMSON.

PALL MALL GAZETTE.—"A book over which it is a pleasure to pore, and which every man of Kent or Kentish man, or 'foreigner,' should promptly steal, purchase, or borrow. . . . The illustrations alone are worth twice the money charged for the book."

TRUTH.—"It will rank as one of the very best volumes in an admirable series."

Sussex. By E. V. LUCAS. With Illustrations by FREDERICK L. GRIGGS.

WESTMINSTER GAZETTE.—"A delightful addition to an excellent series. . . . Such beauty and character has the county, it requires of the writer who would do justice to Sussex a graceful and sprightly pen, as well as fulness of knowledge. Mr. Lucas is well endowed in these things. His knowledge of Sussex is shown in so many fields, with so abundant and yet so natural a flow, that one is kept entertained and charmed through every passage of his devious progress. . . . The drawings with which Mr. Frederick Griggs illustrates this charming book are equal in distinction to any work this admirable artist has given us."

Berkshire. By JAMES EDMUND VINCENT. With Illustrations by FREDERICK L. GRIGGS.

DAILY CHRONICLE.—"We consider this book one of the best in an admirable series, and one which should appeal to all who love this kind of literature."

Oxford and the Cotswolds. By H. A. EVANS. With Illustrations by FREDERICK L. GRIGGS.

DAILY TELEGRAPH.—"The author is everywhere entertaining and fresh, never allowing his own interest to flag, and thereby retaining the close attention of the reader."

COUNTY GENTLEMAN.—"No better study of any well-marked division of the country has appeared."

Shakespeare's Country. By The Ven. W. H. HUTTON. With Illustrations by EDMUND H. NEW.

Hampshire. By D. H. MOUTRAY READ. With Illustrations by ARTHUR B. CONNOR.

WORLD.—"Mr. Moutray Read has written a well-nigh perfect guide-book, and he has been thrice blessed in his illustrator, Mr. Arthur B. Connor."

STANDARD.—"In our judgment, as excellent and as lively a book as has yet appeared in the Highways and Byways Series."

Dorset. By Sir FREDERICK TREVES. With
Illustrations by JOSEPH PENNELL.

STANDARD.—"A breezy, delightful book, full of sidelights on men and manners, and quick in the interpretation of all the half-inarticulate lore of the countryside."

FIELD.—"This volume, in literary style, and happy illustration by the artist, is one of the very best of the series."

Somerset. By EDWARD HUTTON. With
Illustrations by NELLY ERICHSEN.

DAILY TELEGRAPH.—"A book which will set the heart of every West-country-man beating with enthusiasm, and with pride for the goodly heritage into which he has been born as a son of Somerset."

DAILY NEWS.—"Here is a work whose spirit defies pedantic or detailed criticism : here is the book for a Somerset man or a lover of Somerset."

Devon and Cornwall. By ARTHUR H.
NORWAY. With Illustrations by JOSEPH PENNELL and HUGH THOMSON.

DAILY CHRONICLE.—"So delightful that we would gladly fill columns with extracts were space as elastic as imagination. . . . The text is excellent ; the illustrations of it are even better."

South Wales. By A. G. BRADLEY. With
Illustrations by FREDERICK L. GRIGGS.

TIMES.—"A book which may be described honestly as one of the best of its kind which has ever been published."

SPECTATOR.—"Mr. Bradley has certainly exalted the writing of a combined archæological and descriptive guide-book into a species of literary art. The result is fascinating."

North Wales. By A. G. BRADLEY. With
Illustrations by HUGH THOMSON and JOSEPH PENNELL.

PALL MALL GAZETTE.—"To read this fine book makes us eager to visit every hill and every valley that Mr. Bradley describes with such tantalising enthusiasm. It is a work of inspiration, vivid, sparkling, and eloquent—a deep well of pleasure to every lover of Wales."

Cambridge and Ely. By Rev. EDWARD
CONYBEARE. With Illustrations by FREDERICK L. GRIGGS. Also an *Edition de Luxe.* Limited to 250 copies. Royal 8vo, 21s. net.

ATHENÆUM.—"A volume which, light and easily read as it is, deserves to rank with the best literature about the county."

GUARDIAN.—"Artist and writer have combined to give us a book of singular charm."

East Anglia. By WILLIAM A. DUTT. With Illustrations by JOSEPH PENNELL.

WORLD.—"Of all the fascinating volumes in the 'Highways and By-ways' series, none is more pleasant to read. . . . Mr. Dutt, himself an East Anglian, writes most sympathetically and in picturesque style of the district."

Lincolnshire. By W. F. RAWNSLEY. With Illustrations by FREDERICK L. GRIGGS. [*In the press.*

Derbyshire. By J. B. FIRTH. With Illustrations by NELLY ERICHSEN.

DAILY TELEGRAPH.—"The result is altogether delightful, for 'Derbyshire' is as attractive to the reader in his arm-chair as to the tourist wandering amid the scenes Mr. Firth describes so well."

Yorkshire. By ARTHUR H. NORWAY. With Illustrations by JOSEPH PENNELL and HUGH THOMSON.

PALL MALL GAZETTE.—"The wonderful story of Yorkshire's past provides Mr. Norway with a wealth of interesting material, which he has used judiciously and well ; each grey ruin of castle and abbey he has re-erected and re-peopled in the most delightful way. A better guide and story-teller it would be hard to find."

Lake District. By A. G. BRADLEY. With Illustrations by JOSEPH PENNELL.

ST. JAMES'S GAZETTE.—"A notable edition — an engaging volume, packed with the best of all possible guidance for tourists. For the most part the artist's work is as exquisite as anything of the kind he has done."

The Border. By ANDREW LANG and JOHN LANG. With Illustrations by Hugh Thomson.

DAILY TELEGRAPH.—"A fascinating book about a fascinating county."

STANDARD.—"The reader on his travels, real or imaginary, could not have pleasanter or more profitable companionship. There are charming sketches by Mr. Hugh Thomson to illustrate the letterpress."

Donegal and Antrim. By STEPHEN GWYNN. With Illustrations by HUGH THOMSON.

DAILY TELEGRAPH —"A perfect book of its kind, on which author, artist, and publisher have lavished of their best."

Normandy. By PERCY DEARMER, M.A. With Illustrations by JOSEPH PENNELL.

ST. JAMES'S GAZETTE.—"A charming book. . . . Mr. Dearmer is as arrestive in his way as Mr. Pennell. He has the true topographic eye. He handles legend and history in entertaining fashion."

MACMILLAN AND CO., LTD., LONDON.

Lightning Source UK Ltd.
Milton Keynes UK
UKHW021152200219

337573UK00005B/826/P